THE CHURCH IN HISTORY

by

B. K. KUIPER

CSI PUBLICATIONS
Christian Schools International Curriculum Department
under Christian School Education Foundation and
Canadian Christian Education Foundation Inc. grants
Grand Rapids, Michigan   Burlington, Ontario

WM. B. EERDMANS PUBLISHING CO.

Preface

The story of the Christian Church is intensely interesting. It deals with some of the most dramatic episodes in history. For the children of God it is also instructive and inspiring. They regard it as a heritage that should be passed on to their children.

In recognition of this the National Union of Christian Schools (now Christian Schools International) requested Mr. B. K. Kuiper to write a manuscript that could be used for a textbook in church history. He complied, and *The Church in History* was the gratifying result.

Mr. Kuiper brought to his task a lifetime of study and research in this field, as well as his outstanding ability as a teacher of history. He drew from a rich background as he wrote this book. Yet he constantly kept in mind the needs of the student and the general reader for whom he was writing.

The first edition of *The Church in History* was hardly off the press when Mr. Kuiper began to write revisions and to suggest certain structural changes.

Throughout the six printings of the first edition, teachers were both generous with their praise and helpful with criticism. These suggestions caused the Education Committee of the National Union (now Christian Schools International) to appoint a study committee in March, 1960, to determine the advisability of a revision. The report of this study committee led to the appointment of the revision committee, which body determined the nature and extent of the revision and served as consultants throughout.

The addition of a chapter on the Church in Canada, the insertion of sections on the historical development of the sects, the updating of all current material, and the elimination of much detail improved the usefulness of the book.

All of the retained maps have been redrawn and new maps added to correlate with the text. The value of the time lines is obvious. The selection of pictures is broadened, the number doubled, and their quality improved by offset printing. The questions and projects suggested at the end of the chapters should aid the teacher and the pupil in critical thinking on the meaning and relevancy of the contents. A teacher's guide accompanies the text.

It is our fervent hope that those who read this book may learn to love not only church history but also the Church itself, for it is the body of the Lord Jesus Christ.

In Appreciation

Many persons had a part in the publishing of this church history. It is well-nigh impossible to list the names of all those who contributed in some way to the original edition. We wish to acknowledge with gratitude the work of Miss Beth Merizon as the chief editor of the first edition.

For co-ordinating the work of revising *The Church in History,* our sincere appreciation goes to Mr. John S. Brondsema. We are also and especially indebted to Mr. John Rooze for intensive research and rewriting; to Dr. John Kromminga for serving as chairman of the evaluating committee and composing the chapter "The Churches Seek Co-operation and Union"; to Mr. Marvin Schans, Mr. Henry J. Kuiper, and Mr. Martin Vanden Berg for their textual assistance and respective contributions to improve this book as a high-school text.

We wish to thank the Reverend John Vriend for evaluating the chapter on Canada. We acknowledge with gratitude the technical assistance of Mr. Cornelius Lambregtse. The time lines were drawn by Miss Greta Rey and the art work and maps were done by Mr. George Benes.

Contents

PART ONE
WHEN THE CHRISTIAN CHURCH WAS YOUNG

PART TWO
THE CHURCH IN THE MIDDLE AGES

PART THREE
THE CHURCH IN THE REFORMATION

PART FOUR

THE CHURCH AFTER THE REFORMATION

PART FIVE

THE CHURCH IN THE NEW WORLD

Maps

part one

When the Christian Church Was Young

THE NEW TESTAMENT CHURCH IS BORN

THE CHURCH IS TEMPERED

THE CHURCH GROWS INWARDLY

THE CHURCH IS VICTORIOUS

THE CHURCH CONSOLIDATES

THE CHURCH DETERIORATES

THE CHURCH SURVIVES AND GROWS AGAIN

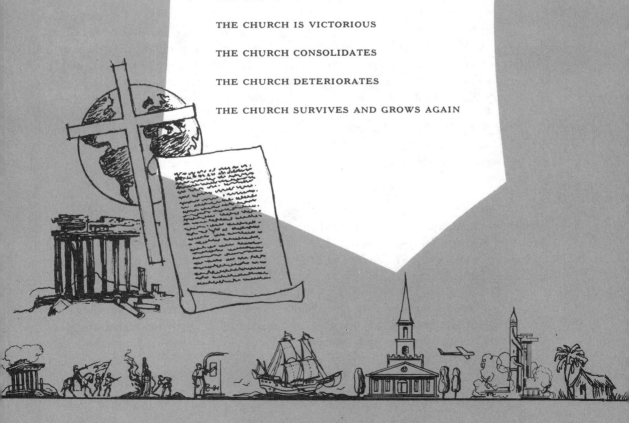

Part One

WHEN THE CHRISTIAN CHURCH WAS YOUNG

In this first part of our book we are going to observe the early growth of the Christian Church. We shall see it develop from one small congregation in Jerusalem to a giant organization reaching into many lands. As the Church grew in numbers and in territory, it developed a form of organization and government. As it grew in its understanding of the truth, it issued carefully worded statements of belief.

Not long after the Church's beginning it began to suffer persecution, first at the hands of the Jews and then at the hands of the pagans. We shall see how the Church was delivered from this persecution and how Christianity became the approved religion of the State.

In this early period, too, the Church had to withstand a great invasion of barbarians from the North, who plundered the towns and cities of the great Roman Empire and overthrew the government. As the first section of our book closes we find the Church carrying on the stupendous task of Christianizing and educating the newly established barbarian kingdoms.

When beginning the reading of each new chapter it will be well to take note of the dates given in the heading, for often a new chapter will cover the same period of time covered in the previous chapter. If we bear this in mind, we shall know just where we are in point of time.

CHAPTER 1

The New Testament Church

Is Born

1. The Background of the Church • Those who know the Old Testament story, the promise of the Messiah, the account of the life of Jesus, and the records of the acts of the apostles have had the finest possible introduction to the history of the Christian Church.

Originally God's revelation was to all men. Only with Abraham, the first Hebrew, did He limit the scope of His promised redemption to the Old Testament people, and even then He assured this father of all faithful that in him all nations of the earth would be blessed. When the New Testament Church was founded, this promise was fulfilled (Galatians 3:8) by the extension of the Gospel to the Gentiles. Now, as at the beginning, all men would come under the preaching of the true religion.

The Hebrew people were the recipients of the Old Testament Truth, and to them

Jesus came as the great final revelation of God (Hebrews 1:1-2). But they rejected their own kinsman as the Messiah. Following their rejection of Him, the Gospel was sent by direction of God to the Gentiles.

Our Christian faith, therefore, has its ancestry in the Hebrew religion. Jesus is the Messiah who is the fulfillment of the promises made to the Old Testament people. Time and again this relation is brought to mind by Matthew. Often when recording some incident in the life of Jesus, he says, "That it might be fulfilled which was spoken through the prophets."

2. The Nature of the Church • When through His preaching, His atoning death, and His resurrection Jesus transformed the Old Testament national "Church" to the Church of the New Testament, He distinctly indicated the spiritual nature of this new institution. He did not arrange for an organization; He taught the principles upon which it should be built. He did not tell His disciples what the mechanical structure of the Church was to be; He sent them out to preach a salvation by faith in His name. Even when He warned about the opposition which they were to experience, He talked not about Roman emperors, but about the "gates of hell."

When He was ready to leave this earth, Jesus promised the Spirit of Truth who would lead the disciples into all truth. Jesus stated that the coming of this Spirit was to be the prearranged sign that His followers should now go out from Jerusalem to the "uttermost parts of the earth." All of these teachings are evidences of the fact that this new Church was to be a spiritual entity—one founded and directed by the Holy Ghost.

3. The Physical Preparation for the Church • Scripture says, "When the fulness of the time came, God sent forth his Son." (Galatians 4:4). Such a statement is a clear indication that the world was prepared by God for the arrival of Jesus to do His redeeming work. In what way was it prepared? What were the conditions in the world when the New Testament Church began and when it first spread out from Jerusalem?

Rome ruled the "world." (See map page 26.) That this fact was of significance to the coming of Christ is evident from Luke's frequent references to the historical events of the Empire. He makes such statements as these: "There went out a decree from Caesar Augustus" and "In the fifteenth year of the reign of Tiberius Caesar."

This great Empire prepared the physical scene for the spread of the Gospel. It gave peace in place of constant tribal warfare; it built a great network of roads and bridges that made travel possible all over the then-known world; it cleared the sea of pirates so that trade by sea and travel by ship became common practice; it protected its citizens from robbers and rioting. All of these conditions favored the easy movement of the messengers of Christ so that along the many roads which Rome had set up for her military purposes the Gospel of peace went out to the world.

4. The Spiritual Preparation for the Church • Not only did these physical conditions help the cause of the new missionaries, but the spiritual and intellectual climate was also readied for their work. Greece had spread her culture throughout the Near East and had "conquered" Rome with her civilization.

The Greek language had become the world language, one that would enable Paul to communicate with all his hearers in that part of the Roman Empire where he did most of his work. When Paul quoted the Old Testament to the Jews whom he met on his journeys, his quotations were from the Septuagint, a Greek version of the Old Testament made as early as two hundred years before Christ.

Greek philosophy had made many people doubt their gods whose strange activities now began to fade into myth and legend. The Roman gods came into disrepute, and many officials of the Empire continued to encourage religion only because such belief served to curtail revolt among the common people. The Roman state religion was clearly a political affair that offered no peace of mind to a disturbed soul. All this left a moral vacuum that boded no good for the world.

Under such conditions the Gospel came with its promise of peace, pardon from sin, rest for the heavy laden. Here was assurance, forgiveness, life, and salvation in Christ. This was the message that struck home, and the fullness of time made the rapid spread of this Word possible.

5. The Expansion of the Church • Many factors caused the Church to be extended. Direct revelation to Peter indicated that Gentiles also were to be included in the Church. The stoning of Stephen and the persecutions by Saul and others scattered the early Christians. Jews of the Dispersion, who had witnessed the events of Pentecost, carried the message of salvation when they returned to their homes.

Official missionaries, such as Paul, brought the Gospel to many pagan communities. Unofficial missionaries, the early converts, were themselves enthusiastic witnesses.

6. The Character of the Church • In the beginning the Church of Jerusa-

Remains of an
Ancient Synagogue
at Kfar Nachum
(Capernaum)

A General View
of Nazareth

lem was known for its spiritual beauty. The members were united by a spirit of love. This was shown in their sharing of material goods and their concern for the welfare of fellow members. They "were of one heart and of one soul."

The young Church was also marred by corruption and dissension. Selfish interest became a stumbling block. Factions, lawsuits, abuses of the Lord's Supper, and other problems faced the Apostolic Church. The Jewish and Gentile Christians often found it very difficult to extend the hand of Christian brotherhood.

In spite of human shortcomings, the Church is the body of Jesus Christ. For it God prepared the world; for it Christ gave Himself; for it the apostles labored and suffered.

Now, with the blessing of the Holy Spirit, the stone cut from the mountain (Daniel 2:35) was about to fill the earth.

1. *What is the Church? What is its work? Who is its head?*
2. *What do the verses from Galatians 3:8–14 indicate about the relation of the Old Testament Hebrew people to the New Testament believers?*
3. *What does the phrase "the fulness of the time" mean with reference to Jesus' coming to earth? (Galations 4:4)*
4. *What work did Jesus do to found His Church?*
5. *What work did the Holy Spirit do for the early Church?*
6. *Why would Pilate write the placard for the cross of Jesus in Hebrew, Greek, and Latin?*
7. *How did Greek culture affect the spread of the Gospel by the early Church?*
8. *Why was it difficult for the Jews to understand that they must go to the Gentiles? How were they convinced that they should do so?*
9. *Is the Church spiritual or physical? Why?*
10. *What was the function of the miracles which were performed in the early Christian Church?*
11. *What was the culture of Greece?*
12. *Philip went to Samaria and founded a church; he also preached to an Ethiopian. Would he have done this before the new message of Christ had come to the Jews?*

CHAPTER *2*

The Church
Is Tempered, 33-313

1. The Heroic Age of the Church • Christ had forewarned His disciples: "They have persecuted me, they will also persecute you."

Throughout the first three hundred years of its existence the Church was tempered in the fires of persecution. This period has been called the *Heroic Age of the Church.*

2. The Apostolic Church Is Persecuted • Many leaders and members of the newly formed Church suffered for their Christian faith. This persecution began already in the history recorded for us in the Bible. Peter and John were imprisoned and persecuted on more than one occasion. Both Stephen and James had died a martyr's death.

Religious News Service Photo

St. Stephen Being Stoned
After an Engraving by Gustave Doré

3. Nero, the First Emperor to Persecute Christians • In the year 64 during the reign of Emperor Nero, fire broke out in Rome. For six days and nights the fire burned. The greater part of the city was laid in ashes. The rumor got around that Nero himself had caused the city to be set on fire. This aroused great hatred in the people of Rome against the emperor. To turn this hatred away from himself Nero accused the Christians of having set fire to Rome. The accusation certainly was not true, but large numbers of Christians were arrested and a terrible persecution followed. Many Christians were even crucified. Some were sewn up in the skins of wild beasts; then big dogs were let loose upon them, and they were torn to pieces. Women were tied to mad bulls and dragged to death. After nightfall Christians were burned at the stake in Nero's garden. The Roman people who hated the Christians were free to come into the garden, and Nero drove around in his chariot wickedly enjoying the horrible scene.

During the persecution of Nero, according to tradition, the apostles Peter and Paul suffered martyrdom in Rome. It is related that Peter was crucified with his head down. This was done at his own request. He said he was not worthy to be crucified in the same manner as his Master. Paul, being a Roman citizen, was beheaded.

The slaughter of Christians at this time was confined to the city of Rome. It was not a general persecution throughout the whole of the Empire.

4. Ignatius, Polycarp, and Justin • For the next one hundred years (from 68 to 161) there were no general persecu-

At one time when Paul was in Corinth, he was dragged by a Jewish mob into the court of the Roman governor Gallio. This governor would have nothing to do with the case and brusquely told the Jews to run along. When the Jews continued to press their charges against Paul, the governor had attendants drive them out of the courthouse.

The initial sufferings were inflicted upon the followers of Christ by the Jews, but in course of time, the attitude of the Roman government toward the Christians underwent a change.

PART ONE: WHEN THE CHRISTIAN CHURCH WAS YOUNG

tions, but in different parts of the Empire many Christians were put to death. Outstanding among the martyrs of this period were Ignatius, bishop of Antioch; Polycarp, bishop of Smyrna; and Justin, the apologist who had written boldly and very ably in defense of the Christians.

Ignatius (67–110) was ordered by the emperor to be arrested and was sentenced to be thrown to the wild beasts in Rome. He longed for the honor of giving his life for his Savior, saying, "May the wild beasts be eager to rush upon me. If they be unwilling, I will compel them. Come, crowds of wild beasts; come, tearings and manglings, wracking of bones and hacking of limbs; come, cruel tor-

tures of the devil; only let me attain unto Christ."

Polycarp was the last one of those who had been personally taught by the apostles. He was arrested and brought into the amphitheater in Smyrna, which was filled with an immense multitude. Since there were no images of gods in the houses of worship of the Christians, the heathen rightly concluded that the Christians did not believe in the existence of the gods, and so they accused them of being *atheists* (people who believe there is no God). The proconsul reminded Polycarp of his great age, and urged him to show his penitence by joining in the cry, "Away with the atheists!" Polycarp

Nero Burns the Christians as Torches in His "Golden House"
From a painting by Henry de Siemieradzki

looked straight at the excited crowd, pointed his finger at them, and cried, "Away with the atheists!"

Then the proconsul said, "Revile Christ, and I will release you."

But Polycarp answered, "Eighty and six years have I served Him, and He has never done me wrong; how can I blaspheme Him, my King, who has saved me? I am a Christian."

To the crowd the proconsul then proclaimed, "Polycarp has confessed himself to be a Christian."

The crowds yelled, "Let him be burned!"

Wood was collected and made into a pile. Polycarp asked not to be fastened to the stake. "Leave me thus," he said. "He who strengthens me to endure the flames will also enable me to stand firm at the stake without being fastened with nails." The woodpile was lighted. While Polycarp prayed with a loud voice, "Lord God Almighty, Father of our Lord Jesus Christ, I praise Thee that Thou hast judged me worthy of this day and of this hour, to participate in the number of Thy witnesses, and in the cup of Thy Christ,"

the flames consumed him. Polycarp's martyr death took place in the year 156.

Justin Martyr (100–166), who was a philosopher, was scourged and beheaded in Rome with six other Christians. In the face of death he bore with joy the witness to the truth. His last words were: "We desire nothing more than to suffer for our Lord Jesus Christ; for this gives us salvation and joyfulness before His dreadful judgment seat. . . ."

5. Persecution Is Continued Under Marcus Aurelius • The emperor Marcus Aurelius (161–180) decreed that the property of Christians should be given to their accusers. It is not difficult to see what would be the effect of this decree. Everywhere there were people who were eager to have the property of the Christians. These came forward with accusations. Persecution became well-nigh universal. Christians everywhere were sought out, brought to trial, and often executed with the greatest cruelty, while their property was taken from them and given to their accusers.

What happened to the Church in Lyons and Vienne in southern Gaul, now

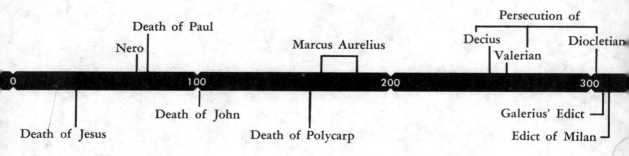

Christian Martyrs in the Amphitheater

France, can give us some idea of the severity of the persecution under Marcus Aurelius. By the most horrible tortures, they sought to make the Christians deny their faith. When at last the persecutors became convinced that no amount of torture would make the Christians deny their faith, they beheaded those Christians who were Roman citizens, and the others they threw to the wild beasts in the arena of the amphitheater.

From far and near the heathen flocked to the amphitheater to see this spectacle. All the condemned met their death with great joy. The last to die was Blandina. She had been a spectator of the death of many others, and she had constantly encouraged and exhorted them to remain steadfast to the end. With joy and thanksgiving she entered the arena. A net was thrown over her. Then she was exposed to the fury of a wild bull. Several times the bull took her upon his horns and tossed her into the air. At last she was dead.

The bodies of the martyrs were burned, and the ashes were thrown into the river Rhone. The heathen said mockingly, "Now we shall see whether there will be a resurrection of their bodies."

6. A Lull in the Storm • With the death of Marcus Aurelius this period of persecution came to a close. For some seventy years the Church on the whole enjoyed rest, with the exception of the persecution under Septimius Severus from 200–211.

For a time this persecution raged with great violence in Alexandria in Egypt. Along with many others, the father of Origen was put to death. Origen, who

Christians
Hunted Down
in the
Catacombs

later became the greatest scholar the Church had produced, was at the time of his father's death a young boy. It was only with the greatest difficulty that his mother restrained him from offering himself for martyrdom.

Another to suffer a martyr's death during this period was Irenaeus, the Church Father who had written the brilliant defense, *Against Heresies.*

7. Efforts Are Made to Destroy the Church • The first emperor who ordered a general persecution with the definite purpose of destroying the Church was Decius. Happily his reign lasted only two years, from 249 to 251. After a brief respite of seven years the Church suffered persecution under Valerian. Thereafter the Church was granted another period of tranquility, which lasted forty years. In the year 303 the emperor

Diocletian started a persecution which was continued by his successor Galerius until the year 311.

The tortures which were inflicted upon the Christians during these persecutions were so gruesome that it is not fit to describe them. Church buildings were demolished and Bibles were burned. These persecutions far surpassed, in the number of Christians who were martyred and in cruelty, anything the Christians had been made to suffer up to this time. These persecutions were a determined and systematic attempt to uproot Christianity completely, and wipe the Church off the face of the earth. An outstanding Christian who suffered martyrdom in these persecutions was Cyprian. Origen also died as the result of the tortures inflicted upon him at this time.

Many Christians in the city of Rome found a place of refuge in the catacombs, which were underground passageways. The ground upon which Rome is built consists of comparatively soft stone. Burying people within the city limits was not permitted. So in many places just outside the city, long, narrow passages or tunnels were dug out of the soft stone for this purpose. There are so many of them that if they were all end to end they would be some five hundred miles long. They wind and cross each other in every direction so as to form a veritable maze. Many of these subterranean passages are thirty or more feet below the surface. In the sides of these galleries or passageways excavations were made row upon row. In these excavations the dead were laid to rest. It was in these catacombs that many Christians hid themselves in times of persecution. There they also laid to rest the mangled remains of their fellow believers who had died as martyrs.

The persecution under Diocletian and Galerius was the most severe of all. But it was also the last. Heathendom had finally exhausted its strength and spent its fury.

8. Galerius Calls a Halt • Emperor Galerius became ill and suffered unspeakable torments. His disease was dreadful and incurable. From his sickbed, which became his deathbed, he issued in the year 311 an edict which granted to the Christians permission to hold their assemblies again. He asked for their prayers in behalf of himself and the Empire.

The edict of Galerius was not a complete victory. What Galerius had granted was only a halfhearted toleration. Nevertheless the complete victory for the Church was near at hand.

1. *How did persecution affect the Church?*
2. *Identify: Galerius catacombs.*
3. *Why did some of the Christians seek to be martyrs?*
4. *Why did the Romans persecute Christians? Notice from the account given that the persecutions were sporadic. In addition, many persecutions were local—in Rome only, or for a time in certain provinces. Relate the answer to the exclusive character of Christianity.*
5. *Why is there so little known of the Christian Church from* A.D. 70 *to* A.D. 300?
6. *Read about the lives of martyrs in Foxe's* Christian Martyrs.
7. *How are the catacombs described by Hawthorne in Chapter 3 of* The Marble Faun?

The Church
Grows Inwardly, 33-325

1. What Is Meant by the Church's Inward Growth • From the above dates you will see that the things to be discussed in this chapter happened in the same period of time as the things treated in the second chapter.

The *inward growth* of the Church has to do with its *doctrine,* or beliefs, and its *organization.* This is vitally important,

for it concerns the truth of God and the system of government within the Church.

Gifted men spent their lives searching out the truths in the Scriptures and defending these truths against the false teachings of the day. In doing this they performed a great service for God and His Church. Certainly we want to know something about these men and about the doctrines, or beliefs, which they championed. We also want to see how the Church developed a system of organization and government.

2. Is Doctrine Important? Many people today do not like doctrine. They say differences of opinion about doctrine have caused much debate and controversy. They say that the many divisions in the Church have been caused by debates about doctrine. Doctrine is not so important after all. What is important is a good Christian life. So runs their argument.

The effect of this kind of talk has been very bad. In many churches ministers teach the people and the children very little doctrine. The result is a great ignorance of Christian truth. The theory that doctrine is not important is not only shallow and foolish, it is also crafty. It is one of the devil's best tricks.

The history of the controversies about doctrine is a very important part of the history of the Church.

3. The Apostolic Fathers • After the time of the apostles the foremost leaders in the Church were the *Apostolic Fathers*. They were called the Apostolic Fathers because they are said to have been taught personally by the apostles. They lived in the first half of the second century. We know the names of five of them. They were Clement and Hermas of Rome; Ignatius of Antioch; Polycarp of Smyrna; and Barnabas, probably of Alexandria. There were two others whose names we do not know.

You will remember that there was much in the teaching of Christ which for a long time the disciples did not understand. From the writings of the Apostolic

Ignatius of Antioch

Fathers we can tell that, more than a hundred years after Christ, they had not as yet penetrated very deeply into the truth revealed in the Bible. Their conception of Christianity was very simple. They thought of Christ chiefly as the revealer of the knowledge of the one true God, and the proclaimer of a law of high and strict morality. The Apostolic Fathers wanted to know the truth about Christ. They thought and wrote about Him.

4. The Apologists • The heathen attacked and persecuted the Christians. They told many false stories about the Christians, accused them of many terrible crimes, and misrepresented the teachings

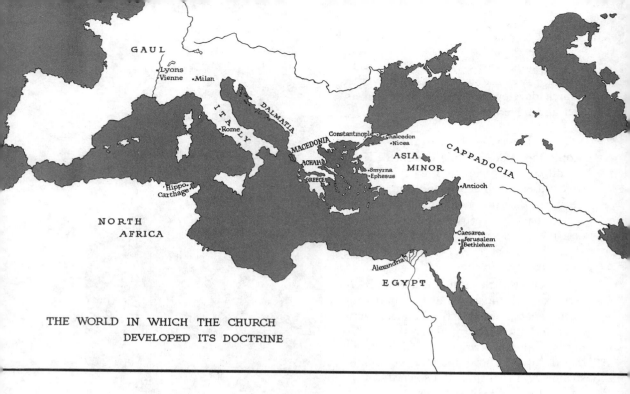

THE WORLD IN WHICH THE CHURCH
DEVELOPED ITS DOCTRINE

of Christianity. In response some Christians wrote books. Because in these books these writers defended Christianity, they are called *Apologists.* An apologist is one who defends what he believes to be the truth. In order to explain Christianity to the educated and cultured heathen and in order to defend it against attacks, they were compelled to make a deeper study of the Bible. In that way the Church made progress in the understanding of Christian truth.

The foremost of these Apologists was Justin. He was born in the ancient town of Shechem in the province of Samaria. There at Shechem was the well of the patriarch Jacob, where Jesus had talked to the Samaritan woman. Justin's father and mother were both heathen. Justin studied philosophy and even after he had become a Christian he continued to wear the man-

tle of a philosopher While living in Ephesus he was converted by the study of the Old Testament prophets. "Straightway," he wrote in one of his books, "a flame was kindled in my soul, and a love of the prophets and of those men who are friends of Christ. Theirs is the oldest and truest explanation of the beginning and end of things and of those matters which the philosophers ought to know, because they were filled with the Holy Spirit. They glorified the Creator, the God and Father of all things, and proclaimed His Son, the Christ. I found this philosophy alone to be safe and profitable."

About the year 153, while in Rome, Justin wrote his famous *Apology.* In that same city, perhaps in the year 165, he was beheaded for his faith. For that reason he is called Justin *Martyr*

Celsus was not one of the Apologists. He was a heathen who was well acquainted with the teachings of Christianity, but he never became a Christian. On the contrary, in the year 177 he wrote a book, *A True Discourse,* against Christianity. Celsus was a man with a very keen mind. He brought all his learning and wit to bear, and used many of the arguments still used by unbelievers today. His was the ablest criticism of Christianity produced by heathenism. It was not until seventy years later that Celsus was answered. But when at last the answer did come, it was overwhelming and crushing. This brilliant apology of Christianity was written by Origen in his book, *Against Celsus.* You will presently hear more about Origen.

5. False Ideas Arise • In the last half of the second century two *heresies* (departures from the truth) became a serious menace. They were *Gnosticism* and *Montanism.* Gnosticism went so far as to maintain that Christ never dwelt on this earth in human form. Montanism taught that Christ's promise of the Comforter had not been fulfilled in the upper room on Pentecost, but that the coming of the Holy Spirit was now at hand and that the end of the world was near. Both of these doctrines were gaining a foothold in the Church. These ideas were entirely contrary to Christian truth. Right doctrine is important. Wrong doctrine will hurt the Church. The Church cannot live with false doctrine. So the last half of the second century was a time of tremendous crisis for the Church.

How keenly the Church felt the deadly nature of these heresies you can tell from the following incident. One of the leading Gnostics was a certain Marcion. After he made his fortune in Constantinople, he moved to Rome. He gave large amounts of money to charity, but he also made strong propaganda for his Gnostic ideas, and gained many followers among the members of the church in Rome. Polycarp, bishop of the church in Smyrna, at one time made a visit to Rome. Marcion and Polycarp had known each other very well back East. When Polycarp happened to come across Marcion on the street, he was going to pass on without speaking. Marcion stopped him and said, "Don't you know me any more, Polycarp?" "Yes," answered Polycarp, "I know who you are. You are the first-born of Satan."

6. The Church Fathers • The first great doctrinal controversy in the Church was about the person of Christ. We know that Christ is the eternal Son of God, the second person in the Trinity, Himself God. But at first this was not so clear to the Church. It took the leaders in the Church a great deal of hard study, thought, and discussion to come to a right understanding of the person of Christ. That we have the right view today we owe to the long and intense labors of the great Church Fathers. Outstanding among these Church Fathers were Irenaeus and Tertullian in the western, and Clement and Origen in the eastern part of the Roman Empire.

Irenaeus was born sometime between 115 and 142. He was reared in Smyrna. There he saw Polycarp and heard him preach. From Smyrna he moved to Lyons in Gaul, now France, in the church of which city he became bishop. In the year 200 he suffered a martyr's death. Irenaeus gave much thought to the Scriptural teaching about Christ. The beginnings of a sound doctrine about Christ are to be found in his book *Against Heresies.*

Tertullian was born sometime between the years 150 and 155 in North Africa in the city of Carthage. Tertullian studied law and practiced in Rome. After his conversion he returned to Carthage, and became a presbyter in the church of his native city. He was a great student of philosophy and history and had an excellent legal mind. In his understanding of Christ he did not advance much beyond Justin and Irenaeus, but he was very gifted in the use of language and so was able to state the true doctrine about Christ more clearly and precisely than anyone before him had done.

Clement of Alexandria (not to be confused with the Apostolic Father, Clement of Rome, who lived a hundred years earlier) was a very able teacher in the theological school in Alexandria.

Origen, a pupil of Clement, became far more famous than his teacher. He was by far the greatest scholar the Church had produced. A deep and original thinker, he wrote many large and learned books. Origen's book, *Against Celsus,* was the brilliant answer to this critic of Christianity. Both Clement and Origen did much through their writings to lead the Church to a better understanding of the person of Christ.

7. A Creed and a Canon Emerge • Out of the Church's struggle with the heresies of Gnosticism and Montanism came three things: a *creed*, a *canon*, and an *organization.* All three of these have been of very great and lasting significance for the Church.

The word *creed* comes from the Latin word *credo*, meaning "I believe." A creed is a statement of belief. The creed that came out of the Church's struggle with Gnosticism and Montanism is known as the Apostles' Creed. It is so called not because it was composed by the apostles, but because it is a summary of the apostles' teachings. No doubt you know that creed by heart. It is the oldest creed of the Church. The Church adopted the Apostles' Creed in order that everybody might know what the Church believed to be true Christian doctrine, in distinction from the false and heretical doctrines of the Gnostics and Montanists.

The word *canon* has many meanings. As we are using it here it means "a list." The canon that came out of the above-mentioned struggle is the canon of the New Testament, that is, a list of the books that belong in the New Testament. In its controversies with the Gnostics and Montanists the Church always appealed to Scripture. But already at that time there were many Christian writings. So it was necessary to know which of those writings possessed absolute authority as inspired writings. Out of all the Christian writings then in existence the Church recognized as inspired those which now make up the New Testament.

8. The Development of the Episcopate • The organization that came out of the struggle with the Gnostics and Montanists is the *episcopal form of church government.* The leaders of these heretical groups also claimed support from the Bible. The Church had to establish its position as the authority who decided the meaning of the Bible. It exercised this authority through its rulers who came to be called bishops. The Church from this point down to the time of the Reforma-

A Meeting of Some
Early Christians in
the City of Rome

tion had the episcopal form of government. There are several churches today which have this form, such as the Roman Catholic, the Greek Orthodox, the Episcopal, and the Methodist churches.

At first the organization of the Church was very simple. The officers were the elders and deacons. The elders were known as presbyters, since *presbyter* is the Greek word for "elder."

In the early Church the presbyters were all of the same rank. But it was natural that in each congregation one of the presbyters should take the lead. He would be president of the board of presbyters, and he would lead in worship and do the preaching. The presbyters were also called overseers. The Greek word for "overseer" is *episcopos,* from which we get our word "bishop." The title of *bishop* was given to the presbyter who in course of time

became the leader of the board of presbyters. So the other presbyters gradually became subordinate to the presbyter who was their overseer, or bishop, and the bishop came to rule the church alone. The Greek word for a man who rules alone is "monarch." For that reason these bishops, who came to have all the authority in a church, were called *monarchical bishops.*

Churches were first established in the cities. The people in the country continued to be heathen when the people in the cities had already become Christians. The Latin word for country people was *pagani.* So the name *pagani* or pagans became equivalent to heathen. From the cities Christianity spread among the heathen, or pagans, in the country. The converts from the country would attend church in the city. The city with its surrounding country district was called a *diocese.* Then the man who at first was bishop only of the city church became bishop of the diocese, and was called a *diocesan bishop.*

You may wonder why all these terms (*presbyter, bishop, monarchical bishop, diocese, diocesan bishop,* and *episcopal*) are taken from the Greek language. You will recall from the first chapter that the world language of that day was Greek, and Christianity first spread in the eastern part of the Roman Empire where Greek was generally used.

Just exactly when the Church came to have bishops we do not know. The de-velopment of the episcopal form of church organization or government came about gradually. It came about in some cities sooner than in others. Churches in certain cities had monarchical bishops be-fore the church in Rome had such a bish-op. Around the year 110 the church in Antioch, from which city Barnabas and Paul had set out on their first missionary journey, had a bishop by the name of Ignatius, and Smyrna had Polycarp as its bishop. Both of these men are said to have been personal disciples of the apos-tles, and both of them are reckoned among the Apostolic Fathers. The first bishop of Rome seems to have been a man by the name of Anicetus. He was bishop of Rome from 154 to 165. By the middle of the second century practically all churches had monarchical bishops.

The bishops were supposed to be the successors of the apostles. That idea

The Ruins of the Corinthian Columns of the Temple of Jupiter at Baalbek, Lebanon

Philip Gendreau

helped immensely to clothe the bishops with great authority. Ignatius considered the bishop to be the great bond of church unity and the great defense against heresy. To the church in Philadelphia he wrote, "Do ye all follow your bishop as Jesus Christ followed the Father. Do nothing without the bishop."

For a long time the churches in the various cities were only very loosely connected with each other. By the year 200 they had become welded into one compact whole. The struggle of the churches with the Gnostic and Montanist heretics had done much to bring this about. All the churches now had in common the Apostles' Creed, the canon of the New Testament as authoritative Scripture, and the episcopal form of church government. The heretics were, of course, outside the Church. They had formed little churches of their own. But the big church was henceforth known as the *Catholic* (or Universal) Church, and also as the *Old Catholic* Church. Later we shall hear of the Roman Catholic Church.

The man who better than anyone else expressed the ideas about the Church which had come to prevail around this time was Cyprian. He was born in Carthage in North Africa around the year 200 and lived in that city all his life. A rich and well-educated man, he became famous as a teacher of rhetoric, or speech. In 246 he was converted. Two years later he became bishop, and in 258 he was beheaded as a Christian martyr. He wrote, "There is one God, and Christ is one; and there is one Church and one Chair." (By *one chair* he meant "one center of authority.") He continued: "He who is not in the Church of Christ is not a Christian. He can no longer have God for his Father who has not the Church for his mother. There is no salvation outside the Church. The Church is based on the unity of the bishops. The bishop is in the Church, and the Church is in the bishop. If anyone is not with the bishop, he is not in the Church."

It was in the midst of persecution that the Church grew in numbers, spread throughout the Roman Empire, and even preached among the barbarian tribes. And it was in the midst of persecution that the Church developed its organization and doctrine. Now it was about to enter a new era.

1. *What do we mean when we speak of Apostolic Fathers? When did these men live?*
2. *Compare the writings about the person of Jesus Christ as they are found*

in the three ecumenical creeds: Apostles' Creed, Nicene Creed, and Athanasian Creed.

3. *Identify: Polycarp, Origen, Gnosticism, Montanism.*

4. *Who were the Apologists? What did they accomplish for the Church by their writings? Look up Volume I of the* Christian Classics *series and read some of Justin Martyr's* Apology. *Notice that it is addressed to Roman officials, philosophers, and men of culture. Why would Justin write to these people particularly? What other Apologists can you name?*

5. *To whom were the books of* Luke *and* The Acts *addressed?*

6. *Why would the Apostles' Creed contain only one statement about the Father, one about the Holy Spirit, but many about the Son? What does this prove about heresy in the early Church?*

7. *Give the meanings of the new words that describe the government of the early Church. Notice the strong movement in the direction of unified government under the bishop. In what way does this development indicate a tendency moving toward the papal control of all the churches?*

8. *Your author mentions Irenaeus and his work* Against Heresy. *Read the selections from that work in Volume I,* Christian Classics.

9. *You may read more about Clement of Alexandria in* Christian Classics, *Volume II. The general introduction tells about his life and work, and excerpts of some of his writings follow. Volume V gives biographical material on Tertullian, Cyprian, Ambrose, and Jerome. All of the writings mentioned in questions 4, 8, and 9 are also found in* The Ante-Nicene Fathers, *Roberts and Donaldson, editors, Eerdmans, 1950.*

CHAPTER *4*

The Church

Is Victorious, 313

1. "In This Sign, Conquer" • In the year 306 the Roman army in Britain proclaimed Constantine emperor. That gave him the rule over Britain, Gaul, and Spain. Maxentius ruled over Italy and North Africa, but he wanted to be emperor over the entire western part of the Roman Empire. More and more openly he showed his hostility to Constantine. Constantine decided to get ahead of Maxentius. Before Maxentius had made prep-

arations for war, Constantine marched into Italy at the head of an army of forty thousand men. At Saxa Rubra, ten miles from Rome and a little north of it, the armies of Maxentius and Constantine met. Between Rome and the army of Maxentius was the Tiber River and, crossing it, the Milvian Bridge. The army of Maxentius was three times as large as that of Constantine, and it contained the Praetorian Guard, the flower

Schoenfeld Collection
from Three Lions

Constantine sees the cross above the sun the evening before the battle at the Milvian Bridge.

of all the Roman armies. Night fell. What the outcome of the battle would be the next day was doubtful.

Constantine found himself in an extremely dangerous situation. He felt the need of supernatural help. He was a worshipper of *Mithra,* as his father before him had been. Mithra was the Persian sun-god, said to be a great fighter and champion of truth and justice. *Mith-*

raism at this time had a great many followers in the Roman Empire. Mithra was most of all a soldier's god.

On the evening before the battle, so the story goes, Constantine saw a cross above the sun as it was setting in the west. In letters of light the cross bore the words: *Hoc Signo Vinces,* which means, "In this sign, conquer."

The next day, October 28 in the year 312, the battle was joined. It was a furious battle. The Praetorian Guards fought like lions. They never gave ground, but their ranks were cut down where they stood. The army of Maxentius was completely defeated. Maxentius himself, attempting to escape over the Milvian Bridge across the Tiber River, was drowned.

2. The Edict of Milan • The battle of the Milvian Bridge was one of the great decisive battles in the history of the world. It made Constantine master of the entire western part of the Roman Empire. But it had another and far more important result. Constantine felt that he had won the battle because he had received help from the God of the Christians, and he became a Christian. He who had been a worshipper of the sun-god Mithra now embraced the religion of Him who is the true light of the world.

In the city of Milan, Constantine in the year 313 issued an edict concerning religion. This edict did not set up Christianity as the only and official religion of the Empire. It did not forbid the practice of heathen religions. But it did more than merely grant toleration to the Christian religion as the decree of Galerius in the year 311 had done. The Edict of Milan put a stop to the persecutions, and proclaimed absolute freedom of conscience. It placed Christianity upon a footing of equality, before the law, with the other religions in the Empire.

3. The Church's Victory Is a Marvel • The Edict of Milan marks the victory of the Church over heathenism. This victory of the Church is one of the most marvelous things in all history. The Church had had its beginning as a very small organization only three hundred years before. It was composed of people who belonged to the small and despised Jewish nation. Many members of this organization were poor people without education or prestige. The message which the Church brought was to many who heard it either a stumbling block or foolishness. Arrayed against the Church were overwhelming numbers, money, learning, culture, social prestige, political and military power: the whole world of that time, Jews and Gentiles, the mighty Roman Empire. Not infrequently the Church was disgraced by serious moral

Schoenfeld Collection from Three Lions

The Baptism of Constantine by Pope Sylvester I
After a painting by Raphael in the Vatican

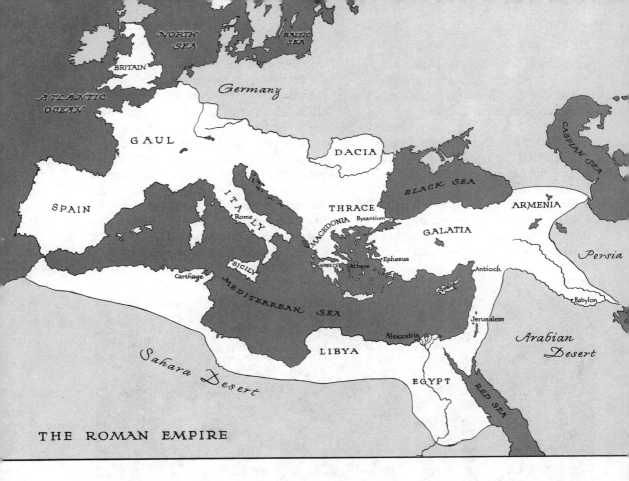

THE ROMAN EMPIRE

lapses of some of its members. It was rent asunder over questions of church discipline. It was harassed from without by strange doctrines and deadly heresies. It was distressed within by heated and bitter controversies over questions touching the very heart of its message. In the midst of these unfavorable conditions, which one would think would have stopped all growth, the Church for three hundred years was subjected to fierce and bloody persecutions.

How was it possible for the Church to emerge victorious from all these conflicts?

Many things can be mentioned in explanation. One thing is that the blood of the martyrs is the seed of the Church. It has always been true that the more martyr-blood there is shed, the more the Church grows and flourishes. But there is only one complete, all-comprehensive answer, and that is Christ and His supernatural care for His Church. The existence of the Church is indeed a marvel.

4. Turning Points in the History of the Church • There have been many events which abruptly changed the course of the history of the Church. One of the first turning points of the early Church was its expulsion from Jerusalem at the time of the stoning of Stephen. The spread of Christianity by the missionary activity of Paul and others may be called a second turning point.

The year 313 marks the third and very decisive turning point in the history of the Church. It was in this year that the Edict of Milan granted Christians the same rights that the followers of other religions had.

There now sat upon the throne of the Empire a man who confessed Christianity. Instead of persecuting the Church, he showered favors upon it. The Christian clergy was relieved of certain unpleasant civil duties. Constantine gave them large grants of money. In Constantinople, Jerusalem, Bethlehem, and other places he erected magnificent church buildings. One of the outstanding features of Christianity is the observance of Sunday as its weekly sacred day. Constantine now forbade Sunday work. However, his personal life left much to be desired and has caused some to doubt the sincerity of his confession.

5. The World Invades the Church • The Edict of Milan proved to have a very definite disadvantage. It was now no longer a shame but an honor to be a Christian. The Christian name now secured many and great material advantages. The Christian name had become a passport to political, military, and social promotion. As a result, thousands upon thousands of heathen joined the Church.

Unfortunately many of these were Christians in name only. The Christianity of Emperor Constantine himself was, if not of a doubtful, at least not of a very high character. What the Church gained in quantity it lost in quality. Constantine's edict of 313 opened the floodgates through which a mighty stream of corruption poured into the Church.

During the first three centuries the Church was extended by peaceful means. The victory over heathenism was won not by fighting, but by enduring suffering. But after 313, Christians at times employed the methods of war to advance their cause. The emblem of the Roman armies had been the eagle. The eagle was now replaced by the cross.

6. The Relation Between Church and State • There is one result of Constantine's conversion which should receive our very special attention. Constantine had granted the Church freedom of religion and many favors. In turn he demanded that the Church should allow him to have a good deal to say about its affairs. The close connection between State and Church, which has deeply colored and to a very large extent given direction to the history of the Church, even down to our own times, dates from the year 313. Many a page in this book will be devoted to the problem of the relation between Church and State. That problem has been the occasion for much disagreement, strife, and even bloodshed. It remains unsolved to this very day.

7. Julian Fails to Revive Heathenism • In the year 361 Julian, a nephew of the great Constantine, became emperor. He had been brought up as a Christian, but had remained a pagan at heart. Now he made it known that he was a heathen. Once more the Roman Empire had a heathen emperor. Because he forsook

Historical Pictures Service—Chicago

Julian Falls in Battle

Christianity he is known as Julian the *Apostate*.

Although he engaged in a certain amount of persecution (Athanasius had said: "It is only a little cloud; it will pass"), he attacked Christianity chiefly by means of his clever pen dipped in biting satire and ridicule. He did his best to breathe new life into heathenism, but in that he failed. The heathen temples stood forsaken, and the heathen altars smoked no more. Heathenism was dead.

In the year 363, fifty years after Constantine the Great had announced the famous Edict of Milan, Julian the Apostate fell in battle against the Persians, mortally wounded in the thigh by a spear. As the story goes, the dying man caught some of the spurting blood in his hand, threw it toward heaven, and exclaimed, "So Thou hast conquered after all, Galilean!"

1. *What might have been Constantine's interest in the Church?*
2. *What were the effects of the Edict of Milan on the membership of the Church? The purity of the Church? The Church's relation to the State and politics?*
3. *Does the Roman Catholic Church still maintain the tradition of a close alliance to governments?*
4. *Why was the Church's victory a marvel?*

CHAPTER *5*

The Church

Consolidates, 325-451

1. The Role of Church Councils • In the course of the Church's history many *councils* have been held. These are meetings of church leaders where important questions are discussed, advice is carefully given, and decisions are made. The first council ever held was the Council of the Apostles in Jerusalem. You remember that it was called to consider problems which arose as a result of the extension of the Church to the Gentiles.

There were various kinds of councils. Some represented a larger number of churches than others. A *provincial* council was a council in which the churches of only one province were represented. In a

national council the churches of one entire country were represented. A *general* council was one in which all churches of all countries were represented. Such a council was also called an *ecumenical* council. The Council of Nicaea in 325 was the first general or ecumenical council.

No agency has done more to consolidate and unify the Church than have the various general church councils. We will take particular note of four of them: the Council of Nicaea (325), the Council of Constantinople (381), the Council of Ephesus (431), and the Council of Chalcedon (451).

2. The Council of Nicaea • The great question which occupied the mind of the Church for some three hundred years was whether Christ, the Son, was as truly and fully God as the Father. Arius and Athanasius, presbyters in the church in Alexandria, were the two champions in the great struggle about this question.

At the time when the fierce controversy was fast coming to a climax, Athanasius was still a young man, but Arius was already far advanced in years. Arius was a pious man of blameless life and an able preacher.

The heathen believe in many gods. Arius thought that to believe that the Son is God as well as that the Father is God would mean that there are two Gods, and that therefore the Christians would be falling back into heathenism. So he taught that Christ, although He is somewhat like God, is after all not fully God.

According to Arius, Christ is the first and highest of all created beings. He does not exist from eternity, and is not of the same substance or essence as the Father. On the other hand, Athanasius taught that Christ is very God.

It should not be thought that this controversy concerning the person of Christ was a debate about an unimportant matter. A question of vital and lasting importance was at stake. What was at stake was nothing less than man's salvation. Christ's work and His *person* are inseparably connected. His work was defined by the angel when he announced: "Thou shalt call his name Jesus; for it is he that shall save his people from their sins" (Matthew 1:21). The value of Christ's saving work depends entirely upon what kind of person He is. Man's condition is so utterly hopeless that he cannot save himself. Only God can save him. If Christ is not God, He cannot be our Savior. It was Athanasius who felt this very deeply. He said, "Jesus, whom I know as my Redeemer, cannot be less than God."

The Arian controversy raged for a long time and with great bitterness. At last the emperor Constantine called a general council to settle the dispute. This council met in the year 325 in Nicaea, a small town in Asia Minor, on the shores of the Bosporus, some forty-five miles from Constantinople. More than three hundred bishops were present. They met in a great hall in the emperor's palace in a setting of pomp and splendor. Among the bishops there were those who bore in their bodies the marks of the tortures they had undergone for the sake of their faith during the severe persecutions.

The outcome of the proceedings of the Council of Nicaea was that the views of Arius were condemned as heresy. A statement of the true doctrine of the person of Christ was adopted as the faith of the Church. That statement elaborated and refined at later councils is known as the *Nicene Creed*. The Church wrestled with the decision of the council for sixty or seventy years and then made it its own.

The Nicene Creed is the first written creed of the Church. In this creed the Church confesses that Christ is very God of very God: begotten, not created; co-substantial with the Father. (Co-substantial means that the Son is of the same substance or essence or being as the Father.)

Thus the Church confessed its belief in the most fundamental article of the Christian faith: the deity of Christ. Ever since Nicaea this has been the faith of all Christians. It is the faith today of the Greek Orthodox and the Roman Catholic Church and of the churches of the Reformation.

3. The Council of Constantinople • The Nicene Council failed to end the Arian controversy. Arius himself and a few other bishops refused to sign the Nicene Creed. There were still many who agreed with Arius and many others who felt that the terms adopted by the council did not adequately express the faith. They received strong support from some of the emperors and certain members of the imperial court. Until the day of his death, Athanasius had to battle continuously for the doctrine of the deity of Christ as expressed in the Nicene Creed.

After the death of Athanasius the leadership in the struggle for *orthodoxy* (right Christian teaching) was taken over by three men, who are known as "the three great Cappadocians." They are so called because they came from the province of Cappadocia in Asia Minor and because these three were among the most outstanding men of the ancient Church. They were Basil of Caesarea, Gregory of Nazianzus, and Gregory of Nyssa. These three men stood firm and strong in defense of the teachings of Scripture.

The Nicene Creed had said nothing about the deity of the Holy Spirit. A second ecumenical council was held in the year 381 in Constantinople. This council reaffirmed the belief of the Church as expressed in the Nicene Creed and also declared its belief in the deity of the Holy Spirit. The doctrine of the Trinity is a fundamental article of the Christian faith. The belief of the Church in Father, Son, and Holy Spirit as the triune God was now fully established. This was the complete and final rejection of Arianism by the Church. From this time on Arianism disappeared.

4. The Council of Chalcedon • Even so, the Church had not yet fully expressed its understanding of the person of Christ. The Scriptures reveal Christ as being not only God but also man. In order that Christ may be our Savior, His full and complete humanity is just as important and necessary as His full and complete deity.

As there had been many different views in the Church about the deity of Christ, so there were many differences of opinion concerning His humanity, and concerning His two natures and their relation to each other. It required much hard study and deep thinking to arrive at a common and clear understanding on these points. Long

The Council of Chalcedon

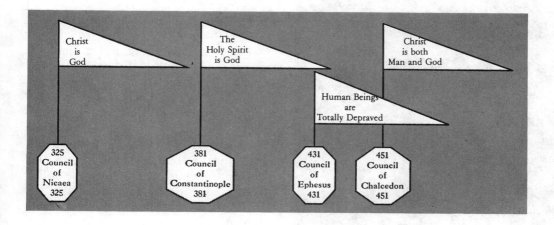

325 Council of Nicaea 325	Christ is God
381 Council of Constantinople 381	The Holy Spirit is God
431 Council of Ephesus 431	Human Beings are Totally Depraved
451 Council of Chalcedon 451	Christ is both Man and God

and severe controversies concerning the doctrine of Christ developed.

At last, in the year 451, a council was held in Chalcedon near Nicaea. This was the fourth ecumenical council. (The third one, the Council of Ephesus, we will discuss at a later point in this chapter.) Some six hundred bishops were present. In the creed formulated by this council, which stands on the same level of importance as the Creed of Nicaea, the Church reasserted its belief in the full and complete deity of Christ, but now also confessed its belief in His equally full and complete humanity. Furthermore the Church confessed the existence of two natures in Christ: the human and the divine. Concerning the relation of these two natures to each other the Church confessed that they exist in Christ without confusion, change, division, or separation. Finally, the Church confessed that while Christ has two natures, He is one person, not two persons.

The two Creeds of Nicaea and Chalcedon are the expression of the most fundamental articles of the Christian faith. The Reformation in the seventeenth century shattered forever the unity of the Church in the West. But it did not reject these creeds, nor did it make any changes in them. These two creeds remain today as the expression of the faith of the Greek, Roman Catholic, and most Protestant churches.

5. Ambrose • In the latter part of the fourth and the first part of the fifth century there were three great leaders in the western part of the Church. They were Ambrose, Jerome, and Augustine. These three men, commonly called the Latin Church Fathers, played an important part in the consolidation of the Church.

Ambrose (340–397) was born in the western part of Germany. His father held a high office there in the Roman government. He was educated in Rome, and early displayed great talents. While still very young he was appointed governor of a large part of northern Italy. His residence was in the city of Milan.

In the days of Ambrose there were still many Arians in the church of Milan. When the bishop of Milan died, both the Arians and the orthodox were determined

Ewing Galloway

Ambrose Rebukes Theodosius

Christian living. This is shown in the way he disciplined his emperor.

Emperor Theodosius was a hot-tempered man. Because the people of the city of Thessalonica had murdered his governor, he had thousands of the inhabitants massacred. Ambrose would not permit the emperor to take communion until he had publicly acknowledged his guilt and declared his repentance. The emperor submitted to the discipline of the Church. The happy outcome of this affair was a great credit to both bishop and emperor.

6. Jerome • Another great leader in the Church, Jerome, was born in Dalmatia around the year 340. Like Ambrose, he received his education in Rome.

Jerome liked to travel. He made many trips to various parts of the large Roman Empire. The last years of his life he spent in Bethlehem, the birthplace of Christ. There he lived as a *monk* (a man who withdraws from the world in order to devote himself entirely to meditation and religious exercise). He lived in a cave next to the cave in which Christ was supposed to have been born. He lived there from 386 until his death in 420.

Some two hundred years before Christ the Old Testament had been translated in Alexandria from Hebrew into Greek. This translation is called the *Septuagint,* because according to an old tradition it was made by seventy men. The Greek New Testament and this Greek translation of the Old Testament had been poorly translated into Latin.

Jerome was about the only western churchman who knew Hebrew, having learned Hebrew from Jewish rabbis when he lived in Antioch and Bethlehem. Je-

to elect a man of their belief as his successor. The meeting held to elect the new bishop became very disorderly. The young governor Ambrose entered the church to restore order. Suddenly a child's voice was heard above the uproar, crying, "Ambrose Bishop!" Ambrose was not a member of the Church, and had not been baptized. Nevertheless he was elected bishop. He considered this a call of God, gave all his money to the poor, received baptism, and was consecrated as bishop. This happened in the year 374.

Ambrose was a strong supporter of the Nicene Creed. He wrote many books, and he is classed among the *Doctors* or great teachers of the Church. He also did much to promote Christian hymnology. He was a very able administrator and was fearless in upholding a high standard of

PART ONE: WHEN THE CHRISTIAN CHURCH WAS YOUNG

rome proceeded to make a new Latin translation of the Bible. He translated the Old Testament not from the Greek Septuagint but from the original Hebrew. This Latin translation of the Bible by Jerome is known as the *Vulgate*. It was Jerome's noblest achievement and to this very day, in its revised forms and translations, it exercises tremendous influence in the Roman Catholic Church.

7. "A Son of So Many Prayers Cannot Be Lost" • The greatest of the Church Fathers was Augustine. He was born in Tagaste in North Africa in the year 354. Africa had already given two other great leaders to the Church: Tertullian and Cyprian.

Monica, Augustine's mother, was a Christian and is one of the famous mothers in history.

Augustine at an early age showed unusual ability. His parents wanted him to become a great man and, although they had to sacrifice to do so, provided him with the best of educational opportunities. But Augustine did not make as good use of these opportunities as he might have done. As a boy he often neglected his studies in order to play. One result was that he did not learn Greek. When he became older and wiser, he regretted this deeply. There were many books which Augustine wanted very much to read in the original Greek. Among these was the New Testament.

When Augustine was about sixteen his parents sent him to school in Carthage. This was the largest city in North Africa, and the best schools were there. Carthage was a very wicked city, full of temptations. Augustine studied hard, but he also plunged into a life of wickedness.

St. Jerome

The most zealous promoter of the monastic life among the Church Fathers was Jerome. Because his life belongs with almost equal right to the history of theology and the history of monasticism, Church art usually represents him as a penitent in a reading or writing posture, with a lion and a skull to denote the union of the literary and monastic modes of life.

All this time Monica was praying for the conversion of her son. Notwithstanding the tearful entreaties of his mother, Augustine left Africa and went to Rome. Sometimes Monica almost despaired. She was greatly comforted by a Christian friend who said to her, "A son of so many prayers cannot be lost."

Notwithstanding his immoral life Augustine was always searching for the

View of a Reconstruction of Rome at the Time of Aurelius

truth. He started to read the Bible but did not find it at all interesting. He liked the books of the great heathen poets and philosophers much better. At this time *Manicheism,* the philosophical system of Manes, a Persian, had many followers throughout the Empire. It was a strange mixture of heathen and Christian thoughts. For nine years Augustine was a Manichean.

When Augustine had been in Rome one year, he received the appointment as professor of rhetoric and public speaking in Milan. At this time Ambrose was bishop in that city. Augustine was very fond of oratory, and he would often go to hear Ambrose preach. At first he was not interested in what Ambrose said, but he went to observe how he used his hands and to admire his oratory.

At this time his mother, Monica, joined him in Milan. A great change was slowly taking place in Augustine's views. He was coming to see the errors of Manicheism. He listened to the sermons of Ambrose with a new attitude.

A certain Potitianus who had been to Egypt told Augustine about the thousands of monks in that country and what holy lives they were leading. The majority of these monks were ignorant men. Augustine felt ashamed that while these uneducated men had mastered their passions he, a learned man, had not been able to do so. He rushed out into the little garden behind the house. The copy of Paul's epistles which he was carrying he laid on the bench beside him. His soul was profoundly agitated. He got up from the bench and flung himself down on the grass beneath a fig tree. As he was lying there he heard a child next door sing the ditty: *Tolle, lege; tolle, lege,* which means, "Take up and read; take up and read."

He got up, returned to the bench, picked up the copy of Paul's epistles, and read: "Let us behave decently, as in the daytime, not in orgies and drunkenness, not in sexual immorality and debauchery, not in dissension and jealousy. Rather, clothe yourselves with the Lord Jesus Christ, and do not think about how to gratify the desires of the sinful nature" (Romans 13:13-14).

This was the turning point in Augustine's life. It was his conversion. From this moment on he was a changed man. The learned professor and accomplished public speaker enrolled as a humble catechumen to be instructed by the bishop of Milan. This happened in the late summer of the year 386. On Easter Sunday of the next year he was baptized.

8. Augustine Defends and Expounds Scripture • Augustine in course of time became bishop of Hippo in his native country of North Africa. Until his death in 430, he devoted himself heart and soul to the service of the Church. He founded the first *monastery* (home for monks) in North Africa. In public debate and with his pen he defended the teachings of the Church against heretics and those who would cause schism, or division, in the Church.

The controversies which occupied so much of Augustine's time and energy were with the Manicheans, the Donatists, and the Pelagians.

The *Donatists* were so called after their leader, Donatus. They were not heretics. In doctrine they were entirely orthodox. But they were schismatics, that is, they caused a division in the Church. During the severe persecution by Diocletian many Christians had denied the faith. The Donatists thought that these should not be readmitted to the Church. Some bishops had surrendered their copies of the Bible to the government officials to be burned by them. The Donatists believed that such bishops were not worthy to administer the sacraments or ordain others as bishops. They withdrew and organized

St. Augustine
After a painting by Botticelli

Historical Pictures Service—Chicago

A fifteenth-century miniature of St. Augustine's *City of God.* The upper inclosure represents the saints who have already been received into heaven; the seven lower inclosures represent those who are preparing themselves for the heavenly kingdom by the exercise of Christian virtues, or who are excluding themselves by committing one of the seven capital sins.

churches of their own. There were many Donatist churches in North Africa.

You will recall from our study of the organization of the Church that when heretics began breaking away and forming churches of their own, the great Church from which they separated took the name of the *Catholic,* or Universal, Church.

Now in Hippo, in North Africa, there were more Donatists than Catholics. Against them Augustine developed his doctrine of the Church and sacraments. He taught that the Catholic Church is the

PART ONE: WHEN THE CHRISTIAN CHURCH WAS YOUNG

only Church. To the Church he ascribed great authority. Said he: "I should not have believed the Gospel except as moved by the authority of the Catholic Church."

In his controversy with Pelagius, Augustine worked out the true doctrine concerning man and the manner of his salvation. *Pelagianism* derives its name from its founder, Pelagius, a British monk who denied that the human race had fallen in Adam. He denied original sin, the total depravity of man, and predestination. Pelagius taught that man is not born corrupt. Babies, he said, are innocent. They become bad when they grow up, through the bad example of others. Against him Augustine taught that every man is conceived and born in sin and can be saved only through the grace of God according to His divine good pleasure. This brings us to the Council of Ephesus, referred to in sections 1 and 4 of this chapter.

The teachings of Pelagius were condemned as heresy by the General Council of Ephesus in 431. In 529 the Synod of Orange condemned the teachings of the Semi-Pelagians—that it is up to the individual to accept or refuse God's offer of grace.

The teachings of Augustine largely dominated the Roman Catholic Church of the Middle Ages; and from this greatest of all Church Fathers, Luther and the other Reformers also received their inspiration.

The two most famous works of Augustine are his *Confessions* and *The City of God*. In his *Confessions* Augustine lays bare the secrets of his early life and the innermost depths of his mind and heart. In *The City of God* he gives his philosophy of history.

9. The Metropolitan and Patriarchal Systems • There was also in the period covered in this chapter a further and extremely important development in the *organization* of the Church. We have learned, in Chapter 3, how the system of monarchical episcopal government became general throughout the Church. Every church, or perhaps it would be better to say every diocese, had its bishop. At first all bishops were of the same rank. No bishop had any judicial power over any other bishops. Step by step, one bishop, the bishop of Rome, acquired power over other bishops and in that way became pope.

First of all the bishops of big churches in the large cities came to be looked upon as being of higher rank than the bishops of smaller churches. They came to be called *metropolitan bishops*.

Then in course of time the churches of five of the cities came to be regarded as having very special importance. These cities were Jerusalem, Antioch, Alexandria, Constantinople, and Rome. The bishops of the churches in these cities came to be called *patriarchs*. The first four cities were all in the eastern and Greek part of the Empire. Rome alone was in the western and Latin part of the Empire.

All the churches naturally held the church in Jerusalem in very high regard. A church had been there when as yet there was no church anywhere else. That church was the mother church. There the Christians had first been persecuted. There the first church council had been held. The church in Jerusalem was unique among all the churches. Gradually, however, the church in Jerusalem was eclipsed by new churches established in other cities.

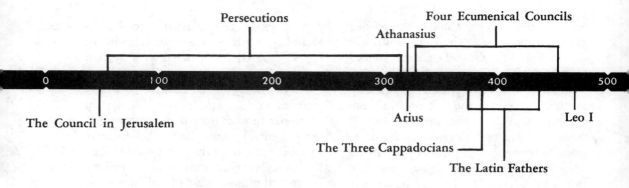

Persecutions

Four Ecumenical Councils

Athanasius

| 0 | 100 | 200 | 300 | 400 | 500 |

The Council in Jerusalem

Arius

Leo I

The Three Cappadocians

The Latin Fathers

Especially after the destruction of Jerusalem by the Romans under Titus in the year 70, and again under Hadrian in the years 132 and 135, the church in that city, as well as all the churches of Jewish Christians in Palestine, declined. The church in Jerusalem continued to exist for a number of centuries, although in a very much weakened condition. Nevertheless, because of ancient hallowed associations going back to the very beginning of the Church, the title of *patriarch* was accorded to its bishop.

Entirely different was the case of the church in Antioch. There the followers of Jesus had first been called Christians. There as well as in Jerusalem Paul had labored. There the work of missions among the Gentiles had its beginnings. The center of gravity in the Church had shifted from Jerusalem to Antioch. The church in Jerusalem had become a grandmother, but the church in Antioch was the mother of a multitude of churches in Asia Minor and Greece. Antioch had many notable bishops, and it had become the seat of an important school of theological thought. Besides, whereas Jerusalem was a small provincial town in an out-of-the-way corner, Antioch was the third city in size and importance in the Empire.

So the bishop of the church in Antioch received the title of *patriarch*.

Although the church in Alexandria could not claim apostolic origin, the evangelist Mark, according to an old tradition, had been active in its founding. It was the second city in the Empire, the greatest seat of learning and culture, and for centuries far more splendid than Rome itself. There, too, flourished a famous theological school, in which Origen, the greatest scholar of the Church up to that time, had taught. So its bishop also was allowed the title of *patriarch*.

Constantinople had originally been called Byzantium, an ancient town situated on the Bosporus. Constantine the Great, the first Christian emperor, had changed his residence from Rome to Byzantium. Then the town was renamed in his honor and called Constantinople. The church there could claim neither apostolic origin nor great antiquity. It owed its importance entirely to the fact that it was located in the city which had become the residence of the emperor. Its bishop also came to be called *patriarch*.

Rome was the first city in the Empire. Not only had Paul labored there, but according to tradition the church in Rome had been founded by the apostle Peter

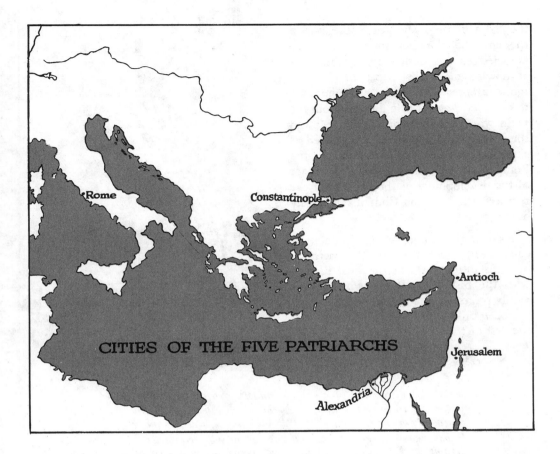

CITIES OF THE FIVE PATRIARCHS

To that apostle Christ had entrusted the keys, and it was claimed that Peter had transmitted the power of the keys to the bishops of Rome.

In almost every controversy the churches—East as well as West—had appealed to the bishop at Rome. In the great controversies about the person and nature of Christ, orthodoxy had gained the victory because of the influence of the West under the leadership of the bishop of Rome. As we have seen, the church at Jerusalem was no longer a leader among the churches; and so its voice bore little weight in these controversies. Between

the patriarchs of Antioch, Alexandria, and Constantinople there was ever the keenest rivalry for supremacy, and none of them was willing to acknowledge the supremacy of the bishop of Rome. But in their rivalry for supremacy they often sought the support of the bishop of Rome.

In all the western part of the Empire there was no church that could even begin to think of rivaling the church in Rome. As far back as around the year 185 Irenaeus had written in his book, *Against Heresies,* that every church must agree with the church in Rome. There was strenuous opposition sometimes to the claim of the bishop of Rome, but in the end the churches in the West acknowledged his supremacy. With this acknowledgment the papacy had come into existence. The bishop of Rome came to be called *pope*, a title derived from the Latin word *papa*, meaning "father"; and the church over which the pope ruled as supreme head came to be known as the Roman Catholic Church. The significance of the development of the papacy for the further history of the Church can hardly be exaggerated.

Against the canon of the Council of Chalcedon, which declared the patriarch of Constantinople to be of equal dignity with the bishop of Rome, Pope Leo I vainly protested. Leo I, who died in 461, has been called the last of the ancient and the first of the medieval popes.

S·LEO·MAGNVS·I·PAPA·ROMA·

Historical Pictures Service—Chicago

Leo I

1. *What is the function of a church council? An ecumenical council?*
2. *What did each of the four great councils mentioned in this chapter accomplish for the Church? What was the date of each council?*
3. *What were the great contributions to the Church made by Ambrose, Jerome, and Augustine?* (The Encyclopedia Britannica *contains excellent articles on each of these three men.*)
4. *What were the reasons for the rise of the bishop of Rome to a position superior to the other bishops?*
5. *The bishops of which cities were his chief rivals?*
6. *Why were these cities of great religious significance?*
7. *Which doctrine of Augustine was strengthened by his controversy with the Donatists? With the Pelagians?*
8. *Why do you think the episcopal form of church government arose rather than the presbyterian?*

CHAPTER 6

The Church

Deteriorates, 100-461

1. Many Evils Are Present • From the above dates you will notice that in this chapter we shall again go through a part of the same period of time already covered in the previous chapters. What has been told you so far is not all that happened during the first five hundred years of the Church's existence. The history of the Church is not a simple but a very complicated story.

What we have learned about the history of the Church so far is, for the most part, very good and inspiring. We saw the Church, heaven-born on the day of Pentecost, growing both outwardly and inwardly. We saw it emerge from bloody persecutions, victorious over heathenism, and firmly establishing its position.

But in this same time also many things happened which are not so pleasant and inspiring. The story we tell about the Church should be a true story. What we learned in the previous chapters is true, but it is not the whole story.

2. Early Signs of Deterioration •
In the epistles of the apostles, and in the
letters to the seven churches in Asia
which Christ himself dictated to John on
Patmos, we can already detect references
to the beginnings of deterioration. The
Apostolic Age came to a close around the
year 100. The apostles were followed by
the Apostolic Fathers. From their writings we can see that the signs of deterioration were disturbing the Church. In the
course of the next four hundred years that
deterioration increased steadily.

By the end of the fifth century the following unscriptural doctrines and practices had become deeply rooted in the
Church: prayers for the dead; a belief in
purgatory (place in which souls are purified after death before they can enter
heaven); the forty-day Lenten season; the
view that the Lord's Supper is a sacrifice,
and that its administrators are priests; a
sharp division of the members of the
church into *clergy* (officers of the church)
and *laity* (ordinary church members); the
veneration (adoration) of martyrs and
saints, and above all the adoration of
Mary; the burning of tapers or candles
in their honor; veneration of the relics of
martyrs and saints; the ascription of magical powers to these relics; pictures, images,
and altars in the churches; gorgeous
vestments for the clergy; more and more
elaborate and splendid *ritual* (form of
worship); less and less preaching; pilgrimages to holy places; monasticism:
worldliness; persecution of heathen and
heretics.

3. The Causes of Deterioration •
You may wonder at this great and sad
deterioration of the Church. Without

tracing the origin and development of
these deteriorations in detail, let us consider some of the causes that were at
work to bring them about.

First of all, there were the Christians
themselves. Every Christian is a saint, but
every saint is a sinner. Even when re-
generated, the sinner still has an inborn
tendency to commit sin and error.

Next, the ancient Church misunderstood
and misinterpreted certain teachings of
the Old Testament, of Christ, and of the
apostles. In a way the Bible is plain. But
because it is the Word of God it is also
very deep. It took the Church centuries
to study out the meaning of the Bible,
and that task is not yet finished.

Finally, there was the heathen *environ-
ment*. For centuries heathenism continued
to exist. The whole life of the people was
saturated with heathen ideas. When
Constantine the Great gave the Christians
freedom of religion, and when he showered favors upon the Church, thousands
upon thousands of heathen flocked into
the Church without having become true
Christians. A flood of worldliness en-
gulfed the Church. It was overwhelmed,
and could not handle the situation. So
many heathen clamored for admission
that the Church was not able to instruct
them all properly in the Christian religion. They took their heathen ideas along
with them into the Church. The moment
of the Church's victory over heathenism
became the hour of the Church's greatest
danger from heathenism.

All heathen religions had their sacrifices, their priests, and their altars. Soon
the Church had its sacrifice, its priests,
and its altars. The heathen had gods innumerable, and their images were to be

Religious News Service Photo

Monks in the Dining Room of Their Monastery

seen on every hand. Soon martyrs and saints take the place of the old heathen gods, and their images and those of Christ and of Mary appeared in the churches. Heathendom was full of superstition. Soon that superstition was transferred to pieces of the cross, and to the relics of saints and martyrs, such as bones and hair and fragments of clothing. Emperor Julian the Apostate called the Christians *bone worshippers.* In many lands among the heathen there were monks. Before long many Christians became monks and nuns.

4. **Monasticism Develops as a Reaction** • Christian monasticism began in Egypt. Its founder was Anthony of Thebes. About the year 270 he took up

the life of a monk in his native village. After some fifteen years he went to live alone in a cave in the desert, and thus became what is known as a *hermit,* one who withdraws from the world and lives alone. Many followed his example. Others lived together in large houses called *monasteries,* in which each monk had his cell.

From Egypt monasticism spread rapidly over the entire East. Sometimes it took very queer forms. In Syria a certain Simon lived for thirty years, until the very day of his death, on top of a pillar or *stylus.* He built several pillars, each one higher than the one before. His last pillar was sixty feet high and the top four feet square. He is known as Simon Stylites. Between the fifth and the twelfth centuries there were many pillar saints in Syria. Athanasius introduced monasticism into the West. Ambrose, Jerome, and Augustine did much to promote it. Monasticism was to be one of the outstanding features of the life of the Middle Ages.

Why did people become monks and nuns? They did so for various reasons, but the original motive was to flee from a world that was wicked in order to lead a holy life.

5. The Church Begins to Persecute Heretics • Almost as soon as the heathen stopped persecution of the Church, the Church began to persecute the heathen and also the heretics. The Church at this time did not torture or put persons to death, but the emperors who were now Christians forbade heathen worship and banished many of the leading heretics.

Sometimes Christians persecuted each other. Through the scheming of Theophilus, bishop of Alexandria, the greatest preacher of the Church was banished to a far distant, miserable little village. This preacher was Chrysostom, patriarch of Constantinople. The name Chrysostom means *golden mouth.* This name had been given to him because he was the most eloquent preacher the ancient Church produced. As an old man, he was exiled to Pontus. He was forced to march barefooted through the hot sand and bareheaded under a blazing sun. He died on the way.

Augustine advocated persecution on the basis of a statement in one of the parables of Jesus: "Compel them to come in" (Luke 14:23). This idea was to bear bitter fruit in the persecution of the Middle Ages and of the time of the Reformation.

1. *List and define the practices which the Church adopted at this time. How are they contrary to Scripture teachings? What harm did they do?*
2. *Was it right for men to leave the evil "world" in which they found themselves and to seek by asceticism to save their own souls?*
3. *Why would the Church persecute those who did not agree with it?*
4. *What would a Roman Catholic say about the "signs of deterioration?"*

CHAPTER 7

The Church Survives
And Grows Again, 376-754

1. A Summary of the Growth of the Ancient Church • The road of the Church's history is a long road. It is almost two thousand years long. By now we have walked some five hundred years down that road. There have been three big turns in that road. The first turn came when the Church, Christ's army, driven out of its original camp in Jerusalem, marched forth into Judea and Samaria and as far as Antioch in Syria. The second turn came when that army under the leadership of Paul invaded the great Gentile world of the Roman Empire. The third turn came when that army, after a bloody war of three hundred years, in 313 gained the victory over heathenism in the Edict of Milan.

We have followed the victorious march of Christ's army from Jerusalem to Spain in the western part of the Roman Empire, that is, from the eastern to the western end of the Mediterranean. We have been in many lands: Palestine, Syria, Asia Minor, Persia, Macedonia, Greece, Italy, Gaul, Egypt, and North Africa. We have been in many cities: Jerusalem, Samaria, Caesarea, Antioch, Smyrna, Nicaea, Chalcedon, Constantinople, Rome, Milan, Bethlehem, Lyons, Alexandria, Carthage, Tagaste, and Hippo. We have been in the studies of learned scholars, in caves in the desert, in the cells of monks, in dungeons, in amphitheaters with wild beasts, in the catacombs, in churches, and in imperial palaces. We have witnessed a great variety of scenes. We have become acquainted with many people. (See maps pages 16 and 26.)

2. Rome Is the Center of a Great Empire • The Roman Empire and the Christian Church came into existence at about the same time. Now the Empire in the West is about to fall, while the Christian Church continues. But the fall of the Empire in the West will have a profound effect upon the whole history of the Church from this time on. It will mark another important turn in the road of the Church's history. Before we go down that

new turn in the road, let us take a look at the Roman Empire as it existed at this time.

The city of Rome had extended its power over Italy, Sicily, North Africa, and Spain. Then its legions turned east and conquered many of the territories of Greece, Asia Minor, Syria, Palestine, and Egypt. Later Rome conquered Gaul (now France), what is now Belgium and the Netherlands, and Britain. Thus the Roman Empire was bounded by the Sahara Desert on the south, by the Atlantic Ocean on the west, by the Rhine and Danube rivers on the north, and by the Euphrates River on the east. (See maps pp. 16, 26.)

From the western waters of the Atlantic and the southern sands of the Sahara, Rome had nothing to fear. East of the Euphrates were the Parthians and the Persians. They often threatened the Roman Empire, but the Romans were always able to hold these enemies in check. Along the northern frontier, however, it was a different story.

3. German Tribes Invade the Empire • East of the Rhine and north of the Danube were German tribes. Behind the German tribes were the Mongolian Huns. The Huns crowded the German tribes. The Germans were barbarians but the Huns were worse. They were fierce horsemen, hideous to look upon. In mortal dread of the Huns, a German tribe, the Visigoths (West Goths) in 376 crossed the lower Danube, exactly one hundred years before the last emperor was removed by Odoacer. It was the first tribe of barbarians to enter the Empire. Soon they were joined by the Ostrogoths (East Goths). The Roman emperor

Valens, in the year 378, gave them battle near the city of Adrianople. The Roman army was annihilated, and Valens was killed. His successor was Theodosius. An able statesman and general, he subdued the Goths. Thereafter the barbarians left the eastern part of the Empire alone. It continued to exist as the Eastern or Byzantine Empire throughout the entire Middle Ages.

Having failed in the East, the Goths, together with other German tribes, attacked the western part of the Roman Empire. The Empire was decaying, but it was large and still had some strength left. It took the barbarians one hundred years, from the crossing of the Danube by the Visigoths in 376 to the fall of Rome in 476, to conquer the western part of the Empire.

These last hundred years of the Empire in the West were a time of great suffering and disaster. It was in those dark days that Ambrose, Jerome, and Augustine lived.

Hosts of barbarians slashed their way through the Empire, leaving a gory trail wherever they went. Matrons, virgins, bishops, and priests were insulted and slain. Churches were destroyed and horses stabled at their altars. The relics of martyrs were dug up. Monasteries were laid waste. Rivers were dyed red with blood. Crowds of men and women were dragged away into captivity. The Roman world was rushing to ruin.

4. The Empire Falls • In 410 Rome was sacked by the Goths under Alaric. For six days and nights the barbarians trooped through the city. Soon the streets were wet with blood. The palace of the emperors and the residences of the

Brown Brothers

The Vandals Pillage Rome

wealthy citizens were stripped of their costly furniture, their precious vessels and jewels, their silken and velvet hangings, and their beautiful objects of art. The city which had plundered the world was now itself plundered.

The awful calamity that had befallen the "Mistress of the World" shocked pagans and Christians alike. Jerome was sitting in his cave in Bethlehem, writing his *Commentary on the Prophecies of Ezekiel,* when he heard the news. He was overwhelmed with anguish and consternation. He believed that the antichrist was

The Huns Invade the Empire

at hand. He said: "The world is rushing to ruin. The glorious city, the capital of the Roman Empire, has been swallowed up in one conflagration. Churches once hallowed have sunk into ashes. Virgins of God have been seized, maltreated, and murdered." He was so struck with horror that he could scarcely pick up courage to work. In his introduction to his commentary on Ezekiel he wrote: "Who could have believed it that Rome, founded on triumphs over the whole world, could fall to ruin; and that she, the mother of nations, should also be their grave?"

The pagans who still remained in the Roman Empire believed that the ancient gods had made Rome great. They blamed the Christians, who had forsaken those gods, for the calamities that had befallen Rome. In answer, Augustine, amid the tremors and rumblings of the stricken Empire, wrote *The City of God,* his greatest book, and Christianity's most brilliant apology.

The Vandals were the next tribe to plunder Rome. After occupying Spain and North Africa, they crossed the Mediterranean Sea and took Rome in the year 455.

Meanwhile the Huns, who had been exerting pressure on all these Germanic tribes, were defeated at the battle of Chalons. Their leader Attila turned toward Rome, but the intercession of Leo I saved the city.

Eventually the barbarians conquered every province of the western part of the Empire: Italy, North Africa, Spain, Gaul, including the Netherlands, and Britain.

The Empire fell, but the Church survived. Many of the barbarian tribes had accepted Christianity and respected the bishop of Rome. The position of the Church was improved by the successes of the bishop of Rome in protecting the people to a certain extent from the worst excesses of the barbarians when the emperor had not been able to protect them.

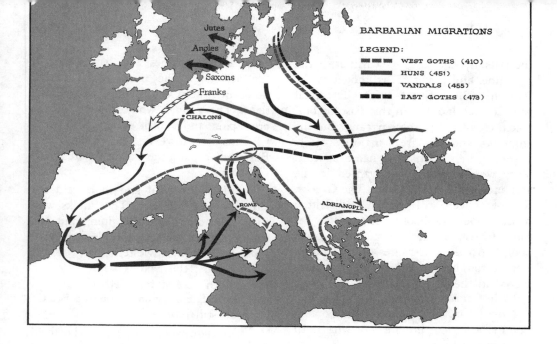

BARBARIAN MIGRATIONS

LEGEND:

▬▬ WEST GOTHS (410)
▬▬ HUNS (451)
▬▬ VANDALS (455)
▬▬ EAST GOTHS (473)

When the smoke and dust cleared away there stood, intact among the blackened ruins of the Empire, the Church, ready to bless and educate the barbarians who had caused this ruin.

5. The Distribution of Peoples • With their invasion of the western part of the Roman Empire and their conquest of Rome in 476, the barbarians brought Ancient History to an end and ushered in the Middle Ages, which were to continue for almost a thousand years until the fall of Constantinople in 1453.

For the understanding of the history of the Church which now follows it is necessary to know what peoples lived in each of the countries at this time.

Let us begin with the *eastern part of the Empire.* It was this part of the Roman Empire that was not conquered and occupied by the barbarians. It embraced

Odacer compels the last
Roman Emperor, Augustulus,
to yield the crown.

*Historical Pictures
Service—Chicago*

the Balkan Peninsula, Asia Minor, Syria, Palestine, and Egypt. It is known as the Eastern or Byzantine Empire. Its capital was Constantinople. In this Eastern Empire there were still some pagans. But the emperors and the great majority of its citizens were Christians in name, at least. They were also highly advanced in the arts and in human thought. The Greeks, when they were still heathen, had written many wonderful books. After they became Christians they wrote other great books. All these treasures of civilization were throughout the Middle Ages preserved in the Eastern Empire, and especially in Constantinople.

Now let us take a look at the population in the various provinces of what until recently had been the *western part of the Roman Empire.*

First of all there was Italy. Originally Italy had been inhabited by a great many different tribes. After Rome conquered all of Italy, its inhabitants were Romanized. They learned to speak Latin, the language of the Romans. Eventually the great majority of people confessed the Christian religion. After the invasion by the barbarians, the Ostrogoths settled in Italy among the native population. The Goths, both the Ostrogoths and the Visigoths, had been converted to Christianity before they invaded the Empire. This had come about through the preaching and teaching of Ulfilas, a bishop who also translated a large part of the Bible into Gothic.

The southern part of Gaul and the northern half of Spain were occupied by the Visigoths. Like their kinsmen, the Ostrogoths in Italy, they had accepted Christianity.

There were besides the Goths many other German tribes who had a part in the invasion. The Burgundians settled down in eastern Gaul. They were Christians. The Vandals who conquered southern Spain and North Africa also were Christians. However, the Goths, the Burgundians, and the Vandals were Arian Christians.

In Northern Gaul and in Britain the situation was different. The Franks who took northern Gaul, Belgium, and the southern Netherlands; the Frisians who lived in the northwestern part of the Netherlands; the Saxons who settled in the eastern part of the Netherlands; and the Anglo-Saxons who conquered Britain were all still heathen.

Then there were the people who lived in *countries which never had been part of the Roman Empire:* the Celts in Ireland; the Scandinavians in what is now Denmark, Norway, and Sweden; the many German tribes east of the Rhine; and beyond them still farther east the tribes in what is now Russia. All these teeming millions scattered over all these vast territories were heathen.

6. The Church Faces a Twofold Task • The Church at the beginning of the Middle Ages differed greatly from what it had been at the beginning of its existence. The conditions which the Church had now to face were also vastly different from those which it had encountered in its early years.

At its beginning the Church was very small and weak, but the people to whom Paul and the other missionaries brought the Gospel were civilized. Those people lived in the Roman Empire. The Roman government maintained peace and order throughout the Empire, and that Empire

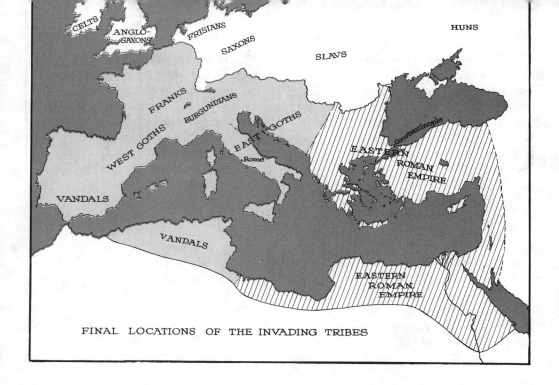

FINAL LOCATIONS OF THE INVADING TRIBES

was covered with a network of excellent roads for travel.

At this later period the Church, although in many ways seriously deteriorated, was large, strongly organized under its bishops, and in possession of a well-worked-out body of doctrines. But the Church now lacked the protection of the one Roman government. In its place had been set up a number of barbarian kingdoms. Some of these kingdoms, like that of the Franks in Gaul and those of the Anglo-Saxons in Britain, were heathen. The tribes living outside the former territories of the Empire were also heathen, and the country in which they lived was wild, uncultivated, and without roads. Besides, all these nations and tribes were barbarous, ignorant, uneducated, and uncultured.

The Church once more, as in its beginning, faced a heathen world. However, there was a difference. The heathen to whom it now had to bring the Gospel were not civilized, but barbarous. And so the Church, standing at the beginning of the Middle Ages, saw set before it a twofold task: that of *Christianizing* and that of *educating* the new nations.

The accomplishing of this task, however imperfectly, within the next thousand years was a remarkable achievement on the part of the Church. In the five hundred years following the invasion of the Roman Empire by the barbarians, that is, by the year 1000, all the new nations of Europe had been Christianized. By the end of the next five hundred years, that is, by the year 1500, new nations with their own cultures had developed, influenced by the medieval civilization they had inherited.

7. The Ancient Civilization Is Preserved • The barbarians were ignorant but not stupid. Stupidity is incurable; ignorance can be cured by education. But the barbarians were not totally ignorant. In fact, they knew many things. They had a religion and a mythology—stories and ideas about their imaginary gods. They had laws and a system of government; they knew how to make a living; they knew how to make war well enough to defeat the Romans; they knew how to make songs and stories. But they did not know how to read or write. Their ignorance was ignorance of books.

When the barbarians invaded the Empire they destroyed *many* but not *all* the books. Thousands of the inhabitants of the Empire were killed, but among those who were not killed were a good many educated people. Some of the learned men who survived the invasion of the barbarians wrote books in which they handed on to the Middle Ages much of the learning of the ancient world.

This is where the monks played an important part. Many of them were educated and could read and write. There were no printed books at this time; all books were written by hand. These manuscripts, or handwritten copies, would wear out, and the only way to replace them was to make copies of them. That is what the monks did as they sat in their cells. By doing this they rendered an invaluable service to civilization. During the first three hundred years after the invasion very few barbarians took an interest in books. These were the Dark Ages. But the monks, by their patient drudgery and persistent industry in copying manuscripts, maintained a supply of books. In this way they provided the means for the education of the new nations at a time when they would be ready for it.

8. The Franks Are Converted • The Franks, under the leadership of their king, Clovis, gradually extended their rule over all Gaul. From that time on

Workroom of a
Manuscript Writer
and Illuminator
of the Middle Ages

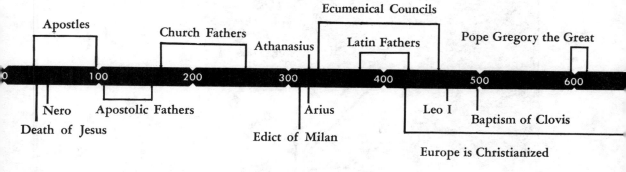

This time line reviews the development of the
young Church which we have studied in Part One.

Gaul was called France. The Franks were the first Germanic tribe to adopt Christianity after the invasion. The story told about the conversion of Clovis is very similar to the story told about the conversion of Emperor Constantine. In the heat of a desperate battle Clovis saw the sign of the cross in the sky. He vowed that he would become a Christian if he won the battle. After the victory was gained, he was baptized, together with three thousand of his warriors, on Christmas day of the year 496 in the city of Rheims.

Heretofore people had accepted Christianity individually. From this time on whole tribes became Christians when their kings became Christian.

Whereas the other German tribes who had accepted Christianity were Arians, the Franks adopted the orthodox Christianity of the Nicene Creed. From the start, therefore, they were in agreement with the Catholic Church, which had prevailed in the Empire, while the other converted German tribes were heretics.

The conversion of the Franks to orthodox Christianity was an event of the greatest importance. It was to have tremendous consequences for the future history of the Church. More than two hundred years were to pass by before the consequences would unfold.

9. The British Isles Are Christianized • Before the fall of the Empire in the West, Christianity was introduced into Britain by Christian Roman soldiers. In the last years of the Empire in the West, a British monk, St. Patrick, became "the Apostle of Ireland." By the time of his death in 461 the Church was firmly established in that country. The Irish monasteries became famous centers of learning; but they owed their greatest fame to their missionary activities.

About a hundred years after the death of St. Patrick, an Irish monk by the name of Columba founded a monastery on the island of Iona, off the west coast of Scotland. From there he set out with a number of companions to do missionary work in Scotland where his labors were blessed, and the Church was planted. Other Irish monks brought the Gospel to the Germans east of the Rhine.

One year before the death of Columba

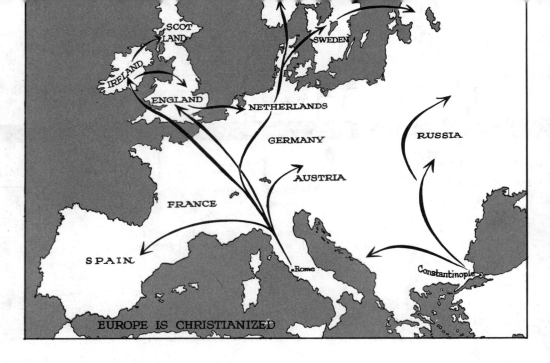

EUROPE IS CHRISTIANIZED

in 597, Pope Gregory the Great sent the monk Augustine with forty other monks to England, which in Roman times had been known as Britain. Since the conquest of Britain by the Angles and Saxons it had become known as *Angleland* or *England*. The Angles and Saxons were fierce heathen. When they conquered Britain in the fifth century they erased every trace of Christianity in the island, and made of it a heathen country again.

More than one hundred years later Pope Gregory's attention, as he walked through the slave market in Rome, had been attracted to some fair-haired, blue-eyed youths. On being told that they were Angles he said: "Not Angles, but Angels." It was then that he decided to send missionaries to England to regain that country for Christ. It took more than a hundred years to re-establish Christianity in England and drive out heathenism.

10. Germany and the Netherlands Are Evangelized • After they were converted, the English became great missionaries. They labored among the heathen in the northern part of the European continent. The greatest of these missionaries was Boniface. He first preached to the Frisians, but without success. Then he crossed the Rhine into Germany, and there he won many converts. One of the greatest gods of the German heathen was Thor. Boniface cut down a big oak which was believed to be sacred to that god. The heathen looked on with awe, expecting that Thor, the god of thunder, would strike him down with lightning. When nothing happened to him the heathen gave up their belief in Thor, and accepted Christianity. Of the wood of the oak the missionary built a chapel. To this day Boniface is known as "the Apostle of Germany."

At the age of 73 Boniface returned to

PART ONE: WHEN THE CHRISTIAN CHURCH WAS YOUNG

Boniface stands by the fallen oak tree which the Germans had regarded as sacred to Thor.

Bettmann Archive

his first field of labor among the Frisians. While baptizing some converts, Boniface and 53 of his companions were murdered by hostile Frisians. That was in the year 754.

Another English monk who labored in the Netherlands, from 690 to 739, was Willibrord. His labors resulted in the establishment of the Archbishopric of Utrecht. That city is even now the headquarters of the Roman Catholic Church in the Netherlands.

By the year 1000 the Christianization of Denmark, Norway, Sweden, and Russia had also made good progress.

11. Gregory Symbolizes the Medieval Church • The most important pope in the days when the new barbarian kingdoms were being built up on the ruins of the Empire in the West was Gregory the Great. He was the first monk to become pope, ruling from 590 to 604. He called himself "the servant of the servants of God," a title used by popes down to the present day.

Gregory the Great stood for all the things which form the most distinctive traits of the Church of the Middle Ages. He was the first of the popes to assume broad political powers. He had more

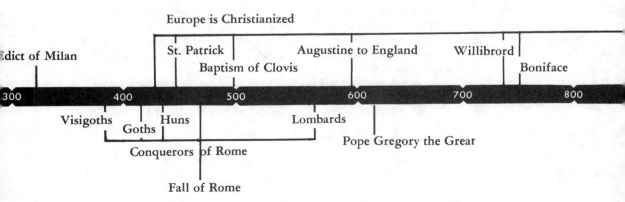

Europe is Christianized

Edict of Milan   St. Patrick   Augustine to England   Willibrord   Boniface

Baptism of Clovis

300 — 400 — 500 — 600 — 700 — 800

Visigoths   Huns   Lombards
Goths
Conquerors of Rome   Pope Gregory the Great

Fall of Rome

power in Italy than had the emperors, although legally and in theory Italy still belonged to the Eastern Empire. Gregory served as secular ruler by appointing heads of cities, by raising armies, and by making peace treaties. He was able to keep the Lombards, who had conquered northern Italy, at bay.

In these activities he was assuming many of the powers which the decaying Roman Empire had relinquished. In years to come the Church, by taking upon itself governing tasks, became the directing power of European politics, using old territorial divisions of the Empire for ecclesiastic administrative units. The Church took up the work of education, of the care of the poor, and of maintaining a semblance of justice. Had the Church not done this, Europe would certainly have experienced a deeper valley of darkness than it did during the difficult days of readjustment to the barbarian invasions. We may object to the methods used, or the type of work it did, but we may not forget that the Church here rendered an exceedingly valuable service to civilization.

Pope Gregory the Great strongly upheld the Roman bishop's claim to power over the entire Church as successors of the apostle Peter. It was Gregory whose work in behalf of missions, as we saw a while back, had such far-reaching results. To him has been ascribed the style of church music known as the Gregorian chant. Gregory taught (1) that the Lord's Supper is a repetition of the sacrifice of Christ, (2) that the saints can be of help to us, and (3) that there is a purgatory.

The Church within five hundred years from its birth conquered the highly civilized heathenism of the Roman Empire. In the course of the next five hundred years, after the fall of the Empire in the West, it conquered the barbarous heathenism of northern Europe.

While engaged in this strenuous, large-scale gospel campaign with its many fierce battles, the Church itself underwent certain great changes, as we shall learn in the following chapters.

1. *Why did St. Augustine write his famous work,* The City of God?
2. *What new tasks presented themselves to the Church when the barbarians had invaded and settled down in the Roman Empire?*
3. *What important work did the monks perform during the dark days of the early Middle Ages?*
4. *What effect did mass conversion have on the purity of the Church?*
5. *Read the splendid short chapter on Pope Gregory I in Cairns'* Christianity Through the Centuries.
6. *Why did the Church survive the barbarian invasion?*
7. *How did the Franks differ from the Vandals as to Christianity? How did this affect the Church?*
8. *Use an encyclopedia or a church history book to find the interesting life story of St. Patrick, missionary to Ireland.*
9. *Note and list the dates and works of Augustine, Boniface, and Willibrord.*

part two

The Church
in the Middle Ages

Part Two

THE CHURCH IN THE MIDDLE AGES

In the second part of our book we are going to follow the Church's history from the time of the Muslim conquest to the dawn of the Reformation.

During this period, known as the Middle Ages, the Church divided into two parts —an Eastern and a Western Church. From that point on our attention focuses on the Latin Western Church.

To the great distress of its leaders, the Church with its huge organization came under the control of the civil government. Repeatedly it tried to free itself and gain control over the State. Popes and emperors schemed for power, and many a dramatic scene took place as the one or the other bowed in defeat.

The Crusades were holy wars, in which the Western Church sent armies of volunteers against the Turks in the East to fight for possession of the Holy Land. The contacts thus made with the ancient and rich civilizations of the East stimulated thought and study in the West. The popes became more interested in pagan culture than in Christian truth. People began to question the teachings and practices of the Church. Some began to spread non-Christian ideas. Others, who were steadfast in the faith, clamored for reform.

The end of this section will find the time growing ripe for a tremendous upheaval in the Church and in the entire western world.

CHAPTER 8

The Church

Loses Territory, 632-732

1. The Curtain Opens on a Scene of Disaster • The eastern part of the Empire escaped the barbarian deluge and for a time enjoyed comparative peace. But for fifty years after the destruction of the Empire in the West, the eastern part had to fight for its life. At first it was kept busy beating off the attacks of the German tribes who tried to cross its borders from the north. After this had been done,

the emperor Justinian was even able to reconquer Italy from the Ostrogoths and North Africa from the Vandals, and regain those provinces for the Empire in the East.

Another fifty years passed. Then the emperor Heraclius had to wage a desperate war with the Persians. In the terrible battle of Nineveh in the year 627 the Persian army was annihilated, and the

Empire in the East was saved. However, this security lasted only a short time. Then calamity befell also the eastern part of the Empire. It was not completely destroyed as had been the western part, but some of its provinces were taken from it. They were never regained. This chapter is the story of that calamity.

The German tribes that conquered the western part of the Empire had come from the North. They were of the same Aryan or Indo-European race as the inhabitants of the Empire, and for the most part confessed the same Christian religion. The Arabs who conquered some of the provinces of the eastern part of the Empire came from the South. They were of a race and religion different from that of the inhabitants of the Empire. The Arab conquerors were Semitic by race and Muslim in religion.

In the foregoing chapter we saw th the Church in the West not only survived the invasion by the German tribes, but thereafter enjoyed extensive growth. In this chapter we shall see that the invasion of the eastern part of the Empire by the Arabs was for the Church in that part of the world nothing short of disaster.

2. Mohammed • The inhabitants of Arabia were descendants of Ishmael, son of Abraham and half-brother of Isaac. They were heathen, worshiping idols and believing in many gods.

In this heathen country of Arabia there was born in the city of Mecca in the year 570 a boy to whom was given the name Mohammed. In his youth he was a shepherd. Later he became a merchant, and with his caravan of camels he traveled to various countries. In his travels he came in contact with Jews and Christians and learned something of their religion. He liked to retire to a solitary place for meditation. There he claimed to have received revelations from the angel Gabriel. The result of his observations and meditations was a new religion called *Islam*. The teachings of Mohammed were later collected and written in a book called the *Koran*, which is the sacred book of the followers of Islam to this day. His fundamental teaching is: There is but one God, and Mohammed is his prophet. The Arabian name for God is Allah. The followers of Islam, called *Muslims*, sum up their religion in the saying: Allah is great, and Mohammed is his prophet.

Mohammed gained a few converts, but most of the people of Mecca, who believed in many gods, did not like his

Mohammed Dictates the Koran

*Schoenfeld Collection
from Three Lions*

Courtesy Arabian American Oil Company

This building, covered with a black curtain, is the Holy Ka'ba in Mecca to which millions of Muslims turn their faces five times every day as they kneel down to pray. Pilgrims kiss the sacred black stone embedded in the wall of the cube-shaped shrine.

teachings. The opposition became so strong that in the year 622 he and his followers had to flee to the city of Medina. This flight is called the *Hegira.* There his teachings were warmly received, and with the help of his converts in ten years' time he made himself master of Arabia.

3. Many Imperial Provinces Are Conquered • Mohammed died in 632, but his influence did not die with him. In the next one hundred years his followers, large hosts of fierce horsemen, swept out of the hot deserts of Arabia, conquered Persia, penetrated into India, overran the imperial province of Asia Minor, twice laid siege, although in vain, to Constantinople itself, and took away from the East-

ern Empire the provinces of Syria, Palestine, Egypt, and North Africa.

The Arabs did not stop in North Africa. They went on, crossed the straits of Gibraltar, and in the years 711 to 718 conquered Spain.

Neither did the Arabs stop in Spain. They crossed the Pyrenees, and penetrated into the center of what for four hundred years had been the Roman province of Gaul, but had now for some two hundred years belonged to the Franks.

The emblem of Islam is the *crescent* (the shape of the moon as it appears at first quarter). This crescent now lay across northern Africa with one point resting on Asia Minor and the other on France. It seemed as if the moon might become full, and that all Europe might become Muslim. The mo-

Charles Martel Halts the Muslim Invasion at Tours

ment was one of the great crises in the history of the Church and the world.

4. **The Battle of Tours** • Once before in 451 Europe had been threatened with a terrible danger. This was even before the fall of Rome. Then Attila and his barbaric Huns were defeated in the battle of Chalons, which is also located in France. Now once more, almost three hundred years later, the whole future of Europe, of the Church, and therefore of the world, was at stake. Islam seemed ready to engulf Christianity.

At this point you must recall that the conversion of Clovis, king of the Franks, back in 496, and the adoption of Christianity by the heathen Franks was an event of the utmost importance. The Franks now came forward as the champions of Christianity.

Charles, the leader of the Franks, sent out a call for every man in all the Frankish lands able to bear arms to come to his aid. There was a general sense of the greatness of the danger threatening all that men held dear. Even Frisians and tribes across the Rhine responded to the call.

A great "Christian" army under the command of Charles met the countless Muslim hosts on the plain of Tours in the year 732. Both sides felt that tremendous issues would be decided by the one single battle that was impending. For seven days the two armies faced each other. Neither side dared to begin the attack. At last on a Saturday in October the battle lines were formed. The Arab army was composed mainly of cavalry; the Frankish army of foot soldiers. The hosts of Islam had behind them one long and unbroken series of victories extending over a hundred years. They had conquered country after country in that time. Why should they not likewise win this battle?

The Franks drew up their army in close order. Nowhere was there a gap in their ranks. All day long, in charge after charge, the wild and expert Arab horsemen swept down headlong and furiously upon the Frankish army. Over their heads fluttered the crescent banners of Islam. It was becoming evident that the crescent was destined not to become full. Helplessly the charges of the Arab horsemen broke against the Frankish army as against a wall. The banners of the cross continued to wave defiantly. When night fell both sides retired exhausted to their camps. Heaps of dead covered the bloody field of Tours. But the most furious attacks of the Arabs had been baffled. As the Franks left the battlefield they still brandished their swords.

Early the next morning the Franks again drew up in battle array, but no Arab horsemen appeared. Fearing an ambush, the Franks sent out searching parties. For miles around no enemy was to be seen. In the deserted Arab camp they found piles of plunder from many lands. The Arabs had retreated behind the Pyrenees into Spain.

Tours was the high-water mark of the Muslim tide. The once heathen and barbarian tribe of the German Franks had saved western Europe for Christianity.

To Charles, the Frankish commander in the battle of Tours, was given the title of *Martel,* which means "hammer." He is known to history as Charles Martel, or Charles the Hammer.

5. The Losses to Islam • The hosts of Islam had been stopped at Tours, but in the wake of their conquests they left behind them the wreckage of many churches in many lands.

By the conquests of Islam the Christain Church was deprived of possible mission fields among many heathen nations. In India today there are many millions of Muslims. Perisa became entirely Muslim. In addition to that, the Arabs had cast up a Muslim barrier across the road from Christian Europe to the heathen nations of the Orient—walls which for many centuries remained insurmountable.

The Church itself had been sadly torn. (It would be well to use the map, p. 67, in studying this paragraph.) The provinces of Syria, Palestine, Egypt, and North Africa, which were wrested by the Arabs from the Eastern Empire, had been the seat of numerous and flourishing Christian churches. Spain, too, had been a Christian land. Consider, for a moment, the long list of casualties: *Jerusalem* in

Muslims take
off their shoes
before entering
the Mosque for
prayer.

Palestine had been the cradle of the Church. In *Bethlehem* Jerome, the greatest scholar of the Church in the West, had given to the Church his translation of the Bible into Latin. *Antioch* in Syria had been the gateway through which Christianity, in the person of Paul, had come into the Roman Empire. It had also been the scene of the marvelous eloquence of Chrysostom, the greatest preacher of the ancient Church. *Alexandria* in Egypt had been the home of Clement; of Origen, the greatest scholar of the Church in the East; and of Athanasius, the father and fearless champion of orthodoxy and the inspirer of the Creed of Nicaea. In *Carthage* and in *Hippo* in North Africa, Tertullian, Cyprian, and Augustine, the greatest of the Fathers of the ancient Church, had taught. In *Seville* in Spain, Isidore, the head of the Spanish Church, had labored mightily and with vast learning to pass on the knowledge of the highly cultured Greeks and Romans of the ancient world to the barbarous German tribes of the Middle Ages.

Syria, Palestine, and *Egypt* to this day remain overwhelmingly Muslim. The few weak Christian churches remaining in those countries lead but a feeble existence. Cairo in Egypt is today the seat of a great Muslim university, the intellectual citadel of Islam. Christian missions in those lands seem to be plowing upon rock.

In *North Africa* the Church was for hundreds of years completely wiped out. No trace of it remained. It is only within the past century that the Church has been reintroduced into North Africa through the colonizing activities of the Spaniards, French, and Italians; but it is a very small, weak, and deformed Church. Islam at the same time remains the religion of the natives. The descendants of the Arabs in North Africa and Spain became known as Moors.

In the continent of Africa Christian missions among the heathen Negro tribes are meeting with strong competition from Muslim missions, and Islam is still spreading.

PART TWO: THE CHURCH IN THE MIDDLE AGES

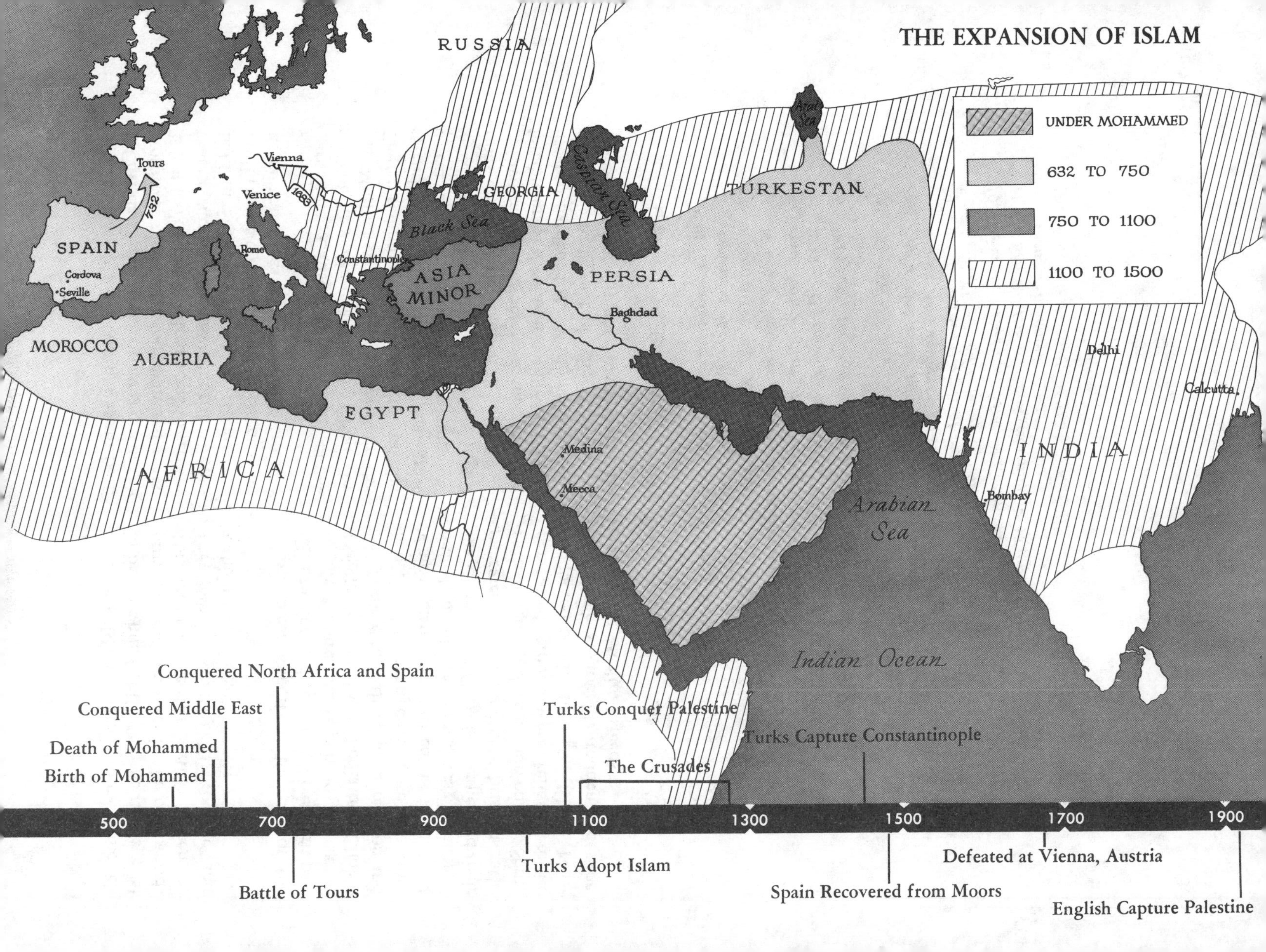
THE EXPANSION OF ISLAM
UNDER MOHAMMED
632 TO 750
750 TO 1100
1100 TO 1500
RUSSIA
GEORGIA
TURKESTAN
Caspian Sea
Aral Sea
Black Sea
ASIA MINOR
PERSIA
Baghdad
Delhi
Calcutta
INDIA
Bombay
Arabian Sea
Indian Ocean
Medina
Mecca
EGYPT
AFRICA
MOROCCO
ALGERIA
SPAIN
Cordova
Seville
Tours
732
Vienna
1683
Venice
Rome
Constantinople
Conquered North Africa and Spain
Conquered Middle East
Death of Mohammed
Birth of Mohammed
Turks Conquer Palestine
The Crusades
Turks Capture Constantinople
500
700
900
1100
1300
1500
1700
1900
Battle of Tours
Turks Adopt Islam
Spain Recovered from Moors
Defeated at Vienna, Austria
English Capture Palestine

The *Spanish peninsula* has again been a Christian land, in the broad sense of the word, for more than four hundred years. But it took eight hundred years to recover that territory. The last Moorish stronghold in Spain was Granada. It was not until the year 1492 that the crescent upon its ramparts was replaced by the cross.

6. The Causes for Defeat • The story of the violence done to the Church by the Muslims is a black chapter in the Church's history. Christ's army in the seventh century suffered its first great defeat, and that defeat was staggering.

What were the causes of this inglorious defeat of the Church?

Civilization had softened the Christian inhabitants of the Empire, while wild desert life had hardened the Muslim Arabs. Monasticism had robbed the Empire of thousands who might have been its defenders. Islam promised to men who fell in battle while fighting for the faith special privileges and pleasures in the next world. This inspired the fierce Arab horsemen. They fought with reckless courage and without fear of death.

But most important, the salt of the Christianity of that day in the eastern part of the Empire had largely lost its savor. (See Matthew 5:13.) The Eastern Church had become formalized in its religion and had failed to evangelize those areas into which Islam now carried its faith. Not only had internal controversy weakened the Church, but Christians expended their energies persecuting other Christians rather than fighting the common enemy. Some persecuted groups were relieved to be conquered by the forces of Islam. Now the Church was roughly trodden under the hoofs of the Muslims' steeds.

1. *What lands were conquered by the followers of Mohammed? Explain the great expansion of the Muslim kingdom.*
2. *Identify: 732, 622, Ka'ba, mosque.*
3. *How was the Church affected by Muslim conquests?*
4. *Find the five pillars or practices of faith of Mohammed.*
5. *What is the theology of Islam?*
6. *Why is the theology of Islam a barrier for the conversion of Muslims to Christianity?*
7. *Why was the conversion of Clovis important?*
8. *Find a book which tells you about the teachings of the Muslims. How do they view the Old Testament and its teachings? What do they believe about Jesus?*
9. *What was the influence of the Moors on literature and architecture? Check on some of Washington Irving's stories.*
10. *Read some selections from the Koran and report on the ideas it presents.*
11. *Where is Islam spreading currently? Why does it seem to spread more rapidly than Christianity?*
12. *Why was the Battle of Tours important?*

CHAPTER 9

The Church

Forms an Alliance, 751-800

1. The Lombards • In the year 568, only fourteen years after the Eastern emperor Justinian regained Italy from the Ostrogoths (see p. 53), the Po Valley in the northern part of Italy was again taken away from the Empire. The members of the German tribe that inflicted this new loss upon the Empire were called the *Lombards* (meaning "Longbeards"). That part of Italy is known even today as Lombardy. The rest of the Italian peninsula continued at least nominally as part of the Empire.

When the Lombards came into Italy they had already been converted from heathenism to the teachings of Arius; later they were to be won over to the orthodox Christianity of the Nicene Creed. Pope Gregory I, eager for their good will, bestowed a crown upon their

Alboin, the first Lombard
king in Italy, enters Pavia.

Three Lions

king. It was called the Iron Crown, because into it had been put what was believed to be one of the nails of the cross.
Here we have a striking illustration of the
unlikely things people in those times
were easily led to believe.

The history of the Church, and especially of the papacy, now became intertwined with the history of the Lombards
and the Franks. The presence of the
Lombards in Italy was a constant threat to
the popes. At no time were they certain
of their safety. The emperors in Con-

stantinople were not in a position to protect the popes against the Lombards.
They were far away, and they had their
hands more than full defending themselves and the Empire against the Arabs.
Moreover, considerable friction had developed between the popes in Rome and
the emperors in Constantinople. So the
popes, when they were being hard pressed
by the Lombards, in their hour of danger
turned for help to the Franks. It was the
Lombards who drove the popes into the
protective arms of the Franks.

Something of the importance of the
conversion in 496 of the Frankish king
Clovis from heathenism to Christianity
was revealed to us, when we saw the
Franks save Europe from Islam. We shall
now see what further important results for
the history of the Church the conversion of
Clovis had through the alliance which the
Church at this time formed with the Franks.

2. Pepin • Clovis was a strong and
influential ruler. The later Frankish kings
of his line were weak. Most of them
were king only in name, while the actual
ruling was done by an outstanding officer.
Charles Martel, the hero of the battle of
Tours, was not king of the Franks. He
was the highest officeholder under one of
these weak kings. In reality he had the
power of a king.

The son of Charles Martel, Pepin the
Short, obtained the same high office his
father had held. But he was not satisfied
with that. He deposed the last king of
the line of Clovis, the feeble Childeric.
He put him in a monastery and placed
himself upon the throne. But he felt that
for this act he should have the sanction,
or approval, of the pope. Pope Zacharias

readily gave his approval, saying that it was only right that he who held the power of king should also have the title. In 751 Pepin was anointed and crowned king.

What had taken place must at the time have seemed something very simple. After all, was it not perfectly natural for Pepin to ask the approval of one as important as the pope? But it was to have far-reaching consequences. From it was drawn the conclusion in later times that the pope had the right to take away and to give kingdoms. It was also a first step toward the re-establishment of the Empire in the West. Out of that grew the tremendous struggle between the papacy and the Empire, which was to make up so large a part of the history of the Middle Ages.

In a way it was the most important event in medieval history.

3. The Pope Becomes a Temporal Ruler • One good turn deserves another, so reasoned Pope Zacharias. He now asked Pepin that he in turn render him a service by helping him against the Lombards, who continued as a constant threat to his power and safety.

Pepin marched with an army into Italy, fought and defeated the Lombards, and compelled them to surrender part of their territory to the pope. In that way began the "States of the Church." The pope now held not only ecclesiastical office, he also had become a temporal ruler. The popes continued to hold temporal power until 1870, when the new Kingdom of Italy was established, and the "States of the Church" were made a part of it.

4. Charles Becomes Charlemagne • Upon the death of Pepin the Short in

Pepin gave the lands which he had won from the Lombard King Aistulf to the pope in a document known as *The Donation of Pepin.* This territory includes areas 1 and 2 on the map. The boundaries of the Papal States were frequently changed by reasons of war or political maneuvers. By the year 1000 the territory over which the pope had control had shrunk to area 1. Pope Innocent III increased the States of the Church to areas 1, 2, and 3. It remained approximately this size for the next six hundred years.

768 his two sons, Carloman and Charles, succeeded him. Carloman died in 771. Then Charles ruled alone, and his real reign began.

On Christmas day of the year 800 Charles was kneeling in St. Peter's Church in Rome. The pope strode up to him, and placed upon his head the imperial crown. By that act the pope made Charles emperor.

It appeared entirely appropriate that Charles should be made emperor. Why? Because he stood for the same three things for which the Roman Empire had

Ewing Galloway

Charlemagne Crowned Emperor by Leo III, A.D. 800

stood. Those three things were *law and order, civilization* or *culture,* and *Christianity.*

Those three things are the greatest things in the world. *Law and order* means peace, the safety of person and property, the assurance that your life and your possessions will not be taken away from you. *Civilization* means knowledge, the refinement of the spirit, the enrichment and adornment of gracious living. *Christianity* means the true religion.

The age of Charles was a time of lawlessness. Murder and robbery were the order of the day. It was a time of barbarism, ignorance, and rudeness. It was also a time when Christianity in western Europe was in a precarious condition. The realm of Charlemagne, which means *Charles the Great,* was a Christian island in an ocean of heathenism and Islam.

The man who on Christmas day of the year 800 was crowned emperor succeeded

PART TWO: THE CHURCH IN THE MIDDLE AGES

in securing for the people of western Europe this invaluable triple blessing of (1) law and order, (2) civilization, and (3) Christianity. That is why he deserves the name Charlemagne.

5. Charlemagne Accomplishes Much • Charlemagne had to fight for these things all his life. He established security and order by making wise laws, and by seeing to it that the laws were enforced.

He fostered civilization and learning by promoting schools throughout his wide domain. But the barbarians as conquerors of the civilized Romans looked down with proud disdain upon learning and culture as something effeminate. Charlemagne established a school in his own residence, the palace school. He set an example by becoming a pupil in that school. He tried to learn to write, but his mighty fist had wielded his hefty battle-axe for so long that his fingers never could learn to handle a pen.

Charlemagne was engaged in war nearly all his life. First he fought the Lombards. He made an end of their kingdom in 777 and set the Iron Crown of Lombardy upon his own head. Next he made a beginning of the work of liberating Spain from the Muslim Arabs. He pushed them back from the Pyrenees to the Ebro River.

Through the greater part of his reign Charlemagne also carried on war with the Saxons. They were a large and powerful Germanic tribe who occupied the northern part of Germany. The Saxons were fierce, untamed, heathen warriors who had never yet felt the conqueror's yoke, and it was only after many hard campaigns that Charlemagne was able to subdue them. He added their territory to his domain and forced them at the point of the sword to accept Christianity.

6. Three Great Empires • When Charlemagne died in 814, there were three great powers or empires in the world. The oldest, but also the weakest, was the Eastern Empire. It embraced the Balkans, Asia Minor, and southern Italy. The largest of the three was the Empire of the Muslim Arabs. It stretched from the border of India through Persia, Syria, and Palestine in Asia, and over all northern Africa up to the Ebro River in Europe. The youngest and the strongest of the three was the Empire of Charlemagne. At his death it consisted of the northern half of Italy; the northeast corner of Spain; all of France, Belgium, and the Netherlands; and a large part of Germany and Austria.

The realm of Charlemagne was truly imperial in size. Since the fall of Rome no such extensive territory had been under

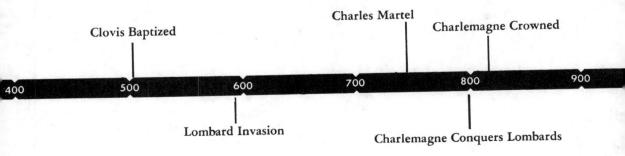

Clovis Baptized

Charles Martel

Charlemagne Crowned

400 500 600 700 800 900

Lombard Invasion

Charlemagne Conquers Lombards

one government in western Europe. Charlemagne was easily the greatest ruler between Justinian and Charles V. He towers above the Middle Ages, and casts his shadow over all the medieval centuries.

Charlemagne's favorite reading was *The City of God* by Augustine. He loved to think of his empire as the Kingdom of God upon earth. The Arab Empire was Muslim. The Eastern Empire was Christian but comparatively small and weak. Of the three empires, that of Charlemagne certainly held the best and brightest promises for the future of the Church and mankind.

7. The Church and the Franks • Pepin, by giving some of the lands of the Lombards to the pope, laid the foundation of the "States of the Church." He made the pope a temporal ruler. (See the map on page 71.)

Charlemagne freed the popes forever from the fear of the Lombards, brought order out of the chaotic conditions of his time, began the expulsion of the Muslims from western Europe; brought the heathen Saxons within the pale of Christendom, and promoted learning and culture.

The pope by crowning Charlemagne emperor restored the Empire in the West. By doing that he set the stage for the gigantic and momentous struggle between Empire and papacy.

The alliance which the Church made with the Franks had borne abundant fruit.

1. *Why were the popes of this period closely attached to the Franks and so to politics and international relations?*
2. *Why was Charlemagne able to accomplish much toward advancing civilization in Europe of his day? How did Charlemagne go about doing this work?*
3. *What is meant by the statement that the pope had become a "temporal ruler"?*
4. *Why is Charlemagne called "the meteor in the dark midnight"?*
5. *What were the Papal States?*
6. *How were the Franks converted to Christianity?*
7. *What was the association of the Lombards with papal policy?*
8. *What were the results of the alliance between the Franks and the Church?*
9. *How did Charlemagne receive the title* Emperor?

CHAPTER 10

The Church

And Papal Development, 461-1073

1. A Review of the Church's Organization • We have seen already in Chapter 3 how natural it was for one of the elders (overseer, presbyter, *episcopos*) to take the lead and receive the title of *bishop*.

The episcopal form of church organization was further developed in the Church's struggle with Gnosticism and Montanism. A centralized structure of church organization was formed to determine what the Bible said and to state the orthodox position, since even heretics appealed to Scripture.

In Chapter 5 we learned that the bishops in the large cities came to be called *metropolitan bishops* and that the bishops of the five most important cities in the Empire acquired the title of *patriarch*. The bishop in Rome gradually came to be recognized by all the other bishops in the West as their superior. By the year 461, the year in which Leo I died, the papacy had become fully established.

As the centuries rolled on there were further developments in the organization or government of the Church. In the time of Charlemagne it became the custom to call the metropolitan bishops *archbishops*. This title the Roman Catholic clergy of that rank still bear today. The archbishop has jurisdiction over the bishops in his territory.

In many denominations, including the Reformed and Presbyterian churches, a minister of a large city church has no power over a minister of a small country church. All ministers are of absolutely the same rank. Yet even today people are inclined to think that the man who holds the pastorate in a prominent city church is perhaps, because of his position, just a little more important than his fellow minister in the country.

It was some such feeling as this that gave the first impulse to the development of the papacy. In all the Roman Empire there was no city that could compare with the city of Rome. It was the city of the Caesars. Rome was the acknowledged mistress of the ancient world. The enormous and unequaled prestige of the city of Rome shed upon the man who was bishop of the church there a luster such as no other bishop had.

Gradually the other bishops got into the habit of appealing to the bishop of Rome for a decision when controversies arose. So it came about that after a while the bishop of Rome began to put forth claims to authority over the other bishops and over the entire Church. They appealed to history to prove that they had long been regarded as the final court of appeal. They even claimed to have Scripture on their side. The belief grew that the church in Rome had been founded by the apostle Peter. Had not Christ said to Peter, "Feed my sheep; feed my lambs," thereby putting Peter in charge of the entire flock? To Peter moreover He had entrusted the power of the keys of the kingdom. That Peter was first in importance among the apostles was generally believed at that time, and the idea grew that the bishops of Rome were the successors of Peter, who was said to have been the first pope. This was the foundation of the papacy. The papal throne is often referred to by the Roman Catholic Church as "the chair of St. Peter."

2. Events in History Strengthen the Papacy • Circumstances in a remarkable way favored the growth of papal power. The whole chain of historical events of that time seemed to lead to a gathering of authority in the bishopric at Rome.

First of all, the barbarians who invaded Italy had come under the spell of Rome. They had accepted Christianity and stood in awe of the bishops of Rome. When the emperor was unable to protect the people, the unarmed bishop of Rome had been able to shield them to a certain extent from the worst excesses of the barbarians. Pope Leo I had been able to restrain, in a measure at least, the fierce Attila and the wrath of the Vandal Geiseric. Rome's extremity had proved to be the pope's opportunity.

The destruction of the Roman Empire by the Germanic invaders gave a tremendous boost to papal prestige. There was no longer an emperor in Rome to overshadow its bishop. The bishop of Rome now held the most important office in the entire West.

Through the work of missionaries sent out from Rome, churches were founded among many tribes in the north of Europe. The great missionary Boniface, the Apostle of Germany, had stood in very close relation to the bishop of Rome, and

A Fresco in the Vatican by Raphael Showing Pope Leo Meeting Attila

had carried on his mission work in his name. A person who is converted under the preaching of a certain pastor will always hold that minister in special esteem. The churches founded through the labors of the Roman missionaries naturally regarded with gratitude amounting to veneration the head of the church in Rome, which had sent these missionaries to them.

The Muslim conquest of Syria, Palestine, and Egypt removed forever the patriarchs of Antioch, Jerusalem, and Alexandria as rivals to the bishop of Rome. The Muslim conquest of North Africa removed the bishop of Carthage as possible rival in the West to the bishop of Rome.

The Church had suffered some grave disasters, but those very disasters brought increasing power and authority to the head of the church in Rome. They all had the tendency to elevate, in the eyes of men, the bishops of the church in Rome to the headship of the entire Church.

3. Papal Power Aided by Deceit • The papacy was also aided by the scheming efforts of men who, through deceit and fraud, succeeded in strengthening the pope's position and authority. Two instances will show how deceit was used to accomplish this.

Around the time of Charlemagne there appeared a strange document. It was called the "Donation of Constantine." It told that the emperor Constantine was cured of leprosy by the prayers of Pope Sylvester. Thereupon Constantine out of gratitude to the pope decided to remove his residence from Rome to Byzantium on the Bosporus, the city later called Constantinople. His object in doing this was

Historical Pictures Service—Chicago

This ninth-century mosaic represents St. Peter as giving the scarf, symbol of holy office, to Pope Leo III, and the standard, symbol of royal power, to Charlemagne.

that the secular government of the emperor might not cramp the spiritual government of the pope. On leaving Rome Constantine, according to this document, ordered all officeholders in the Church to be subject to Pope Sylvester I and to his successors upon the papal throne. Furthermore he transferred to the popes the city of Rome and all the provinces, districts, and cities of Italy and of the western regions. So, according to this document, Constantine bestowed upon the popes sovereignty over the western half of the Empire.

Then somewhere around the middle of the ninth century there appeared a second mysterious document. It was called the "Isidorian Decretals," because these decretals, or decisions, were claimed to have been collected by Isidore of Seville. This document consisted of decisions of popes and councils from Clement of Rome in the first century to Gregory II in the eighth. Bishops, according to this document, could appeal directly to the pope, and neither bishops nor popes were subject to the control of secular governments. The "Donation of Constantine" was included in these decretals.

The whole *hierarchical* system (a series of rulers, each subject to the one immediately above) was the result of a growth extending over several centuries. But this document, the "Isidorian Decretals," represented it as something complete and unchangeable from the beginning. The great purpose of this document was to show that all the rights claimed by the popes in the ninth century had been exercised by the popes from the earliest times.

For hundreds of years these documents were accepted at face value and regarded as genuine. Nicholas de Cusa in 1433 was the first one to suggest that the decretals were a forgery. After that they came to be called the "Pseudo-Isidorian Decretals." (Pseudo means "false," or "pretended.") In 1440 Lorenzo Valla

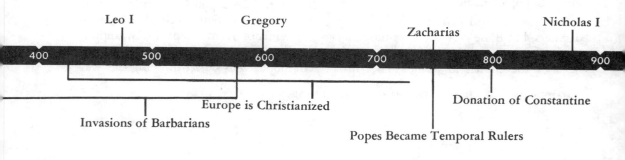

proved that the "Donation of Constantine" was a forgery. Today Catholic scholars agree with Protestant scholars that both documents are spurious.

Fictitious documents were nothing new. But these two are among the most colossal frauds ever carried out. However, the time when they were foisted upon the world was an age of extreme ignorance, and throughout the medieval centuries they were generally accepted as genuine. This gave the papacy sufficient time to establish and entrench itself.

When in 1054 the eastern and western parts of the Church formally separated, the patriarch of Constantinople and the bishop of Rome could no longer be considered rivals. The bishop of Rome, now known as the pope, was supreme in the West. The patriarch of Constantinople was supreme in the East.

4. Pope Nicholas I • Nicholas I, who occupied the papal throne from 858 to 867, did much to lay the foundation of papal power and prestige in following centuries. The writings of St. Augustine had great influence throughout the Middle Ages. His book *The City of God* was the inspiration of the emperor Charlemagne. It had likewise made a deep impression upon the mind of Pope Nicholas

Pope Nicholas I

I. It was his ambition to apply its ideas to the life of his day.

He believed that the bishops are the agents of the pope, that the pope is the ruler of the entire Church, and that the Church is superior to all earthly powers. Nicholas I was able to make good his claims for the papacy only to a very limited extent. But he left these claims behind as an ideal after which later popes were to strive. The popes who came closest to fulfilling them were Gregory VII and Innocent III. But no pope ever made greater claims to papal power than did Nicholas I.

1. *List the reasons for the rise of the Roman bishop to a position of pope.*
2. *To know how the fraudulent character of the "Donations" and "Decretals" was discovered, look up the name of Valla in an encyclopedia. Be sure to note how he argued his point.*
3. *Find out from a good encyclopedia what great work Nicholas I did as pope and what powers he exercised.*
4. *How did the "Donation of Constantine" strengthen the papacy?*

CHAPTER 11

The Church

In Bondage to the State, 885-1049

1. Europe in Disorder • In 843 the Empire of Charlemagne was divided among his three grandsons. One of them obtained the land east of the Rhine known in history as the East Frankish Kingdom; this was the beginning of Germany. Another obtained the land west of the Meuse and the Rhone; this was known as the West Frankish Kingdom and included, roughly, what is now France, Belgium, and the Netherlands. The third obtained the long but narrow strip of land in between the other two territories. It included Italy and was called the Middle Kingdom.

Charlemagne had created order out of chaos. But his successors did not succeed in protecting their people from new enemies who now appeared. The Slavs and Hungarians upon their fleet horses attacked from the East. From Scandinavia in the North came the wild Norsemen in

"Lord, deliver us from the Norsemen!"

Three Lions

their swift ships. They sailed up the rivers and made landings in the Netherlands and France. Being heathen they took special delight in plundering and burning churches and monasteries. They also murdered many of the inhabitants. For three hundred years there rose from the Christian lands of Europe the prayer: "Lord, deliver us from the Norsemen."

Europe was again plunged into disorder. Out of the disorder of these times arose *feudalism.*

2. Feudalism Develops • A knowledge of feudalism is necessary for the understanding of the history of the Church in the Middle Ages, because for a large part of that period the people of western Europe lived their lives under that system. Due to the invasion of the barbarians there were in the early Middle Ages no large cities. Most people lived in the

country, and land was the chief form of wealth. Feudalism was a system based upon a peculiar way of holding land.

The kings who succeeded Charlemagne soon discovered that they were not able to protect themselves and their kingdoms against the invading barbarians. As a security measure each of these kings divided his kingdom among his leading warriors, on the condition that they give him military aid whenever called upon to do so. Upon this same condition each of these newly made kings or princes divided his estate among lesser nobles. These nobles in turn granted sections of land to still lesser tenants, and so on down.

Charles, Louis, and Lothair received areas now France, Germany, and Italy, respectively, in the division of Charlemagne's Empire in 843.

THE DIVISION OF CHARLEMAGNE'S EMPIRE

The interrelationships of the feudal system are illustrated by these two photographs. On the left the clergy collects its tithe of wine. On the right monks are receiving feudal lords at the door of their monastery.

Those who received land upon the condition of military aid and service were called *vassals*. A vassal might in turn give some of the land he had received to others on the same terms. The lands which were held upon these conditions were called *fiefs*.

It frequently happened that pious people gave land to churches or monasteries. Bishops, archbishops, and heads of monasteries (called abbots) in that way became landowners. This also brought them into the feudal system. At last everybody in Europe was in the feudal system. Emperors looked upon the popes as their vassals—a fact which foreshadowed serious trouble for the Church.

At the top of the feudal system were the men who were nobody's vassals; they were lords only. At the bottom of the system were the men who were not lords over anybody; they were simply vassals. In the middle of the system were men who were both lords and vassals. They were lords to those below them, and vassals to those above them.

Lords were under obligation to give protection to their vassals, and vassals were obliged to give service, especially in war, to their lords. So feudalism was in effect a system of mutual aid.

The political result of feudalism was *decentralization*. There were no countries unified under a strong central gov-

PART TWO: THE CHURCH IN THE MIDDLE AGES

The Count of
Paris defends
his castle
against the
Normans, 886.

Courtesy
French Embassy Press
and Information Division

ernment. Every country of western Europe was broken up into a large number of small principalities ruled over by nobles. These noble lords had the power of a king, each in his own domain. That made a king weak. The king was only the chief noble or lord among many. If a number of lords or nobles combined, they might be stronger than the king. A number of nobles did sometimes combine and fight the king, but more often they fought each other. It is not surprising that the Norse invaders had comparatively easy going in this disorganized territory.

3. The Normans • Many of the Norsemen did not go back from their marauding expeditions to their homes in Denmark and Norway. Large bands of them made permanent settlements in

northwestern France. They very quickly adopted the language, customs, and religion of the country in which they settled. The Norsemen who settled in northwestern France came to be called Normans, and that part of France to this day is called Normandy.

The Normans soon set out on military expeditions of their own. William, duke of Normandy, invaded England in 1066, defeated the English in the battle of Hastings, and conquered their land. The Normans also conquered southern Italy.

4. Italian Feudal Lords Control the Popes • Italy, like the other countries of Europe in which feudalism came to prevail, instead of having one central government ruling over the entire country, was split up into a large number of small

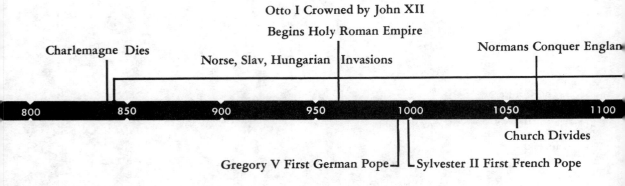

Otto I Crowned by John XII

Begins Holy Roman Empire

Charlemagne Dies

Norse, Slav, Hungarian Invasions

Normans Conquer England

| 800 | 850 | 900 | 950 | 1000 | 1050 | 1100 |

Church Divides

Gregory V First German Pope — Sylvester II First French Pope

principalities, each one ruled over by some lord or noble.

These Italian feudal lords were continually fighting each other for supremacy. Whichever noble family gained control of Rome for a time dictated the appointment of the pope, for the popes were elected by the clergy and people of that city. Often very wicked men, entirely unfit for office in the Church, were elected popes. This was especially true during the tenth century. It was then that the papacy touched its lowest point. The Church was in bondage to secular rulers. Often the noble who won out deposed the pope elevated to the office by the noble who had been in control before. Then he would put a new man on the papal throne. In this way one pope followed another in rapid succession. Between the death of Stephen VI in 891 and the accession of John XII in 955 there were no less than twenty popes. This was indeed a time of shame, disgrace, and confusion for the Church.

5. The Popes Depend on German Emperors • Once more the pope looked longingly beyond the Alps for aid. This time it was Pope John XII, who called to

his aid Otto I, king of the Germans. This Otto was a strong man. Many of the dukes of Germany had acted as independent sovereigns, but Otto made them his vassals. He accomplished this with the help of the bishops and the abbots of the large monasteries. These bishops and abbots controlled extensive landed estates. Their forces, joined to those of the king, were strong enough to put down any combination of dukes. Down to the time of Napoleon the bishops and abbots of the Catholic Church in Germany were not only officeholders in the Church, but also temporal rulers. Otto's power as king rested upon his control over the appointment of bishops and abbots. This was called *lay investiture*. (Investiture was the giving to a man who was elected bishop a ring and a staff as symbols of his office. When a layman—a man who had not the authority of the Church—gave someone these symbols and made him bishop, the act was called *lay investiture*.) Naturally Otto always appointed as bishops and abbots men who were willing to support him.

This Otto came to the rescue of Pope John XII. The pope showed his appreciation by crowning Otto emperor on

PART TWO: THE CHURCH IN THE MIDDLE AGES

February 2, 962. Thus was restored the Empire in the West, which had collapsed under the weak successors of Charlemagne. From that time on it was known as the *Holy Roman Empire*. The Empire was henceforth connected with Germany. It continued to exist until 1806, when Napoleon made an end of it.

By calling Otto I, king of Germany, to his aid, John XII opened a new era in the history of the papacy.

Until this time the popes had all been Italian. Now this tradition was broken. Otto III placed his tutor, Gerbert, archbishop of Rheims, upon the papal throne in 999. He was the first French pope, and the most learned man of his time. Gregory V, who had preceded him, was the first German pope.

6. The Papal Office Is Sold • Now the Church was once more to be plunged into the depths of disgrace. The Italian party, the nobles of the Tuscan family, which happened to be in control at the time, made Benedict IX pope in 1033.

This Benedict was only twelve years old at the time, and he turned out to be one of the worst characters ever to occupy the papal seat. His conduct was so bad that the nobles of the Crescenzio family, who were rivals of the Tuscan party, were able in the year 1045 to drive him out of Rome. In his place they made Sylvester III pope. Soon, however, Benedict came back and resumed the pontificate. But after a time he grew tired of it and brazenly sold the office of pope for one thousand pounds of silver to a man who now became Gregory VI. (This sinful practice of giving or obtaining an appointment to a church office for money is called *simony*.) News of this shameful transaction leaked out. There was a loud outcry. As a result Benedict refused to surrender the papal office which he had sold. There were now three popes—Sylvester III, Benedict IX, and Gregory VI.

This was the Church of which all Christians are descendants. Both Protestants and Catholics should grieve over these days.

1. *How did abbots and bishops become vassals of the king?*
2. *Explain the advantages and disadvantages of the feudal system.*
3. *Explain these terms: simony, lay investiture.*
4. *How did the Church become dependent upon the German emperors?*
5. *Find information about life on the manor in the feudal days.*
6. *How did feudalism affect the relation between the State and the Church?*

CHAPTER *12*

The Church
Is Divided, 1054

1. Europe in the Year 1000

2. The Germanizing of the Western Church

3. The Church Separates Into Two Parts

4. The Eastern Church Is Quiescent

1. Europe in the Year 1000 • The Empire in the West died, but the Church survived and grew. The Church made gains in northwestern Europe but suffered severe losses to Mohammedanism in the South. We should at this time take a brief look at the conditions in Europe in the year 1000. (The maps on pages 53 and 67 will be helpful.)

In the West the Church by the year 1000 was to be found in Italy, France, the Netherlands, England, Germany, Austria, Denmark, Norway, Sweden, Ireland, Scotland, and Russia.

In Italy, which had been the core of the Empire, German tribes settled among the original population and mingled with it through marriage, but the old Roman stock continued predominant.

In Gaul, a former province of the Empire, German tribes settled among and mingled with the Romanized Celts and the Romans. In that territory the upper hand was gained by the Germanic tribe of the Franks. Then Gaul came to be spoken of as France.

In the Netherlands, after the Romans departed without leaving behind much

Schoenfeld Collection from Three Lions

In Russia, Christianity is introduced to Olga, widow of Igor, who had been Emperor of
Russia. She was baptized in 957.

trace of their occupation, the population
consisted of Franks in the south, Saxons
in the east, and Frisians in the north and
west. All three of these tribes belonged
to the Germanic race.

In England, after the departure of the
Romans, the Romanized Celts were replaced by the Germanic Angles and Saxons. Under Roman occupation this country was called Britannia. Now it came to
be called England after the Angles.

Germany, Austria, Denmark, Norway,
and Sweden never had been part of the·
Empire. The population of these countries was purely Germanic.

Ireland and Scotland never had belonged to the Empire. The Celts of Ireland and the Picts of Scotland were non-
Germanic.

Russia was Christianized by missionaries
from Constantinople, who established the
Greek Orthodox Church in that country.

2. The Germanizing of the Western Church • As you can see by a glance
at the foregoing section, the Church in
the West had become largely Germanic.
It had its origin among the Latin speaking Romans, but had been passed on to
the invading German tribes.

Philip Gendreau

The gradual separation of the eastern and western sections of the Empire and of the Church can be illustrated by the difference in the architecture of their churches. The Byzantine style of St. Basil's Cathedral in Moscow, on the left, shows the buoyancy and fantasy which characterized architecture of the East. The Gothic architecture of England's most famous church, Westminster Abbey in London, shows the influence of the ponderous, solid architecture of the West.

The Germanic tribes had no civilization. Through the Church, Rome also passed on to the uncivilized German tribes its Latin language, literature, and civilization. For that reason the Church in the West, although its membership was now largely Germanic, came to be called the Latin Church.

So at the entrance to the Middle Ages we have a most remarkable condition of affairs. There now was in the West a Church with a Latin language and literature, but with the majority of its members belonging to the Germanic race.

The Germanizing of the Church marks a major turn in the Church's history. For in a Church so made up of different elements, a process of fermentation (like the action of yeast on dough) was sure to set in. That fermentation in the centuries to come was going to produce great results.

3. The Church Separates Into Two Parts • In the East the situation was entirely different. There the Empire did not fall under the blows of the German barbarians, but remained standing for another thousand years. It is true, as related

PART TWO: THE CHURCH IN THE MIDDLE AGES

in the preceding chapter, the Empire in the East lost Syria, Palestine, and Egypt to the Muslim Arabs. The Church in those provinces was reduced to a most feeble state. But in that part of the Eastern Empire which remained standing, in Asia Minor and the Balkan Peninsula, the Church remained intact. The language of the Church in the East was Greek.

We have now come not merely to another decisive turn, but to a fork in the road. This is something entirely new in the history of the Church. Up to this time the Church had been one. Now, after having been one for a thousand years, the Church in 1054 was divided. In that year the two parts of the Church, the Greek Eastern part and the Latin Western part, separated from each other.

This separation could have been fore-seen and predicted. In the long period of a thousand years since the founding of the Church on Pentecost Day, many points of difference between the two parts of the Church had cropped up. On the whole the differences were trivial and unimportant.

But the differences in the character of the people who made up the two parts of the Church were not trivial. The eastern section of the Church was distinctly more oriental in character, so that its point of view on many problems of the Church was quite different from that of the western section. When the Empire was separated into its two parts for purposes of administration, the two areas tended to grow apart in other respects also, particularly when the western section through the papacy sought to exercise authority

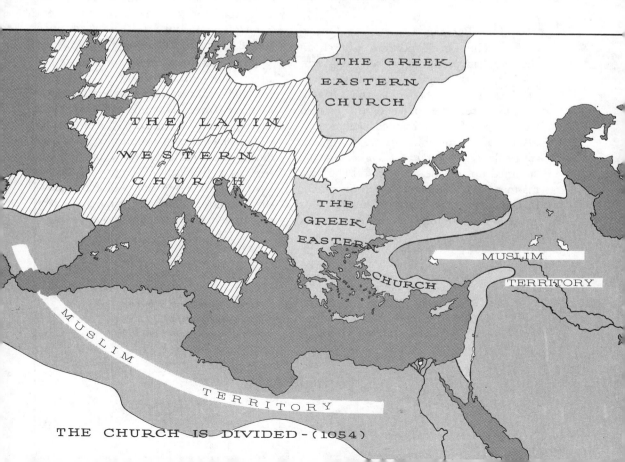

THE CHURCH IS DIVIDED - (1054)

A miniature painted about the year 1000 shows John of Damascus writing. Opposite him is an illuminator.

within the realms of the patriarch of Constantinople. So, over many years, these two areas drifted apart, till an occasion arose when they made a formal break in relations. You will learn the immediate causes of this separation in a later chapter.

4. The Eastern Church Is Quiescent • The Greek-speaking Church in the East had produced, as we have seen, many great theologians, such as Clement of Alexandria, Athanasius, and Origen. The last great theologian of the Eastern Church was John, surnamed Damascenus after the city in which he was born. In his book, *The Fountain of Knowledge,* he summed up in a neat and comprehensive manner the whole preceding development of theology in the Eastern Church. This great work of John of Damascus was translated into Latin. Thus knowledge of the theology of the Greek Church in the East was passed on to the Latin Church in the West.

But the Greek Eastern Church of the eleventh century was composed of an old and exhausted people. It became like a stagnant pool, and after this it dropped almost entirely from sight.

From now on we shall concentrate our attention upon the Latin Western Church. We shall find that the Church in the West was far from stagnant. In this Latin Church, composed so largely of the young and virile Germanic peoples, we shall find during the Middle Ages now opening before us a life full of vigor. There we shall find not a stagnant pool, but a sea— the waters of which are often lashed by roaring winds into mountainous waves.

1. *Why did the civilization passed on by the Romans to the Germanic invaders begin to "ferment"?*
2. *Why is the Church in Russia called the Greek Orthodox Church?*
3. *Why did the Eastern Church become "like a stagnant pool"?*
4. *What is meant by the "Germanizing of the Western Church"?*
5. *Identify:* The Fountain of Knowledge, *Eastern Church.*

CHAPTER 13

Monasticism

And the Cluny Reform

1. The Inner Life of the Church • Thus far we have said very little about the inner religious or spiritual life of the Church. Because of the presence of sin in the hearts of all men, the inner life of the Church has not been altogether true and perfect.

In the earliest days imperfection began to creep in. How soon the spiritual beauty of the first Christian church, the one in Jerusalem, was marred by Ananias and Sapphira! In the second Christian church, the one in Samaria, there was Simon the Sorcerer to whom religion was "a racket."

From his attempt to buy the gift of the Spirit for money the name *simony* has come. This practice became very common, especially in the Church of the Middle Ages.

Because of the shortcomings of the Church, people both inside and outside have always found much fault with it. Much of the criticism is unintelligent and unfair. Every Christian is a saint, but every saint to the end of his life remains a sinner. Besides, there always have been many church members who were not actually Christians.

The monastery known as *Montserrat* is Spain's holiest shrine.

At times the spiritual life of the Church did sink to a very low level. But always the life of Christ, which dwells in the Church, has reasserted itself.

2. The Growth of Asceticism and Monasticism • We have already seen in Chapter 6 how the early Church deteriorated and how monasticism developed as a reaction. The general misery of the Middle Ages and the low point to which religious life in the Church had fallen gave added reasons for men to seek spiritual satisfaction. There seemed to be a revival of religion. Unfortunately it was not a healthy revival. People did not return to the pure teachings of Scripture. Instead they turned to *asceticism.*

Asceticism means extreme self-denial. In practicing asceticism the Christians denied themselves the comforts and pleasures of life and turned to religious medi-

tation and the performance of religious forms and rituals.

This general ascetic life, which was not organized nor separated from society, often led to other stages. We have seen how already in the fourth century men separated themselves from society and became hermits. This form of monasticism was widely practiced in the Eastern Church. It was only suitable for men and often unsuitable for the colder European climate.

In the West cloister life developed. This is monasticism in the usual sense of the word. In their monasteries and convents the monks and nuns practiced asceticism. They abstained from the possession of earthly goods. The monk did not eat and drink more than was absolutely necessary. Many monks ate nothing but bread, and drank only water. Frequently monks fasted; that is, for a period of time they

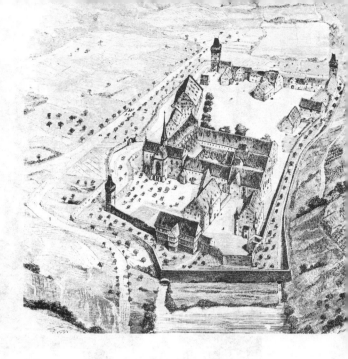

Medieval monasteries were often self-sufficient social communities. Note the fields and orchards. The walls afforded protection as well as privacy for this French monastery.

did not eat at all. Monks also chastised themselves by beating themselves with whips or scourges. All monks and nuns abstained from marriage. And while leading such a life of asceticism, the monks and nuns devoted their time to praying, reading religious books, and meditating on what they had read.

A final step in the development of monasticism was the formation of monastic orders, unions of a number of cloisters under one rule and a common government. We shall learn more of these orders later.

3. Monasticism Is Based on Error • The monks of the Middle Ages rendered great services to the cause of civilization.

Amidst the tide of barbarism that flooded the western part of the Empire, the monasteries stood as islands of refuge. They served as inns for the weary traveler and as hospitals for the sick. They were centers of agriculture and learning.

But monasticism was based upon the recognition by the Church of a higher and

The Sisters of Charity sing in unison at their chapel at the Rue du Bac, Paris.

Three Lions

The Refectory of a Carthusian Monastery

Only on Sundays and feast days are the monks permitted to meet here for repast under the eyes of the abbot. At this time they may break their vows of silence and talk a little with each other. Once a week they must fast on bread and water, and on Fridays they must refrain even from partaking of this nourishment.

lower morality. If one wished to be a Christian in a higher sense one should become a monk or nun. Monks and nuns were called "the religious." This differentiation between a higher and a lower morality is a false distinction.

Even today Roman Catholic priests who serve in regular churches, that is in the world, are called *secular* priests. Those who enter a monastery are called *religious*

priests. The underlying error of monasticism as a method of attaining holiness is thinking that the sinful heart is cleansed by fleeing from this world.

In the ninth century in many monasteries the monks no longer observed the rules of asceticism. These monasteries shared in the general decay of the times and became breeding places of wickedness.

The Church believed that it was enough for the ordinary Christian to observe certain outward ceremonies prescribed by the Church. He should learn the Lord's Prayer and the Apostles' Creed. He should confess his sins. All were to observe the Lord's Supper, which was thought to impart grace in a magical manner.

The Christianity of the great masses was largely on the surface. Observing forms and practices was considered sufficient for the common Christian. But monks and nuns, so it was thought, could go far beyond this.

4. The Monastery at Cluny • However, in every age there have been true Christians. There were many true Christians even in the dark tenth century. The spiritual decline of the Church filled their hearts with sadness. One of them, William the Pious, duke of Aquitaine, founded a new monastery at Cluny in eastern France in 910. In this monastery the rules of asceticism were strictly observed. The Cluny movement spread far and wide to other monasteries. For the next two hundred years the great Cluny reform was a powerful force in the improvement of the religious life of the Church. The principles and methods of monasticism were wrong, but its motives were truly religious. The Cluny movement, although it took an erroneous form, was nevertheless an expression of a genuine spiritual awakening. In the time of its highest prosperity it ruled over two thousand monastic establishments.

It was this Cluny movement which produced the great Hildebrand, who as pope became known as Gregory VII. We shall hear much about him, for through him Cluny had a tremendous influence on the Church.

1. *Read Paul's statements in Colossians 2:16-23 and Jesus' statement in Matthew 16:24. Do these state that men must abstain from certain foods or pleasures to develop the piety which the monastics sought?*

2. *What contributions did the monastics make toward civilization? Did these contributions fit the original objectives of monastic life?*

3. *What practices in the Church of this time encouraged the belief that observing outward ceremonies was sufficient?*

4. *Cluny stood as a light in the dark period of church history you are studying. What made this monastery different from the others of its time?*

5. *How are asceticism and monasticism related? On what error is monasticism based?*

6. *List the four stages of monasticism.*

7. *What is the distinction between the two levels of religious service developed during the Middle Ages?*

CHAPTER 14

The Church Makes Efforts
To Free Itself, 1049-1058

1. Stages in the Roman Church • Before we go on with the story of the Church we should recall four things: (1) It was early apparent that the church in Rome was to take a place of special importance in the history of the Church. (2) The gradual rise and growth of the papacy took place through the bishopric of Rome. (3) During the tenth and the first half of the eleventh centuries the papacy was brought into bondage to the State, and became utterly corrupt. (4) As a reaction to the low spiritual conditions in the Church, there took place a religious revival. This revival had its beginning with the founding of the monastery at Cluny.

2. The Cluny Reformers Enlist the Aid of Henry III • The Cluny movement aimed at a reform of the clergy, the monks, and the papacy. This reform movement reached into many monasteries in every country of western Europe. It stirred the hearts and minds not only of thousands of monks, priests, and bishops, but also of numerous laymen. In fact, it was a layman, the Duke of Aquitaine, who had founded the Cluny monastery.

As you will remember, three men at one and the same time tried to occupy the papal throne. One of them was the wicked and utterly unworthy Benedict IX, who had sold his office for money. To make an end of this scandal, and to restore the papacy, the Cluny reformers now called in the help of the German emperor Henry III, the head of the Holy Roman Empire.

This emperor was one of the thousands of laymen who had come under the spell of Cluny. He was a truly religious man. A synod held under his leadership deposed Sylvester III. It also compelled Gregory VI to resign and banished him to Germany. Another synod deposed Benedict IX. There was not room on the papal seat for three men at once. Trying to sit on that chair at one and the same time, all three fell off.

To get away from the Italian corruption in Rome, Henry then had a German bishop chosen as pope under the name of Clement II. This pope and also the next one died soon. Henry then appointed his cousin Bruno, bishop of Toul, to be pope as Leo IX.

3. Pope Leo IX • Leo IX, who was pope from 1049 to 1054, was a leading supporter of Cluny. It was for this reason that the emperor had appointed him. He was full of reforming zeal, and he got busy at once.

The first thing he did was to bring about a great change in the *College of Cardinals*. From early times there had been in Rome leading or cardinal bishops. The cardinals are the personal assistants and advisers of the pope. In many ways the college of cardinals is to the popes what the cabinet is to presidents or prime ministers.

When Leo IX became pope, he found that the College of Cardinals was made up entirely of Romans. These cardinals represented the noble families, who for so long had controlled and corrupted the papacy and were entirely out of sympathy with the Cluny reform movement. The new pope appointed to the College of Cardinals men who were in hearty accord with Cluny. Moreover, he chose the new cardinals from various parts of the Church. Thus he surrounded himself with advisers whom he could trust, and who represented not merely the one church in Rome but all the churches throughout Christian Europe.

In many other ways the new pope vigorously promoted reform. He traveled through France and Germany, held synods, and everywhere enforced papal authority. In all he did, he had the cordial co-operation of Hugo, who was abbot of Cluny. There were three points on which he laid special stress. He forbade priests to marry and to practice simony. Leo also insisted that no one should obtain a church office without the choice of the clergy and people.

Philip Gendreau

A View of Istanbul

The three Mosques in this photograph are St. Sophia, left; the Mosque of
Mahmoud, foreground; and the Mosque of Sultan Ahmed, right. Asia is in the
background.

4. The Schism Between East and West • But Leo's term as pope had also its troublous side. You will remember that, although the eastern and the western parts of the Church had for a long time been drifting apart, they were up to this time still united. It was while Leo was pope that the two parts of the Church separated from each other. Pope Leo IX of Rome became involved in trouble with Michael Cerularius, the patriarch of Constantinople. In 1054 he sent representatives to Constantinople with a letter which they laid upon the high altar of the St. Sophia Church. In that letter Pope Leo

IX excommunicated Cerularius. The patriarch in turn excommunicated the pope. That was the *schism,* or division, of the Church into the Greek Eastern and the Latin Western Church.

5. The Cluny Reformers Face a Dilemma • On the death of Leo IX, Emperor Henry III appointed another German to the papacy. This man took the name of Victor II. He was pope for only two years, from 1055 to 1057. In 1056 Henry III died unexpectedly. Victor II was an adherent of the Cluny reform party, but at the same time he had been

　　　　　　　　　　PART TWO: THE CHURCH IN THE MIDDLE AGES

very much devoted to Emperor Henry III. At the time of the emperor's death his son was a boy of only six. Victor brought about the acceptance of this boy as successor to the imperial throne under the regency of his empress mother, Agnes.

The Cluny reform party now saw itself placed before a dilemma. It had succeeded in breaking the bonds in which the papacy had been held by the Roman nobles. But it had been able to do so only with the help of the German emperor. In reality the papacy had only exchanged masters. For the time being the Cluny reformers had tolerated the imperial bondage for two reasons. (1) It seemed to be the only way to break the bonds in which the Italian nobles had held the papacy. (2) They much preferred the imperial bonds. Emperor Henry III had, it is true, dominated the papacy as completely as the Roman nobles had done before him. But the latter had been bitterly hostile to reform, whereas the emperor had promoted it.

Now, however, the Holy Roman Empire had at its head the empress mother Agnes as regent. She was weak. Her strong husband, Henry III, was dead. Her son, who one day would ascend the German imperial throne as Henry IV, was as yet only a little six-year-old boy.

The Cluny reformers believed that circumstances were now favorable for breaking also the imperial bonds.

6. Pope Stephen X • The reform party was now in control also in Rome. And a new pope, Stephen X, was chosen by the Roman clergy under the leadership of the Cluny reformers, without imperial dictation or influence. The mother regent, Agnes, was not even consulted.

Stephen himself was a strong reformer. He declared that appointment to church office, in order to be official and valid, must be made by the Church, not by laymen. He expressed very firmly his disapproval of *lay investiture*. (See p. 84.)

The power of the German emperor rested upon his right to appoint and invest bishops favorable to him. If the right of appointment and investiture should be taken away from the emperor, his power would be greatly weakened. It could not be expected that the emperor would give up this right without offering strong opposition. If the pope should try to carry out the policy he had announced, it would surely result in a great conflict between pope and emperor.

The pope did not bring the impending conflict to an issue. He was afraid to do so. Instead he asked the regent mother, the empress Agnes, to give her approval of his occupancy of the papal throne. He obtained her approval, but almost immediately thereafter he died.

7. Hildebrand Selects the Next Pope • Upon the death of Pope Stephen X a situation of great difficulty arose for the Cluny reform party. The Roman nobles tried to regain their power over the papacy. Only a week after the death of Stephen they elected one of their own number pope with the title of Benedict X.

The reform cardinals had to leave Rome and seek safety in flight. The outlook for the Cluny party was very dark. It looked as if the conditions that had prevailed in the tenth century and in the days of Benedict IX might return. But help came in an unexpected way.

Leo IX, before he had even begun his rule as pope, did something which no one

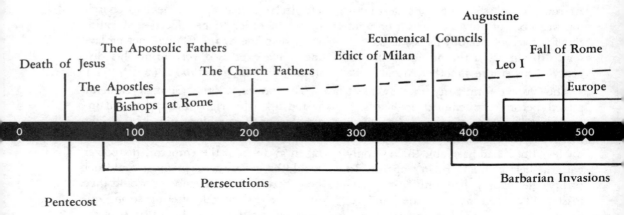

Death of Jesus

The Apostles

Bishops at Rome

The Apostolic Fathers

The Church Fathers

Edict of Milan

Ecumenical Councils

Augustine

Leo I

Fall of Rome

Europe

0   100   200   300   400   500

Pentecost

Persecutions

Barbarian Invasions

noticed particularly at the time, and to which the pope himself did not attach any unusual significance. No one could have known its importance at the time.

When Pope Gregory VI was banished to Germany, he was accompanied into exile by a young man named Hildebrand. When Leo, having been appointed pope by the emperor Henry III, journeyed to Rome to occupy the papal throne, he took this Hildebrand back with him from Germany to Rome, made him subdeacon, and put him in charge of the financial affairs of the papacy. It was this Hildebrand who, in this black hour when all seemed lost, stepped into the breach and saved the day.

First of all he looked around for a man who, as a sympathizer with the Cluny movement, would in his opinion make a good pope. He picked the bishop of Florence as his candidate. Next he lined up the Duke of Tuscany and a part of the people of Rome to back his candidate. He succeeded in interesting only a minority of the people, but a representative of this minority party succeeded in gaining the

consent of the regent empress Agnes to the election of Hildebrand's candidate.

Then Hildebrand rallied the reform cardinals who had fled. They chose Hildebrand's candidate as pope. The new pope assumed the title of Nicholas II.

The soldiers of Duke Godfrey of Tuscany made Nicholas master of Rome, and established him firmly upon the papal throne. But from now on the *real* power behind that throne was Hildebrand. He is one of the outstanding men of history.

8. Hildebrand's Early Life • Hildebrand was born in Italy around the year 1020. His family was poor and lived in very humble circumstances. An uncle was abbot of the Cluny Monastery of St. Mary in Rome. In that monastery Hildebrand acquired his education.

Gregory VI, who had bought the papacy from the wicked Benedict IX in order to rid the Church of a very bad pope, was one of the very few able clerics living in Rome at that time. He took Hildebrand into his papal service and with him when he was banished to Ger-

PART TWO: THE CHURCH IN THE MIDDLE AGES

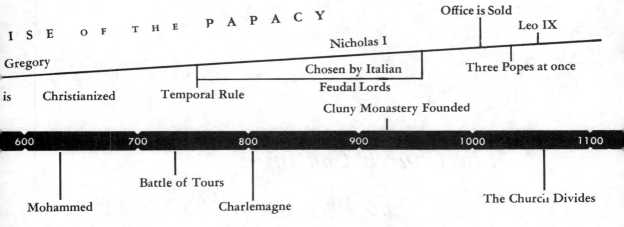

RISE OF THE PAPACY

Gregory

...is Christianized

Temporal Rule

Nicholas I

Chosen by Italian Feudal Lords

Cluny Monastery Founded

Office is Sold

Leo IX

Three Popes at once

| 600 | 700 | 800 | 900 | 1000 | 1100 |

Mohammed

Battle of Tours

Charlemagne

The Church Divides

many. Later when Hildebrand was made pope in 1073, he chose Gregory VII as his papal name to express his gratitude to his earliest benefactor.

While in the Rhine country, Hildebrand gained first-hand knowledge of the evils afflicting the Church in Germany.

He learned that secular rulers quite openly appointed to church offices men who paid the highest price, even though they might be entirely unfit. In Germany he became acquainted with the man who was to become Leo IX. Leo took him back to Rome.

1. *Identify: schism, college of cardinals, papacy.*
2. *Why would an emperor be able to discard and set up popes at this time?*
3. *What basic method of reforming the papacy did Leo IX introduce?*
4. *What were the reasons for the disagreement between the Eastern and the Western Catholic Churches?*
5. *Why did the reform party wish to break the emperors' control of the papacy?*
6. *Why did the emperors object to the Church's claim to invest bishops?*
7. *How did Hildebrand manage to keep his reform program under way? See Schaff's* History of the Christian Church, *Volume V, for additional explanation of this reform movement.*
8. *How did Emperor Henry III aid the Cluny reform movement?*
9. *List three ways in which Pope Leo IX freed the Church from the Italian nobles.*
10. *What was the dilemma that faced the Cluny reformers?*
11. *Hildebrand was the power behind the papal thrones of all the popes from Leo IX to his own papacy. List these popes with their dates.*
12. *Why would the Church object to lay investitures?*

CHAPTER 15

The Church Continues
To Free Itself, 1059-1073

1. Hildebrand Practices Clever Diplomacy • Hildebrand had been successful in defeating the Roman nobles by putting a reform pope on the papal throne. But a difficult problem still remained. The papacy had been freed from bondage to the Roman nobles, but not from the German emperor. Now Hildebrand wished to free the papacy and the Church also from this bondage. But he felt that the papacy could not get along without the support of some government. The problem was to find a government able and willing to support and protect the papacy without wishing to control it.

Hildebrand looked about him. There was Duke Godfrey of Tuscany. He could be counted on. But Tuscany's strength was not enough. In southern Italy were the Normans. But Pope Leo IX had been in disagreement with them. Disputes about possessions in southern Italy between them and Leo IX had even led to war, in which Leo had been defeated and made a prisoner. However, the clever diplomacy of Hildebrand won them over. Upon his advice Pope Nicholas II recognized their conquests in southern Italy. They in turn became the pope's vassals. That put them under the feudal obligation to render protection to the pope. Hildebrand also gained for the pope the support of the democratic party in northern Italy.

Hildebrand felt that the pope, bolstered by these governments, could now afford to take a firm stand on the all-important question of the day. In a synod held in Rome in 1059 Nicholas II definitely forbade lay investiture.

2. A New Method for Electing a Pope

• The most important thing to take place while Nicholas II was pope was the establishment of a new method of electing men to the papacy. The new method was decreed at the Synod of 1059. With certain refinements it is still in use today.

The object of this new method was to take the election of popes, and therewith the control of the papacy, out of the hands of the Italian nobles and also out of the hands of the emperors.

The new method was to be as follows. On the death of a pope the cardinal bishops were to nominate his successor. Only after the cardinals had thus made their selection were they to seek the approval of the clergy and people of Rome.

The decree in vague language spoke of "the honor and reverence due our beloved son Henry." (This Henry was none other than the young Henry IV.) But these were only polite words. The decree said

Three Lions

These mitres are symbolic of the various offices of the pope. He may wear only a few of them, the rest being brought forward only symbolically during certain stages of ritual.

nothing about the participation of the emperor in the election.

The decree also laid down the rule that a pope may be chosen from any part of the Church; that if necessary the election may be held in some place other than Rome; and that no matter where the man elected pope may be at the time, he will at once come into possession of all the powers of his office.

3. Pope Alexander II

• The change in the method of electing popes brought about by this decree was revolutionary. The decree was designed to free the papacy and the Church from all political control. To the extent to which this new method of electing popes was actually carried out in practice, this decree broke the bonds in which Church and papacy had heretofore been held by the State.

Soon after the adoption of the decree, Pope Nicholas II died. Would it be pos-

This photograph shows part of the Rhine country, Germany, where Hildebrand was taken by Gregory VI and from which he returned with Leo IX.

Philip Gendreau

sible to put into practice the new method of election?

Hildebrand was now the recognized leader of the Cluny reform party. He brought about the election of Alexander II to succeed Nicholas II. But the bishops in Germany and in Lombardy, and of course the Italian nobles, did not like the new method. Their combined influence secured from the empress-regent the appointment of the bishop of Parma under the title of Honorius II.

Honorius came close to winning out in the contest that followed. What saved the day for Hildebrand and the Cluny reform party this time was an upset in Germany in 1062. Anno, archbishop of Cologne, kidnapped Henry IV and was made his guardian in the place of his mother, the empress Agnes. This man Anno was very ambitious. He estimated that the reform party would best serve his purpose. So he recognized Alexander as the rightful pope. Again Hildebrand had won.

The new pope in many ways made good his claim to power, but it was Hildebrand standing behind the papal throne who inspired his actions. Alexander succeeded

in making two of the most powerful archbishops in Germany do penance for simony. He would not allow Henry IV to get a divorce from his queen. Duke William of Normandy was contemplating an enterprise which was to result in the Norman conquest of England. Before launching his attack upon England he asked the pope for his approval. Alexander gave his sanction to the enterprise, and also to the activities of the Normans in southern Italy, which eventually resulted in their conquest of Sicily. In this way Alexander strengthened his position.

4. Hildebrand Becomes Pope • For twenty-four years, under six successive popes, Hildebrand had been the power behind the throne—the heart and the brains of the papacy. Now, in these tremendously critical circumstances, he himself was made pope in 1073. This came about as a complete surprise, and took place in a highly irregular manner.

Hildebrand was conducting the funeral services of Alexander II in the Basilica of St. John Lateran. By acclamation the crowd suddenly and unexpectedly proclaimed him pope. Amidst scenes of the wildest enthusiasm the people carried him to the Church of St. Peter. There he was consecrated and placed upon the papal throne, without having been elected by the cardinals according to the decree of 1059. Later, however, the cardinals legalized Hildebrand's irregular selection by formally electing him pope in the prescribed way.

5. The Relation Between Church and State • Up to the time of the conversion of Constantine there was no such problem as that of the relation of Church and State.

There have always been a Church and a State. Among heathen nations the relation between kings and priests was not a problem. In practice the kings usually dominated the priests; sometimes the priests dominated the kings. Among Israel the Church was not a separate institution; Church and State were intertwined. The Church came into existence as a separate institution on the day of Pentecost. But from that day until the conversion of Constantine the Church was a persecuted institution. Constantine's conversion completely changed the situation. The Church became recognized by the State as a sepa-

Hildebrand—Gregory VII

rate institution. At the time when the entire Roman Empire became at least in name Christian, Church and State were really two parallel institutions. Then there arose in course of time the problem of the proper relation between the two.

There are three possible solutions to the problem of the proper relation between Church and State: (1) Church and

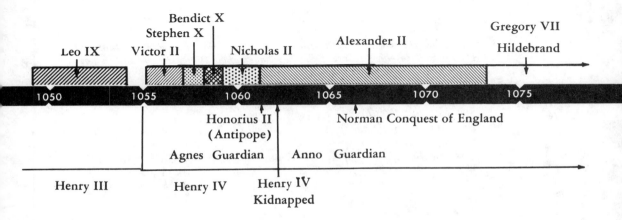

State should be on the same level, (2) the State should be above the Church, or (3) the Church should be above the State.

In the East the second solution came to be adopted. The emperors of the Eastern Empire obtained complete control over the patriarchs of Constantinople and the Eastern Greek Church.

In the West the problem caused the most violent clashes of opinion between those who wished the State to be above the Church, and those who wanted the Church to be above the State. Only a few wanted the two institutions to be on the same level.

Here we observe one of the differences between the Eastern and the Western Church. The early settlement of this problem in the East explains why the history of the Eastern Church is comparatively dull, while the long contest for superiority makes the history of the Western Church lively and exciting.

6. The Stage Is Set for a Terrific Struggle • In the West also the Church for a time came under the control of secular rulers: Italian nobles and German emperors. Control over the Church by the emperors in fact goes back to Charlemagne and the very first Christian emperor, Constantine himself. However, the Cluny reform party put forth strong efforts to free the Church and the papacy from their bondage to the State, and scored considerable success.

But the popes were not satisfied with freeing the Church from its bondage to the State. They wanted to go still further —to put the State into bondage to the Church.

The next chapter will show how this situation developed into a terrific struggle between Pope Gregory VII and Emperor Henry IV. This struggle was going to be, in the highest degree, epic and dramatic.

1. Identify: Synod of 1059, basilica.
2. What was clever about Hildebrand's diplomacy?
3. Why would the new method of electing a pope free the Church from imperial control?
4. Though the Church sought to free itself from imperial control, it nevertheless courted the favor of political leaders like Duke William of Normandy. Why did it do so?
5. List three happenings to prove Pope Alexander II made good his claim to power.
6. How did the Church authorities get around the irregular election of Hildebrand to the papacy? Did they have much choice in the matter, or could they have nullified his selection by the people?
7. What is the official position of the Roman Church on the relation of Church and State? What is the position of the Constitution of the United States on this question?
8. Look up information in leading periodicals about the conclave that elected the most recent pope. Has the method changed since 1059?
9. The opening chapter of In the Shoes of the Fisherman by Morris L. West, William Morrow and Co., 1963, tells of the election of the imaginary Pope Kiril I. The entire novel deals with the work of the papacy.

CHAPTER 16

The Church Is Forced
To Compromise, 1073-1122

1. Hildebrand Inspired by Cluny Ideas • No one on seeing Hildebrand would have gotten the idea that he was an unusual man. His figure was very small, his voice weak, and his whole appearance unimpressive. Yet he was one of the most remarkable characters of all the Middle Ages. He had a powerful mind, an inflexible will, dauntless courage, and a fiery soul.

Like Pope Nicholas I and so many other aspiring men of medieval times, Hildebrand had come under the spell of St. Augustine's greatest book, *The City of God*. In the monastery in Rome he had become imbued with the Cluny reform ideas. Throughout his life the ideas and ideals derived from these sources were his inspiration. They aroused in him all the tremendous energies which lay hidden within his nature.

The highest ideal of his life was derived from Augustine's *City of God*. That ideal was the establishment of the Kingdom of God on earth. Hildebrand believed that the divinely prepared and appointed agency for the realization of this ideal is the Church. He furthermore believed that the head of the Church on earth is the pope as Christ's *vicar* (representative). In his view the pope is above all—above princes, kings, and emperors. Everybody is subject to him. The pope himself is answerable only to God.

For the realization of these ideas Hildebrand had already been working for more than twenty years as the power behind the throne of six popes. Now that he himself had become pope he continued to use all his marvelous energies and powers in working for the realization of these ideas.

In doing this he was not moved by self-interest. He could not be bribed or bought, as could so many bishops and other church dignitaries of his day. Hildebrand was not moved by ambition or vainglory. No doubt his motives were not always entirely pure. Whose are? Sometimes he was unscrupulous in the use of means; that is, he was determined to gain his end, even if he had to employ a wrong method in order to accomplish what he believed to be a good thing. It is also

true that he loved to rule. It was in his blood. But fundamentally he was moved by a sincere and strong desire to serve God and the Church, and thus promote the cause of God's Kingdom in this world.

The popes had vast treasures at their disposal. Hildebrand could have lived a life of self-indulgence, luxury, and idleness—as some popes before and after him did do. Instead of that he was always immersed in hard and fatiguing labors. He lived very simply and was a real ascetic.

2. The Struggle for the Right of Investiture • In order that the Church might be a fit agency for the establishment of God's Kingdom on earth, the Church and the clergy, Hildebrand felt, should be reformed according to Cluniac standards. In order to clear the way for reform the Church had to be freed from its bondage to the State, and the State had to be made subject to the Church. That meant that the right of investiture would have to be taken away from the emperors, and be lodged in the popes.

As long as emperors and other secular rulers could appoint their men to church office, and invest their appointees to bishoprics with the symbols of holy office, the Church could expect that such men would seek the interest of their leaders rather than that of the Church.

On the other hand the emperors could not give up their power of investiture without very seriously undermining and weakening their position. We should remember that at this time the feudal system prevailed. Like other countries, Germany was divided into many parts ruled over by dukes, counts, and other nobles. Often these nobles came in conflict with the emperor. If a number of them com-

Schoenfeld Collection from Three Lions

At the Council of Bishops, January, 1076, Emperor Henry IV declares that
Hildebrand must come down from the papal throne.

bined, they might be more powerful than the emperor. The bishops and abbots in Germany were also great feudal lords. With their help the emperor could hope to keep the nobles in check. If the right of the investiture of bishops were taken away from the emperor, he would lose his control over them, and he would no longer be able to count on their support. Deprived of their help he might lose his throne and crown to the nobles.

For both popes and emperors the right of investiture was therefore a matter of life and death. But both could not have it at the same time. For if the pope did not have it exclusively, he could not hope to reform the Church. But if, on the other hand, the emperor did not have it exclusively, he would run great risk of losing his throne. The struggle between papacy and empire had been smoldering a long time. It was precisely over the question of the right of investiture that the bitter struggle between Pope Gregory VII and Emperor Henry IV now burst into flame.

3. Henry IV Challenges Pope Gregory VII • During the first two years of Gregory's pontificate, Henry IV maintained friendly relations with the pope, at least on the surface. This was because rebellious nobles caused him great difficulties and made his position as king of Germany very weak. The pope, emboldened by Henry's weakness, in 1075 again forbade investiture by laymen. But later in that same year Henry gained a brilliant victory over his enemies. This changed the picture. Henry now felt strong enough to defy Gregory. Directly in violation of the decree against lay investiture he conferred investiture upon three bishops.

What would the pope do now? Would he overlook Henry's violation of the decree?

In December of the year 1075 Gregory sent Henry a letter in which he poured out all his fury. The message dictated final terms, and opened the hostilities between pope and emperor.

The letter began: "Bishop Gregory, servant of the servants of God, to King Henry, greeting and apostolic benediction, that is if he be obedient to the Apostolic Chair as beseems a Christian king. Considering and carefully weighing with what strict judgment we shall have to render account for the ministry entrusted to us by St. Peter, chief of the apostles, it is with hesitation that we have sent unto thee the apostolic benediction."

The pope continued by pointing out to the emperor his sins. He reminded him that he was entirely under the authority of St. Peter and St. Peter's successor, the pope. Gregory admonished Henry not to be puffed up because of his recent victory.

Gregory told Henry that because of his offenses he deserved to be *excommunicated* (cut off from membership in the Church), and deposed from his office as king. Unless he repented he would be punished.

At the time the emperor received the pope's letter he was flushed with victory. He was young, proud, and headstrong. As he read the letter he became more and more angry.

The emperor called a council of bishops. It met in Worms on the 24th of January, 1076. Upon the bidding of the emperor the council declared that it no longer recognized Gregory as pope. This decision of the council was announced to the pope by letter.

The letter began: "Henry, king not through usurpation but through the ordination of God, to Hildebrand, at present not pope but false monk."

The thrust of this sentence was that Hildebrand had obtained the papacy by illegal means and force. This was a conclusion drawn from the way in which he had become pope. You will remember that, although he had been elected by the spontaneous acclamation of the people, the cardinals later had made his election legal and proper. It was therefore not true that Hildebrand, as Henry implied, had become pope by usurpation.

The emperor's letter continued: "Thou, therefore, condemned by the judgment of all our bishops and by our own, descend and relinquish the Apostolic Chair which thou hast usurped. Let another ascend the throne of St. Peter who shall not practice violence under the cloak of religion, but shall teach the sound doctrine of St. Peter."

4. The Pope Excommunicates the Emperor • As can well be imagined, Gregory was not slow in countering the emperor's blow. In a council held in Rome on the 14th of February he issued a solemn sentence deposing the emperor.

Said the pope in the sentence: "Blessed Peter, prince of the apostles, lend me, I pray thee, a favoring ear. It is because I am thy representative that thy grace has descended upon me, and this grace is the power granted by God to bind and loose in heaven and in earth. Strong in this faith, for the honor and defense of thy Church, on behalf of Almighty God, Father, Son, and Holy Ghost, by virtue of thy power and authority I deprive Henry son of the emperor Henry [Henry III], who has opposed thy Church with unheard-of insolence, of the government of the whole kingdom of Germany and of Italy; I release all Christians from the oath which they have made to him or that they shall make to him. I forbid everyone to obey him as king."

5. The Emperor Pretends Submission

• The emperor sent an appeal to the people of Rome urging them in the most vehement language to banish the "monk Hildebrand" from their city. The pope sent a message to the people of Germany telling them to choose someone else as king unless Henry repented.

The emperor's appeal was completely ignored by the people of Rome. The pope's appeal on the other hand met with a strong response in Germany. The great feudal lords were glad that they now had a pretext for discontinuing their obedience to the emperor. The mass of the people in Germany hated Henry because he had ruled very oppressively.

In October, 1076, the German nobles held a meeting. Many wanted to depose Henry as king at once. All wanted to humble him.

At last the nobles decided that another meeting should be held in Augsburg on the second of February of the next year, under the presidency of the pope. There they would give Henry a

chance to clear himself of the things of which he was accused. If within one year Gregory had not freed him from the ban of excommunication, Henry was to forfeit the throne. In the meanwhile he was to live under guard in the city of Spires.

Henry's position was desperate. He felt his crown slipping. He was willing to agree to anything to save it.

To the pope he wrote: "In accordance with the advice of my subjects, I hereby promise to show henceforth fitting reverence and obedience to the apostolic office and to you, Pope Gregory. And since I have been accused of certain grave crimes, I will either clear myself by presenting proof of my innocence or by undergoing the ordeal, or else I will do such penance as you may decide to be adequate for my fault."

6. The Emperor Sets Out for Italy

• At the same time that the emperor thus humbled himself before the people of Germany and the pope, he was busily scheming how he might regain his former position.

To be excommunicated meant to be cut off from the membership of the Church. When a king was excommunicated his people were no longer under obligation to obey him. He lost his kingdom. To have

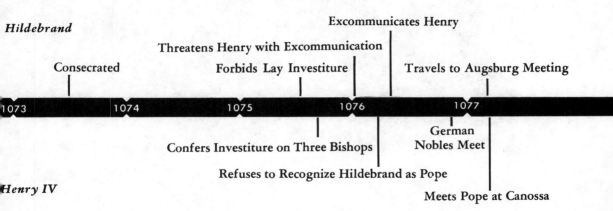

Hildebrand

Excommunicates Henry

Threatens Henry with Excommunication

Consecrated · Forbids Lay Investiture · Travels to Augsburg Meeting

1073 · 1074 · 1075 · 1076 · 1077

Confers Investiture on Three Bishops

German Nobles Meet

Refuses to Recognize Hildebrand as Pope

Henry IV

Meets Pope at Canossa

the *ban* (decree) of excommunication removed and to be restored to membership, a man had to receive absolution of his sins from the proper church officer. Before the church officer could grant absolution the man had to do penance and give proof of repentance.

The doing of penance was a common thing in the Middle Ages. There was a definite form for doing penance fixed by custom. The penitent had to be dressed in a certain way, and he had to fast while doing penance.

It was absolutely necessary for Henry to obtain the pope's absolution and to be freed from the ban of excommunication before the year was over. He contrived to escape from Spires, and with his wife, Bertha, his little son, and a few faithful followers he set out for Italy. It was in the dead of winter. The air was bitterly cold, and the passes of the Alps were choked with snow.

In the meantime the pope had started out upon his northward journey to attend the meeting which was to be held in Augsburg. As he was traveling through Tuscany rumors reached him that Henry was approaching at the head of an armed force. Gregory turned aside, and took refuge within the strong walls of the castle of Canossa.

7. **The Emperor Waits** • On the morning of the twenty-fifth day of January, 1077, Henry climbed the hill to the castle of Canossa, and knocked at its outer gate. The gate was opened to him,

Emperor Henry IV at the Gate of Canossa

and he was led through the gates of the first and the second walls. But the gate in the third wall remained closed. There he stood all day long in the courtyard before that third gate. All day long he fasted. Over his ordinary clothes he wore the garb of a penitent, a coarse woolen robe. He was bareheaded and barefooted. Thus he stood in that courtyard in the cold and the snow. The shades of night were falling, and still the inner gate remained closed. There would be no opportunity any more that day to see the pope.

The next morning Henry appeared again. Again he stood all day long barefoot in the snow. By nightfall the gate in the third wall was still closed, and once more Henry returned to his lodging, a miserable lodging for an emperor.

The next morning saw Henry standing again as a penitent in the courtyard of Canossa. The long weary hours dragged on. The noon hour struck. Still nothing happened. Then, when the afternoon was drawing to a close, on the twenty-seventh day of January, 1077, the inner gate slowly opened, and Henry was told to enter.

Three Lions

Gregory Lifts the Ban of Excommunication

8. The Pope and Emperor Meet • There in the farther end of the room sat Hildebrand, once a poor boy, born of a lowly family, now a little, wizened old man, insignificant in appearance. But he was Pope Gregory VII.

There entered Henry. He was young, tall, powerfully built, impressive even in the penitent's garb. He was Emperor Henry IV.

Here was drama.

In tears the emperor prostrated himself to the ground. He kissed the pope's foot and implored his forgiveness. Gregory granted Henry absolution, and lifted the ban of excommunication.

9. The Real Drama of Canossa • Why did the pope keep the emperor standing for three days barefoot in the snow? Was it to humiliate him to the utmost limit? That is the way the ever memorable scene at Canossa has often been represented. The expression "to go to Canossa" has become proverbial for submitting to the deepest humiliation. But that representation rests upon an entirely wrong conception of what happened at Canossa.

Henry's kingdom was at stake. If he had waited, and appeared before the council in Augsburg with the ban of excommunication hanging over his head, he would have been lost. So he risked everything, crossed the wintry Alps, and headed off the pope on his way to Augsburg.

Next, when Henry appeared not at the head of an armed force as had been rumored, but as a penitent, Gregory did not know what to do. When a man comes as a penitent, absolution *must* be granted. The word of Christ and the ordinances of the Church demand it. Gregory was torn between his Christian and ecclesiastical duty and political considerations. That is why he kept Henry waiting. For three whole days Gregory hesitated. A mighty struggle was going on inside him during those three days. The emperor had put the pope "on the spot." The real drama of Canossa was enacted not outside in the courtyard, but inside the castle in the mind and soul of Gregory.

In the end Henry literally wrung absolution from Gregory, and therewith the restoration of his kingdom. By humbling himself before the pope, the emperor gained a great diplomatic victory over the German nobles. Emperor Henry had "stooped to conquer."

10. The Struggle Continues • Canossa was not the end of the fierce struggle between Henry and Gregory. It was only the most spectacular act in the drama.

Confusion now reigned. Germany and Italy were divided into two warring camps. Henry's opponents in Germany in 1077 elected Rudolph of Swabia to be king. So now there were two kings, or a king and an anti-king. In 1080 Gregory again put Henry under the *ban,* as the decree of excommunication is called. But this time it had little or no effect. The tide had turned against the pope. Most of the bishops declared Gregory deposed, and elected another pope, known as an *antipope.* In the same year, in a battle between Henry and Rudolph, the latter was wounded and bled to death. Civil war continued to rage. Unspeakable cruelties were committed on both sides. Germany was overrun and laid waste.

Now that Rudolph was dead, Henry gathered an army, marched into Italy, besieged Rome, and took it. He installed the anti-pope of his own choice, who then crowned him emperor. When Gregory heard of Henry's approach, he fled into the castle of St. Angelo on the left bank of the Tiber, and sent a call for help to the Normans in southern Italy. They came, and Henry fled. In revenge against the Romans for having surrendered the city to the enemies of the pope, the Normans plundered Rome and committed fearful excesses. The pope was not responsible for this, but it filled the hearts of the Romans with hatred for him. This made his further residence in Rome impossible. When the Normans returned to southern Italy, Gregory went with them.

He died on the way, in Salerno in 1085, a broken man. His last words were: "I have loved righteousness and hated iniquity; therefore I died in exile."

11. The Concordat of Worms • After the death of Gregory the struggle about investiture continued for some thirty-five years.

In 1122 the contestants, weary with the long-drawn-out struggle, came to an agreement known as the *Concordat of Worms*. It was a compromise. According to the terms of this Concordat the popes from this time on were to invest the bishops with the symbols of their spiritual office, and the emperors were to bestow upon them their feudal estates by a touch with the scepter.

1. *Identify: Canossa, Concordat of Worms, anti-pope, ban, council of bishops.*

2. *State clearly in your own words Hildebrand's concept of the papacy.*

3. *Hildebrand sometimes used wrong means to accomplish his ends. Is this ever permissible? (See Schaff's* History of the Christian Church, *Volume VI, p. 41.)*

4. *Why was the struggle over lay investiture such an important one to both emperor and pope?*

5. *Notice that Henry IV did not dare oppose the pope until he was able to gather his own political strength. What circumstances gave him occasion to meet the strength of the papacy?*

6. *Why was the pope's edict to the Germans supported, and Henry IV's disregarded? What should have been the real reasons for their decisions?*

7. *What did excommunication mean to any person in the Church? What special difficulty would this impose on a king or emperor? Was the reaction of Henry to the ban of excommunication a fear of spiritual punishment? What motives and means may a church use in its discipline?*

8. *Why was the pope obliged to give Henry IV absolution? Show that the Church had a higher morality than the political leaders.*

9. *Was Henry sincere? Must the church today accept the profession of faith or the confession of sin of anyone who comes?*

10. *Why did Pope Gregory VII make Henry IV wait outside the castle for three days?*

11. *Why was Hildebrand's second excommunication ineffective?*

12. *Why did the Romans blame Hildebrand for the sack of Rome?*

13. *What motivated Hildebrand throughout his life? Why do men seek positions of leadership?*

CHAPTER 17

The Church
Inspires the Crusades, 1096-1291

1. The Setting for the Crusades • The Church had its origin in the East. There during the first centuries of its existence it developed its greatest strength. There it established the great fundamental Christian doctrines in the Creeds of the Ecumenical Councils. From the East the Church expanded into the West. For more than a thousand years all orthodox Christians lived together in one Church, united in the bonds of a common faith.

Then in 1054 the Church was divided into the Greek Eastern and the Latin Western Church. When in 1073 Hildebrand became pope as Gregory VII, the deep wound dealt the Church by the schism between East and West was still fresh and bleeding. It was the fondest wish of Gregory VII to heal the wound.

Not only was the Church divided, it was also torn by war, and thousands of its members were conquered. Islam, like Christianity, had its origin in the East. The Muslim Arabs took away from the Eastern Empire the provinces of Syria, Palestine, Egypt, and North Africa. From Africa they swept victoriously with the speed of a whirlwind through Spain into the heart of France. There are Tours their impetuous advance was checked in 732 by Charles Martel.

With the passing of the centuries the Arabs lost their strength. They were supplanted in the East by the Turks. These also were Muslims. By 1070 they had taken over from the Arabs Palestine and Syria, had invaded Asia Minor, and were very seriously threatening Constantinople itself and what there was left of the Eastern Empire and Church.

Here was a most remarkable combination of events. The schism between East and West had taken place in 1054. The Turks were threatening Constantinople by 1070. Gregory became pope in 1073.

Gregory was anxious to heal the schism. He was gravely concerned about the Eastern Empire and Church because they were hard pressed by the Turks.

In his hour of need the eastern emperor appealed to Gregory for help against the Muslim Turks. The emperor, who ruled the Eastern Church, promised that if the pope would help him he would put an end to the schism brought about by Patriarch Michael Cerularius.

The appeal of the eastern emperor stirred the pope mightily. It set him on fire. Here was an opportunity such as seldom in the course of history presents itself to any man. Pope Gregory thought he might be able to accomplish three things of major importance at one and the same time. He might be able to save the Eastern Church from the Muslims; heal the grievous wound of the schism by re-uniting the Eastern and Western churches; and then establish the universal, world-wide rule of the papacy. It was a bold and magnificent plan.

Soldiers of the Arab Legion guard the Church of the Holy Sepulchre in Jerusalem in 1954. The Church contains the Chapel of Golgotha, the Stone of Unction, the Chapel of the Holy Sepulchre, the Greek Cathedral, the Chapel of Apparition, and the Chapel of Invention (discovery) of the Cross. The first church was built in 336, demolished in 614, rebuilt in 616 and destroyed in 969 to be rebuilt again in 1037. In 1056 the Crusaders erected a large Romanesque church embracing all holy places and chapels. This church was destroyed in 1244, rebuilt in 1310, restored in 1400 and 1717, destroyed again in 1808 and rebuilt in its present form in 1810. The steel braces over the entrance were added to keep the building from collapse.

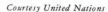

Courtesy United Nations

Pope Gregory VII, the ecclesiastical Napoleon of the Middle Ages, was ready to march in person at the head of an army of fifty thousand soldiers, and lead them "against the enemies of God, even to the tomb of Jesus Christ." But this was not to be. Gregory became involved in the struggle with Henry IV about investiture, and he was thereby prevented from carrying out his plan.

However, Gregory was the first man to conceive of a crusade, or "war of the cross." No pope ever led a crusade personally, but all those that were undertaken later were inspired by the popes.

2. The Turks Are Hostile Toward the Pilgrims •
The Christianity of the masses after the conversion of Constantine, and even more so in the Middle Ages, appears to have been largely formal. As we have seen, it consisted in learning the Apostles' Creed, the Ten Commandments, and the Lord's Prayer; in a belief in the magical power of the sacraments, the ideal of asceticism, the veneration of saints and their relics, and in pilgrimages to their shrines.

Pilgrimages to the Holy Land and its sacred places were especially popular. Away back in the fifth century Jerome had made his home in Bethlehem (see page 34). The great majority of the Christians in western Europe were not much concerned over what the Muslims did to the Eastern Church, from which they were now separated. But the thought that the Holy Land with its sacred places was in possession of infidels was an unbearable insult to the Christian Church.

The Christian pilgrims to the Holy Land had always gotten along well with the Arabs. The attitude of the Arabs

Urban II Proclaims the First Crusade

toward the pilgrims was much the same as that of today's resort owners toward tourists. To the Arabs, Christian money was just as good as Muslim money. They did a very profitable business with the pilgrims.

When the Seljuk Turks took the Holy Land away from the Arabs, the situation changed. The Turks were fanatics in religion. They hated the Christians *because they were Christians*. They would have nothing to do with the pilgrims. They did not want their money. They made it difficult for them to visit the sacred places. Pilgrims upon their return told about their bad treatment at the hands of the Turks. Their reports fanned into flame the resentment which had long been smoldering in the hearts of the Christians of western Europe. This state of popular sentiment opened the way for Pope Urban II to launch the first Crusade.

3. Pope Urban II Initiates the First Crusade • Urban II, who was pope from 1088 to 1099, was a man altogether different from Gregory VII. Gregory was small, insignificant in appearance, and not a public speaker at all. Urban came from a very prominent family; he was tall, handsome and impressive, and a great orator. He was not a man to lead armies, but he was a master of mass psychology.

In the fall of 1095 Urban went to Clermont in France. He let it be known that he was going to speak about the Holy Land and the Turks. When he ascended the platform he saw before him a sea of eager and expectant faces. His powerful and eloquent voice held the multitude spellbound. He spoke to them of the birth of Jesus. He pictured to them Jesus growing up, being baptized, going up and down the Holy Land teaching and doing good. He made them see the arrest of Jesus, His crucifixion, death, and burial. Feelingly he spoke of all the scenes and places in the Holy Land rendered sacred by the sojourn there of the Savior. He forcefully denounced the desecration of those places by the infidels, and the ill treatment of the pilgrims. The huge multitude began to boil with anger.

He went on and whipped the crowd into a frenzy. He called upon them to go to the Holy Land and rescue Jerusalem and the tomb of Christ from the hands of the Turks. To all those who would go he promised a greatly reduced period of time in purgatory. (Purgatory is an imagined place of suffering, where the Catholics believe souls must go to be purified before they can enter heaven.) To all those who should die while serving in the war against the Turks, Urban promised heaven.

Crusaders on the March

Godfrey of Bouillon,
Raymond IV of Toulouse,
Bohemond of Tarentum,
and Tancred of Hauteville
lead the first Crusade, 1096–1099.

The vast multitude was electrified. The thousands assembled at Clermont on that day exclaimed and chanted in wild enthusiasm: "God wills it! God wills it!"

The pope had red cloth cut up into little strips. These strips were sewn together into the forms of crosses. A cross was affixed to the sleeve of every one who said he would take part in the undertaking.

The Latin word for "cross" is *crux*. That is why the undertaking was called a "crusade," and the participants "crusaders."

The Crusades were military expeditions engaged in by the Christians of western Europe with the purpose of wresting the Holy Land and its sacred places from the hands of the Muslims.

The wars engaged in by the Muslim Arabs and Turks for the purpose of spreading their religion were to them holy wars. Now the Christians of western Europe

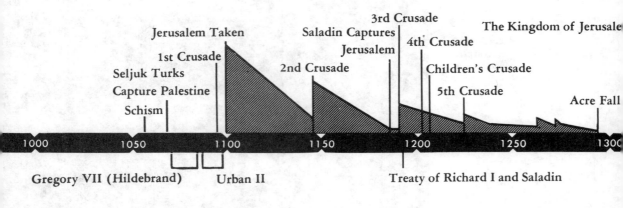

Schism
Seljuk Turks Capture Palestine
1st Crusade
Jerusalem Taken
2nd Crusade
Saladin Captures Jerusalem
3rd Crusade
4th Crusade
Children's Crusade
5th Crusade
The Kingdom of Jerusalem
Acre Fall

1000   1050   1100   1150   1200   1250   1300

Gregory VII (Hildebrand)   Urban II   Treaty of Richard I and Saladin engaged in the Crusades. To them they were holy wars because they were inspired by the Church and had a religious motive.

4. The Immediate Results of the Crusades • The first Crusade, which got under way in 1096, regained Jerusalem. The Kingdom of Jerusalem was set up there and was ruled by the military leaders who had won the fight. Soon these Europeans were quarreling among themselves and even making treaties with the Muslims they had come to conquer. Though the first Crusaders' kingdom lasted for eighty-eight years—until 1187 —it was by no means a strong and flourishing government. Many of its people lived on friendly terms with the natives of the country, who were frequently employed for activities of building or farming, which the Christian foreigners found difficult to perform.

Subsequent Crusades, like the second in 1147, were launched in order to give aid to the shaky and threatened Kingdom of Jerusalem. In 1187 Jerusalem was captured by Saladin, Sultan of Egypt and Syria, and the third Crusade was formed by Richard I of England, Philip of France, and the emperor Frederick Barbarossa. Barbarossa drowned, Philip returned to France, and Richard I (the Lion-Hearted) gained only a treaty with Saladin that Christians could visit the Holy Sepulcher.

Most historians count eight Crusades and a tragic Children's Crusade. With intervals they continued over a period of two hundred years. None of these accomplished the purpose of the Crusades, and as time went on, it became more and more difficult for the popes to whip up enthusiasm for such movements, so that by the

Brown Brothers

**The Storming of Antioch
on June 3, 1098**

middle of the 1200's they had faded out of the historical scene. It was not until the First World War that the English took Palestine away from the Turks.

5. The Motives of the Crusades • The Crusades were unquestionably an expression of religious fervor, both on the part of the pope and on the part of the people. They were also an example of a perverted view of religion. The religious esteem in which the Christians of the Middle Ages held the Holy Land and its so-called sacred places can be likened to their veneration of the relics of saints.

The crusader followed the lead of the Church which asked for the conquest of the Holy Land. He did not ask the question, "Is such an activity a part of my service to God?" Few, if any, asked such a question, since the common people at this time were sadly lacking in education. So we admire the crusader for his zeal but not for his deep religious insight. In religion, as well as in any other area, we are responsible not only for enthusiasm, but also for being right.

1. *Identify: Kingdom of Jerusalem, Seljuk Turks, Holy Sepulchre.*
2. *What circumstances united to create a grand opportunity for Gregory VII?*
3. *What was the relation of pilgrimages to the crusade movement?*
4. *What conditions in Europe made it possible for a pope to stir up the people so that thousands upon thousands would leave their work and homes to go to war against the Muslims? Would it be possible to get people to do this today?*
5. *Find a book of source reading on the Middle Ages and read the report of contemporaries on the Crusades. See Thatcher and McNeal,* Sourcebook for Medieval History, *New York: Charles Scribner's Sons, 1905.*
6. *Find information about the Children's Crusade.*
7. *What is the basic meaning of the word* Crusader? *What is the meaning of the word today?*
8. *Look up the story of Peter the Hermit's activities in the first Crusade.*
9. *Look up the stories of the militant orders, such as the Knights Templar, which were founded to protect pilgrims in Palestine.*

CHAPTER *18*

The Church Rises
To Its Height of Power, 1198-1216

1. Another Emperor Humbles Himself • All the efforts of Gregory VII to establish the supremacy of the papacy over kings and emperors had failed. Even Gregory's victory over Henry IV at Canossa was empty. Yet the scene at Canossa was ever in the minds of succeeding popes. In their mind's eye they saw Emperor Henry bowing in deep humiliation before Pope Gregory. This

Emperor Frederick Barbarossa kneels at the feet of Pope Alexander III on July 24, 1177. Frederick took the cross in May, 1189, set out on the third Crusade, but was drowned crossing a river in Cilicia.

Three Lions

scene stimulated them to constant attempts to attain the ideal to which Gregory had devoted his life.

The Church rose to heights of power under Pope Alexander III. With this pope the mighty emperor Frederick Barbarossa carried on a bitter conflict. At last the emperor had to give in to the pope. When in 1177 the emperor came into the presence of the pope under the porch of the Cathedral of St. Mark in Venice, he spread his cloak upon the pavement, kneeled upon it, and kissed the pope's foot. Alexander made Frederick rise, and gave him the kiss of peace.

On the seventh day of August the two met again, this time in Anagni, Italy. The emperor Frederick now solemnly renounced the anti-pope whom he had installed in Rome, and recognized Alexander as the lawful pope. When Alexander mounted his horse the emperor held the stirrup, and he walked alongside the horse for some distance holding the bridle.

History does seem to repeat itself. Exactly one hundred years after his great-grandfather, the emperor Henry IV, had humbled himself before Pope Gregory VII at Canossa, the emperor Frederick Barbarossa humbled himself before Pope Alexander III in Venice and Anagni.

2. Innocent III • The Church rose to her greatest height of power under Innocent III, who was pope from 1198 to 1216. He belonged to a very outstanding Roman family. His education had been of the best. In Paris he had studied languages, and in Bologna, law. He was an eloquent speaker and an excellent musician and singer. At the youthful age of twenty-nine he was made a cardinal, and when only thirty-seven years old, in 1198, he was elected to the papacy.

Pope Innocent had a most exalted idea of the papacy. In two letters he said: "The Lord gave Peter the rule not only over the universal Church, but also the rule over the whole world," and "No king can rule rightly unless he devoutly serves Christ's vicar."

3. Innocent's Rise to Power • There were five factors that helped Innocent to realize so nearly the papal ideal: the example of Gregory VII, the "Donation of Constantine," the Crusades, the principle of *ratione peccati,* and favorable political circumstances in the Europe of his day. Let us look at each of these in turn.

Although the gigantic efforts of Gregory VII to establish the power of the Church over the State had ended in failure, he left his mighty example behind as an incentive to following popes.

Although the "Donation of Constantine" was a false document, it was for centuries accepted as genuine, and it thus furnished Innocent with a strong legal basis for his claims of papal power.

The Crusades were a manifestation of the unity of Christian Europe against the Muslims. All the Crusades were inspired by the popes. The popes bade the kings and emperors to lead these Crusades, and they obeyed them. Thus the pope appeared in the eyes of the world as the head of all Christendom.

Ratione peccati is Latin, and means "by reason of sin." The popes admitted that kings and emperors are supreme in the purely political sphere. But they maintained that they, the popes, were supreme in the religious and moral sphere. Now the popes claimed that if temporal rulers engaged in political actions which were morally wrong, the popes had not only the right but also the duty to interfere and call these temporal rulers to account. But since every political action has a moral side, the principle of *ratione pec-*

cati gave the popes supreme power also in the political field. It made them dictators over kings and emperors.

As to the political circumstances of the time, they, too, were favorable to Innocent. They made it possible for him to enforce his claims to universal power. The northern Italian towns had grown rich from trade and were willing to join the pope in fighting the emperor. Frederick Barbarossa had died on a Crusade, his son reigned only a few years, to be followed by a three-year-old grandson, Frederick II. France and other nations were beginning to feel a national unity, but no ruler could challenge Pope Innocent III.

4. The Papacy Reaches Its Greatest Height • When Innocent became pope, he restored at once to the papacy the patrimony of St. Peter, as the Papal States were called. This territory across the middle of the Italian peninsula had been gradually shrinking as various popes had to make sacrifices of land to the Holy Roman Emperor in order to gain his protection. For the next six hundred years the boundaries of the Papal States or States of the Church remained what Pope Innocent III made them.

The pope lost no time in proclaiming to the world that he would tolerate no opposition from temporal powers. John Lackland, king of England, dared to oppose Innocent. In 1208 the pope placed England under an *interdict.* That meant that in all England no church service could be held. The next year King John was excommunicated. His subjects were no longer required to obey him. He was deprived of his throne. In 1213 he submitted to the pope. He had a legal docu-

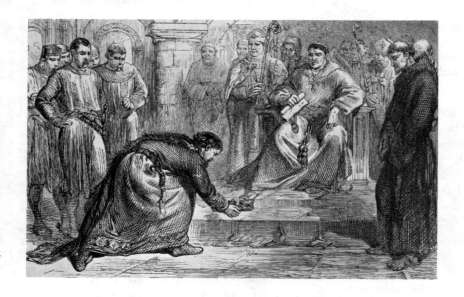

King John
presents his
crown to
Rudolph, the
pope's legate.

ment drawn up, which in a solemn ceremony he handed over to Rudolph, the legate or representative of the pope. The document read: "We grant to God, to his holy apostles Peter and Paul, to our mother the Holy Roman Church, and to our Lord Innocent and to his Catholic successors . . . our kingdoms of England and Ireland, with all their rights and dependencies, in order to receive them anew, as a vassal of God and of the Roman Church. In testimony whereof we take the oath of vassalage before Rudolph . . . and our heirs will always be obliged to take the same oath. And as a sign of our being vassals, we and our successors will pay annually to the Holy See, besides the denarius of St. Peter (Peter's pence), seven hundred marks for England and three hundred marks for Ireland, derived from the royal revenues." Thereupon King John committed his crown and scepter to Rudolph. After keeping them for five days as a sign of sovereignty, Rudolph returned them to the king. England was now a self-acknowledged vassal of the pope.

One after another the emperor and all the kings, lords, and princes of Europe acknowledged the pope as spiritual lord. And all but the king of France acknowledged him also as feudal and temporal lord. They declared themselves to be his vassals and held their kingdoms as fiefs of the Church.

For a time even the Eastern Empire became a fief of the Roman Church. The object of the Crusades was to take the Holy Land away from the Muslim Turks. But the fourth Crusade was deflected from this purpose. Instead of taking Jerusalem, the crusaders on their way to the Holy Land captured Constantinople, and set up what is known as the Latin Kingdom. The rulers of this Latin Kingdom acknowledged them selves to be vassals of the pope.

The majority of the princes of Christendom became vassals of the Church. Thus it was that during the rule of Innocent III, from 1198 to 1216, the Church rose to its greatest height of temporal power.

5. The Lateran Council • But the ideals of Pope Innocent III went beyond the desire for temporal power. In 1215 he held an ecumenical council in the Lateran Church in Rome. In summoning this council Innocent declared: "Two things I have especially at heart, the reconquest of the Holy Land, and the reform of the Church universal."

More than four hundred bishops, eight hundred abbots and priors, and a great host both of the clergy and of the laity were present at the meeting. Seventy-one *primates,* the highest ranking clergy, were also present. They included the patriarchs of Constantinople and Jerusalem, envoys from Emperor Frederick and from the kings of France, England, Aragon, Hungary, Jerusalem, and Cyprus, and representatives of Italian cities. "The whole world seemed to be there."

The Council determined on a new crusade, which the pope offered to lead in person. The Waldensian and Albigensian heresies, of which we shall hear more a little later, were condemned. Punishment of all unrepentant heretics was pre-scribed. It was decreed that the granting of indulgences should be restricted. Bishops were instructed to appoint competent men to preach and to provide free instruction in grammar and theology for poor scholars. It was ordered that Jews and Saracens should wear a distinctive costume. No Jews were to hold public office which would give them authority over Christians.

This Lateran Council of the year 1215 marked the high point in the rule of the most powerful of the popes, Innocent III. The following year he died.

6. The Need for Reform • Innocent had declared that one of the purposes for which he had called the Lateran Council was to reform the Church. There was indeed great need of reform. To the Christian mind of that time reform of the Church meant chiefly reform of the clergy and the monks. The religious and spiritual condition of a very large proportion of the clergy was deplorable. The Church in the course of time had accumulated enormous wealth. To many of the

The Fourth Lateran Council, convened by Innocent III in 1215, was one of the most brilliant councils ever held. Over 1500 persons attended.

Three Lions

clergy a church office was nothing but an easy and pleasant way of making a living. Bishops enjoyed fat incomes. Many utterly worldly men managed to become bishops. A clerk at Paris said: "I can believe everything, but I cannot believe that any German bishop can be saved." Pope Innocent wrote: "The prelates in southern France are the laughingstock of the laity."

Yet it must not be thought that there were no good and sincere Christians in these dark days of the Church. The many hymns that were written during the Middle Ages testify to a deep spiritual life. One of these hymns, familiar to most of us, is the beautiful "O Sacred Head, Now Wounded," written by the monk Bernard of Clairvaux. To the pope, Bernard wrote: "Who will permit me to see before I die the Church of God so ordered as it was in the old days, when the apostles cast their nets to fish for souls and not for gold and silver?" Some of the things he wrote were later of great help to Martin Luther in finding peace for his heart.

The feeling that the Church was in need of a general reformation was shared by all the more earnest Christians. It was this feeling that gave rise to many new monastic orders. These new orders were a condemnation of the laxity that had gradually crept into the old orders. Some of the new orders were the Camaldoli, the Carthusians, the Cistercians, and the two most important—the Franciscans and the Dominicans.

The number of monks and nuns increased rapidly. Peter the Venerable, abbot of Cluny, said: "The innumerable multitude of monks covers almost all the lands. It fills the cities, castles, and fortified places. What a variety of garbs and customs in this army of the Lord which has taken an oath to live according to the rule, in the name of faith and charity!"

The Templars and the Hospitalers and the Teutonic Knights were three military monastic orders established in Palestine. Their purpose was to protect the pilgrims traveling to the sacred shrines in the Holy Land and to care for them when sick. The first two remain Roman Catholic orders to the present. The Teutonic Knights maintained their headquarters in Acre until its fall in 1291, but as early as 1226 had gone to Hungary and Prussia. Here they battled the Slavs and Tartars and gave much effort to the conver-

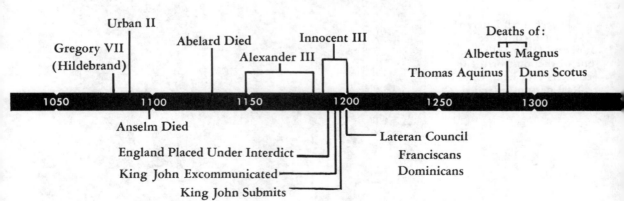

sion of the Baltic lands. At the time of the Reformation, the Grand Master, Albert of Brandenburg, became Protestant and dissolved the order.

7. The Dominican Order • Dominic was a monk who had been born and educated in Spain. Accompanying his bishop to southern France, he began to preach in order to bring back into the Roman Catholic Church those who had withdrawn and were teaching other doctrines. It is claimed that he performed several miracles. He established a nunnery where converts to the Roman Church could find a shelter and poor girls of noble blood could receive an education.

At the Lateran Council of 1215 he sought from Pope Innocent III recognition of a fraternity which he had established. At that time the fraternity counted only sixteen members. Pope Innocent readily granted the recognition.

The Dominicans adopted the name of "Preaching Friars." This was the name Innocent had used in speaking of them. This name denoted their ideals. They were to preach. In order to be able to do this they were to be *friars,* a name derived from the word *frater,* or brother. They were not to be monks. They were to live not secluded in a cloister, but in the midst of the hustle of life.

The growth of the Dominican Friars was very rapid. Dominic died four years after he had sent them out. By that time the Order was already organized in eight provinces, and it had established sixty convents.

The Dominicans adopted the vow of poverty. They became a *mendicant* order, which means that they were an order of begging friars.

Franciscans were called Minorites from the designation *Fratres Minores,* and in England they were popularly called Grey Friars from the color of their dress.

In course of time the Dominicans acquired a great reputation for learning. The university towns were the special fields of their activity. Soon Dominicans were teaching as professors in all the leading universities of western Europe. Their most illustrious scholars were Albertus Magnus and Thomas Aquinas. Because of their learning the Dominicans came into control of the *Inquisition,* a court established to root out heresy. We shall hear more about the Inquisition in a later chapter.

8. The Franciscan Order • Francis of Assisi was born in Italy in the year 1182. His father was a rich merchant, and Francis gave himself over to a life of pleasure. When he was about twenty years old he fell dangerously ill and was converted. From that time on he devoted himself to poverty and charity. Other men of like mind joined with him. When they were twelve in all they, too, as Dominic had done, applied to Pope Innocent III at the Lateran Council of 1215 for approval of their organization. The pope granted their request, and the *Minorites* or Friars Minor (lesser), as they called themselves in their humility, began their work.

Francis insisted upon absolute poverty. The brethren were to labor with their hands, but were not allowed to receive wages in money. They were not to take thought for the morrow, and they were to give to the poor all that was not absolutely necessary for the day.

Francis of Assisi loved all created things, and would preach to the birds. He adopted "My Lady Poverty" as his mistress, and sang her praises. He was very eloquent, and by his preaching swayed the minds and hearts of men.

The order of the Franciscans, or Minorites, grew with astonishing rapidity. It soon spread throughout the civilized world.

9. The Mendicant Orders Do Much Good • In many ways the two mendicant orders of Dominican and Franciscan Friars were similar, and they were both very popular.

The Friars wandered all over Europe under the burning sun or in chilling blasts. They rejected alms in money, but received thankfully whatever coarse food might be offered them or endured hunger uncomplainingly. They busied themselves untiringly in the work of snatching souls from Satan and lifting men up from the sordid cares of daily life.

The Friars also engaged in missionary work among the heathen, schismatic Christians in the East, heretics, and Mohammedans.

On the right of this general view of a section of Assisi, Italy, is the famous monastery and church of St. Francis, who founded the order of the Franciscans.

Philip Gendreau

Pierre Abelard, French philosopher and teacher who became a monk, was widely known for his brilliance and learning. At the monastery which he built after his retirement in Champagne, he often lectured in theology to very attentive audiences. He lived from 1079 to 1142.

They emphasized the dignity of manual labor, the duty of Christians to care for those who are in want, and the need of reform in the lives of the clergy. Both these orders exist today. They are strong and active.

10. A Revival of Culture Begins • During the period of the Crusades thousands of people of western Europe traveled to many distant lands. the people of the eastern Empire and the Muslims of Spain and of the eastern countries were far more civilized than the people of western Europe. Contact with the Near East through the Crusades immensely stimulated the mental life of the people in the various countries of western Europe.

From the twelfth century on the medieval darkness of western Europe was gradually being dispelled. Many universities sprang up in Italy, Germany, France, and England. These universities could boast of teachers of great learning and mental acumen, such as Anselm, Abelard, Peter the Lombard, Albertus Magnus, Thomas Aquinas, and Duns Scotus. These men are called *Schoolmen* and the learning they imparted is called *scholasticism.* This learning was a mixture of theology and philosophy. Thomas Aquinas' massive work *Summa Theologica* was a synthesis of classical and Christian thought and is the basis of Catholic teaching today.

Medieval men also built many wonderful cathedrals. Some of the most illustrious are those of Milan, Rheims, and Cologne.

This cultural revival did also affect the Church. The Church is in the world, and any major change in the world is sooner or later felt in the Church.

1. Identify: Minorites, Preaching Friars, interdict, Schoolmen.
2. Write an imaginary letter in which Pope Alexander tries to convince Emperor Frederick Barbarossa that the pope's authority is final and supreme.
3. Write an imaginary response in which Barbarossa tries to convince Alexander that the pope has no civil authority in Germany.
4. Find a list of the popes and figure the average time for the reign of the pontiffs. Why is it quite short in duration?
5. What great work did the Lateran Council accomplish?
6. What were some outstanding virtues in St. Francis' life?
7. List the activities of the mendicant orders and show how these activities reflected the condition of the Church of that day.
8. Find information about the stigmata in connection with St. Francis' life.
9. What do the decisions of the Lateran Council reveal about the conditions in the Church of that day?
10. What evidences did this period show of the revival of culture?

The Famous Cathedrals of Cologne, Germany (above); Rheims, France (right); and Milan, Italy (below)

CHAPTER 19

The Church
Declines in Power, 1294-1417

1. Pope Boniface VIII • Generally speaking the popes from Innocent III to Boniface VIII, that is throughout the thirteenth century, were successful in maintaining the temporal power of the Church. A rapid decline began with the rule of Boniface VIII.

Here we have an example of how the character and personality of a leader may influence the course of history. Boniface was a man of considerable learning and overbearing arrogance. His installation as pope was attended with great pomp. As he mounted his horse, a king held one of the stirrups, and a second king held the other stirrup. This man was pope from 1294 to 1303.

Boniface soon got into trouble with Philip the Fair, king of France, about taxation of the clergy. King Philip imposed a heavy tax upon the clergy in France. The pope forbade the clergy to pay this tax. The king retaliated by forbidding the exportation from his kingdom of gold, silver, and precious stones. In that way the king cut off the revenue the pope had been receiving from France.

The pope issued several *bulls*. A bull is an official papal pronouncement or declaration. It is called a bull because to such a papal document there was always affixed a round leaden seal, called in Latin a *bulla*. Papal bulls are always written in Latin. These papal bulls are named after their opening words.

In the bull *Unam sanctam* (One holy) the pope said: ". . . the Church has two swords at its command, the spiritual and the temporal. . . . Each of these is the power of the Church, but the former should be drawn by the Church and by the hand of the *Pontiff* [or pope]; the latter by the hand of kings and soldiers, but on behalf of the Church, at the command and with the authorization of the Pontiff. One of these swords must be subordinate to the other, that is to say, the temporal power must be subordinate to the spiritual power. It belongs to the spiritual power to establish the temporal power and to judge it if it goes astray. . . . It is necessary for salvation for every human creature to submit to the Roman Pontiff." For Scriptural proof of his right to universal dominion the pope cited Jeremiah 1:10: "Behold, I have set thee over nations and kingdoms."

Pope Boniface hurled the ban of excommunication at King Philip of France as Pope Gregory VII had hurled the ban at Emperor Henry IV. By that means Gregory had brought the emperor to terms: but the ban hurled by Boniface did not have the desired effect.

How should one account for it that the same means did not in both cases have the same effect? The times had changed.

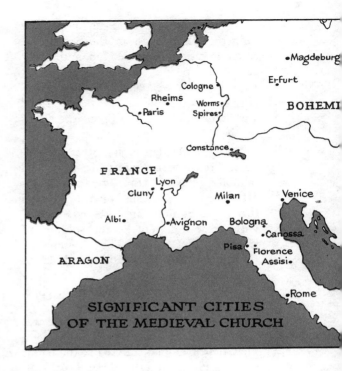

SIGNIFICANT CITIES OF THE MEDIEVAL CHURCH

In the time of Gregory feudalism prevailed, and the nobles were strong. They often rebelled against their king. Henry's excommunication furnished them with an excuse for withdrawing their obedience. In that way the emperor was rendered helpless. There was nothing for him to do but submit himself to the pope. In the time of Boniface, as one of the many results of the Crusades, feudalism had fallen into decay, the nobles had lost much of their power, and a strong spirit of nationalism had sprung up in the hearts of the people of France. When Pope Boniface excommunicated their king, they did not withdraw their allegiance and forsake him. They loyally clung to him and backed him up, so that King Philip the Fair of France was in a position to defy Boniface.

In any struggle between pope and king the effectiveness of the ban of excommunication depended upon the attitude of the people. If they supported the pope it was a weapon of well-nigh irresistible power. But if the people sided with their king, that weapon lost all its power.

It was at Anagni in Italy that the emperor Frederick Barbarossa in 1177 had humbled himself before Pope Alexander III. It was in that same town of Anagni that Pope Boniface in 1303 was treated with great indignity by the soldiers of King Philip of France. The king sent two representatives with a band of soldiers to Anagni to arrest the pope. The populace of Anagni rose up in defense of the pope. The soldiers beat and buffeted him, but they could not arrest him. Boniface was an old man of eighty-seven. The complete defeat he had suffered at the hands of King Philip, and the physical maltreatment that had been inflicted upon him, were too much for him. Broken in spirit, he died a few days after his return to Rome.

2. A New Era • No pope had ever stated the papal claims to power in such extravagant form as the arrogant Boniface VIII had done in his various bulls. No pope ever suffered so complete and humiliating a defeat. But it was not only his defeat; it also marked the beginning of the decline of the power of the Church. It ushered in a new era.

In 1309, when Pope Clement V decided to leave Rome and accepted King Philip the Fair's offer to come and settle in France, he selected Avignon as the new seat of the Papal Court. In 1348, Pope Clement VI acquired Avignon from the House of Provence and the city remained the property of the Roman Church until 1791 when it was returned to France. This immense fortified Palace of the Popes is a real fortress, including luxurious apartments, chapels, courtyards, and gardens.

Boniface had entirely failed to understand and estimate correctly the strength of the new spirit of nationalism. The States-General of France, composed of the three estates of the realm—the nobles, the clergy, and the commons—declared that in civil matters the pope had no authority, and that the king had no superior but God.

3. The "Babylonian Captivity," 1309-1376 • In 1309 the papal seat was removed from Rome to Avignon in Provence, immediately adjacent to France. Here the popes resided until 1376. This period of residence of the popes in Avignon is known as the "Babylonian Captivity of the Papacy." It is called a captivity because during this time the popes were completely under the domination of the French kings. It is called the Babylonian captivity because it lasted just about seventy years, as did the captivity of the Israelites in Babylon in Old Testament times. During this period all the popes were Frenchmen.

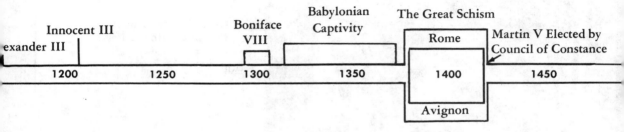

Innocent III
exander III

Boniface
VIII

Babylonian
Captivity

The Great Schism

Rome

Martin V Elected by
Council of Constance

1200   1250   1300   1350   1400   1450

Avignon

King Philip the Fair of France had dealt the papacy a heavy blow. The Babylonian Captivity further undermined the prestige of the papacy. Because the popes in Avignon had to dance to the tunes played by the French kings, the people in other countries lost respect for them. The condition of the papacy in this time resembled its condition in the tenth century, when the popes were under the domination of the Italian nobles.

Besides, nationalism was rearing its head also in other countries. Certain princes in Germany had the right to elect the king. They declared that the German emperor derived all his powers through them from God and not from the pope. The principle that the German emperors were independent of the papacy, as far as their election and exercise of their governmental powers was concerned, became a part of the German constitution. In England in 1366 during the reign of Edward III, Parliament put an end to English vassalage to Rome. It repudiated the claims of the popes upon England as a fief to the Roman Church. The English refused to pay the tribute pledged by King John to Pope Innocent III.

Many of the popes of the Babylonian Captivity led wicked lives. While in Avignon they maintained a very luxurious court. This cost a great deal of money.

To obtain the money the popes brazenly and in the most scandalous manner sold the office of bishop and indulgences, and in many other ways exacted a heavy toll from the members of the Church. This came to be felt as an unbearable burden in all the countries of western Europe. Many people began to say that the pope was the antichrist.

In all these ways the Babylonian Captivity caused the papacy to lose a great deal of prestige.

But worse was still to come.

4. The Great Schism, 1378-1417 • The Italians were greatly dissatisfied with the residence of the popes in Avignon. They wanted Rome to become again the seat of the papacy. This resulted in an open rupture in 1378 between the Italian and the French party. Each party elected a pope. Now there were two popes: one in Rome and one in Avignon. This is known as the Great Schism, which lasted from 1378 to 1417.

The popes denounced, excommunicated, and *anathematized* (pronounced curses upon) each other. To all true and sincere Christians it was a sad spectacle. The reverence in which the papacy had been generally held received a rude shock, from which it never fully recovered.

In 1409 a council was held in Pisa to

Catherine of Siena
Pleading with the Pope
to Return from
Avignon to Rome

Courtesy Metropolitan Museum of Art
Historical Pictures Service—Chicago

heal the Schism. The Council deposed both popes, and elected Alexander V as the new pope. Neither of the deposed popes would give up his office. Now there were three popes.

Under these confusing circumstances none of the three was fully recognized as pope. At last in 1417 the Council of Constance elected an Italian cardinal pope as Martin V. The other three popes, weary of the troublesome state of affairs, gave Martin their support. And so the Church in western Europe once more had one head, and the Great Schism was healed. But the wounds which the papacy and the Church had suffered in consequence of the Babylonian Captivity and the Great Schism continued to throb for a long time.

1. *Identify: Avignon, Anagni, papal bulls, 1417.*
2. *How would you answer Boniface's claim to power when he quoted Jeremiah 1:10?*
3. *Explain why the excommunication of Philip of France proved to be ineffective.*
4. *What historical events led to the Babylonian Captivity? What were the effects of this experience on the papacy?*
5. *What was the Great Schism? What effect did it have on the papacy?*
6. *How did the Babylonian Captivity lead to the Great Schism?*
7. *List the councils that tried to settle the Schism and tell how the Council of Constance finally succeeded. Schaff's* History of the Christian Church, *Volume II, will be helpful.*

LIST OF POPES FROM LEO I TO THE PRESENT

The Roman Catholic Church lists forty-eight popes before Leo I. The popes in bold type are mentioned and indexed in this textbook.

440–461	**Leo I**
461–468	Hilary
468–483	Simplicius
483–492	Felix III
492–496	Gelasius I
496–498	Anastasius II
498–514	Symmachus
498	Laurentius*
514–523	Hormisdas
523–526	John I
526–530	Felix IV
530–532	Boniface II
530	Dioscorus*
532–535	John II
535–536	Agapetus I
536–538	Silverius
537–555	Vigilius
555–560	Pelagius I
560–573	John III
574–578	Benedict I
578–590	Pelagius II
590–604	**Gregory I†**
604–606	Sabinianus
607	Boniface III
608–615	Boniface IV
615–618	Deusdedit
619–625	Boniface V
625–638	Honorius I
640	Severinus
640–642	John IV
642–649	Theodorus I
649–655	St. Martin I
654–657	Eugenius I
657–672	Vitalianus
672–676	Adeodatus
676–678	Domnus I
678–681	Agatho
682–683	Leo II
684–685	Benedict II
685–686	John V
686–687	Conon
687–692	Paschal*
687	Theodorus*
687–701	Sergius I
701–705	John VI
705–707	John VII
708	Sisinnius
708–715	Constantine I
715–731	**Gregory II**
731–741	Gregory III
741–752	**Zacharias**
752	Stephen II
752–757	Stephen III
757–767	Paul I
767–788	Constantine II
768–772	Stephen IV
772–795	Adrian I
795–816	**Leo III**
816–817	Stephen V
817–824	Paschal I
824–827	Eugenius II
827	Valentinus
827–844	Gregory IV
844–847	Sergius II
847–855	Leo IV
855–858	Benedict III
855	Anastasius
858–867	**Nicholas I**
867–872	Adrian II
872–882	John VIII
882–884	Marinus
884–885	Adrian III
885–891	**Stephen VI**
891–896	Formosus
896	Boniface VI
896–897	Stephen VII
897	Romanus
897	Theodorus II
898–900	John IX

* indicates Antipope
† Gregory I is called Gregory the Great
§ Gregory VII is known as Hildebrand
‡ Sylvester II is known as Gerbert

900–903	Benedict IV
903	Leo V
903–904	Christopher
904–911	Sergius III
911–913	Anastasius III
913	Lando
914–929	John X
928–929	Leo VI
929–931	Stephen VIII
931–936	John XI
936–939	Leo VII
939–942	Stephen IX
942–946	Marinus II
946–955	Agapetus
955–964	**John XII**
963–965	Leo VIII
964–965	Benedict V
965–972	John XIII
973–974	Benedict VI
974–983	Benedict VII
983–984	John XIV
984–985	Boniface VII
985–996	John XV
996–999	**Gregory V**
997–998	John XVI
999–1003	**Sylvester II‡**
1003	John XVII
1003–1009	John XVIII
1009–1012	Sergius IV
1012–1024	Benedict VIII
1012	Gregory VI*
1024–1033	John XIX
1033–1045	**Benedict IX**
1045–1046	**Sylvester III**
1044–1046	**Gregory VI**
1046–1047	**Clement II**
1048	Damasus II
1049–1054	**Leo IX**
1055–1057	**Victor II**
1057–1058	**Stephen X**
1058–1059	**Benedict X**
1059–1061	**Nicholas II**
1061–1073	**Alexander II**
1061	Honorius II*
1073–1085	**Gregory VII§**
1080–1100	Wibertus
1086–1087	Victor III
1088–1099	**Urban II**
1099–1118	Paschal II
1100	Theodoricus*
1102	Albertus*
1105–1111	Sylvester IV*
1118–1119	Gelasius II
1118–1121	Gregory VIII*
1119–1124	Calixtus II
1124	Celestine*
1124–1130	**Honorius II**
1130–1143	Innocent II
1130–1138	Anacletus II
1138	Victor IV*
1143–1144	Celestine II
1144–1145	Lucius II
1145–1153	Eugenius III
1153–1154	Anastasius IV
1154–1159	Adrian IV
1159–1181	**Alexander III**
1159–1164	Victor IV*
1164–1168	Paschal III*
1168–1178	Calixtus III*
1178–1180	Innocent III*
1181–1185	Lucius III
1185–1187	Urban III
1187	Gregory VIII
1187–1191	Clement III
1191–1198	Celestine III
1198–1216	**Innocent III**
1216–1227	Honorius III
1227–1241	Gregory IX
1241	Celestine IV
1243–1254	Innocent IV
1254–1261	Alexander IV
1261–1264	Urban IV
1265–1268	Clement IV
1271–1276	Gregory X

1276	Innocent V
1276	Adrian V
1276–1277	John XXI
1277–1280	Nicholas III
1281–1285	Martin IV
1285–1287	Honorius IV
1288–1292	Nicholas IV
1294	Celestine V
1294–1303	**Boniface VIII**
1303–1304	Benedict XI
1305–1314	**Clement V**
1316–1334	John XXII
1334–1342	Benedict XII
1342–1352	Clement VI
1352–1362	Innocent VI
1362–1370	Urban V
1370–1378	Gregory XI
1378–1389	Urban VI
1378–1394	Clement VII
1389–1404	Boniface IX
1394–1423	Benedict XIII
1404–1406	Innocent VII
1406–1415	**Gregory XII**
1409–1410	**Alexander V**
1410–1415	**John XXIII**
1417–1431	**Martin V**
1417	Clement VIII
1431–1447	Eugene IV
1439–1449	Felix V
1447–1455	Nicholas V
1455–1458	Calixtus III
1458–1464	Pius II
1464–1471	Paul II
1471–1484	Sixtus IV
1484–1492	Innocent VIII
1492–1503	**Alexander VI**
1503	Pius III
1503–1513	Julius II
1513–1521	**Leo X**
1522–1523	Adrian VI
1523–1534	Clement VII
1534–1549	**Paul III**
1550–1555	Julius III
1555	Marcellus II
1555–1559	Paul IV
1559–1565	Pius IV
1566–1572	Pius V
1572–1585	Gregory XIII
1585–1590	Sixtus V
1590	Urban VII
1590–1591	Gregory XIV
1591	Innocent IX
1592–1605	Clement VIII
1605	Leo XI
1605–1621	Paul V
1621–1623	Gregory XV
1623–1644	Urban VIII
1644–1655	Innocent X
1655–1667	Alexander VII
1667–1669	Clement IX
1670–1676	Clement X
1676–1689	Innocent XI
1689–1691	Alexander VIII
1691–1700	Innocent XII
1700–1721	Clement XI
1721–1724	Innocent XIII
1724–1730	Benedict XIII
1730–1740	Clement XII
1740–1758	Benedict XIV
1758–1769	Clement XIII
1769–1774	**Clement XIV**
1775–1799	Pius VI
1800–1823	**Pius VII**
1823–1829	Leo XII
1829–1830	Pius VIII
1831–1846	Gregory XVI
1846–1878	Pius IX
1878–1903	Leo XIII
1903–1914	Pius X
1914–1922	Benedict XV
1922–1939	Pius XI
1939–1958	Pius XII
1958–1963	**John XXIII**
1963–1978	Paul VI
1978–1978	John Paul I
1978–	John Paul II

CHAPTER 20

The Church
Is Stirred from Within, 1200-1517

1. Struggle and Change • As we in our study approach the end of the Middle Ages, we find the conditions characterized by decay and chaos. The epic struggle between papacy and empire was the great drama of the Middle Ages. Now the Holy Roman Empire was fading out, and a spirit of nationalism was arising in the various sections of Europe. The political structure was chaotic.

In the struggle the papacy also received serious wounds. The Medieval Church was a vast and mighty structure. It symbolized unity. But this symbol was shattered in the sordid spectacle of the Great Schism. This situation was not comprehensible to the common people.

The Crusades not only did much to break down the feudal system, but they stimulated the economic and intellectual life of the West. There came into existence groups of people who began to hold and spread ideas which were in conflict with the doctrine and government of the Church.

Not only was the outer framework of the Church being shaken, but the life of the Church was being stirred from within.

2. The Albigenses • You will remember that Manicheism had its origin in Persia and spread from there through the Roman Empire, and that for a time the great Church Father Augustine came under its influence. Later Augustine gave up the teachings of the Manicheans and combatted them. His opposition did much to eradicate Manicheism from the West; but in the East it lingered on. During the Crusades, Manichean ideas came back into western Europe through Bulgaria along the new trade routes opened by the crusaders.

These ideas sprouted abundantly, especially in southern France. There the town of Albi became a hotbed of these ideas, and the people there who held these ideas came to be called *Albigenses*. A more inclusive name for these new Manicheans is *Cathari*.

Like the Manicheans the *Cathari* were *dualists*. This means that they believed that there is a good and an evil god. The visible world, the world of matter, is the work of the evil god. In this material world souls are held in bondage as prisoners from the kingdom of the good god.

Some of the Albigenses rejected the Old Testament. They considered it to be the work of the evil god. Others accepted the Psalms and the Prophets. All believed that the New Testament came from the good god. Since they believed that all material things are evil, they thought that Christ did not have a real body, and that He did not die a real death. They did not reverence the cross because it is a material thing. They rejected the sacraments, because their elements are material. They did not have church buildings, because they are built of material things. The Albigenses were heretics.

3. The Waldenses • The Albigenses were definitely hostile to the Church. That cannot be said of the Waldenses. They were followers of Peter Waldo, a rich merchant of Lyons. He believed that the Bible and especially the New Testament should be the only rule of faith and life for the Christians. Around the year 1176 he sold all his goods and gave his money to the poor. He and his followers learned large portions of the New Testament by heart. Two by two, dressed in simple woolen garments and barefooted, they went about preaching. On Mondays, Wednesdays, and Fridays they fasted. They would not swear an oath or shed blood. They used only the Lord's Prayer. They did not believe in purgatory or in prayers and masses for the dead. They considered prayers offered in a house or in a stable just as effective as those offered in a church. They practiced lay preaching by both men and women.

*Schoenfeld Collection
from Three Lions*

Peter Waldo
From the Luther Monument at Worms, Germany

4. The Church Resorts to Persecution • The Albigenses and the entirely different Waldenses grew so numerous that in the areas in which they lived they became a real threat to the very existence of the Roman Catholic Church. Their presence had a great effect upon the Church. The Church pronounced them to be heretics. It was largely to oppose their preaching that the Dominican and Franciscan Orders of Preaching Friars were organized. As these two orders grew very rapidly they acquired a place of the utmost importance during the later Middle Ages. They became the armies of the popes.

The preaching of the Dominican and Franciscan Friars had some, but not a very great, success in winning the heretics back to the Church. And so various church councils decided, in no small measure under the influence of the teachings of Augustine, to use methods of force. The Church began to persecute heretics. The *Inquisition* was introduced with the Dominicans in charge of it.

The Inquisition was a Roman Catholic court whose business it was to root out heresy. Anybody suspected of heresy was brought before this tribunal conducted by Dominican Friars. The Friars would question the suspected one. If they discovered that he held heretical ideas they would ask him to *recant* or deny his heretical beliefs. If he recanted he would go free. If he would not recant, but steadfastly persisted in his heretical opinions, he was abandoned by the Church to the officers of the civil government. That is, he was surrendered to the civil government to be punished, for "the Church does not shed blood." Punishment most frequently took the form of death by fire. The heretic was burned at the stake. This *Medieval* Inquisition is not to be confused with the *Spanish* Inquisition of a later date.

If a man accused of heresy would not answer the questions put to him by the Dominican examiners, he would be tortured until he confessed or died as a result of the torture.

Many Albigenses and Waldenses fell victims to the Inquisition. But their number in southern France was so great that the task of destroying them was too big for the Inquisition. Then the popes resorted to other measures. They preached a crusade against the heretics. Some of

Pope Innocent III
Urging the War
Against the
Albigenses

Historical Pictures
Service—Chicago

the nobles responded to the call of the popes. They marched at the head of their armies into southern France. For twenty years "blood flowed like water." The country was devastated by war of the most savage kind. What had been the fairest province of France was turned into a wilderness, and its cities into ruins. The Albigenses were rooted out.

The Waldenses found a place of refuge in the high valleys of the Alps. They still live there today. At the time of the Reformation they accepted its teachings and became Protestants. Of the Christians who broke away from the Roman Catholic Church during the Middle Ages, they are the only group that has survived to the present time. They are carrying on evangelistic work in Italy today with considerable success.

5. John Wycliffe • In the latter part of the Middle Ages there arose many in-

dividuals who criticized the doctrine and government of the Roman Church. The two who were by far the most important were John Wycliffe and John Huss.

Wycliffe was born in England in the year 1320. He studied at the University of Oxford, and later became professor in that institution. In 1376 he began to criticize the clergy. He said that wealth and political power had so corrupted the Church that a radical reform was necessary. The Church, he said, should return to the poverty and simplicity of apostolic times. The pope he called the antichrist. He declared that the Bible rather than the Church should be the only rule of faith. But the Bible in general use in the Catholic Church was written in Latin and could not be read by the people. It was the translation made from the Hebrew and the Greek into Latin by Jerome, known as the Vulgate. In order that Christians in England might be able to read the Bible

John Wycliffe
Sending Forth
His Followers,
the Lollards

for themselves, Wycliffe translated it into the English language. He also wrote many books.

Wycliffe's followers carried his teachings and the newly translated Bible into many parts of England. Naturally the pope and the clergy were uneasy about this. They did all they could to destroy Wycliffe. But a large portion of the English people and among them many powerful nobles were in hearty sympathy with the reformer. These nobles protected him so that he did not fall into the hands of his persecutors. Wycliffe died in peace on the last day of the year 1384.

The teachings of Wycliffe continued to be spread over England after his death, not only by means of his writings, but also by the preaching of his disciples, who came to be known as *Lollards*. They were people who denounced the pope and his clergy, practiced poverty, and acknowledged the Bible as the only standard of doctrine.

As the followers of Wycliffe increased in influence, the opposition of the clergy likewise increased. At last the bishops succeeded in getting a law passed which condemned heretics to be burned. From one end of England to the other the Lollards perished as martyrs in the flames. But it was difficult to uproot them entirely. In the fifteenth century fires were still kindled. Gradually, however, the growth of Lollardism was checked. Thinner and thinner grew the ranks. Finally those who were left were driven into hiding. But Lollardism lingered on in secret to the time of the Reformation.

6. **John Huss** • The teachings of Wycliffe spread far beyond the shores of England. In Bohemia John Huss accepted them with enthusiasm. Huss, who was born around 1369, had been trained for the priesthood. He became dean of the theological faculty at the University of Prague, in the capital of Bohemia, and later was made head of that institution.

When Huss became acquainted with the writings of Wycliffe, he began to preach with boldness against the corrup-

PART TWO: THE CHURCH IN THE MIDDLE AGES

tion of the clergy. Long before the birth of Huss, strong opposition to the Roman Church had developed in Bohemia. The Waldenses were especially numerous in that country. So the preaching of Huss met with a hearty response among both the common people and the nobility. Huss won almost the whole of Bohemia to his views.

Huss taught many ideas which later became the main teachings of the Reformers. He taught that the holy Catholic Church consists of the total number of the predestinated. He distinguished between being *in* the Church and being *of* the Church. He taught that one could be in the Church and yet not be a real member of it. Of the universal Church Christ alone is the head. Popes and cardinals are not necessary to the government of the Church.

It should be remembered that this was the time of the Great Schism. The bitter conflict caused by it in the Church was now at its height. The two popes at this time were John XXIII in Avignon, and Gregory XII in Rome. Pope John XXIII was hard pressed by the king of Naples,

who was the protector of Pope Gregory XII. John promised indulgences to all who would come to his aid against the king of Naples. Before this, Huss had been a strong believer in indulgences. On one occasion he had spent his last cent to buy one. Now he condemned the selling of indulgences as an abominable practice contrary to the teachings of the Bible.

Immediately Pope John excommunicated Huss. The latter treated his excommunication with contempt, declared it to be null and void, and appealed from the pope to the Council.

Late in the year 1414 a general council assembled in Constance. It had been called by the emperor Sigismund for the purpose of making an end of the Schism and bringing about the necessary reforms in the Church. The emperor invited Huss to attend the Council, and promised him a safe-conduct. Relying upon the emperor's promise of safety Huss accepted the invitation. A few weeks later he was put into prison by Pope John XXIII for heresy.

Huss, supported by the Bohemians and the emperor himself, protested vehement-

John Huss administers Holy Communion in both the bread and the wine.

Brown Brothers

**John Huss Is Burned
at the Stake**

ly against his arrest. The answer was that his arrest was entirely canonical, that is to say, it was in accordance with the canons, or rules, of the Church. That was only too true. According to canonical law of the Roman Catholic Church, heretics have no rights. To deceive heretics and betray them is a pious act. Promises made to heretics need not be kept.

Huss was left to languish in prison for more than eight months. Then, without having been given an opportunity to defend himself, he was brought from the dungeon to the cathedral in Constance. There, on the sixth of July, 1415, in the presence of the bishops and the emperor he was degraded. First he was dressed in the vestments of a priest. Then one by one every article of priestly attire was removed with curses that were considered appropriate. Thereupon a paper cone was placed upon his head. Upon this paper cap three ugly devils had been painted. The cap bore the inscription: "Here is the Heresiarch."

Huss was led forth from the cathedral to a place before one of the city's gates. There a high stake had been erected and surrounded with firewood. He was tied to the stake with cords which had been thoroughly soaked in water. The wood was kindled. Flames licked his body and Huss died a martyr's death.

A crusade was organized against the followers of Huss, and for many years Bohemia was ravaged by war. But the spirit of reform lived on, and when the Reformation began in Germany, opposition to the Roman Church was still strong in the land of Huss.

7. Three General Church Councils • In the period from 1409 to 1449 three general church councils were held: in Pisa in the year 1409, in Constance from 1414 to 1418, and in Basel from 1431 to 1449. The threefold purpose of these councils was (1) to heal the Great Schism, (2) to bring about reforms in the Church, and (3) to suppress heresy. It must be remembered that at this time councils were considered infallible and were the final authority of the Church.

The Council of Pisa accomplished nothing that proved to be effective. The Council of Constance, by appointing Martin V

The Turks slaughter the helpless Christians in the Great Church of St. Sophia, Constantinople, in 1453.

as the legal pope, was successful in healing the Great Schism. In addition to burning Huss, it ordered that the writings of Wycliffe should be burned and that his body should be dug up and burned.

One of the main objects of the Council of Basel was to restore the unity of the Church in Bohemia where terrible slaughter had failed to stop the Hussite movement. In 1436 an agreement was reached with the Hussites. It allowed certain freedom of preaching; resolved that attempts should be made to reform the lives of the clergy; and permitted all members of the Church of Bohemia, who so desired, to partake not only of the bread but also of the wine in Communion. The Council had negotiated with heretics on equal terms and had granted special privileges to those who had openly defied the authority of the Church.

This Council also made an agreement with representatives of the Eastern Church which seemed to have healed the Schism of 1054. The Greek representatives agreed to accept the doctrines of the Western Church in exchange for help against the Mohammedan Turks who were threatening the very existence of the Eastern Empire and Church.

When reports of the agreements reached the East, there arose bitter protests. The representatives were denounced as heretics. Ten years later, in 1453, the Turks captured Constantinople. That put an end to all further attempts at reunion of the Eastern and Western churches.

8. The Renaissance • When the German barbarians overran and conquered the western provinces of the Roman Empire, the ancient Graeco-Roman civilization was well-nigh trampled out in the West. But the barbarians did not conquer the eastern provinces of the Roman Empire. For a thousand years (from 476 to 1453), that is, all through the Middle Ages, while western Europe became steeped in ignorance and barbarianism, the ancient civilization was preserved in the Eastern or Byzantine Empire.

It is true that in the West the lamp of learning occasionally received a meager supply of oil. In the time of Charlemagne there had occurred a revival of learning. Then also men coming back from the Crusades, through their contact with the Greeks in the East and also through their contact with the Arabs in Spain, had brought with them to the countries of western Europe some knowledge of ancient civilization.

But the real revival of learning, called *the Renaissance,* came about in the following manner. Trade and commerce had developed during the period following the Crusades, and many towns sprang up in Europe. In the bustling life of these cities there came into existence a class of people who were interested in learning and culture. Capitalists who had great wealth sponsored the men of learning, who in turn revived many of the ancient documents which had not been known to men of the Middle Ages but were part of the culture of the Greek and Roman world.

This revival of learning had wide consequences for Europe. The Greek language became a new subject of interest; the writing of elegant Latin was an attainment widely sought; the publication of ancient writings was considered a calendar event.

In Italy the men of the early Renaissance were flagrantly irreligious and immoral. The whole movement seemed to revolt against the asceticism of medieval times. Men were out to explore man's new freedom from restraint and from ignorance.

When this Renaissance movement moved into northern Europe it changed character. It took on a religious aspect.

The Basilica of St. Peter in Rome is the world's largest church, covering six acres. Some eighty thousand people can stand in the building, which is 700 feet long and 450 feet wide. Raphael and Michelangelo were two of its famous architects.

Brown Brothers

The Interior of St. Peter's

Men began to show particular concern for New Testament Greek and for Hebrew. The works of the early Church Fathers were published and came out in the new form—the printed book. With the new language equipment and these new materials available for study, one might well expect new insights, and they did appear.

This Renaissance learning was highly significant in furnishing the Reformation leaders with the historical background necessary to prove that the Church of their day had departed from the simple faith of the fathers and had encumbered religious practice with innumerable forms, customs, and rituals which had no significant place in the apostolic Church.

Many of the popes of the second half of the fifteenth century also became very liberal *patrons,* or supporters, of the Renaissance. They supplied students of Greek and Latin literature, writers, architects, and painters with funds so that they could devote themselves to literature and art without financial worries. It was during this period of the Renaissance popes that the Vatican was built in Rome. The Vatican is the palatial residence of the popes, with its beautiful gardens, its famous Vatican Library and Sistine Chapel, and the magnificent St. Peter's Church.

The ancient Greek and Latin scholars, whose writings were now again studied for the first time in centuries and with unbounded enthusiasm, were pagans. A study of their works resulted in a revival of paganism. The popes of this period were more interested in this revived pa-

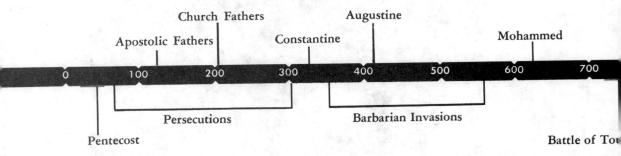

Apostolic Fathers

Church Fathers

Constantine

Augustine

Mohammed

0   100   200   300   400   500   600   700

Pentecost

Persecutions

Barbarian Invasions

Battle of Tou

ganism of the Renaissance than in Christianity. Many of them, especially Alexander VI, were very wicked men. Their splendid and luxurious court, their patronage of art and literature, and their great building projects cost immense sums of money. By various schemes they managed to make great amounts of gold flow into the papal treasury from the several countries of western Europe. The irreligion and the luxurious manner of life of the popes and their heavy exactions of money caused great dissatisfaction with the papacy and the Church, especially in the countries north of the Alps.

In Florence, Italy, a priest by the name of Savonarola preached boldly against the wickedness of his time. He did not spare Pope Alexander VI. He was, however, in no sense a reformer of the Church. He did not attack the Catholic system, but only the moral abuses of his day. In 1498 he was hanged, and his body was burned.

9. The Brethren of the Common Life • Around 1350 there arose in the Netherlands and Germany another attempt to reform the Church. This movement was that of the Brethren of the Common Life. It was founded by Gerhard Groote. He preached to large multitudes of eager listeners, and the result was a great revival of religion.

The Brethren of the Common Life

Savonarola preaches against luxury in Florence, Italy.

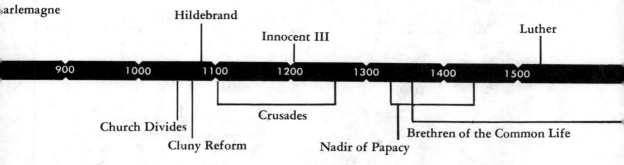

arlemagne   Hildebrand

Innocent III

Luther

| 900 | 1000 | 1100 | 1200 | 1300 | 1400 | 1500 |

Crusades

Church Divides

Cluny Reform   Nadir of Papacy

Brethren of the Common Life

were strong believers in Christian education. They hoped to bring about reform in the Church by means of education. From their schools came many men who did much to promote learning and piety. Luther attended one of their schools in Magdeburg for one year. Three other pupils of the Brethren of the Common Life who deserve special mention are John of Wessel, Erasmus, and Thomas à Kempis.

John of Wessel was one of the leading scholars and thinkers of his time. From 1445 to 1456 he was a professor in the University of Erfurt in Germany, from which school forty-nine years later Luther received his degree of Master of Arts. Many called John of Wessel "the light of the world." He attacked indulgences. He clearly taught the doctrine of justification by faith alone. He said, "He who thinks to be justified through his own works does not know what it is to be saved." He also taught the closely related doctrine that the elect are saved by grace alone, and wrote, "Whom God wishes to save He would save by giving him grace, if all the priests should wish to damn and excommunicate him." He did not accept the Roman Catholic doctrine of transubstantiation—the belief that when the priest pronounces the sacramental words, the bread and wine

are changed into the actual body and blood of Christ. Of him Luther later said, "If I had read the works of Wessel beforehand, it might well have seemed that I derived all my ideas from him."

Of course, the Roman Catholic Church did not approve of John of Wessel. He was tried for heresy before the Archbishop of Mainz. After having attempted to defend himself, he recanted. But he was cast into prison, where he died in October, 1489.

The most famous pupil of the Brethren of the Common Life was Erasmus. He lived at the same time Luther did. He used his great learning and sharp pen to ridicule the ignorance of the monks and the many abuses in the Church. But that was as far as he went. He never joined Luther in the great Reformation movement. It was said: "Erasmus laid the egg [of the Reformation] and Luther hatched it."

Another man who was deeply influenced by the spirit of this great movement was Thomas à Kempis. He lived in the Netherlands near the city of Zwolle, and he wrote *The Imitation of Christ*. This little book has held its place in the front rank of devotional literature down to our own day. It is one of the famous books of the world. It advises one to read the Bible and flee worldly vanities.

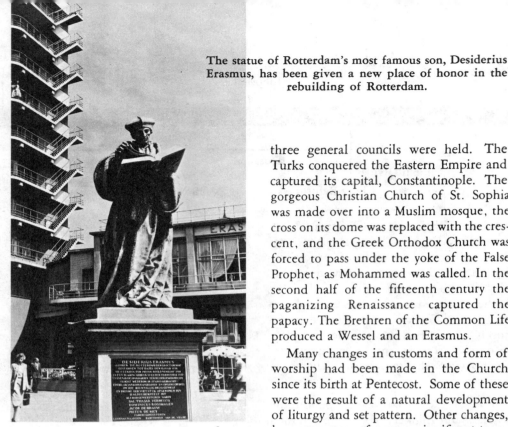

The statue of Rotterdam's most famous son, Desiderius Erasmus, has been given a new place of honor in the rebuilding of Rotterdam.

Courtesy Doeser Fotos, Laren

10. The Threshold of the Reformation

10. The Threshold of the Reformation • For more than three hundred years the Church had violent turmoil in many areas. There had been the Albigenses and the Waldenses. In the fourteenth century Pope Boniface VIII was humbled, his successors were captives for seventy years, and then the papacy was rent by schism. In England Wycliffe and the Lollards caused great commotion, as did John Huss and the Hussites in Bohemia. Dominicans and Franciscans became a power in the Church. The Inquisition was introduced. Heretics were burned, and their lands were devastated. In the first half of the fifteenth century three general councils were held. The Turks conquered the Eastern Empire and captured its capital, Constantinople. The gorgeous Christian Church of St. Sophia was made over into a Muslim mosque, the cross on its dome was replaced with the crescent, and the Greek Orthodox Church was forced to pass under the yoke of the False Prophet, as Mohammed was called. In the second half of the fifteenth century the paganizing Renaissance captured the papacy. The Brethren of the Common Life produced a Wessel and an Erasmus.

Many changes in customs and form of worship had been made in the Church since its birth at Pentecost. Some of these were the result of a natural development of liturgy and set pattern. Other changes, however, were of a more significant type: changes in doctrine, and even in the concept of the Church's mission and place in the world.

Men had come to think of the Church as a hierarchy of officials, from parish priests to bishops to cardinals and to the pope. These were thought to be the rulers, not only of the Church as an organization, but also of the entire civilized world. They assumed that their place was between God and the people, commissioned by the former, to be obeyed by the latter.

From this position they not only served as administrative agents of the government, but themselves assumed the right to change or make new doctrine. So there had come into the beliefs of the official

Church many teachings not found in Scripture, but based on what men called holy tradition, and announced as dogma by the papacy. Such teachings included the doctrines of purgatory, of transubstantiation, of indulgences and perhaps most significant, the doctrine of the pope as the direct apostolic successor of Peter.

Now when men of the Renaissance period began to look back into the history of the early Church by studying the Church Fathers, they noticed that these Fathers knew nothing about many teachings now accepted. They also began to read Scripture in the original languages and found that the Bible itself frequently contradicted teachings which the Church had proclaimed basic. So doubts arose in the minds of many leaders, particularly among the university men. These did frequently express their disagreement with the Church, but such action was extremely dangerous. The Church carried a sword, not for ornament, but for use, and dissenters quickly felt the sting of the Inquisition. When the Reformation broke over Europe, it came as a climax to the voices of these reformers, and at a time when the social, political, and intellectual climate was ready for a change. At this crucial point Luther entered the scene and led a movement that shook the Church to its foundations.

The inscription under this portrait of Thomas à Kempis reads *Super omnia, et in omnibus requiesces, anima mea in Domino semper, quia ipse Sanctorum aeterna requies* (Book III, Chapter 21 of *The Imitation of Christ*). There have been more than 3,000 editions of this famous work.

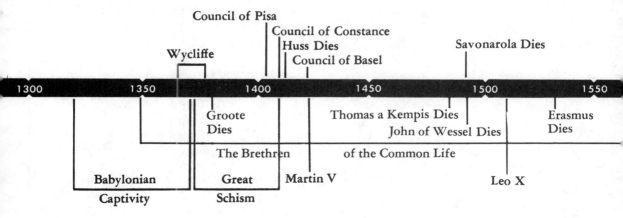

1. *Identify: Inquisition, Lollards, Renaissance, Vatican, heresy, Savonarola, John of Wessel, Erasmus, Thomas à Kempis.*

2. *Why did the Catholics consider both the Cathari (Albigenses) and the Waldenses heretical? Would you agree?*

3. *List as many of the pre-Reformation reformers as you can. Also list the schools with which they were associated. Does this listing indicate something about the character of the reform movement?*

4. *List the attitudes of all of these reformers to the Bible. What translations were made at this time? What was the attitude of the Church toward these translations into the vernacular languages?*

5. *Why should the pope who died in 1963 be called Pope John XXIII and not Pope John XXIV?*

6. *What important concessions were granted the Hussites?*

7. *Why did the attempt to settle the rupture between the Eastern and Western churches fail after an apparent initial success?*

8. *Read an account of the trial of heretics or a description of such a trial in Coulton's* Inquisition and Liberty, *Boston: Beacon Press, Paperback, 1959.*

9. *Was excommunication such as John XXIII used against Huss a sacred pronouncement or a religious weapon used to suppress opposition?*

10. *The account of the Council of Constance in Schaff's* History of the Christian Church *will give an interesting insight into the moral conditions of the Church.*

11. *Erasmus was a highly significant man during this period. Consult one of your library's volumes that discusses his work.*

12. *Read a few of the splendid short devotionals of Thomas à Kempis in his popular book,* The Imitation of Christ. *Is this volume distinctly Roman Catholic or more generally Christian?*

13. *Why was development of trade and commerce influential in the Renaissance movement?*

14. *The* Encyclopedia Britannica *has a splendid article on the Renaissance and also a beautiful section on Renaissance art.*

part three

The Church in the Reformation

Part Three

THE CHURCH IN THE REFORMATION

We have come to a high point in the history of the Church. In 1517, and the years that followed, a series of events occurred which ushered in a new era in world history. In that period the power of Rome over the Christian Church was challenged, men broke away from its tyranny, and Christian liberty was at last restored.

The men who led the way in this great Reformation were men of strong faith and convictions, high intelligence, and great moral and physical courage. They risked their lives and sacrificed all ordinary pleasures to work untiringly for the purity and freedom of the Church of Jesus Christ.

The period of the Reformation was an exciting and heroic one. The people were no less courageous than their leaders. War and persecution did not turn them aside. It was a time of high thinking and perilous living.

In spite of all opposition from the Catholic Church, the Reformation spread—through Germany, Switzerland, France, the Netherlands, England, Scotland, Norway, and Sweden. The fetters that had bound the people to a religion of superstition and fear had at last been broken, and the Church was once more free to worship God "in spirit and in truth."

CHAPTER 21

The Church

Is Shaken, October 31, 1517

1. A New Era Opens • The Reformation came "in the fulness of time." It was not a movement that began merely because a man named Luther revolted against certain teachings of the Church. Rather, it was prepared over a long period of time and came into full flower when the conditions were ripe for its develop-

This study of Martin Luther was executed by the great German painter Holbein.

ment. In the previous chapter we traced some of the preparatory movements for this great reform.

2. The Central Importance of the Sacrament of Penance • The Church in medieval times put great emphasis on sin and its punishment in purgatory and hell. Purgatory, according to the Church at that time and the Roman Catholic Church today, is a place to which those who are to enter heaven are assigned for a period of cleansing by fire before they are fit for entrance. The more faithfully the believer went through the rites and ceremonies on earth, the shorter would be his time of suffering in purgatory.

According to the Roman Catholic Church there are four sacraments which deal with the forgiveness and removal of sin and the cancellation of its punishment. These are *baptism,* the *Eucharist, penance,* and *anointment of the sick* (formerly called *extreme unction*).

In Luther's day the sacrament of penance occupied a central place in Catholic religious practice. The heart of this sacrament was the priestly act of absolution (pardoning of sins and release from the eternal punishment upon such sins). It involved three acts by the penitent sinner receiving this sacrament: (1) contrition, (2) confession to a priest, and (3) satisfaction.

After witnessing an expression of contrition for mortal sins committed and hearing a confession of these sins, the priest would grant absolution. This word of absolution declared to the penitent sinner the forgiveness of his sins, his release from eternal punishment, and his restoration to the state of grace.

The priest would then decide what satisfaction the sinner should make. Satisfaction usually consisted in something the penitent should do. It took a great variety of forms, but it was always in the nature of a penalty for sins committed. Most often satisfaction was made by the saying of a prescribed number of prayers, by fasting, by giving alms, by going on a pilgrimage to some shrine, or by taking part in a crusade. Frequently it also involved pain.

3. Indulgences • In process of time a certain development took place in this system of penance. The Church permitted the penitent to substitute the payment

of a sum of money for other forms of penalty or satisfaction. The Church would issue to the penitent an official statement that he had received release from other penalties through payment of money. Such a document or papal ticket was called an *indulgence.*

Money thus paid in place of other penalties amounted to what we would call a fine. Not only could one buy indulgences for oneself, one could also buy indulgences for relatives and friends who had died and passed into purgatory, and in this way shorten the time they would otherwise have to spend in the place of purification.

The practice of granting indulgences was based on the Catholic doctrine of *works of supererogation.* Works of supererogation were works done beyond the demands of God's law. These works earned a reward. Christ by His life of perfect holiness had done more than was necessary for the salvation of man. In that way Christ had earned what amounted to a rich treasury of merits laid up in heaven.

The saints had added much to this fund of merits. The Church taught that the Gospel not only imposes commands upon man, but that it also comes to us with *counsels of perfection.* It based this teaching upon the story of the rich young ruler. He said that he had observed all the commandments. "Jesus said unto him, If thou wouldest be perfect, go, sell that which thou hast, and give to the poor, and thou shalt have treasure in heaven" (Matthew 19:21). The Church taught that if he had heeded Jesus' admonition, he would have performed a work of supererogation, and would have merited great reward. The saints had done that. They had sold their goods and given them to the poor or to the Church. All these were added to the merits stored up in heaven.

The fund of merits earned by works of supererogation was in charge of the pope as Christ's vicar on earth. Much as we draw a check against our account in the bank, so the pope, for the benefit of sinners who were short of merits, could grant indulgences by drawing upon this fund of merits in heaven.

This system worked out to the great satisfaction of all concerned. It pleased the people. They found it easier to buy an indulgence than to undergo other penalties. And they preferred paying a sum of

money for the soul of a dear one in purgatory to saying many prayers for that
soul. To shorten the soul's sojourn in
purgatory to any worthwhile degree took
an enormous number of prayers.

The system pleased the Church. The
sale of indulgences was a source of huge
income. It kept money flowing into the
pope's coffers.

More and more frequently the popes
issued indulgences. Although they raised
the price, the people bought them in ever-
greater quantities. As the indulgence business grew, abuses attendant upon it also
grew. At the time of which we are now
speaking, Tetzel, an eloquent Dominican
Friar and high-pressure salesman, was
peddling indulgences in an unusually scandalous manner near the Saxony border in
the neighborhood of Wittenberg. In his
sales talk he said, "The moment you hear
your money drop in the box, the soul of
your mother will jump out of purgatory."

It was Tetzel's conduct that made Luther speak up concerning indulgences.

How did this come about? The story will
have to be delayed until we get acquainted
with Luther, the man who was to kindle
the fires of the Reformation.

4. Luther's Early Life • Martin Luther was born in Eisleben, Germany, on
November 10, 1483. When Martin was
still a baby, the family moved to Mans-
feld. His parents were pious people. The
father had become interested in the min-
ing industry. He slaved and saved in order to make it possible for his promising
son to have an education.

Martin received an elementary and high
school education and attended college in
Erfurt. From the University of Erfurt he
obtained his Master's degree in 1505. His
father was very happy on this occasion.
In accordance with the wishes of his father Luther now took up the study of law
in the same university. Half a year later
he suddenly dropped that study and entered the Augustinian monastery in Erfurt.

Luther's father was a man of strong will and fiery temper. To see his son a famous lawyer had been the great ambition of his life. Now his son, whom he dearly loved, had in gross ingratitude, as he thought, disappointed his fondest hopes and long-cherished expectations. He was not only disappointed; he was furious.

But Martin was equally strong-willed. He might have retraced his steps. But in spite of his father's terrible anger he persisted in his course. After a trial period of half a year, he took the vow. Brother Martin was now a monk. He fully believed at this time that he would be a monk for life.

Instead of law Luther now studied theology, and in 1507 he was ordained as priest. The next year he was sent from Erfurt to Wittenberg to become a tutor in the university in that place. While there he obtained his first degree in theology, that of Bachelor of Bible.

After one year in Wittenberg Luther was transferred back to Erfurt. There he received his second degree in theology, that of *Sententiarius*. He was called upon to teach the *Sentences* of Peter Lombard, the standard textbook of theology. At the youthful age of only twenty-six years, Luther occupied an important position.

While teaching in Erfurt, Luther was sent to Rome as companion to an older brother on business for his monastic order.

He visited all the famous shrines. On his knees he climbed the *Scala Santa,* the stairway which was said to be the one which Jesus had climbed to reach Pilate's judgment hall. This stairway was supposed to have been brought from Jerusalem to Rome. There is a story that when halfway up the stairway Luther heard a voice within him say, "The just shall live by faith." He got up from his knees and walked down. It has been said by many that this was Luther's conversion, but that is not correct. Luther's conversion took place late in 1512 in his own cell in the tower of the Black Cloister in Wittenberg, not in 1511 on the steps of the *Scala Santa* in Rome.

Religious and moral conditions were very bad in Rome at that time. Much of what Luther saw and heard there shocked

The House in Eisleben, Saxony, in Which Luther Was Born

Brown Brothers

Luther Reading in His Cell at Erfurt
From a painting by Sir Noel Paton

his moral sense. Years later his memories of his visit to Rome did much to stiffen him in his opposition to the hierarchy. But at this time his faith in the Roman Church remained unshaken. He came back still a loyal Catholic.

Soon after his return, Wittenberg became his permanent residence. For the rest of his life he lectured on the Bible in the university at Wittenberg. He also began to preach, and the degree of Doctor of Theology was conferred upon him. From 1512 to 1517 he did what every professor does, he studied and lectured.

5. Luther's Conversion • Such, in short, had been Luther's outward career up to 1517. What had been his inner development during this time?

Luther was of a deeply religious nature,

and from childhood on he had absorbed the teaching of the Church of his day. He was greatly concerned about the salvation of his soul. Under the influence of the Church's teaching he came to the conclusion that the best way to gain salvation was to flee the world. That is why, in spite of the bitter grief and anger of his father, he had buried himself in a *cloister* (a residence for monks or nuns) and become a monk.

In the monastery he lived a life of strictest asceticism. With all his might he tried to earn salvation by his good works. He cheerfully performed the humblest tasks. He prayed and fasted and chastised himself even beyond the strictest monastic rules. He wasted away till he looked like a skeleton. His cell, even in the severest cold of winter, was unheated. He often spent the night in vigils and only occasionally slept on a mat.

He was oppressed with a terrible sense of his utter sinfulness and lost condition, and this cast him into the deepest gloom of black despair. No matter how hard he tried, never, it seemed to him, had he done enough to earn salvation. In a letter he wrote to the pope after his conversion he said: "I often endured an agony so hellish in violence, that if those spells had lasted a minute longer I must have died then and there."

But from time to time rays of light fell into the darkness of his soul. He found some comfort in the writings of Bernard of Clairvaux who stressed the free grace of Christ for salvation. The vicar of Luther's monastic order, Johann von Staupitz, spoke to him many a word of cheer. Some of the writings of Augustine helped him. Above all he began to study the Bible.

Sometime toward the end of the year 1512, Luther was sitting in his cell in Wittenberg with his Bible open before him. He had begun to study Paul's letter to the Romans, and coming to Romans 1, verse 17, he read, "The righteous will live by faith." He paused. He pondered. Then joy unspeakable flooded his heart. The burden of his soul rolled away. Up until now he had tried to earn salvation by his good works, but never had he been able to feel that he had done enough. Now God had spoken to him. Luther had learned that man is saved not by *works* but by *faith*. Romans 1:17 had become to him the "gate to Paradise."

That was Luther's conversion.

6. The Ninety-five Theses • It will be easy for you now to understand how Tetzel's conduct led Luther to talk about indulgences. Luther's soul was now filled with peace and joyful hope. He began to look at life round about him and at the Church with new eyes. He began to see the many abuses in the Church, and more and more clearly and boldly he spoke out against them.

The traffic in indulgences had long been the cause of great scandal. Now Tetzel was hawking indulgences at the very gates of Wittenberg in a most shameless manner. Luther saw that the people were being deceived for eternity.

He went up to his cell in the tower of the Black Cloister, took his pen, and wrote out his views about indulgences in ninety-five *theses,* that is, in ninety-five statements or propositions. Then around noon on the thirty-first day of October, 1517, he went out and nailed these ninety-five theses to the door of the Castle Church in Wittenberg. In this way he

Religious News Service Photo

Luther nails his ninety-five theses to the Castle Church door.

made his views about indulgences known to the public.

This act of Luther was not the Reformation. But it was the first in a series of acts which were to lead up to the Reformation.

7. Luther Is Already a Man of High Attainments • Luther is often spoken of as being at this time only a simple and obscure monk. This is by no means true to fact. Surely, Luther was young at this time. He was only thirty-four years old. But he was experienced and accomplished far beyond most young men of his age. He had lived in Magdeburg, Eisenach, and Erfurt. He had been to Cologne, and to Leipzig, and had crossed the Alps and traveled to Rome. He had met a great number and a great variety of people. In Rome he had seen Pope Julius II. He had read and studied the writings of many great men.

He was prior of his monastery and district vicar over eleven other monasteries. He had to appoint and remove priors; he had to instruct, counsel, and comfort brother monks beset with temptations, and discipline those who misbehaved. He had to attend to the repair of buildings and the auditing of accounts. He had to take care of legal matters pertaining to these monasteries.

He was a Master of Arts and a Doctor of Theology. He was one of the great preachers of all times. By now he had been teaching for nine years, and had gained a high reputation as a teacher. He was one of the first theological professors in Germany to base his lectures in the Old and New Testaments on the original Hebrew and Greek texts. He was also one of the first professors in Germany to lecture in the German language instead of in Latin.

Luther was favorably known to his prince, the elector Frederick the Wise, and he carried on correspondence with some of the most prominent men of his time.

No, Luther at this time was not a simple or obscure monk!

8. He Is Still a Catholic in Good Standing • It should be borne in mind that when Luther published his ninety-five theses, he was a member in good standing of the Roman Catholic Church.

Luther himself was baptized, brought up, and confirmed in the Catholic Church. He attended its services, went to mass, made confession regularly and often, bought indulgences, visited shrines, revered relics. He prayed to the saints and to Mary. He believed that they could intercede for him, and also that they had power to work miracles.

Luther was a monk, an ordained priest, a preacher, and a professor in the Roman Catholic Church.

9. Posting of Theses Is a Common Practice • When Luther nailed his theses to the door of the Castle Church, he did nothing unusual. The door of the Castle Church served as the University bulletin board. In posting these theses he invited any doctor of theology who might so wish, for the purpose of clarifying the truth, to debate with him publicly on the value of indulgences. This procedure was very common.

10. The Ninety-five Theses Are Widely Read • When Luther published his ninety-five theses he did not say to himself, "Now I am going to start the Reformation." No man was more surprised than Luther himself at the results of his action. No one accepted Luther's challenge. It was not until two years later that an opponent presented himself.

What did happen? That is a long but interesting story. Wittenberg was located in Saxony whose ruler at this time was the elector Frederick the Wise, a very pious Catholic. He had collected more than five thousand relics from all over Christendom. To house these relics Frederick had built the Castle Church.

Wittenberg's famous *Schlosskirche* is part of a fortress.

Brown Brothers

The day after Luther had nailed his theses to the door of the Castle Church was All Saints' Day. On that day, as was customary, the relics in the Castle Church were solemnly displayed. From far and near people came to see them, and to be benefited by the graces attached to them. They naturally saw the large sheet of paper tacked to the door, and they stopped to read it. When they came home they told their neighbors what they had read. These told others. In this way the news spread like wildfire.

Printing had recently been invented. The theses, which had been written in Latin, were translated into many languages, printed, and carried with unbelievable speed to every country of western Europe. Within two weeks the theses of Luther became known throughout Germany. Four weeks after their publication they were read all over western Europe. They had a tremendous and immediate effect. They almost stopped the sale of indulgences.

The archbishop of Mainz, who was to receive a share of the proceeds from the sale of indulgences by Tetzel, naturally did not like this. He sent a copy of the theses to Pope Leo X in Rome. The pope at first did not think it was a serious matter. He simply asked the general of Luther's monastic order to advise that monk in Wittenberg to keep quiet.

Tetzel with the assistance of a friend published a set of theses defending the sale of indulgences. Mazzolini, a Dominican monk and inquisitor in Rome, wrote a book in which he severely criticized the conclusions of Martin Luther. John Eck, a theological professor, answered Luther in a pamphlet. Luther soon published his answer in another pamphlet. Luther's friends did not rise to his defense; they thought he had been too rash in his criticism. This made Luther feel bad.

In April, 1518, the monasteries connected with the Augustinian Order held their annual meeting in Heidelberg. Luther found the opposition much stronger than he had expected. However, the discussion was frank and friendly, and this put Luther into a happier frame of mind.

Upon his return from Heidelberg to Wittenberg he wrote a general answer to all his opponents. This book bore the title *Resolutions*. It was very carefully written and was addressed to the pope. In it Luther defended his theses point by point.

11. Their Real Significance Is Recognized • In his theses Luther did not attack indulgences themselves, but only the abuses connected with their sale. Already Wycliffe and Huss had protested against these abuses. But the Church was quick to see that the thrust of Luther's protest was more far-reaching. By raising the question of indulgences, Luther, guided by the Spirit of God, had laid his finger on the most sensitive spot in the whole Catholic system of his day.

It was from the sale of indulgences that the Church and its head, the pope, received an immense income. And furthermore, the Catholic system had declined to the point where it placed all importance on the sacraments and the priests. The Roman Catholic Church held that only the priest could adminis-

ter the sacraments; and without the sacrament of penance, without absolution and indulgences, there was no salvation. Man's salvation, his eternal weal or woe, lay in the hands of the priest. And so the Church, through the priests, had a strong hold on the people.

That is why, by raising the question of indulgences, Luther shook the Church. What he said in his theses had the tendency to loosen the priests' hold on the people. Now the Church was not merely stirred. It was shaken to its very foundations.

12. The Reformation's Fundamental Elements • Before we outline the important events of the Reformation, we should sketch the elements of its teachings which all the leaders of the movement considered fundamental ones.

1. The Reformation leaders went back to the Apostolic Church, as described in the New Testament, to find there the spirit and practice of the Church as they believed it should operate. The republishing of the works of the early Church Fathers—Jerome, Cyprian, Origen, and Athanasius—was a great aid to them. Au-

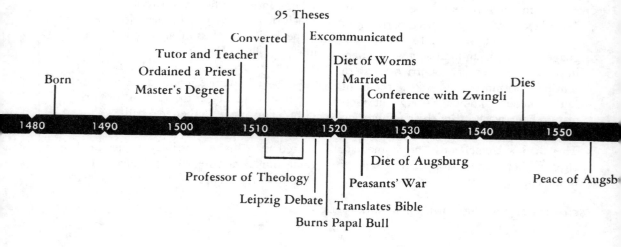

Large sums of money were needed by the pope to construct and furnish magnificent buildings. This is a view of the Vatican Library.

Brown Brothers

gustine was a favorite of most of the reformers. From these men they learned the simple character of the early Church and found it widely different from the adorned service of their own day. They therefore sought to eliminate the forms, customs, and traditions in the formal keeping of which men had come to trust for salvation, and to stress the preaching of the Word as the Gospel of salvation by grace alone.

2. Closely related to this aspect of reform was the stress on the priesthood of all believers. This meant that men went directly to God; they did not gain salvation through the Church, but became members of the Church when they became believers. The Roman Catholic Church used the name priest for clergyman, which meant that they stood, as in Old Testament times, between man and God. The reformers spoke of all men as priests, personally speaking to God, without the mediation of the Church.

3. All the reformers thought of the Church as the community of believers rather than the hierarchy of officials. This concept was already evident in Huss, one hundred years before Luther, and persisted all through the Reformation days. They thought of the Church as an organism, a living body of which each believer was a member; they did not think of it as an organization made up of officials. Organization they did consider necessary for efficient functioning, but they did not think of it as the dispenser of divine grace.

4. Many church leaders in the days before the Reformation had urged the distribution of the Bible to the common people. Wycliffe had translated large portions of the Vulgate into English. Tyndale had translated the Bible. But the Roman Catholic Church had bitterly opposed unofficial translations. Tyndale paid for his offense with his life, being burned at the stake. Now all the reformers accepted the Bible as the final authority on

all questions of faith and morals. Luther translated the whole Bible; Zwingli copied in handwriting all the letters of Paul from Erasmus' Greek text; Lefèvre translated the New Testament into French, as did John Calvin. Whether a reformation principle was to be accepted or not was determined by the support one could find for it in Scripture. That became the touchstone; and of course this led to a careful study of the Bible as the source for all religious teaching.

1. *List specific practices to which Luther objected. Write a brief statement giving the reasons for his objections.*

2. *From one of the many fine biographies of Luther trace some of the stages of his reformation thoughts. Why did his insights come gradually?*

3. *Write a short summary of those events that show that the Reformation was in the making for a long time. Be sure to add dates to your summary, so that the time involved in this movement becomes clear.*

4. *List important religious practices of the Roman Catholic Church that centered around penance and write one explanatory statement for each.*

5. *How did the practice of issuing indulgences rise out of these practices? Why would men think of indulgences as paying for sins?*

6. *What is meant by the treasury of merits?*

7. *List and describe in your own words the basic elements of the reformation movement.*

8. *Identify: Tetzel, works of supererogation, Scala Santa, Wittenberg, Sentences of Peter Lombard, ninety-five theses, mass.*

9. *Read the ninety-five theses. (See Schaff,* History of the Christian Church, *Volume VII; or* The Banner, *October 25, 1963.) Write out the five that are of the greatest interest to you.*

CHAPTER 22

The Church Is Convulsed, 1517-1521

1. Luther Is Summoned to Rome •
From this time on Luther lived in a glass house. Everything he did or said was watched with eagle eyes by friend and foe. Luther was a great talker. He was living in an age of violent passions and brutal outbursts of bad temper. In the heat of argument both he and his oppo-

nents tended to exaggerate, and critics must read with discretion all that was said and done by both sides. Much of his conversation at meal times was written down by admiring students, and later published as *Luther's Table Talk.*

Luther's theses struck the pope some hard blows in two tender spots: his power and his purse. When therefore the pope learned that the General of the Augustinian Order had completely failed to silence Luther, he decided to take matters into his own hands. In July, 1518, he issued a summons to Luther to appear before him in Rome. If Luther had gone to Rome it would have meant his certain death. Heresy was taken very seriously in those times. It was the greatest of all crimes. A heretic deserved death by fire.

But Luther had a faithful, wise, and powerful friend in Elector Frederick. For many years the German people had had many and great grievances against the *curia,* or papal government. The elector Frederick had forbidden Tetzel to peddle indulgences in Saxony. He did not wish money from his country to go into the coffers of the pope. The University of Wittenberg was the elector's very special

pet, and Luther was its most famous and popular professor. So Frederick brought all his influence to bear in Rome to have the papal summons canceled.

Circumstances at this time were in Frederick's favor. Emperor Maximilian was old and sickly. It was evident that a new emperor would have to be chosen soon. There were three candidates: Charles, king of Spain; Francis, king of France; and Frederick, elector of Saxony. The pope wanted Frederick to become emperor, because he thought that he would be able to manage Frederick much more easily than either of the other two. So the pope listened to Frederick, and canceled the summons for Luther to come to Rome.

2. Cajetan Fails to Silence Luther •
At this time a *legate,* or delegate, of the pope, Cajetan, was in Germany to attend a *diet* in Augsburg. (A diet was a national meeting of all the princes, the prelates, and other leading men in Germany.) The pope sent Cajetan a letter empowering him to order Luther to appear before him in Augsburg. Cajetan was to hear him and demand that he re-

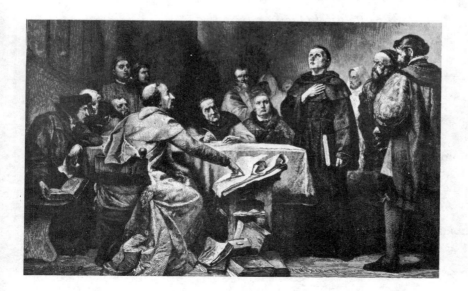

Luther
in Augsburg
Before Cardinal Cajetan

cant. If Luther would not recant he should be sent bound to Rome. If Cajetan should fail to arrest Luther, he should put him and his followers under the ban. Up to this time the pope had said only that Luther was suspected of heresy. Now he declared him to be a notorious heretic.

To go to Augsburg would therefore be very dangerous for Luther. But again his prince came to his aid. Although only with the greatest difficulty, he obtained from the aged emperor Maximilian a safe-conduct for Luther.

Luther had three interviews with Cajetan in Augsburg in October, 1518. The discussion became hot and furious at times. Close friends of Luther tried to persuade him to settle things peaceably by giving in. But Luther refused to recant. He left Augsburg secretly by night.

Cajetan, finding himself unable to handle the situation, now requested the pope to settle the points in dispute once for all by an official pronouncement. The pope did so by issuing a bull in which he declared, without mentioning names, that certain statements which certain monks had made about indulgences were heretical. That meant that from then on Luther could no longer claim that those questions had not been decided officially by the Church.

3. Von Miltitz Is Seemingly More Successful • The pope next decided to send a special representative into Germany for the purpose of arresting Luther. By now Pope Leo had come to realize that this could not be done unless he had the co-operation of Luther's faithful friend, Frederick the Wise, elector of Saxony. He chose a man who he thought would be most acceptable to Frederick.

Historical Pictures
Service—Chicago

**A Painting by Raphael
of Pope Leo X**

His name was Charles von Miltitz. He was a close acquaintance of Spalatin, the elector's private secretary, and was Frederick's own agent at the papal court in Rome.

Before presenting his credentials to Frederick, Von Miltitz sought a private interview with Luther and Tetzel. He could not get to see Tetzel, but he did have a talk with Luther. The result of these conversations was that Luther promised not to speak about indulgences any more, if his opponents would agree not to do so. He also promised to write a submissive letter to the pope. The pope was so well-pleased with the letter that on March 29, 1519, he sent Luther a very friendly letter in return. He now called him his dear son, invited him to come to Rome to make his confession, and offered to pay the expenses of the journey.

4. Eck Challenges Luther to a Debate

If the pope had supported Von Miltitz, and if both sides had remained still, there is no telling how far the reconciliation of Luther with the Roman Church might have gone.

But at this time the pope's attention was distracted from his differences with Luther. He had become deeply absorbed in another matter. In January, 1519, the emperor Maximilian died. A new emperor had to be elected and the pope was greatly concerned about the selection. He had to work hard for the election of Frederick. The election campaign occupied his mind entirely to the exclusion of everything else. For fourteen months he failed to push the charge of heresy against Luther. Meanwhile, the two opposing sides in Germany did not remain silent.

One of Luther's fellow professors of theology at Wittenberg University, Andreas Carlstadt, came out with a set of theses against Eck. Eck, you will recall, had written a pamphlet against Luther's ninety-five theses. Eck answered Carlstadt with some counter theses in which he advanced an extreme view of papal supremacy. Luther then took up the cudgels and published twelve theses. In the twelfth he declared that the claim of the Roman Church to supremacy over all other churches rested only on weak papal decrees of the last four hundred years, but that in all the eleven hundred years before no such supremacy had existed.

An attack like that on the authority of the pope had never before been heard. It caused a tremendous sensation. Eck could not possibly ignore it. He challenged Luther to debate with him on the question of the supremacy of the pope.

The supremacy of the pope had been one of Luther's earliest and most cherished beliefs. His mother had taught him as a little boy that the Church is the pope's house, in which the pope is the house-father. The nine months until the debate with Eck in July, 1519, Luther spent in hard study. He had to find arguments against many things he had always held to be true, and which he had only recently found to be false. He plunged into the study of church history and canon law. *Canon law* consists of the decretals or decisions of popes and general councils. Luther was dismayed to find that many decretals were forgeries. Thus he saw another pillar of the Roman Catholic system cracking before his eyes.

5. The Leipzig Debate

In Leipzig the atmosphere was tense. A company of armed burghers stood guard at the duke's palace where the disputation was to be held. In the inns at mealtime an armed guard was posted at every table to keep the Leipzig and Wittenberg students from fighting.

On the fourth of July, 1519, Eck and Luther faced each other. As far as the learning and speaking ability of the two opponents was concerned the debate was just about a tie. But Eck out-maneuvered Luther. He drove him into a corner, and finally got him to say that some of the teachings of Huss had been unjustly condemned by the Council of Constance. As soon as Luther made this statement, Eck had achieved his purpose. He had made Luther take his stand openly on the side of a man officially condemned by the Church as a heretic. When Luther ad-

The Leipzig Debate with Dr. Eck

mitted that he did not think Huss wrong in all respects, a wave of excitement swept over the audience. Duke George of Saxony said so loud that everyone could hear it, "God help us; that is the pestilence!"

Luther's arguments had been historical. He called to mind that the Eastern Greek Church is a part of the Church of Christ, and that it had never acknowledged the supremacy of the bishop of Rome. The great councils of the early Christian centuries knew nothing of papal supremacy. But no reasoning on Luther's part could save him after he had taken his stand on the side of the condemned heretic, Huss.

One result of the Leipzig debate was that Luther greatly strengthened his cause among his followers. He made them feel certain that their position was right. Luther also won many new followers, one

of whom was Martin Bucer, who became an important leader of the Reformation, and who helped to shape the views of John Calvin.

As is usually the case, neither debater was able to change his opponent's views. However, the debate did much to clarify Luther's ideas for himself. This was undoubtedly the most important result.

This debate was also an important stage in the Reformation movement. It made it clear to everybody that reconciliation between Luther and the Roman Catholic Church would be impossible.

6. The Storm Gathers • Luther had rejected the supremacy of the pope and the infallibility of councils. His break with the Roman hierarchical system was now complete. Luther was in the thick of the battle. From now on it was to be a life-and-death struggle between him and the Roman Church. Soon after the Leipzig debate Eck went to Rome to ask Pope Leo to issue a bull excommunicating Luther. The pope was more than willing.

The first thing Luther did was to publish an account of the Leipzig debate. Soon pamphlets and letters followed in great abundance. In May, 1520, he published a pamphlet with the title, *On Good Works.* This was only a little book, but it had a far-reaching effect. In it he applied to practical, everyday life his newly won conviction that *man is saved by faith alone.* "The noblest of all good works," he said, "is to believe in Jesus Christ." We must serve God in the midst of the world by faithfully performing the tasks of our daily occupations. Shoemakers, housekeepers, farmers, and businessmen, if they do their work to the glory of God, are more pleasing to Him than monks and nuns.

This was one of Luther's most important and fundamental teachings. It was also the widest possible departure from ancient and medieval asceticism, and it became one of the most distinctive traits of Protestant Christianity.

The period between the Leipzig debate in July, 1519, and the Diet of Worms in April, 1521, was a hectic time for Luther. Every incident that took place, every friend he made, every book he read carried him forward from one position to another.

Two books especially which he read at this time influenced him powerfully. Several Hussites had been present at the debate. Two of them, after that memorable meeting, had written to him and sent him one of the works of Huss. He had no

time to read it just then, but when early in 1520 he read it, he learned that Huss had taught the same things that he, Luther, had come to believe, and he avowed himself to be a disciple of the Bohemian.

The other book which influenced Luther profoundly at this time was a work by the brilliant Italian humanist Lorenzo Valla, who proved beyond the possibility of contradiction that the "Donation of Constantine" was a forgery. This discovery roused Luther to such a passion that he scarcely doubted any longer that the pope was the antichrist.

7. Excommunication • On June 15, 1520, Pope Leo ratified and signed the bull excommunicating Luther. The bull began with the words: "Arise, O Lord, plead thine own cause; remember how the foolish man reproacheth thee daily; the foxes are wasting thy vineyard, which thou hast given to thy vicar Peter; the boar out of the wood doth waste it, and the wild beast of the field doth devour it." These opening words are quotations from the *Psalms* and the *Song of Solomon.*

The bull mentioned forty-one propositions, which it said were Luther's, and which it condemned as "heretical or scandalous, or false or offensive to pious ears, or seducing to simple minds, and standing in the way of the Catholic faith."

The bull called upon all faithful people to burn Luther's books. It forbade Luther to preach. He and all who followed him were ordered to recant publicly within sixty days. If they did not, they were to be treated as heretics. The bull ordered the government to seize and imprison Luther and everyone who followed him. All towns or districts that sheltered them would be placed under the interdict.

The publication of the bull in Germany was entrusted to Eck. He soon found out that it was easier to prepare the bull than to get it published. He could get permission to do so in only a few places. At Erfurt the students seized all the copies they could lay hands on and threw them into the river.

Luther came out with a tract:*Against the Execrable Bull of Antichrist.*

8. Three Great Reformation Treatises • All Germany hung breathless on Luther's every word. His books circulated far and wide and were eagerly bought and read. In his day there were no newspapers, so he poured out small books or pamphlets, which were like editorials or magazine articles. Luther used the press as a means of molding public opinion. It was chiefly by means of the press that Luther gained the support of vast numbers of followers, not only in his own country of Germany but also far beyond its borders.

To cushion the shock of the papal bull, and to rally the German nation around the standard of revolt against the Roman hierarchy, Luther published three works in the latter half of the year 1520. They are known as "The Three Great Reformation Treatises."

The first, *To the Christian Nobility of Germany,* was a trumpet call to do away with the abuses fostered by Rome. In the second, *The Babylonian Captivity of the Church,* Luther exposed the falsity of the Church's claim that men could be saved only through the priest and the Roman system of sacraments. The third, *The Liberty of a Christian Man,* is a very

THE LAND THAT LUTHER TRAVELED

Martin Luther
Burning
the Pope's Bull
Against Him

*Historical Pictures
Service—Chicago*

small work of only thirty pages, but it contains the whole sum of the Christian life.

9. Luther Burns the Pope's Bull • Writing against Rome, however, did not satisfy Luther. He decided to do something more. If the pope ordered his writings to be burned, he would burn the pope's writings.

On December 10, 1520, a large crowd of students, professors, and citizens assembled outside the walls of the city of Wittenberg. One of the professors kindled the pile. Luther placed the books of canon law (church law) on the burning wood. Then amid solemn silence Luther placed a copy of the bull on the fire, and said: "As thou hast wasted the Holy One of God, so may the eternal flames waste thee." He waited until the books and the bull were consumed. Then with his friends and colleagues he returned to the town.

Some hundreds of students remained behind. Under the spell of the solemnity of the occasion they sang, as they stood around the dying fire, the *Te Deum* (We Praise Thee, O God). Then youthful mischievousness got the upper hand, and they sang funeral dirges in honor of the burnt papal decretals and bull.

10. Luther Is Summoned by the Emperor • Pope Leo was almost at the end of his rope. He had exhausted all ecclesiastical means to bring Luther to his knees. There was only one thing left that he could do. He turned for help to the highest secular authority, the emperor.

The pope had been unsuccessful in his efforts to have Frederick the Wise elected emperor. Frederick himself, feeling that he could not afford the expenses incidental to the imperial office, had thrown his weight in favor of Charles, king of Spain. During the days of the Leipzig debate Charles was elected emperor.

This Charles, known to history as Charles V, had inherited the Austrian domains and Spain. As king of Spain he also ruled over the Netherlands, a 'large

PART THREE: THE CHURCH IN THE REFORMATION

part of Italy, and the parts of America discovered only twenty-nine years before by Columbus. Now that he had been elected also emperor of Germany, he ruled over a larger territory than any man since Charlemagne.

To this powerful monarch Pope Leo appealed for help in an attempt to bring Luther either to obedience or to the stake. Charles V was a devout Catholic, and Leo prevailed upon him to summon Luther before the Diet—the council of German rulers—which was to be held the next year in the city of Worms.

11. The Diet of Worms • Protected by the safe-conduct of the emperor, Luther started for Worms on April 2, 1521. Luther believed that he was going to his death. To Melanchthon, one of his colleagues at the university, he said at parting, "My dear brother, if I do not come back, if my enemies put me to death, you will go on teaching and standing fast in the truth; if you live, my death will matter little."

His journey was like a victory parade. Everywhere he went crowds lined the roads and streets to see the man who had dared to stand up for Germany against the pope, and who, so they thought, was going to his death for his faith.

At four o'clock in the afternoon of Wednesday, April 17, Luther appeared before the Diet. In the midst of a scene of pomp and splendor, before the throne of an emperor who was the most powerful to appear in many centuries, stood a poor and powerless priest, offspring of peasant parents. Charles V and Martin Luther saw each other for the first time.

Charles was at this time a youth of twenty-one. Luther, now thirty-seven

years old, was a man in the prime of life. He wore the black robe of an Augustinian monk. The crown of his head was newly shaven, according to the custom of priests, and was fringed with short, thick hair. At Luther's side stood his legal counsel, Jerome Schurf. Pointing to the books on a little table, an official asked Luther: "Are those your writings; and do you wish to retract them, or do you adhere to them and continue to assert them?"

Religious News Service Photo

The trunk of the famed Luther Elm in Worms, Germany, has been transformed into a lasting monument in honor of the sixteenth-century reformer. According to legend, the tree furnished shade for Luther when he was on the way to the fateful Diet of Worms in 1521. The trunk, dead since 1949, has been transformed by a German sculptor, G. Nonnenmacher, into a 36-foot-square basrelief which shows Luther before the Diet.

Historical Pictures Service—Chicago

Luther Before the Diet of Worms

Luther spoke. With precision he first repeated the two questions. Thereupon he answered the first question in the affirmative. The second question he answered by begging the emperor graciously to allow him time to think it over, in order that he might answer the question without injury to the Word of God and without peril to his soul.

The members of the Diet went into conference. After a short consultation it was announced that the emperor had decided to grant Luther's request. He was to give his answer in twenty-four hours. Then the meeting was adjourned.

12. The Political Question Is Settled • Luther's first appearance before the Diet had been brief and simple. But it had great historical significance.

The papacy during the last two hundred years had suffered many severe defeats in its struggle with the secular powers. Pope Leo X now wished the Diet of Worms to handle Luther's case in such a way that the old papal claim—that the spiritual (papal) authority is superior to the secular (royal and imperial) authority —would be recognized. In other words, Pope Leo X tried to bring down two birds with one stone. He tried to manipulate the handling of Luther's case by the Diet of Worms in such a way that suppression of heresy by the Diet would at the same time elevate papal authority above imperial authority.

The pope had excommunicated Luther. He wanted the Diet, that is to say really the emperor, to condemn and to punish Luther as a heretic without any further ado. He wanted the emperor, the secular ruler, to be merely a tool of the spiritual ruler, the pope. He wanted the emperor merely to execute the pope's orders without asking any questions. On the other hand, if the Diet first heard Luther, even if it then did condemn him—and it was a foregone conclusion that it would—it would then do so not because the pope said so, but because the Diet itself decreed his condemnation. That is why the papal party did not want the emperor to give Luther a hearing.

Luther's request for time to think it over seemed reasonable and also entirely innocent. But it was far from innocent. His request for time involved the request to be heard the next day by the Diet. And that request was momentous. The Diet had been in session a long time before Luther's appearance. The papal party, under the leadership of the very skillful and crafty papal nuncio Aleander, had been working day and night, and had left no stone unturned to prevent Luther from being heard by the Diet. When the Diet decided to grant Luther's request, the pope lost his game.

On the political issue, the question was whether the pope or the emperor should be supreme. The Catholic emperor and all the German princes, also the Catholic princes, sided with Luther against the pope. Thus for one brief moment Martin Luther, a poor man, risen from total obscurity, and a heretic excommunicated by the pope, stood forth as the champion of the emperor and of a united German empire against the foreign Italian pope.

On the day of Luther's first appearance before the Diet the political question had been settled. The religious question remained.

13. Luther's Second Appearance Before the Diet • The following day, Thursday, April 18, Luther appeared before the Diet for the second time. Dusk was gathering. Torches were lit. Their flames cast weird shadows in the now gloomy hall.

Many of those present took notes on what Luther said that day, but we have not a single complete account of Luther's address. All the accounts we have are only summaries. First Luther spoke in Latin. Then he was asked to repeat in German.

The hall was packed. The flaming torches gave out their heat. The ventilation was poor. The air was getting to be almost unbearably close.

When Luther had finished, the official told him that he had not spoken to the point. The question was whether he would recant or not. The emperor demanded a plain answer. Then Luther said, "If the emperor desires a plain answer, I will give it to him. It is impossible for me to recant unless I am proved to be wrong by the testimony of Scripture. My conscience is bound to the Word of God. It is neither safe nor honest to act against one's conscience. Here I stand. God help me. I cannot do otherwise."

The torches had burned down. The

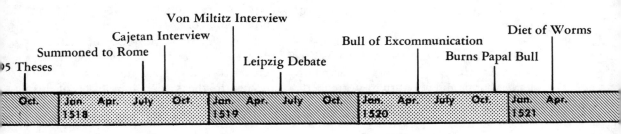

Von Miltitz Interview

Cajetan Interview

Diet of Worms

Summoned to Rome

Bull of Excommunication

Burns Papal Bull

95 Theses

Leipzig Debate

Oct.	Jan. Apr. July Oct.	Jan. Apr. July Oct.	Jan. Apr. July Oct.	Jan. Apr.
	1518	1519	1520	1521

Religious News Service Photo

Luther Is Carried Off

He was forbidden to preach. It was planned that after the safe-conduct expired he would be seized and put to death as a pestilent heretic.

There is a very small gate in the wall of Worms. By that gate Luther left the city on the night of April 26. It is pointed out to tourists today as Luther's gate.

After a few days rumors spread that Luther had suddenly disappeared. Nobody seemed to know what had become of him. Luther's enemies rejoiced, but among his friends there was consternation. The great painter Albrecht Dürer of Nuremberg wrote in his diary: "Luther, the God-inspired man, has been slain by the pope and his priests as our Lord was put to death by the priests in Jerusalem. O God, if Luther is dead, who can expound the Holy Gospel to us?" In Worms excitement ran high. The imperial court was in an uproar. Aleander, the papal nuncio, was told he would be murdered even if he were clinging to the emperor's bosom.

This is the true story of Luther's disappearance: On April 28 Luther reached Frankfort on the Main. On May 1 he reached Hersfeld, where he preached. On May 2 he entered Eisenach. The next day he preached there. On May 3 he rode through the beautiful forests of Möhra. On the morning of May 4 he preached in the open air. After dinner he continued his journey. And then, in the heart of the forest, five masked riders suddenly swept down upon him, lifted him out of the cart, and rode off with him back in the direction of Eisenach.

This was done by order of Luther's prince, the elector Frederick the Wise. Frederick had ordered the riders to take Luther to the safe hiding place of his

hall was getting dark. The emperor gave a sign that the meeting was over. He left his throne and went to his private apartments. The other members of the Diet also went to their lodgings.

Luther turned and left the tribunal. A number of Spaniards broke out into hootings. Then many of the German nobles and delegates from the towns formed a circle around Luther, and escorted him back to his lodgings.

Several conferences were held with Luther during the next few days, but it was found impossible to come to an agreement.

14. Luther Is Carried Off to Wartburg Castle • Luther was ordered to leave Worms and to return to Wittenberg.

Wartburg Castle, famed refuge of Martin Luther in Eisenach, East Germany, has now come under the control of Dr. Karl Hossinger, known as a loyal member of the Socialist (Communist) Party in East Germany.

Bildarchiv
Foto Marburg

castle, the Wartburg, whose wooded rocky heights overlooked the pretty little town of Eisenach. Here Luther stayed for ten months while the storm quieted. Writing occupied most of his time.

Luther was a volcano whose eruptions from 1517 to 1521 caused the quakes which convulsed the Church, first in Germany, but soon also in many other countries of western Europe.

1. *You will notice from this chapter that Luther's ideas were developing out of the conflict which was begun by the ninety-five theses. Which ideas now come into prominence? Why did these particular ones develop?*

2. *Questions 1 and 2 of the study aids of Chapter 21 are appropriate here also.*

3. *What political issues influenced the papal relation to Luther?*

4. *What were the results of the Leipzig debates?*

5. *Identify: Cejetan, Von Miltitz, the Wartburg, Luther's Table Talk.*

6. *Why did Luther use the press for his purposes? What did this use of popular appeal imply about the attitude of the people toward the papacy?*

7. *List the three great treatises of Luther and indicate the important thought of each one.*

8. *What was the significance of Luther's burning of the papal bull?*

9. *What was the Diet of Worms supposed to decide? Was this a Church meeting or a political meeting?*

10. *Why was Luther's request for time to rethink his position so important?*

11. *Why did Prince Frederick find it necessary to capture and hide Luther secretly? What would be involved if a public announcement that he had hidden Luther had been made?*

CHAPTER 23

The Church
Is Reformed in Germany

1. The Reformation • The events we have observed so far, centering around Luther's life, were, however, not the Reformation. They were things that led up to and paved the way for the Reformation.

What, then, was the Reformation? It was first of all a reformation of the Church. It consisted of changes for the better made in the Church. Every church teaches certain doctrines, and has certain forms of government, of worship, and of life. The changes for the better had to do

with every one of these various aspects of the Church.

But it was not only a change *in the Church*. The Reformation brought about certain changes also *outside* the Church. The Church deals with what is most fundamental in life. Men carry their religious convictions with them and reflect them in every phase of life. Consequently, what was first of all a reformation in the Church also wrought changes in the political, economic, social, and cultural life of the nations which accepted its principles. The result has been that right down to our own day there is a vast difference in almost every way between Catholic and Protestant nations.

2. Luther Restores Christian Liberty

Luther's character was made up of strangely contradictory traits. He was at the same time very *radical* and very *conservative*. Luther was the man who was to bring about a tremendous change in the Church; but he was very slow in discarding the old and substituting the new. At first he made only a few changes. In this he showed great wisdom and tact.

Luther's followers were not always as wise as he was. While he was in hiding in the Wartburg Castle, some of his followers in Wittenberg were trying to make many and radical changes. This led to confusion, conflict, and disorder. As a result, Luther left his hiding place against the advice of Elector Frederick the Wise; and in spite of the fact that he was under the sentence of death, he returned to Wittenberg. For eight successive days he preached, and thereby restored order.

Step by step many important changes were introduced. The papacy was rejected. The distinction between clergy and laity was discarded. Said Luther: "All believers are priests. There are only two and not seven sacraments. The sacraments are not indispensable to salvation." Thus Luther rang the death knell of what is the very heart of the Roman system. He broke the yoke of Rome under which believers had groaned for centuries, and established Christian liberty. For us who have never been under the yoke of Rome it is impossible to realize what this meant for the Christians of Luther's day. Praying to the saints and to Mary was done

away with, as were also the worship of images, the veneration of relics, pilgrimages, religious processions, holy water, outward asceticism, monasticism, prayers for the dead, and belief in purgatory.

While Luther changed many things, his conservative nature led him to adopt the principle that everything in the old Church that was not directly forbidden in the Bible should be retained. For example, the side altars and the images were removed, but the Lutheran Church kept the main altar with candles and picture of Christ.

The Roman Catholic Church teaches that the Lord's Supper is a sacrifice, and that to offer a sacrifice a priest is required. It teaches that when the priest pronounces the sacramental words, the bread and wine are miraculously changed into the actual body and blood of Christ. This is called the doctrine of *transubstantiation* (a change in substance). The priests alone are allowed to partake of the wine, for fear the laity might spill some of it and shed Christ's precious blood anew. The laity is allowed to receive only the bread, in the form of a wafer called the *host,* which is placed upon the tongue by the priest.

Luther denied the sacrificial character of the Lord's Supper. He denied that every time the Supper is celebrated Christ is offered anew upon a thousand altars as a sacrifice. He taught that Christ was offered once for all as a sacrifice upon the cross. There was therefore no place in the Church for priests. Since Luther's day Protestant churches have had ministers of the Word, rather than priests; and at the Lord's Supper all members partake of both the bread and the wine.

Although Luther denied that the bread

is changed into the body of Christ, he nevertheless taught that Christ's body *is* present in the Lord's Supper because, said he, since Christ's ascension, His body, like His godhead, is present everywhere.

3. A Form of Church Government Is Developed • Luther was not greatly concerned about the form of church organization or government. The form of government which he did adopt was not first of all based upon the teachings of Scripture, but was developed to meet the conditions within the Church at that time.

Luther introduced a system of church visitors. When these visitors inspected the various churches it became evident to everybody that there was an urgent need for reformation. The Roman clergy had shamefully neglected their duties. Both people and priests were almost unbelievably ignorant of religious truth. Most priests were totally unable to preach. They could only mumble masses. As a result of church inspection by the visitors, a set of *Regulations* was drawn up for the guidance of church life.

The Lutheran Church does not have bishops. The denomination has officers who are called superintendents. They exercise somewhat the same functions as bishops. The congregation is the basic unit of Lutheran government, which is usually administered by a church council consisting of the pastor and a number of elected lay officers.

The most characteristic feature of Lutheran church government is the place it gives to the State. Luther to a great extent adopted the principle that the State should be above the Church. He did that largely under the influence of circumstances. His own personal safety he owed,

humanly speaking, entirely to the protection of his prince, the Elector of Saxony. Likewise it was possible for the Protestant Church to exist only in those German lands which were ruled by princes who had accepted Protestantism. Due to this circumstance Luther gave these Protestant princes a great deal of authority in the affairs of the Church. For a short time Luther hoped that there would arise in Germany a national Protestant Church embracing all the German people. That hope, however, was never realized. Some German lands remained Roman Catholic. Even the Protestant Church in Germany was divided into a number of territorial churches.

In various ways and under varying circumstances the Church in the course of the sixteenth century was reformed also in the Scandinavian countries of Denmark, Norway, and Sweden. In these countries the Church adopted the Lutheran type of Reformation.

The victory of the Reformation in Denmark and especially in Sweden was going to be of decisive importance in the wars of religion which followed the Reformation.

4. Materials for Study and Worship • While Luther was in hiding in the Wartburg for ten months—from May 4, 1521, to March 3, 1522—he did not spend his time in idleness. He translated the Bible into the German language, the language of his people. In the Roman Catholic Church the Bible was studied only by the church leaders and scholars. Luther held that every man has the right and the duty to read and study the Bible for himself. In the church services Latin language was replaced by German.

Martin Luther in His Study

Philip Gendreau

Luther also did a great deal for education. To relieve the dense ignorance of the people he labored tirelessly for the establishment of schools everywhere. In order that the children might become thoroughly grounded in evangelical doctrine, Luther wrote his *Shorter Catechism*. It was only a very small book; yet it was one of the great Reformer's most important works. Luther's Shorter Catechism was the doctrinal dish on which generation after generation of Lutheran children were reared. The new Church also needed a new hymnbook. One of the most remarkable things about this very extraordinary man Luther is that in the midst of his terrific combat with Rome and when he was already forty years old, he blossomed forth as a poet and wrote many of the hymns for the new hymnbook. A large number of Luther's hymns have no great poetic beauty. But he wrote one hymn that will live forever. That is "Ein' feste Burg ist unser Gott," known to us as "A Mighty Fortress Is Our God."

Luther retained the idea that there is only one, true, visible Church. He did not think of himself and his followers as having left the Church. The Romanists were the ones who had departed from the New Testament Church. Luther did not feel that he had established a new church. All that he had done was to reform the Church that had become deformed.

It was considered desirable that the Lutheran Church should present to the world an official statement in which it declared its faith. Such a statement was drawn up, and handed in to the Diet of Augsburg in 1530. This statement of the Lutheran faith has become known as the *Augsburg Confession*. It was the first confession or creed to be formulated since the ancient Church formulated the Christian faith in the creeds of the Ecumenical Councils.

The Augsburg Confession did not replace the creeds of the ancient Church. The Lutheran Church believed wholeheartedly in the doctrines of the ancient Church as formulated in the Apostles' Creed, and in the Creeds of Nicaea and Chalcedon. The Augsburg Confession was based upon and included them, but at the same time it enlarged upon and expanded them.

5. Luther Has Many Helpers •
Luther soon had many helpers. His closest friend and most helpful co-worker was Philipp Melanchthon. In 1518, at the extremely youthful age of twenty-one, he had become a professor of Greek in Wittenberg University. He was therefore associated with the Reformation movement practically from the beginning. While Luther was in the Wartburg, Melanchthon published the first systematic presentation of Luther's ideas under the title of *Loci Communes*. He was one of the most learned men of his day, and was called the Preceptor of Germany. The Quiet Reformer, as he was called, exercised a moderating influence on late Lutheranism.

Another friend and valuable assistant was Spalatin, the private secretary of the Elector of Saxony. Surprisingly, in spite of Prince Frederick's high regard and friendship for Luther, the prince and Luther never met. Spalatin acted as intermediary between the two.

On June 13, 1525, Luther received a very special helper, for on that day he married Catherine von Bora. She had been a nun. Luther had been a monk-priest.

On becoming a monk or a nun a person must take the vow not to marry. For more than three hundred years it had been one of the greatest laws in the Roman Church that a priest must not marry. This practice among priests of refraining from marrying is known as *celibacy* of the clergy.

When Luther married, many priests, monks, and nuns followed his example; thus another step was taken in the Reformation movement away from Rome.

1. *What are some of the differences between the Roman Catholic countries and the Protestant countries?*
2. *Why did Luther's church regulations call for an extensive educational program?*
3. *Why was Luther's form of church government closely related to the civil government?*
4. *Luther wrote over fifty hymns. Can you find some of these, other than "A Mighty Fortress"? Notice that he wrote both words and music to many of these hymns.*
5. *Identify: Augsburg Confession,* Loci Communes.
6. *You will find the life of Philipp Melanchthon very interesting. Find some facts about this scholar that show his influence in Luther's life.*
7. *Luther had a very happy family life. Find some of the letters that Luther wrote to his wife or to his children. They will give you an interesting insight into the life of Luther. (See Schaff's* History of the Christian Church, *Volume VII, p. 464.)*

CHAPTER *24*

The Reformation in Switzerland

1. Ulrich Zwingli • On January 1, 1484, there was born in Wildhaus in the German-speaking part of Switzerland a boy who was to become known to history as Ulrich Zwingli.

Zwingli's experience differed greatly from that of Luther. He never lived as a monk in a convent. He did not have Luther's deep consciousness of sin, and he knew nothing of Luther's fearful spiritual struggle to gain salvation. Luther emerged out of the darkness of medievalism, and had been educated in scholastic theology; he studied the great writings of the Church Fathers and other works written under the influence of the medieval Church. Zwingli received his education under the influence of the Renaissance, that is, under the influence of the new interest in the ancient writings of the Greeks and Romans, which had recently been brought to the western world.

Zwingli studied in Basel, Bern, and Vienna. In 1506 he received the degree of Master of Arts. Thereupon he entered the service of the Church. In 1519 he became pastor of the church of Zurich, the most important city in that part of Switzerland. He was also chaplain in the army of the city of Zurich.

At first Zwingli stood strongly under the influence of Erasmus, with whom he became personally acquainted. He made a thorough study of the New Testament

and of the Church Fathers. Originally he had no intention of attacking the Roman Church. Like Erasmus, he hoped to bring about improvements gradually through education. He first arrived at certain reformatory ideas independent of Luther. Later he came under Luther's influence, and moved further and further away from the position of Erasmus.

2. Zwingli Reforms the Church in Switzerland • In 1518 Zwingli attacked indulgences. The stand Luther took in the Leipzig debate and his burning of the papal bull inspired Zwingli to make a systematic attack on the Roman Church.

Images were removed from the church buildings in Zurich. The mass was abolished. Altars, relics, and processions were discarded. The government of the church and the care of the poor were placed in the hands of the city council. The school system was reformed.

From Zurich the Reformation of the Church spread to several of the Swiss cantons; but many cantons remained Catholic.

3. Zwingli Differs from Luther • Zwingli differed from Luther in his idea of the Lord's Supper. As we have seen,

The Zwingli Memorial
at Zurich, Switzerland

At the conference at Marburg, Luther and Zwingli failed to come to agreement in their ideas concerning the Lord's Supper.

Ewing Galloway

Luther took the words, "This is my body," literally. He taught that the body of Christ, having become everywhere present at His ascension, is actually present in the bread and wine. Zwingli taught that the body of Christ is now only in heaven, and that the words "This is my body" mean: "This signifies my body." According to Zwingli the bread and the wine are only symbols of the body and blood of Christ, and the Supper is only a memorial ceremony.

In October, 1529, Luther and Zwingli held a conference in Marburg, but the two leaders of the Reformation could not come to an agreement.

For a time Zwingli had considerable influence in Switzerland and southern Germany. But after his death in battle in 1531 the Protestants in that region inclined more and more toward Calvin.

4. John Calvin • The third Reformer was John Calvin. He was born July 10, 1509 in Noyon, a little town in northern France, near Paris. His father was a secretary to the bishop of Noyon, and a man of some means. Through his father's influence young John was appointed to a chaplaincy already when he was eleven.

This benefice was exchanged for two better-paying ones as they became available. It was a common custom to appoint a boy to a church office, collect the salary, and pay a portion of it to an adult priest who did the work. An archbishop of Rheims was only five when he received the office.

Because of the early death of his mother, Calvin was brought up in the household of a nobleman in the neighborhood of his own home, and absorbed there something of the refined manners of the aristocracy. At thirteen years of age he went to Paris to continue his education.

5. Calvin's Youth in France • Although we have focused our attention on the events of Luther in Germany for the past two chapters, you will recall that the Church had been in turmoil for many years in many countries. In 1512, when Luther was still unknown, Professor Jacques Lefèvre of the Sorbonne in Paris published a Latin translation of, and commentary on, the epistles of Paul. It is God who saves "by grace alone," said the professor. One of his pupils, Guillaume Farel, saw with the eye of faith what his teacher was telling him.

Many others in France rediscovered the

The Birthplace
of John Calvin
in Noyon, France

truths of God's Word. Churches were changed. Margaret, the king's sister, was converted. The new faith spread throughout the country.

As in all lands, this raised fierce opposition. Lefèvre's writings were condemned in 1525, as were the writings of Luther and a little book by Margaret. Anyone found possessing such writings could expect to pay dearly. Into such a Paris came John Calvin in 1523.

Calvin drove himself to master all his studies: the classical languages, logic, the writings of the Church Fathers, law. After three years in Paris and one in Orléans, he went to Bourges to study under a famous law professor. In each city he gained influential friends as well as knowledge: Nicolas Cop in Paris, Wolmar in Orléans, and Theodore Beza in Bourges. At his father's wish, Calvin changed from the study of theology to that of law. On his father's death, Calvin decided to practice neither, but to live the life of a scholar in Paris.

Late in 1533 Nicolas Cop, now rector of the University of Paris, made his annual All Saints' Day address. The speech sounded like the ideas of Erasmus and Luther. It was rumored that Cop had written it with the advice of Calvin. Both had to flee for their lives. John Calvin escaped through a back window while some friends talked to the bailiffs in the front.

6. Calvin Becomes a Leader and Writer • When had these ideas taken over Calvin's heart? He had heard them from his brother, his cousin, his Greek teacher Wolmar, and many others. He had seen the ideas in action in the home of his landlord and in the fires of the martyrs. "God by a sudden conversion subdued . . . my heart," he writes in a later book. But when, or the exact circumstances, we do not know.

A year of wanderings followed. Calvin was hunted from city to city. He often used assumed names such as Charles

PART THREE: THE CHURCH IN THE REFORMATION

Torture
of the
Huguenots

Brown
Brothers

d'Esperville or Martianus Lucanius. Everywhere he went he taught small groups in secret places. A new torture was devised about this time, a device to lift the victim in and out of the fire, roasting him slowly instead of burning him all at once. Nowhere in France was a Protestant safe.

The wanderings ceased for a time in 1535 when Calvin found rest in Basel, Switzerland. His time was spent formulating the truths of the Bible in an orderly way. In the spring of 1536 he published his *Institutes of the Christian Religion*. This work is the greatest exposition of evangelical truth produced by the Reformation. Calvin was only twenty-six years of age when he wrote this famous book.

Notice the date and the dedication on this title page of the first edition of Calvin's *Institutes*.

It was written, first of all, as a catechism, an explanation of the fundamental teachings of the Protestant movement. Upon second thought Calvin judged that his book could do double service by explaining to the king of France, Francis I,

CHRISTIA
NAE RELIGIONIS INSTI-
tutio, totam ferè pietatis summã, & quic
quid est in doctrina salutis cognitu ne-
cessarium, complectens : omnibus pietatis studiosis lectu dignissi-
mum opus, ac re
cens edi-
tum.

PRAEFATIO AD CHRI
stianißimum REGEM FRANCIAE, qua
hic ei liber pro confessione fidei
offertur.

IOANNE CALVINO
Nouiodunensi autore.

BASILEAE,
M. D. XXXVI.

Courtesy
French Embassy Press and
Information Division

that the people being persecuted in France were not radicals or revolutionaries, but firm believers in the Bible. Calvin asked for consideration of his work as proof that his fellow believers were worthy of better treatment than that which they were being given in France.

The whole book, but particularly the dedication, was written in classic Latin and later was translated into elegant French. In a very short time it became known as the leading statement of the evangelical faith, for it set forth in splendidly organized and logical form just what the teachings of the Protestant movement were. Even today the *Institutes of the Christian Religion* are widely recognized as one of the ablest expositions of the teachings of Scripture.

After some time Calvin decided to go to Strassburg in southwestern Germany, there to pursue the quiet life of a scholar. Because of the alarms of war he took a roundabout route. It was a frail young Frenchman, with pallid face but lustrous eyes and a refined and scholarly air, who, toward evening on a warm day in August, 1536, walked through the gates of Geneva. Little did he dream of the important task to which God was about to call him.

7. Farel Brings the Reformation to Geneva

• Geneva is located on the western tip of beautiful Lake Geneva in the French-speaking part of Switzerland. Near by, through a pass in the Alps, runs an important trade route connecting Italy, Germany, and France.

To this city of Geneva the French evangelical preacher Guillaume Farel had first come in October, 1532. Farel was a zealous and influential promoter of the Reformation. As a result of his visit to a synod of the Waldenses in one of the high valleys of the Alps, many of these people accepted the principles of the Reformation. Before that, he had helped to bring about the Reformation in Bern and Neuchâtel, and in some of the smaller towns and surrounding districts. On the occasion of his first visit to Geneva, Farel had failed to get a foothold there. But he was not one to give up. He had returned to Geneva in December, 1533, and this time he was more successful.

When Farel came to Geneva the Catholics were still in the majority. But during the following months the fiery preaching of Farel turned the tide in favor of the Reformation. In the summer of 1535 Farel seized the Church of La Madeleine and the Cathedral of St. Peter. Then an *iconoclastic* (image-destroying) riot swept the city. In all the churches the images were demolished, the mass was abolished, and the monks and nuns were driven out. On May 21, 1536, the General Assembly of the citizens voted in favor of the Reformation and made Protestantism the official religion of Geneva.

All through this time Geneva was in revolt against its bishop, and against its lord, the Duke of Savoy. The waves of political and religious turmoil were running high. Farel was of a fiery temper, and gifted with eloquence and a powerful voice. But he did not feel himself equal to the task of bringing peace and order to the distracted city. Then he heard that Calvin had come to Geneva. It came to Farel as a revelation that this young Frenchman of twenty-seven was just the man for the place. Farel hurried to the inn where Calvin was stopping for the night.

When Calvin entered Geneva he did not think anyone in that city knew of him. He himself was a total stranger there, and of the situation in Geneva he knew little or nothing. He was therefore greatly surprised when Farel came to see him. He had not expected callers. But the fame of his *Institutes* had preceded him. The first edition of that work was only a small book, but in the few months that had passed since its publication it had made him, young as he was, a man of European renown.

Farel told the stranger what was on his mind. Calvin shook his head as he moved uneasily in his chair. But he asked Farel to give him a complete picture of the situation in Geneva, and to tell him in detail just exactly what he wanted him to do. The longer Calvin listened to Farel, the less inclined he felt to fall in with his plans. He realized that if he should yield to Farel's entreaties, it would mean that he would become involved in a critical situation full of the greatest difficulties. His timid nature shrank from the hurly-burly of fierce and prolonged struggles. He had his mind set on going to Strassburg. There in that haven of safety he would in peaceful seclusion devote all his time to studying and writing. He did not need a job. His father left him money enough to supply his modest wants. When he entered Geneva that evening he had no idea of staying. It was "accident" that had brought him. All he wanted there was sleep.

Farel insisted that Calvin stay in Geneva. He needed his help in establishing the work of the Reformation more firmly in that city. Calvin went on resisting the old preacher's passionate pleadings.

Here, in this Geneva inn that summer

Religious News Service Photo

Guillaume Farel

night of the year 1536, high drama was being enacted. Here was a clashing of two determined wills. The outcome of this contest would have its influence on the world's history down to the end of time.

At last Calvin pleaded as his reasons for declining Farel's request his youth, his inexperience in practical affairs, his general unfitness for the work, and his need of more study. He told Farel that this was his last word, and that he considered the discussion closed. Then the old man rose from his chair, and, straightening himself out to his full height as his long beard swept his chest, he directed his piercing look full at the young man before him and thundered: "May God curse your studies if now in her time of

CHAPTER 24: THE REFORMATION IN SWITZERLAND

"May God curse your studies if now in her time of need you refuse to lend your aid to His Church!"

need you refuse to lend your aid to His Church."

Hearing these words, Calvin was struck with terror, as he himself said later. He was visibly shaken. In Farel's voice of thunder he heard the voice of God. Then and there he ceased struggling and yielded to Farel's pleadings. Calvin consented to stay in Geneva.

This is another instance of a man of ordinary ability enlisting a man of genius in the service of the Master. As Barnabas brought Paul, so Farel brought Calvin into the service of the Church.

8. Almost All Protestants Were Lutherans • As Wittenberg was the city of Luther, and Zurich of Zwingli, so Geneva became the city of Calvin.

When Calvin began his work in Geneva in 1536, almost all of the people of northern Europe were either Catholics or Lutherans. Nineteen years had passed since Luther posted his ninety-five theses in Wittenberg. Luther was now past the height of his great career and was to live just ten years longer. The Reformation in

Germany after this time did not gain much more ground. Roughly speaking, southern Germany remained Catholic, although there were many Protestants there; and northern Germany became Protestant, although many of its people remained Catholic. After the death of Zwingli many of his followers, especially in southern Germany, went over to the teachings of Luther, and practically the entire population of Norway, Sweden, and Denmark embraced Lutheranism. In the other countries, too, Protestants during the early years of the Reformation were called Lutherans.

One important exception must be noted. Soon after the Reformation began, a group of people known as Anabaptists spread their teachings in various countries of Europe.

9. Calvin Works with Farel in Geneva • Calvin's life from the time that he came to Geneva to the time of his death falls into three parts: his first stay in Geneva from August, 1536, to April, 1538; his stay in Strassburg from May,

1538, to September, 1541; and his second stay in Geneva from September, 1541, until his death in May, 1564.

Calvin began his work in Geneva in a very modest way as assistant to Farel. The next year he was appointed one of the preachers.

Then Calvin and Farel laid before the city council three proposals which had been formulated by Calvin: (1) the Lord's Supper should be administered monthly, and every person not leading a good Christian life should be disciplined —if necessary, to the point of excommunication; (2) a Catechism which had been composed by Calvin should be adopted; and (3) every citizen should subscribe to a recommended creed, which had probably been drawn up by Farel.

The first proposal was Calvin's first attempt to make of Geneva a model community, a "city of God," and to secure the freedom of the Church from the State.

The proposals soon aroused bitter opposition. Then Calvin's opponents won the city election, and they decided to bring matters to a head. The form of worship in the neighboring city of Bern differed somewhat from that in use in Geneva. For some time past Bern had wished to have it adopted in Geneva. Now the city council insisted on introducing this form of worship. Calvin and Farel did not think that the differences were very important. But they refused to introduce the liturgy of Bern, because it was being imposed upon the Geneva church by the civil government without consultation with the church officers. This they regarded as an improper curtailment of the independence and liberty of the Church by the State. When they would

not give in they were banished from the city. Their banishment took place on the twenty-third of April, 1538.

It seemed as if Calvin's work in Geneva, so reluctantly begun less than two years before, had come to a sudden end in complete failure before it had gotten well under way.

10. Three Years of Peace in Strassburg • Farel went to Neuchâtel, where a few years before he had helped to introduce the Reformation. From this time until his death he served the church in that city as pastor.

Martin Bucer, who had been won for the Reformation by Luther during the great Leipzig Debate, invited Calvin to Strassburg. Calvin gladly accepted this invitation. It brought him to the city where he had been so eager to go in the first place.

After the eighteen months of struggle and conflict in Geneva, Calvin enjoyed three years of peace in Strassburg. Here he married Idelette van Buren, a woman from the southern Netherlands. In this

EUROPE AS CALVIN KNEW IT

Courtesy French Embassy Press
and Information Division

John Calvin

city Calvin had the opportunity to become acquainted at firsthand with the followers of both Luther and Zwingli, who had preceded him in the great work of the Reformation. He became pastor of the church of the French refugees, followers of Luther in France who had fled to Strassburg to escape persecution. He also gave lectures in theology. So for three years Calvin in large measure realized his ideal, the quiet life of a scholar. At the same time, as pastor of a church he gained practical experience.

These three years in Strassburg were for Calvin very fruitful years. He had a good deal of time for studying and writing, and he grew much in intellectual and theological stature. He prepared a greatly enlarged edition of the *Institutes.*

He also wrote a *Commentary on Romans.* This work at once placed him in the front rank of interpreters of Scripture.

At this time the emperor Charles V in Germany was putting forth very strenuous efforts to bring the Protestants and the Catholics together in order to restore the unity of the Church. Under his direction a number of conferences were held. Strassburg sent Calvin as one of its representatives. Nothing came of these conferences, but they served to make Calvin personally acquainted with many of the leading Lutherans. Calvin and Luther never met, but Calvin and Melanchthon became warm friends.

11. Calvin Returns to Geneva • After the departure of Calvin from Geneva all was confusion and disorder there. Cardinal Sadoleto, a very able man, thought there might be good fishing in troubled waters. In elegant Latin he wrote a clever address in which he tried to persuade the people of Geneva to return to the fold of the old mother Church. To offset this appeal of the cardinal, Calvin, setting aside all hard feeling against the Genevans, in no less polished Latin wrote a brilliant *Reply to Sadoleto.* This *Reply* held Geneva steady for the Reformation.

However, things were going from bad to worse. The party that had secured the expulsion of Calvin made a treaty in 1539 whereby it surrendered the independence of Geneva to the city of Bern. In the election of the following year this party was defeated, and the men who had negotiated the treaty with Bern were condemned as traitors. The party which was friendly to Calvin was again in power, and Geneva asked Calvin to return.

Photo Zimmer—Meylan, Geneva

The Nave

Religious News Service Photo

Photo Zimmer—Meylan, Geneva

**The Chapel
of the Maccabees**

The Cathedral of St. Peter was built between 1160 and 1220 on the site of previous basilicas and the still earlier pagan temples of the Roman days. The people of Geneva had reformed their worship here before Calvin arrived. For thirty years Calvin preached in St. Peter's. The 223-foot spire was added in 1899.

He had no desire to leave peaceful Strassburg for stormy Geneva. It was only with the greatest difficulty that he was at last prevailed upon to do so. Amid great rejoicing and an enthusiastic ovation Calvin entered Geneva a second time, on September 13, 1541.

We can similarly see the wonderful providence of God in bringing John Calvin to Geneva. This free and independent city with its democratic institutions was at that time, of all the places in the world, the most admirably fitted to be the scene of the great reformatory labors of Calvin. His entire life up to this time was one long preparation for the task which was now awaiting him in Geneva, and which was to be of world-wide significance.

12. His Great Work in Geneva • Upon his return to Geneva Calvin drew up a *Church Order,* a set of rules for the governing of the church. This Order was readily adopted. It was based upon the teaching of Scripture that Christ has ordained four offices in the Church: pastors, teachers or professors, elders, and deacons.

The cornerstone of Calvin's form of church government is the office of elder. Elders are chosen from among the members of the church. Together with the minister or pastor they form the consistory. The elders' office is to watch over the purity of doctrine and life of the members of the church, of each other, and of the minister. To the consistory Calvin assigned the right of discipline of the members of the church to the point of excommunication. If a case demanded any further penalty, it was to be turned over to the civil magistrate.

Luther, under the force of circumstances, had allowed the German territorial princes a great deal of power in the affairs of the Church. Calvin's ideal, on the other hand, was a Church free and independent from the State. For Calvin the freedom of the Church was concentrated in the Church's right of excommunication without outside interference.

Upon one occasion, certain citizens of Geneva whom the consistory had excommunicated came into the church armed. Their plan was to force admission to the communion table. They threatened Calvin's life if he should refuse to administer the sacrament to them. Protectingly Calvin stretched out his hands over the bread and wine, and declared that they would be able to take of it only over his dead body. By sheer moral courage and strength he made them desist from their attempt to gain admittance by force to the communion table.

Bitter opposition often arose against the strict discipline of the Church over the moral life of the members. More than once it looked as if Calvin would be expelled a second time from Geneva. What in the end saved the day for Calvin

was the influx into Geneva of refugees from other countries and the case of Servetus.

Servetus was a learned Spanish physician who had published a book attacking the doctrine of the Trinity. He came to Geneva and was arrested. He was tried, found guilty, condemned as a heretic, and burned to death on October 27, 1553. All the leading Protestant theologians, even the mild and softhearted Melanchthon, fell in with the common practice of the Roman Catholic Church of that time, and approved of his death. Calvin's opponents had done all they could to hinder the trial of Servetus. Because they had tried to protect a man whom everybody condemned as a great heretic, they were now thoroughly discredited. Their power of opposition was broken.

Men suffering persecution for the sake of their Protestant religion fled from many countries to Geneva. They were all staunch supporters of Calvin. When they were made citizens of Geneva, Calvin was able to count on a government heartily loyal to him. From 1555 on Calvin was master of Geneva.

Under his leadership the consistory of the church in Geneva passed rules and laws designed to control completely the lives of the citizens of Geneva, and to make of that city a Christian city, a "city

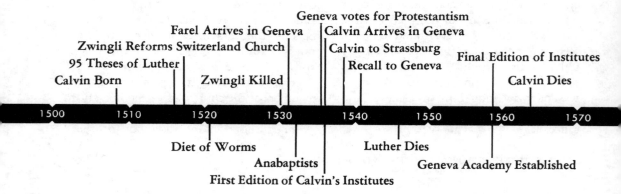

Geneva votes for Protestantism
Farel Arrives in Geneva | Calvin Arrives in Geneva
Zwingli Reforms Switzerland Church | Calvin to Strassburg
95 Theses of Luther | Recall to Geneva | Final Edition of Institutes
Calvin Born | Zwingli Killed | Calvin Dies

1500   1510   1520   1530   1540   1550   1560   1570

Diet of Worms | Luther Dies
Anabaptists | Geneva Academy Established
First Edition of Calvin's Institutes

Calvin
Conferring with
the Geneva
Council

of God." The civil government of Geneva could be relied on to put into effect the rules made by the consistory.

Calvin's greatest achievement in the final years of his life was the establishment of the Geneva Academy, the first Protestant university anywhere. Calvin realized the need for an educated ministry. From his study of the Scriptures he also realized that God's glory involves more than merely saving souls. This world is God's world. The way men deal with each other is of concern to God. Therefore, government workers, doctors, lawyers, and all others needed a training that recognized and honored God.

The university was built not with a fortune given by a king, but by the sacrificial giving of the common people of Geneva. Calvin selected his faculty with the greatest care, and from its beginning in 1559 the Geneva Academy enjoyed the highest reputation. Soon nine hundred boys were enrolled, coming from all over Europe. It wasn't long before the king of France sent an official warning to Geneva complaining of all the preachers coming from this headquarters of Protestantism.

Theodore Beza was called to be the first rector of the Academy. Calvin had first met Beza as a twelve-year-old lad who was being tutored by Wolmar when Calvin was studying in Bourges. Beza became Calvin's right-hand man and was pastor of the Geneva Reformed Church for forty years after Calvin died.

1559 also saw the publication of the third and final edition of the *Institutes*. It was five times as large as the first edition of 1536.

By means of the men trained in his university; by means of his pattern of church government; through his writings, foremost among which were his *Institutes* and his commentaries on the Bible; and by means of his correspondence which he carried on with leading men in all European countries, Calvin gained followers everywhere. His influence extended even into Italy, Hungary, Poland and western Germany.

This man, who was simply a minister of the Gospel and theological professor, acquired an influence which was and remains international in extent. Through him the light of the Gospel radiated from the little city of Geneva into every corner of Europe. Calvin was the only international Reformer.

That Calvin could do so enormous a work is all the more amazing because he was frail of body, and much of the time suffered exceedingly from a complication of painful diseases. But his will triumphed over all difficulties and obstacles, God working with him. Worn out with his difficult and extensive labors, Calvin died May 27, 1564. He was not quite fifty-five years old.

His coat of arms was a hand holding a flaming heart. His motto was: "Cor meum tibi offero Domine prompte et sincere." Freely translated this means: "My heart for thy cause I offer thee, Lord, promptly and sincerely." Calvin's life was in keeping with his motto.

13. How Calvin and Luther Differed • Luther and Calvin were in agreement on the doctrine of *predestination*, that God has from eternity chosen those who are to inherit eternal life. They both derived this doctrine from Augustine, and through him from Paul.

Calvin differed from Luther in the matter of form of worship. Luther retained as much as possible of the form of worship of the Roman Church. He retained everything that is not expressly forbidden by the Bible. Calvin departed as far as possible from the form of worship of the Roman Church. He permitted only what is expressly commanded by the Bible. Both, however, made the sermon the main thing in the church service. Both provided for congregational singing; but Luther stressed hymns while Calvin emphasized the Psalms.

Calvin differed from Luther in the form of church government. Luther allowed the State a great deal of power over the Church. Calvin denied to the State any power over the Church. He actually gave to the Church power over the State. Calvin laid much more stress on church discipline than did Luther. Both provided for the care of the poor through the deaconate.

Luther and Calvin both believed that everyone had the right and the duty to read and study the Bible for himself. And to make this possible for the people Luther translated the Bible into German; Calvin translated it into French. Both were great masters of language, and each by his Bible translation did much to mold his own native language.

Both Luther and Calvin set great store by education. Luther was first of all a professor at Wittenberg University, but he also preached. Calvin was first of all a minister and preacher in the Geneva church, but toward the end of his life he also became a professor in the University of Geneva, of which he was the founder.

Religious News Service Photo

John Calvin lived here at what is now No. 11 Rue Jean Calvin until his death in 1564.

Both were deeply convinced that the members of the Church should be thoroughly grounded in doctrine. To provide for this training they both wrote catechisms.

Calvin differed from both Luther and Zwingli in the doctrine of the Lord's Supper. With Zwingli he denied the *bodily presence* of Christ in the bread and wine as taught by Luther. But to Calvin the Lord's Supper was much more than a mere memorial ceremony, as taught by Zwingli. Calvin taught that Christ is actually and really present in the bread and wine, and is by faith actually and really partaken of by the communicant, not bodily but *spiritually*.

Both Luther and Calvin believed in salvation by faith alone. For Luther the doctrine of salvation by faith alone was the doctrine with which the Church stands or falls. For Calvin the doctrine of predestination was the heart of the Church.

Luther put emphasis on the salvation of man; Calvin on the glory of God.

14. Heroes of Faith • Luther and Calvin are among the outstanding men of the Church. Luther was the bold leader whose dangerous work of reform started the Reformation. Though it is true that much had been done before his day to prepare the way for his work, he nevertheless merits the praise of Protestantism and receives the condemnation of Catholicism for his leadership of this reforming movement. We could list his great contributions to the Reformation, such as his bold leadership, his translation of the Bible, and his forceful writings in defense of the faith; but we could perhaps best quote Luther himself who said, "The die was cast; and so I did not want to do anything else than what I did. I began to put all my trust upon the Spirit who does not carry on a lazy business."

John Calvin's work and leadership were of a different nature but also highly significant. He was among the second generation of reformers who, therefore, had a foundation for operation in previous reformers like Luther and Bucer, and he could move on to new advances of understanding and interpretation in his *Institutes* and Commentaries. He was a

In 1909, the 400th anniversary of Calvin's birth, the first stone was laid of the *International Monument of Reformation*. The center of the 325-foot monument is occupied by the statues of the four Reformers who were present in Geneva in 1559: Farel, Calvin, Beza, and Knox. See pages 258 and 259 for a reproduction of the entire monument.

master at explaining the Scriptures, so that even today, after three hundred years of scholarly activity in this field, his work is still esteemed as of first rank.

Zwingli's short life did not allow him a large place among the trio of leaders, but these three men stand as the bold servants of God who led the reform of the Christian Church, back to the fundamental teachings of faith, and to the study of the Bible. If, as a result of their reform, the Church organization was irreparably split, that was not their intention; they sought purification and return to apostolic teaching, not revolution and dissension. And certainly it is far more important that the Church of God be Scriptural than that it be united under one organization.

1. *In what way did the differences in background and training between Luther and Zwingli evidence themselves in the reformation ideas of each man?*

2. *State specifically the difference between Luther's and Zwingli's views of the Lord's Supper.*

3. *Why was Zwingli's influence as a reformer less extensive than Luther's or Calvin's?*

4. *How did Farel convince Calvin that he should stay to work in Geneva?*

5. *Was Calvin an originator of reformation ideas? Did the fact that he followed Luther by about fifteen years affect his work or were other factors more important?*

6. *What, basically, are the Institutes? What prompted Calvin to publish them? What are the major divisions?*

7. *What good results came from Calvin's banishment? Why was he recalled to Geneva?*

8. *What was Calvin's form of church government?*

9. *How were Church and State to be related under Calvin's system?*

10. *Find in a reference book the widespread influence of Servetus in fields other than theology. Why was he executed?*

11. *Discuss Calvin's widespread influence.*

12. *In what ways were Luther's and Calvin's basic ideas of reformation similar? In what ways did they differ?*

13. *Identify: Cardinal Sadoleto, Nicholas Cop, iconoclastic riots, 1536, Farel, Charles d'Esperville, Lefèvre.*

14. *Make a list of ten men you consider greatest in the Church from the time of Paul to Calvin.*

15. *Calvin is sometimes called "The Pope of Geneva." Is this title appropriate? If Christians are a majority in a city, have they the right to restrict the activities of non-Christians?*

16. *Why is Beza given such a prominent place on the International Monument of Reformation?*

The Anabaptists

1. Conrad Grebel • The Anabaptist movement, starting in Switzerland, spread almost instantaneously over many countries and ran as a side current to the main stream of the Reformation. These Christians, who called themselves "the company of the committed," were not primarily interested in writing creeds or in forming organizations. They were devoted students of the Bible who felt that the reformers were not moving fast enough in purifying the Church and applying the principles taught in the Scriptures.

Conrad Grebel was a prominent member of the church in Zurich. He had been led to the evangelical faith by Zwingli and heartily approved his work of reformation. But it was not long before he and others of like mind felt keenly disappointed with both Zwingli and Luther.

For several years they had met in each other's houses for Bible study as Zwingli had urged his followers to do. In January, 1525, in one of their meetings a man by the name of Blaurock asked Grebel to baptize him again, although he had been baptized in infancy. Grebel complied. Thereupon Blaurock rebaptized the others. This was several months before Zwingli abolished the mass and formally set up the Swiss Reformed Church.

Because of their practice of rebaptism, these people came to be called Anabaptists. However, although rebaptism was their most obvious characteristic, their most fundamental mark was their idea of the Church. That idea went down deep to the very roots of Church and State and the question of the proper relation between these two organizations.

2. Origin of the State-Church Bond • The Anabaptist movement was in part a reaction against the close ties of Church and State. This bond came about by the *mass* conversions during the days of Constantine and Clovis and the Christianizing of the pagan barbarians during the Middle Ages. Most citizens of the State felt that they were members of the Church. This type of membership brought much of the world into the Church.

Membership in the Protestant churches was also due in large part to mass "conversions." The decisions of the city councils or princes to join the reformation movement brought cities and states *as a whole* into the Protestant churches. Because most of the citizens of the State were also members of the Church, the bond between Church and State was very strong.

These mass changes in affiliation gave the Protestant churches much grief. The external aspects of Catholic ritual were easily changed, but the personal lives of many had not been touched. Many members used the doctrine of salvation by faith only, without good works, as an excuse for loose living. In his last years Martin Luther lamented over the low morality of the great mass of those who had gone over to the Protestant Church.

Much in the same way in which the Catholic Church had failed in its efforts to Christianize the heathen, so Luther and Zwingli had partially failed in their work of reforming the Church.

One of the distinctive teachings of the Anabaptists came from their reaction to this State-Church bond. They insisted that membership in the Church be limited to those who consciously committed themselves to Christ. They objected to easy membership in the Church by way of the State.

3. Separation of Church and State • When Church and State are closely connected, false doctrine is an offense not only against the Church but also against the State. Heresy is then a crime and should be punished by the government with the utmost severity. This is the view that was held not only by Catholics, but by Protestants as well. The Anabaptists, because of their doctrine of separation of Church and State, stood for liberty of religion and for a "free church." They opposed the establishment of any faith by law.

The early Anabaptists taught that Christians, as much as possible, should keep themselves separate from the world. They admitted that in this present life some kind of government is necessary, but they taught that believers should have no part in it. Consequently, according to them, a Christian should not hold government office because this involved "the use of the sword," should not be a soldier, should not take an oath, and should not sue in the courts. You can see that the Anabaptists were considered radicals in their day.

4. The Anabaptist Ideal of the Church

The Anabaptists were quite in accord with the general principles of the Reformation when Luther and Zwingli announced them. Even today they agree with major Christian doctrines of the Fatherhood of God, the deity of Christ, the Church as a body of converted believers, the Bible as God's authoritative Word, and the second coming of Christ.

However, soon after the Reformation had developed into a widespread movement, these people began to express their disapproval, because they believed that the reform movement had not gone far enough in its return to early church teachings. It should, they insisted, go back completely to the faith and practices of the Apostles.

The Anabaptists had a high regard for Christ, His Word, His Church, His commandments, especially those which Christ Himself stressed—love, holiness, self-denial, lowliness, and peaceableness. Because they took the Great Commission seriously, they had a passionate missionary concern. You can see why they called themselves "the company of the committed."

In the New Testament record they found a Church free from the State, and composed only of believers, with no mention of infant baptism. To their minds, infant baptism and the close union between Church and State were at the bottom of all the terrible corruption in the Church. They felt that children of believers prior to the age of accountability were already in the Kingdom of God without any ceremony.

5. Community of Goods

With amazing rapidity groups of Anabaptists sprang up in many cantons of Switzerland, in Austria, Bohemia, southern Germany, and all the way down the Rhine valley into the Netherlands. In Switzerland they were known as the Swiss Brethren; later, in the Netherlands, as Mennonites.

The picture of the members of the newly born church in Jerusalem sharing their goods had a magnetic charm for some Anabaptists, especially in Moravia. In 1533 a Swiss Brethren minister, Jacob Hutter, joined and later became pastor of the Austerlitz Anabaptists. Before he was burned at the stake in 1536, he had introduced a strict discipline of communal living. Each unit was called a *Bruderhof,* a "brother-estate." Today there are also over one hundred Bruderhofs in Alberta and Manitoba.

6. The Anabaptists Are Persecuted

Because of their doctrinal, political, and social views, the Anabaptists were extremely obnoxious to both Catholics and Lutherans. Infant baptism had been the universal practice of the Church for ages. To Catholics the baptism of infants is so important that if it seems a baby may die and no priest is available,

PART THREE: THE CHURCH IN THE REFORMATION

Johann Gutenberg shows his partner, Johann Fust, a proof from their press. Gutenberg (1400? to 1468) was the first European to print with movable type cast in molds. He lived in Mainz, Germany. His famous first Bible, often called the Mazarin Bible, is known also as the 42-line Bible, because most of the pages are 42 lines long. It was printed in three volumes. The Library of Congress has a complete set of this rare and treasured publication.

they insist upon anybody present performing the rite. The refusal to baptize infants and rebaptizing adults was something unheard-of and in the highest degree reprehensible. Anabaptist refusal to co-operate with the Church-State, and their socialistic tendencies made them suspect. They were generally regarded as a revolutionary sect, dangerous to society. The Catholics blamed this on the teachings of Luther. That made the Lutherans hate the Anabaptists.

Soon relentless persecution of the Anabaptists by Zwinglians, Lutherans, Calvinists, and Catholics broke out. They were imprisoned, fined, drowned, burned at the stake, tortured, and persecuted in all the manners of the day for such crimes as refusal to pay tithes, to attend church, to refrain from Bible study groups in private homes, to refrain from preaching, and other offences against the Church-State. All of these, of course, were crimes against the State in those days. Thousands of them were put to death.

7. The Kingdom of Münster •
One of the most tragic episodes in the entire history of the Christian Church was the attempt of certain radicals to set up an Anabaptist kingdom at Münster in Westphalia, Germany.

Münster

Three Lions

Melchior Hofmann, a furrier by trade, was at first an enthusiastic follower of Luther. In course of time he worked out a weird interpretation of Scripture by which he confounded the unlearned. He was opposed not only by the state churches but also by the Swiss Anabaptists. He predicted that Christ would return to earth in 1533. Multitudes in the Netherlands followed him, including Jan Matthys, a baker from Haarlem. Hofmann was imprisoned in Strassburg and died there.

Matthys declared that he was the prophet Enoch whom Hofmann had said would appear just before the return of Christ. In 1533 the followers of Matthys made themselves masters of Münster, and Matthys soon took charge. He proclaimed that Münster was going to be the New Jerusalem with community of goods and without law. From Germany and the Netherlands thousands streamed into the city.

Soon Münster was besieged by an army of Catholics and Lutherans. After granting a short period of "grace" to leave the

city, the Anabaptists killed without mercy all those suspected of being out of sympathy with them. Matthys was killed in battle in April, 1534, and John of Leyden took charge. He introduced the practice of polygamy and in the autumn of 1534 assumed the title of *king*.

Meanwhile the siege went on. For more than a year these Anabaptists defended themselves with fanatical courage. Toward the end of the siege their sufferings were indescribable. At last, on June 24, 1535, the city was taken. A terrible massacre followed. The leaders were horribly tortured.

8. The Mennonites • The excesses and fanaticism of these few radicals had discredited the movement, and for a time it seemed as if their cause was lost. But under the guidance of Menno Simons, a Dutch reformer, a moderate group of Anabaptists flourished during the second half of the sixteenth century.

Simons had been ordained a Catholic priest in 1524 in his own province of

PART THREE: THE CHURCH IN THE REFORMATION

Friesland. In his first year he began to doubt the doctrine of transubstantiation. Various events caused him to search the Scriptures, the ancient authors, and the writings of Luther and the other reformers. It was not until 1536 that he left his Roman appointment and united with the Frisian Anabaptists. He traveled widely throughout the Netherlands and the neighboring parts of Germany, everywhere organizing his followers into churches, and teaching and exhorting them by preaching and writing.

In course of time the name *Mennonites* instead of Anabaptists came to be applied to these people. They were peaceful, industrious, prosperous, and highly respected citizens. While the Anabaptists were almost universally rejected during Reformation days, today they are honored as having been pious Christians whose major contribution was the doctrine of a believers' church which included the separation of Church and State.

9. The Amish • In 1693 a division occurred in the congregations of the Swiss Brethren. Jacob Ammann felt that the shunning of excommunicated members was a biblical command (I Corinthians 5:11). Others felt that this applied primarily to the Lord's Supper. Following the rupture, the followers of Ammann set up a rigorous church discipline which has caused them to maintain a unique traditional way of life. Settlements of the Amish are found today in Pennsylvania, Ohio, Indiana, Iowa, and Ontario.

1. *What principles of the Reformation did the Anabaptists emphasize?*
2. *Which teachings of the Anabaptists are the same as those of all devout and sincere believers?*
3. *Why would one of the basic teachings of the Anabaptists be on the relation of State and Church and religious liberty?*
4. *What advantage and disadvantage to the Church is the clear statement of doctrine in the form of a creed?*
5. *Identify: Menno Simons, Melchior Hofmann, community of goods, Conrad Grebel, Münster.*
6. *Why did the Anabaptists oppose Luther and Zwingli?*
7. *What were the geographic centers of Anabaptist activity?*

CHAPTER 26

The Reformation

In Western Europe

1. The Preparation in France • Like all great movements, the Reformation had its roots far back in history. The preparation for the Reformation stretched over many centuries.

The same forces that were at work in other countries of western Europe were at work also in France to prepare the soil for the seed of the Reformation. Among these were: the Babylonian Captivity; the

Great Schism; dissatisfaction of the earnest members of the Church with the many abuses existing in the Church, which led to the calling of the three General Councils; the Renaissance; and the writings of Erasmus.

Then there was a preparation in France peculiar to that land. In the southern part of France the influence of the Albigenses and the Waldenses still lingered.

PART THREE: THE CHURCH IN THE REFORMATION

Finally there was an immediate preparation by Lefèvre, Luther, and Calvin.

Jacques Lefèvre was a student of the ancient Greek and Roman writings. He was also a Bible scholar. In 1512 he published in Latin a *Commentary on the Epistle to the Romans,* in which he denied that good works can earn salvation. He taught that man is justified by faith. He wished the people to know the Bible, and so he translated most of the New Testament into French. He was especially interested in reaching the common people. He wanted the Church to preach Christ in a simple way. Lefèvre has sometimes been called "the little Luther."

However, Lefèvre and his followers would never have brought about the Reformation in France. They had no intention of breaking with Rome. They wished to keep most of the old forms and beliefs, and bring about a reform simply by correcting the most glaring abuses.

2. Luther Has Wide Influence in France • Luther gave the impetus to the Reformation in France first by means of his writings. A book containing nearly all that Luther had published up to October, 1518, was imported into France. This book aroused widespread interest. Two years later a student in Paris said that no books were bought more than those of Luther. Writings of Luther kept pouring in from Frankfort, Strassburg, and Basel. They were written in Latin and could be read only by the learned. But soon they made their appearance in French translations. A Roman Catholic bishop said that the common people were led astray by the lively style of the heretic.

The Catholic theologians in France became alarmed. They started to publish tracts to counteract the reformation movement. The Greek New Testament of Erasmus and Lefèvre's translation into French were condemned as blasphemies against Jerome and the Holy Ghost.

But the reformation movement could not be stopped. It found followers first of all in the cities. The early recruits of the Reformation in France were merchants and artisans. But the reading of the Bible and the books of Luther soon became a practice among the middle and higher classes. Under the inspiration of Margaret, the king's sister, small, private groups were organized at the royal court to read the Bible in secret. Many short tracts which made propaganda for Luther's ideas continued to be published.

The "Lutheran contagion" continued to spread. It found advocates among all classes except among the great nobles. No exact figures are available, but in 1534 it was estimated that there were thirty thousand followers of Luther in Paris alone.

So far it was chiefly Luther who inspired the reformation movement in France. But Zwingli and other German and Swiss Reformers also exercised some influence. Protestantism in France was still weak. As yet it was not more than a protest against the deformation of the Roman Church. The followers of Luther lacked all organization, and there was no unified leadership.

For a while it seemed as if Farel might supply the much-needed leadership. He was learned, eloquent, and full of fiery zeal. He persuaded Olivetan, a relative of Calvin and an excellent Greek scholar, to make a French translation of the New Testament. This translation was a great help. Nevertheless the reformation movement in France remained confused.

Suddenly the year 1536 saw a great change.

3. Calvin Provides Leadership •
In 1536 Erasmus and Lefèvre died. Their deaths spelled the end of the Christian Renaissance movement, the aim of which had been *reform* but not a *reformation* of the Church.

But also in the same year, 1536, Calvin published his *Institutes* and began his labors in Geneva. With the publication of this small volume Calvin, the French refugee in Basel, in one leap took his place at the head of the reformation movement. With the publication of the *Institutes* the reformation movement in France received in Calvin its leader and organizer.

If an idea is to gain followers, it must be well-presented. If the followers are to become a power, they must be well-organized. Up to 1536 the Reformation in France had gained numerous followers through the writings of Luther and others. But not until Calvin settled in Geneva and began to write in French were the ideas of the Reformation presented in a form that appealed especially to French-

men. Calvin gave a better presentation of the cause than any of those before him. He also furnished a definite organization. He supplied a clear statement of doctrine, a form of public worship, and a system of church government.

Calvin was a born leader of men. He followed up his books with personal appeals. He carried on a very extensive correspondence with Protestants in France. He took great pains with the composition of his letters, and displayed great skill in using this means of impressing his ideas more firmly upon the minds of his followers.

4. The Reformation in France Matures •
It was not long before there was a well-organized church in Paris. To avoid persecution, its members met secretly in small groups in private houses. By 1559 there were many Protestant churches throughout the land, and it has been quite reliably estimated that by this time one sixth of the population of France had become Protestant. Some of the foremost men of France joined the reformation movement.

In May, 1559, the Protestant churches

The Huguenots are hunted down.

From the painting by M. Leloir

of France held a synod in Paris. This synod adopted a creed known as the *Gallic Confession*.

This synod also organized the Protestant churches in France on a national scale. Here again Calvin provided the model. The country was divided into districts. At stated times the churches within a district were to hold meetings to which each church in the district was to send as its representative a minister and an elder. Then there was to be a national synod to which every church in the country was to send a minister and an elder.

It was also around this time that the Protestants in France came to be called by the name by which they are known to history. Up to this time they were called Lutherans, and sometimes Calvinists. From this time on they were called *Huguenots*.

5. The Preparation in the Netherlands •
The same forces that prepared the way for the Reformation in Germany and in France were at work also in the Netherlands. But there was besides these an activity peculiar to the Netherlands, namely, that of the Brethren of the Common Life. You will recall how the Brethren in their work to reform the Church preached to great multitudes and also established excellent schools where Christian training was given. John of Wessel, who received his early training in one of these schools, attacked indulgences and taught that justification comes by faith alone, just as Luther did later on.

The writings of Luther and his heroic example became known in the Netherlands at an early date, and the number of his followers in the Low Countries multiplied rapidly. But the reformation movement in the Netherlands was for a long time even more confused than it had been in France. Of those that joined the Reformation some were Lutherans, some were Zwinglians, and others were Anabaptists. In the Netherlands, as in France, there was for a long time no unified leadership.

6. Calvin Becomes the Main Influence •
The man who with his clear mind and organizing ability brought order out of chaos in France, did the same thing in the Netherlands. Naturally the influence of this great Reformer was felt in the Netherlands later than in France.

A change occurred almost immediately in France upon the publication of the *Institutes* in 1536. It was not until about 1550 that the people of the Netherlands began to feel the impact of Calvin's superior mind. But when once Calvin's ideas became known they achieved a swift victory. Before long Luther and Zwingli and the Anabaptists receded into the background. At first many students from the Netherlands had gone to Luther's university at Wittenberg, but after this they went to Geneva. Gradually those Protestants who followed Zwingli and Calvin were called *Reformed*. They differed with Luther primarily on the Lord's Supper and felt that they had carried the Reformation to a higher point. All Protestants of the Reformed faith will always love and revere Luther for his heroic initiative in the mighty struggle for freedom from Rome; but they see their spiritual father not in Luther but in Calvin.

The Church in the Netherlands also gave written expression to its faith. In 1561 Guido de Brès drew up a confession of faith, which is known as the

The painting *Work of the Dragon-ade* by A. de Neuville shows the persecution Protestants suffered in this time.

nus translated into Dutch the *Heidelberg Catechism,* which had first been published in the German language. This famous catechism was written by Zacharias Ursinus, professor at the Heidelberg University, and Caspar Olevianus, the court preacher in Heidelberg. This, too, became one of the creeds of the Reformed Church in the Netherlands. Dathenus translated the Genevan Psalter, which was long used in the Reformed Church of the Netherlands.

All this time Charles V, who was lord of the Netherlands, was persecuting the Protestants. The persecution was so fierce that it was not safe to hold synodical meetings in the Netherlands. For this purpose they had to leave their own country. In 1571 a synod was held in Emden in East Friesland just across the border in Germany. Here a church order was adopted after the model of that of Geneva.

With the adoption of creeds, psalter, and church order the organization of the Reformed Church in the Netherlands was for the most part completed, and that church was firmly established.

Belgic Confession and also as the "Netherlandish Confession" or the "Thirty-seven Articles." Two years later Dathe-

1. List the pre-reformation and reformation leaders who had influence in France from Peter Waldo to John Calvin. State briefly the extent of the influence of each.
2. What did Calvin do for the Church in France?
3. Why would the adoption of creeds, psalter, and church order serve to organize the Church in the Netherlands? What were the sources of these instruments?
4. Identify: Lefèvre, Huguenots, Guido de Brès, Gallic Confession.

CHAPTER 27

The Church Is Reformed
In Scotland, 1557-1570

1. The Preparation in Scotland • In the Reformation era Italy and France were foremost in civilization and culture, but not far behind were Switzerland, southern and central Germany, the Netherlands, and England. In the countries along the outer rim, however—in Spain, Portugal, Hungary, Poland, northern Germany, Ireland, and Scotland—the light of the new day had not yet fully dawned. Those countries were still partly shrouded in the shadows of the Middle Ages.

Scotland at this time was a poor country, ruled over by a weak king and feudal lords who were constantly fighting one another. The clergy was perhaps more corrupt than in any other country. During the fifteenth century universities had been founded in St. Andrews, Glasgow, and Aberdeen; but they could not compare in scholarship with the great universities on the Continent.

Rumors of the great and strange new things going forward in Germany reached

Scotland. Several young Scotchmen visited Luther's university at Wittenberg. When they returned they sowed the seed of Luther's doctrines in the soil of their native country. Others also imported and distributed some of Luther's writings. Tyndale's and Coverdale's English translations of the Bible were circulated. The early Protestants in Scotland met for worship and instruction in private houses.

2. Calvin's Influence Felt through Knox • Gradually, as in France and in the Netherlands, the influence of Calvin overshadowed that of Luther also in Scotland. The transition from Lutheranism to Calvinism took place under George Wishart. However, not Wishart but John Knox was destined to be the great Reformer of Scotland.

John Knox was born in Scotland some time between 1505 and 1515. He received a university education and was ordained a priest. When in 1547 the French

John Knox

fleet captured St. Andrews, Knox, together with others, was made prisoner. For nineteen months he toiled as a galley-slave. Day after day he had to ply the oars in the hot, smelly hold of a French ship. Sometimes he was made to feel the lash, and constantly he was pestered with suggestions that he should pray to the image of Mary.

After his release from the rowing bench, Knox went to England for five years. Here he was of help to archbishop Cranmer in formulating the *Forty-two Articles,* the Protestant creed adopted by the Church of England. Cranmer appointed Knox and others to be chaplains in ordinary to the king to go to the various districts of the kingdom to indoctrinate both clergy and people with the principles and purposes of the Reformation.

After his stay in England, Knox went to Geneva. He was much impressed with the teachings of Calvin and adopted his system. In August, 1555, Knox paid a short visit to his native Scotland, and preached with great feeling against the mass. To Mary of Lorraine, who was at this time regent of Scotland, he sent a letter urging her to favor the Gospel. Mary, who was a strong Catholic, took the letter as a joke. She soon learned that Knox was far from joking—that he was in dead earnest. By the time she realized this, Knox had left Scotland again and returned to Geneva. She sentenced him to death and burned him in effigy, that is, she burned an image of him.

The Reformed party was slowly making headway in Scotland. From Geneva, Knox served his fellow believers with advice. In 1557 the leaders of the Protestant party drew up a "Common Band," known as the First Scottish Covenant.

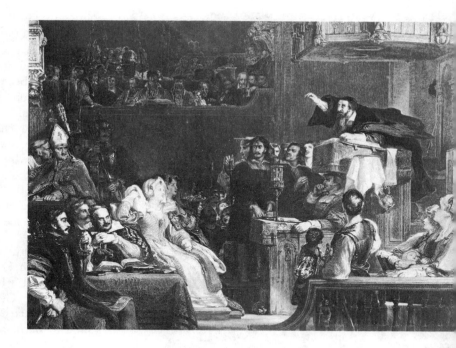

John
Knox
Preaching

Brown
Brothers

They pledged themselves to do all in their power to further "the most blessed Word of God and His Congregation." Under the protection of the "Band," or Bond, Reformed churches were established openly. "The Lords of the Congregation" felt that they needed the help of Knox, and they requested him to return from Geneva. On May 2, 1559, Knox came back to Scotland.

3. Knox Revolutionizes Scotland • After Knox returned to Scotland the Reformation in that land swept forward. The preaching of Knox was powerful. His style was direct, vigorous, and plain. Frequently he employed sparkling wit and cutting satire. Of his preaching it was said: "Others lop off branches, but this man strikes at the root." In the pulpit he

was so energetic that he seemed likely to pound it to pieces and fly out of it.

The preaching of Knox was like a spark in a keg of gunpowder. Wherever he preached there followed an iconoclastic explosion. Images were broken and monasteries stormed by the mob. He wrote: "The places of idolatry were made level with the ground, the monuments of idolatry consumed with fire, and priests were commanded under pain of death to desist from their blasphemous mass."

In 1560 the Scottish Parliament decreed a change of religion. Protestantism instead of Catholicism was made the religion of the country. A Calvinistic confession of faith, largely the work of Knox, was adopted. The pope's authority and all jurisdiction by Catholic prelates

In many countries followers of the Reformation destroyed the images and altarpieces and other symbols in the churches. This painting of iconoclasts at work in the Netherlands is by A. de Neuville.

was abolished, and the celebration of the mass was forbidden.

Maintenance of the true religion was declared to be the prime duty of government. Ministers were paid by the State. The Church was not to take a hand in politics unless it concerned some matter touching upon religious life or practice.

Under this plan of Knox the relation of Church and State remained practically what it had been under the popes—the Church was considered supreme in spiritual matters, and the State in civil affairs. The only real change was that for the pope, Knox was substituted; and that the Protestants who were formerly suppressed, now suppressed the Catholics. This idea of the relation of Church and State also underlies the original form of Article 36 of the Belgic Confession.

4. The Church in Scotland Is Organized • In December, 1560, a meeting was held which is regarded as the first Scottish General Assembly. This body, in January of the next year, presented to Parliament a church order, the *First Book of Discipline.*

The *Book of Discipline* applied to the churches of the entire country of Scotland the system which Calvin had worked out for the one church in the city of Geneva. In each parish or local church the minister, together with elders chosen from the members of the church, constituted what was called a *session.* Meetings in which the churches of a limited area were represented by delegated ministers and elders were called *presbyteries.* Meetings in which larger groups of churches were represented by delegated ministers and elders were called *synods.* And meetings in which all the churches of the country were represented by delegated ministers and elders were called *general assemblies.*

For the conduct of public worship Knox prepared a *Book of Common Order.* To a great extent this order of worship was based on the form for public worship

PART THREE: THE CHURCH IN THE REFORMATION

used by the church of English refugees in Geneva. That in turn was based on the form designed by Calvin. This form of worship consisted in prayer, reading of Scripture, the sermon, congregational singing, and the taking up of an offering. *The Book of Common Order* contained prayers for special occasions. They were models and their use was not compulsory. Ample room was left for entirely free prayer.

The Church organized by Calvin in Geneva was extremely influential. It became the pattern for the Huguenot Church in France, the Reformed Church in the Netherlands, and the Presbyterian Church in Scotland.

5. The Church Is Firmly Established • Mary, queen of the Scots, was an unyielding Catholic. She was a woman of ability and of great personal charm. In the first three years of her reign she made considerable progress in regaining for the Roman Church the ground that had been lost. But the cause of the Reformation was saved in the end by Queen Mary's mistakes. Her unwise acts and immoral life threw Scotland into confusion and the Roman Catholic Church into disrepute. The leaders as well as the people in general turned to Protestantism. By the year 1570 the Presbyterian Church was firmly established in Scotland.

Two years later, on November 24, John Knox died.

Knox's career had been stormy; but he had shown himself to be a great fighter, a man of dauntless courage. He had reformed the Church in Scotland. And furthermore, by reforming the Scottish Church, John Knox, more than any other man, molded the character of the Scottish nation.

1. *How did the beginnings of the Reformation in Scotland differ from the beginnings in other countries?*
2. *Why did violence and destruction attend a change of religious practice in Scotland?*
3. *What was the relation of Church and State in Scotland?*
4. *Outline the type of church government the Calvinists set up in Scotland.*
5. *Identify: Mary of Lorraine, George Wishart, First Scottish Covenant.*

CHAPTER *28*

The Church Is Reformed
In England, 1534-1563

1. John Wycliffe

2. Tyndale Translates the Bible

3. Henry VIII Becomes Head of the Church

4. Henry Makes Other Changes

5. Edward VI

6. The Catholic Reaction Under Bloody Mary

7. Thomas Cranmer

8. The Reformation Under Elizabeth

1. John Wycliffe • The Reformation in England ran a course different from that in any other country, and the outcome was different. It went through a number of stages under four successive rulers: Henry VIII, 1509–1547; Edward VI, 1547–1553; Mary, 1553–1558; and Elizabeth, 1558–1603.

The stirring in the Church during the fourteenth and fifteenth centuries had in a general way prepared England for the Reformation as it had other countries. But on this island there had been a very special preparation such as, outside of Bohemia, no other country had experienced. It was over England that the morning star

Religious News Service Photo

John Wycliffe

In the early years of the reign of Henry VIII (from 1511 to 1514), Erasmus had lectured at Cambridge University. He had made many friends in England, and his writings, with their biting criticism of the abuses in the Roman Church, were widely read.

In England, as in other countries, the Reformation received its direct impulse through the writings and the bold stand of Luther. Four months after Luther published his theses Erasmus sent them to his English friends John Colet and Sir Thomas More. Thereafter many of Luther's books were imported into England. Lutheran doctrine invaded the two great English universities of Oxford and Cambridge. At Cambridge a number of young men met regularly to discuss the new ideas. From year to year the number of Englishmen who embraced the teachings of Luther increased.

of the Reformation had risen in the person of John Wycliffe (1320–1384). The Council of Constance had condemned Wycliffe as an archheretic. It had ordered his body dug up out of its grave in the peaceful churchyard of Lutterworth, his bones to be burned, and the ashes to be strewn over the waters of the Severn River. The river had carried Wycliffe's ashes out to sea, but his ideas continued to work as a leaven.

The Council of Constance had also ordered Wycliffe's writings to be burned, but they had not all been destroyed. Many of the men who became leaders in the reformation movement in England were acquainted with his writings. When at last the Reformation broke through in England, it followed in some respects the lines laid out by Wycliffe.

2. Tyndale Translates the Bible • From the beginning the Word and the Spirit of God have been the two greatest factors in the history of the Church. The preaching of Jesus and the apostles was rooted in the Old Testament. Later the Old and New Testaments came to be the one source of knowledge of Christian truth, the only rule for faith and conduct.

The translation of the Bible into various languages has been one of the most influential factors in the history of the Church. Even today missionaries, as soon as they are able to do so, translate the Bible into the language of the people to whom they bring the Gospel. The Seventy translated the Old Testament from Hebrew into Greek about three centuries before the birth of Christ, and produced the *Septuagint*. Jerome translated the Bi-

Schoenfeld Collection
from Three Lions

**William Tyndale Translating
the Scriptures**

ble from Hebrew and Greek into Latin, and produced what is known as the *Vulgate*. Wycliffe translated the Bible into the English of his day. Translations of the Bible were among the most powerful agencies for the promotion of the Reformation. Luther translated the Bible into German; Calvin made a French translation. The translation of the Bible into Dutch was a great help to the Reformation in the Netherlands. Now Tyndale set to work to translate the Bible into English.

William Tyndale was educated at Oxford and Cambridge. He became acquainted first with the ideas of Erasmus, then with those of Luther, and at last also

with those of Zwingli. He decided to place the Bible within reach of the people of England. The common people could not, of course, read the Latin Bible. Copies of Wycliffe's translation into English were not numerous, and besides, in the course of two centuries the English language had undergone such great changes that his translation was no longer understood.

Tyndale's work was published in Germany in 1525. It was a very excellent translation of the New Testament from the original Greek, not from the Latin Vulgate as Wycliffe's had been. The first edition was six thousand copies. In the ten years following, seven editions appeared. Next he translated parts of the Old Testament. Tyndale accomplished all this in the face of fierce opposition and bitter persecution. Finally his enemies caught up with him, and on October 6, 1536, Tyndale suffered a martyr's death near the city of Brussels. His translation did much to further the cause of the Reformation in England and also in Scotland. God's Word again proved to be more powerful than the sword.

In 1535 another English version—this time of the whole Bible—was published. This translation was the work of Miles Coverdale.

3. Henry VIII Becomes Head of the Church • The Reformation in England had many peculiarities. One was that in England there was no single, great, outstanding leader. England had no Luther, Zwingli, Calvin, or Knox. Another peculiarity of the English Reformation was that changes were made in the Church in England not by an officer of the Church but by the king.

PART THREE: THE CHURCH IN THE REFORMATION

In the course of history a strong national feeling had developed in England. The people were against any domination by a foreigner. During the Renaissance the papacy had become secularized; it had become more and more interested in the things of this world. To the English people, therefore, the pope appeared to be little more than an Italian prince. Consequently, although the great majority of the English people were still good Catholics, they were beginning to resent more and more the rule of the pope over the Church in England. They did not like to send to Rome all the money that the pope demanded.

In spite of these factors, it is probable that for many years no changes would have been made in the Church in England if it had not been for the fact that the king wanted a divorce.

Henry VIII applied to the pope for a divorce from his wife, Catherine. He wanted to marry Anne Boleyn. Much time passed and still the pope did not give his decision. At last the king's patience grew thin. He made up his mind to take things into his own hands. He was a very powerful king, able to control Parliament. In 1534 he had Parliament pass a law which decreed that the king "justly and rightfully is and ought to be the supreme head of the Church of England." This law is called the *Act of Supremacy*.

The Act of Supremacy introduced an important change in the Church of England. It was a change in the Church in only one respect—not in doctrine or form of worship, but in the government of the Church. And it was a change in the government of the Church only in this one particular: that the pope as head of the Church was replaced by the king. It was

a big change, but it could not be called a Reformation.

Henry VIII regarded Luther as a heretic. As early as 1518 Henry had written a book against heretics entitled, *The Seven Sacraments*. For that service the pope had bestowed upon him the title of "Defender of the Faith." When Henry VIII made himself head of the Church in England in place of the pope, he did not feel that he had ceased to be a good orthodox Catholic.

Powerful king that he was, Henry could not have pushed the pope aside if he had not had the support of the nation. The Catholics felt as the king did. They believed that in spite of the change that had been made they could still be good Catholics. Those who favored the ideas of Luther, on the other hand, looked upon the change as a first feeble step in the direction of the Reformation.

But not all Englishmen were willing to submit to the Act of Supremacy. So Henry had another law passed, the *Law of Treason and Heresy*. This law stated that to hold any doctrines other than those of the Catholic Church was heresy, and to refuse to acknowledge the king as head of the Church in England was treason.

Under the Law of Treason and Heresy a number of persons were put to death. Monks were executed for denying the supremacy of the king. Two very prominent men, John Fisher, bishop of Rochester, and Sir Thomas More, one of England's most illustrious scholars, were also executed. Both had refused to take the oath of supremacy. For his opposition to the Act of Supremacy the pope had rewarded Bishop Fisher by making him a cardinal. A cardinal wears a certain kind of red hat. In a fit of fury the king ex-

Ewing Galloway

This painting of Henry VIII by Hans Holbein hangs in Warwick Castle.

erned by bishops, under the king as supreme head. Hence the Church of England or the Anglican Church is also called the Episcopal Church.

Later in the reign of Henry VIII some changes were introduced in doctrine, form of worship, and certain practices. Monasteries were discontinued; and relics were no longer displayed or regarded as sacred. There were many small monasteries and a few large ones in England. Together they possessed immense wealth in land and in jewels and gold. That land the king parcelled out among his favorites. By doing this he created a new landed aristocracy, which was very loyal to him.

The relics were gross frauds. Among the things that were claimed to have been preserved were a part of Peter's hair and beard, stones with which Stephen was stoned, the hair shirt and bones of Thomas, and the ear of Malchus that Peter had cut off. At Maidston there was a crucifix which could turn its head, roll its eyes, move its lips, foam at the mouth, and shed tears. When it was removed a mechanism was discovered inside, which the priests had manipulated. Scattered all over England were pieces of wood said to be fragments of the cross. There were enough of these to fill three carts. The removal and destruction of these things during the reign of Henry VIII was a heavy blow at medieval superstition.

England was not a Protestant nation at the close of the reign of Henry VIII It is perhaps safe to say that in London and the southeastern part of England the majority of the people were Lutherans. But the west and north of England were still almost solidly Catholic. That included probably about three-fourths of the population.

claimed that he would send the bishop's head to Rome to get the hat. The seventy-six-year-old bishop was beheaded in June, 1535. Sir Thomas More had been a zealous Catholic and had caused many English Lutherans to be sent to the stake. Now the tables were turned. More was beheaded in July.

4. Henry Makes Other Changes • When the king became the supreme head of the Church, the rest of its organization remained what it had been when the pope was supreme head. The Church of England, or the Anglican Church, as it is also called, has ever remained a church gov-

5. Edward VI • Upon the death of Henry VIII in 1547 his son Edward VI succeeded to the throne. Since Edward was a boy of only nine years of age, his uncle, the Duke of Somerset, was made regent.

Throughout the reign of Henry VIII sentiment in favor of the Reformation had been steadily growing in England. The regent Somerset and his new government leaned toward the Reformation. So during the brief reign of Edward VI the Reformation made considerable progress in England. No further changes were made in the form of government of the Church of England, but changes were made in its doctrine and form of worship.

Almost at once, in 1547, Parliament passed a law which provided that all communicants should be allowed to partake of the wine as well as of the bread. Early the next year it was decreed that images should be removed from the churches. A year later celibacy of the clergy was done away with, and marriage for priests and the higher clergy was declared lawful.

In 1549 Parliament passed the *Act of Uniformity*. This Act made the use of the *Book of Common Prayer* compulsory in church services. It is known as the *First Prayer Book of Edward VI*. This Prayer Book substituted the use of the English language in the service of the Episcopal Church for the Latin used in the Roman Church. Fundamentally it is still today the Prayer Book of the Church of England.

The First Prayer Book of Edward VI did not satisfy anyone. Those who continued to cling to Catholicism did not like the changes that had been made. For those who wanted a Reformation the changes did not go far enough. In 1552 Parliament passed a new Act of Uniformity. The First Prayer Book was revised. Most of the Catholic practices in worship were now discarded. Prayers for the dead were dropped. A communion table took the place of the altar. In the Lord's Supper common bread was used instead of the wafer. Exorcism (casting out of evil spirits) and anointing went out of use. The form used in the administration of the Lord's Supper was based upon Zwingli's belief that the bread and wine are symbols of Christ's body and blood.

The Reformation made progress also in the matter of doctrine. A new creed was formulated by Cranmer, archbishop of Canterbury. With the help of six other theologians, of whom Knox was one, it was put into final shape, and then adopted as the creed of the Church of England under the name of the *Forty-two Articles*. In general this creed was even more definitely Protestant than the Prayer Book.

The Reformation in England seemed to have complete victory within its grasp.

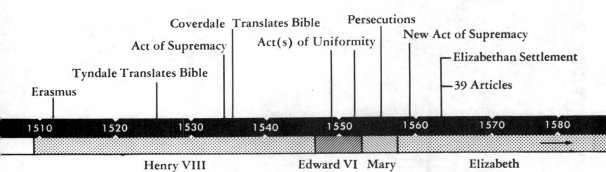

Then suddenly its triumphal march was halted, and Catholicism regained much of the ground it had lost since the reign of Henry VIII.

6. The Catholic Reaction Under Bloody Mary

Edward died of tuberculosis in 1553, when he was only sixteen years old. His sister Mary succeeded him to the throne of England.

Mary was strongly Catholic. She proceeded to set the clock of the Reformation in England back at least twenty-five years. The laws regarding the Church which Parliament had passed during the previous reign were repealed. The form of worship in use during the last year of Henry VIII was restored. Bishops and all the lower clergy who were known to favor the Reformation were removed from office. Many leading Protestants fled to the Continent, where they were warmly received by Calvin. Among the Lutherans they met a chilly reception, because they did not believe in Christ's bodily presence in the Lord's Supper.

Cardinal Pole, who had fled to the Continent during Henry's reign, returned to England. Parliament voted the restoration of the authority of the pope over the Church in England. It re-enacted the laws against heresy, and repealed the legislation of Henry VIII with reference to the Church. The work of the Reformation in England was entirely undone. The Church was again as it had been before 1534, with one exception. The property that had belonged to the monasteries was allowed to remain in the hands of the new possessors.

The year 1555 was a terrifying year for the Protestants in England. Before the year was over, seventy-five persons in various parts of the land were put to death by fire. The most notable victims of Mary's persecution were the two bishops Hugh Latimer and Nicholas Ridley. As the flames curled around their bodies Latimer spoke courage and comfort to his fellow martyr: "This day we shall light such a candle, by God's grace, in England, as I trust shall never be put out." Mary was not yet satisfied. Her next victim was Cranmer, archbishop of Canterbury.

7. Thomas Cranmer

Although the dominant personalities in the story of the Reformation in England were its political rulers, there was one man of the Church who worked valiantly to promote Protestantism. In 1532 Henry VIII appointed Thomas Cranmer the first Protestant arch-

The Future Queen Elizabeth in the Tower During the Days of Bloody Mary

Thomas Cranmer, Archbishop of Canterbury, at the Traitor's Gate on the Way to His Martyrdom

Religious News Service Photo

bishop of Canterbury. Prior to his archbishopric Cranmer was a preacher at the University of Cambridge. He had traveled on the Continent where he had met the pope, the emperor, and Lutheran leaders who had strengthened his pro-Reformation leanings.

Because of his strong feelings on nationalism and on the need for reforming the Christian religion, Cranmer heartily approved the decision of Henry VIII to end the rule of the Roman pope over the Church of England. After the death of Henry VIII, Cranmer became the moving force of the Reformation in England. Under his direction many changes took place. All communicants were allowed to partake of both bread and wine at the Lord's Supper. All images were removed from the churches.

Cranmer strengthened the movement by bringing to England from Germany such Protestant leaders as Peter Martyr and Martin Bucer to teach at Oxford and Cambridge. Since many of the clergy were continuing to use the old rites and practices of Romanism, Cranmer had the

king's privy council permit him to send out chaplains as visiting lecturers to instruct both the clergy and the people. You recall that John Knox was one of those who was sent out. Cranmer was also the chief writer of the Book of Common Prayer and of the Forty-two Articles.

Late in the year 1555 he was excommunicated in Rome. Cardinal Pole was appointed to the office which had thus fallen vacant. Cranmer now weakened. He declared that he recognized the authority of the pope over the Church in England as it had recently been restored by law. But Mary was bent on Cranmer's death. Knowing Cranmer's weakness she hoped that he might be made to renounce Protestantism publicly before he died. It was believed that this would do great harm to the cause of the Reformation. Cranmer did sign a statement in which he denied Protestantism. The time of his execution in Oxford was set for March 21, 1556. Just before he was to die he renounced his denial, and once more and in the strongest terms declared his Protestant faith. In dramatic fashion he showed

Queen Elizabeth signs the
new Supremacy Act

how he felt about his denial of the principles of the Reformation. The hand which had signed the denial he held in the flames until it was burned to a crisp. Then the flames scorched his body, and he died the death of a martyr and a hero.

Mary continued her persecution until the day of her death on November 17, 1558. She had caused almost three hundred people to be burned. Her persecutions earned her the name of Bloody Mary.

8. The Reformation Under Elizabeth • Mary was succeeded by her sister Elizabeth. Under Mary her life had been in danger, and she had outwardly observed the Catholic ritual. But Eliza-

beth had been educated under the supervision of Cranmer and was a Protestant at heart. It was now possible for her to make the Reformation victorious in England. The persecutions of Mary had been aimed at the total destruction of Protestantism, but they had done more to arouse anti-Roman sentiment than all previous legislative enactments of Parliament. Here again the blood of the martyrs proved to be the seed of the Church.

Against strong opposition Parliament on April 29, 1559, passed a new Supremacy Act. For a second time, and now for good, the government rejected all authority of the pope over the Church of England.

Next the Second Prayer Book of Edward VI was revised. The prayer against the pope was dropped. The matter of the bodily presence in the bread and wine of the Lord's Supper, one of the principal doctrines of the Catholic Church, was left an open question. The earlier Prayer Book had definitely stated that kneeling at the Lord's Supper did not imply adoration of the host (as the Catholics call the wafer used in communion); this declaration was now dropped to please the Catholics. These compromises seemed wise at the time, but were the source of much dissatisfaction and conflict in later years.

In 1563 there was a slight change in the creed. The Forty-two Articles were reduced to thirty-nine. These now famous *Thirty-nine Articles* are the official creed of the Church of England today.

Changes had now been made in the doctrine, the worship, and the government of the Church in England. The adoption of these changes is known as the *Elizabethan Settlement*. Therewith the Reformation in England came temporarily to a halt, but as we shall see in Chapter 34, it was later continued—and in a far more radical fashion.

The Catholics were now a small minority.

On the surface it would seem that the Reformation in England was the work of the government, of kings and queens. It appears to have been political rather than religious in its interests. Yet the kings and queens could never have carried the Reformation through, if there had not been a powerful religious undercurrent in the life of the English nation.

1. Comment on this statement: *Whenever men of this period went back to a careful study of the Scriptures they became heretics to the Church.*

2. Why would men be punished for translating the Scriptures into the language of the people, when the Church of Rome itself recognized the Bible as authoritative?

3. How did the development of nationalism affect the cause of the Reformation in England? What was the reason for the Act of Supremacy?

4. Did Henry VIII actually want reform of doctrine for the Church? Why was he known as "Defender of the Faith?"

5. After reading the section on Henry VIII's execution of Fisher and More, answer the question, "Were these men guilty of heresy or of treason?"

6. How was Henry VIII's attitude toward monasteries related to nationalism?

7. Note how under Mary the people of England were expected to adjust their religious faith to the rule of the Queen. Why did men look upon the king or queen as having authority in such matters?

8. The Elizabethan Settlement was a compromise. Was Elizabeth primarily concerned with what was right?

9. Identify: William Tyndale, Archbishop Cranmer, Thirty-nine Articles, Book of Common Prayer, Law of Treason and Heresy.

10. How did the Reformation in England differ from the Reformation in Scotland?

CHAPTER *29*

The Roman Church
Undertakes Reform, 1545-1563

1. *Reform Is Universally Desired*

2. *Ximenes*

3. *Charles V Chooses Aleander*

4. *Pope Adrian VI*

5. *The Council of Trent*

1. Reform Is Universally Desired • The disgrace of the Babylonian Captivity (1309–1376), the scandal of the Great Schism (1378–1417), and the many and gross abuses which disfigured the life of the Roman Church had been a sore grief to all true Christians. From every country of western Europe there arose loud and insistent cries for a thoroughgoing reform.

The answer to these cries for reform had been the three general councils of

Pisa, Constance, and Basel (1409–1449). These general councils were a bitter disappointment to all upright Christians. They accomplished nothing in the way of reform. On the contrary, the situation became worse.

All the evils and abuses that afflicted the Church were centered in the *curia,* that is, the papal government. Soon after the Babylonian Captivity and the Great Schism, the papacy came under the influence of the paganizing Renaissance. The

PART THREE: THE CHURCH IN THE REFORMATION

popes became worldly Italian princes, patrons of art and literature. Pope Leo X was an elegant gentleman, highly polished, deeply interested in the paganizing culture of the Renaissance. Leo was a man of blameless moral life, but he was thoroughly worldly, without interest in religion. After he had been ordained pope he said, "Now let us enjoy the papacy." His great project was the building of the splendid St. Peter's Church in Rome. The project required immense sums of money. To raise that money he organized the sale of indulgences on a huge scale.

It was at this time that Luther lifted up his mighty voice. And it was because of the widespread and passionate desire for reform that Luther's actions met with such tremendous and instantaneous response. For more than two hundred years the desire for reform had been rising like the waters of a flood. For all that long time Rome had been successful in casting up a dam to hold that flood in check. The higher the popes built the dam, the higher the waters rose. At last Luther broke the dike and the mighty waters of the Reformation flooded western Europe.

2. Ximenes

2. Ximenes • A generation before Luther started the Reformation in Germany, Ximenes had accomplished a reform in Spain.

For seven hundred years the Christians in Spain fought to drive out the Muslim Arabs, or Moors. Granada, the last Moorish stronghold in Spain, was finally taken from them in 1492. This centuries-long struggle of the Spanish Christians against the Muslims had bred in them a spirit fanatically religious and patriotic. This spirit was particularly

Courtesy Embassy of Spain

This outstanding example of Moorish architecture is the Giralda Tower in Seville, Spain.

strong in Ferdinand and Isabella, by whose marriage Spain had been united into one kingdom.

Queen Isabella undertook to bring about a reform in the Church in Spain. She entrusted this work to the three leading churchmen. One of these was Ximenes, a Franciscan monk who later became archbishop of Toledo. He it was who really planned the reform and carried it to a successful conclusion.

The reform was a reform of the clergy and of the monks. In all the monasteries Ximenes enforced strict discipline. The priests were likewise forced to live up to high moral standards. Those who lacked ability or were hopelessly ignorant were removed from office. For the others he established new schools for the study of theology. All those who opposed Ximenes were swept out of his way by the secular power of the queen. Isabella also protected Ximenes from interference by the pope. The outcome was that the Church in Spain acquired a devoted and able clergy.

But for the rest everything remained the same in the Church in Spain. The pope continued to be acknowledged as the head of the church. The hierarchy remained. The Catholic conceptions of priesthood and sacraments remained. The sacred ceremonies, decrees, ordinances, and sacred usages were left untouched. Catholic doctrine was left unchanged. The monasteries did not dissolve as in Germany, nor were they suppressed as in England.

What Ximenes had brought about in Spain was a reform, not a reformation.

3. Charles V Chooses Aleander •

At the Diet in Worms in 1521 the three outstanding persons were Charles V, Luther, and Aleander. Charles was the grandson of Ferdinand and Isabella. He had been brought up in the strict Catholicism of his grandmother. He was king of Spain and emperor of Germany. Aleander was the representative of the unreformed papacy.

For a short time Charles hoped to use Luther to bring about a reform in the entire Church, as his grandmother Isabella had used Ximenes to bring about reform in the Church in Spain. Charles knew that Luther had violently attacked the papacy as an institution and the Catholic

system of priests and sacraments. Charles hoped that Luther would forsake this extreme position. But at the Diet of Worms, Luther maintained that church councils could err and had erred, and that he could prove it. Upon hearing this, Charles waved his hand as a sign that the session of the Diet was closed. Luther had chosen. His break with Rome was beyond repair.

From that moment on Charles set his face like flint against Luther and the Reformation. He made up his mind to ally himself with Aleander as the representative of the papacy. His first move would be to crush Luther and the Reformation. Then, having crushed Luther and the Reformation with the help of the papacy, he would turn against his ally, make himself master of it, and impose the Spanish reform upon the entire Church.

4. Pope Adrian VI •

Soon after the close of the Diet of Worms the opportunity presented itself to Charles to try to work out his plan. Pope Leo X died. The cardinals who met to elect a new pope were deadlocked for a long time. The only way to break the deadlock was to accept the candidate offered by the emperor Charles. This they finally did, and the emperor's man became pope under the title of Adrian VI.

Pope Adrian was a Dutchman from Utrecht and had been Charles' tutor. He was a pious and strict Catholic, in thorough agreement with Ximenes. He became known as the Dutch Ximenes.

Pope Adrian tried, according to the emperor's wishes and his own ardent desire, to introduce the Spanish reform in Rome. But he failed miserably in his attempt. There were several reasons for his failure. He did not feel at home among the Italians, did not know their ways, and did not understand their language. They in turn did not understand him. Adrian was a good but simple man. He thought it would be easy to introduce the Spanish reform in Rome. Until he came to Rome he had no idea how deepseated and far-spread the corruption of the papacy actually was. To do away with the abuses connected with the sale of indulgences would cut off millions every year from the pope's revenue. The papal court was a vast machine with thousands of employees and hangers-on. To introduce the Spanish reform would deprive all these thousands of their jobs and income.

At every turn he made, he faced unexpected obstacles and sly opposition. The smooth Italian papal courtiers laughed behind his back at the pious but simple Dutchman. In Rome there was no Isabella to sweep away opponents as there had been for Ximenes in Spain. After a brief rule of twenty months, Adrian, exhausted by his fruitless struggles, died in 1523.

On his tombstone the cardinals caused these words to be chiseled: "Here lies Adrian VI whose supreme misfortune in life was that he was called upon to rule." He was the last non-Italian pope.

Pope Adrian did something unusual during his tenure. He commissioned one of his messengers to go to Germany and admit that the papal government in Rome was the chief source of corruption in the Church. As could be expected, this admission was ridiculed by the papal court at Rome. But it was a great act on the part of the honest and simple Dutch Adrian. And it was important, because

Pope Adrian VI

it was done by him in his official capacity as pope.

This act marks the beginning of a reform in the Roman Church. There were at that time a few spiritually minded men occupying high positions in the papal court. The example of Pope Adrian VI and his efforts to reform the Roman Church awakened in them a new zeal for reform.

5. The Council of Trent • Meanwhile, abuses continued to flourish in the Roman Church, and the Reformation spread. Emperor Charles was anxious to reunite the Protestants and the Catholics. He arranged a number of conferences in which leading Protestant and Catholic theologians took part. They discussed their differences but could not reach an agreement. Earnest Christians in the Roman Church continued to clamor for reform.

Finally Pope Paul III summoned a council. It met in a little city in the mountains of northern Italy called Trent from 1545 to 1563, although not continuously. There were two interruptions of several years. The Council of Trent is a milestone in the history of the Roman Catholic Church, for it marks a triumph for the papacy.

The Protestant churches in Germany, Switzerland, France, the Netherlands, England, and Scotland had formulated creeds in which they declared their faith. Now the Council which met in Trent formulated a creed for the Roman Church. A catechism was also adopted. Many of the abuses that had caused so much trouble were corrected. Provision was made for the better education of the Roman clergy. The supremacy of the papacy was established more firmly than ever.

A great reform had been brought about in the Roman Church, but that Church had not changed its essential character. Over against Protestantism the Roman Church in the Council of Trent had definitely and strongly upheld and reasserted its Catholic system. This self-reform of the Roman Church is often called the *Counter Reformation.*

For a number of years the heat of the Reformation had rendered the religious condition of the Church fluid. Now it had become solidified, and the lines were hard-set.

The churches of the Reformation now found arrayed against them a reformed and revived Roman Church. A terrific struggle was about to take place between Protestantism and Catholicism.

1. *Why had reform of the Church through reforming councils failed? What was generally the attitude of the Curia to reform?*

2. *How was Ximenes able to carry on reform in Spain? How did his reform movement differ from Luther's?*

3. *What was the relation of Charles V to the papacy? What were his intentions concerning its reform?*

4. *Why did Adrian VI fail to institute reform in the Church of Rome?*

5. *What specific reforms did the Council of Trent introduce? Why was it possible to get reforms such as those instituted now, when such were not possible previously?*

6. *How did the Council of Trent affect Protestant-Catholic relationships? Are Catholic relations to the separated Protestant churches the same as those to the separated Eastern Orthodox churches? See* The Riddle of Roman Catholicism *by Pelikan, Abingdon Press, Nashville, 1959, pp. 50 ff., 67 ff., and elsewhere.*

7. *What do you think of the idea of calling the Reformation by the name Protestant Revolution and calling the Counter Reformation the Catholic Reformation?*

8. *Make a list of the ecumenical councils with a brief statement of the main purpose of each. See the index of this book, or "councils" in* The New Shaff-Herzog Encyclopedia of Religious Knowledge.

CHAPTER 30

The Protestant Churches
Fight for Their Lives, 1546-1648

1. Charles V Tries to Uproot the Reformation • To understand the bitter struggle which was about to take place between the Catholics and the Protestants we shall have to review some things we already know. The emperor Charles never said much. He would think carefully before he spoke. But once, and perhaps only once in his life, he spoke right from the heart. That was immediately after the Diet of Worms, where Luther had defied the pope and emperor. Then the emperor vowed, "To root out heresy I shall stake my crown and my life." He kept his vow.

The emperor issued against Luther the Edict of Worms. That edict ordered his arrest and death. Luther would have been burned at the stake, as so many heretics before him had been, had not Frederick the Wise protected him.

This portrait of Charles V, Emperor of the Holy Roman Empire, was painted by Titian at Augsburg in 1548.

Immediately after the Diet of Worms the Reformation movement was still only a small and tender sapling. If the emperor had had his hands free, he could have pulled it up by the roots. But he had a war with France on his hands. Later he had to defend the Empire against the Turks.

At last, having defeated all his enemies, Charles was free to give his attention to the followers of Luther in Germany. In 1546, the year that Luther died, Charles launched his attack on the Protestants. But twenty-five years had passed since the Diet of Worms, and the Reformation had had time to grow. The sapling had become a tree. Now it would require lusty blows with an axe to cut it down. At first the emperer won some victories. It looked very dark for the cause of the Reformation. Charles even captured Wittenberg, the place where Luther had started the Reformation, and where he had lived and labored.

Just as the emperor was beginning to make progress against the Lutherans he suffered a sudden change of fortune. Maurice of Saxony, who was at first one of his staunchest supporters, turned against him. He might have made the emperor prisoner, but he let him escape. Asked why he did that, Maurice answered, "I did not have a cage good enough for so fine a bird."

In 1555 the emperor found himself in such straits that he was forced to make the Peace of Augsburg with the Lutherans. The German Empire consisted of a large number of countries ruled over by princes. By the Peace of Augsburg each prince in Germany received the right to choose between Lutheranism and Catholicism. The people in each country had to accept the religion chosen by their prince.

2. The Reformation Movement Halts • For a time Protestantism swept everything before it. This was in large part due to the furious, headlong attack of Luther, aided by Zwingli, Calvin, and a host of lesser Reformers and also by the carelessness of the popes and the continuing corruption of the Roman Church. As a result the gigantic old edifice of the Roman Church was rocking on its foundations. For a while it seemed that it might collapse in utter ruin.

Then, as suddenly as it had started, the Reformation movement was brought to a dead standstill. There were many causes.

The first was Luther's stand in the Peasants' War of 1525. The peasants in Germany were heavily oppressed by the nobles and higher clergy. They rose up in protest in the name of "God's justice." They had a right to protest, and Luther was in sympathy with them. But when under the leadership of fanatics they began to kill and destroy, Luther turned against them and urged the government to put down their uprising with a firm hand. From that moment the lower classes turned their backs upon Luther and the Reformation. Thereafter the Reformation was confined to the middle and upper classes in Germany.

The second cause was the influence of the Anabaptists. Some of the early Anabaptists were fanatics. They went much further in their opposition to Catholic doctrine and practice than either Luther or Calvin. They threatened to upset not only the old ecclesiastical order, but also the social and political order. The Romanists were not slow to see their opportunity. They said that the doctrines of the Reformation would upset all order and authority not only in the Church but in the State and society as well. This caused many of the upper classes to remain in the Roman Church.

A third cause was the division among the Protestants. Again the Romanists were not slow to take advantage of this development. To choose intelligently and sincerely between Luther, Zwingli, and Calvin required prayerful study and thinking. The Romanists induced many who were too lazy and indifferent or unable to think for themselves to stay in the Roman Church, and let the Church do the thinking for them.

A fourth cause was the misapplication of Luther's central doctrine of justification by faith alone without good works. This misapplication led to moral conditions even worse than they had been under Rome. Many turned the "liberty of a Christian man" into license. They reasoned that if salvation was not earned by good works there was no need to live a good life. The Romanists used this sad development as an argument against Luther's doctrine. This development was a bitter disappointment to Luther himself.

This development in the land of Luther may have been one of the things that steeled Calvin's hand when he introduced his strict church discipline in Geneva. His reason for doing this may partly have been his desire to prevent German conditions in Geneva, and thereby ward off moral reproach against the Reformation.

Another cause was the separation of the Protestants. The Protestants in France, the Netherlands, and Scotland were doctrinally united by their Calvinistic creeds, but they were geographically far apart. The Lutherans were doctrinally separated from the Calvinists, and the Peace of Augsburg separated them politically also, since it applied only to the Lutheran Protestants in Germany.

3. A Revitalized Catholicism • A major cause for the slowing down of the Reformation movement was the reform and revitalizing of the Roman Church. This Church was once more ready to move forward. It had equipped itself with three new and powerful weapons: the Index, the Spanish Inquisition, and the Order of Jesuits, organized by the Spaniard Ignatius Loyola. Divided and inwardly weakened, Protestantism was

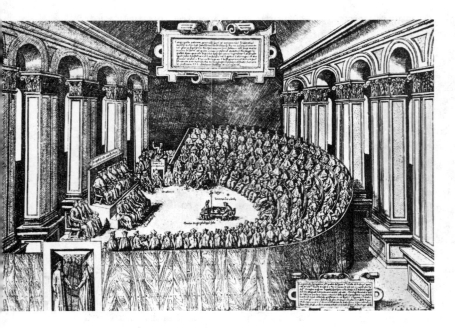

A Session
of the Council
of Trent

From a copper
engraving
published
in Vienna
in 1565

now opposed by this unified Catholicism which had recovered from the shock of the reformation movement.

In addition to the many actions of the Council of Trent which we studied in the previous chapter, this Council also decided to draw up a list of forbidden books. This list, called the *Index,* was to protect the Catholic reader from books the Catholic Church regarded as false or harmful. In the early days of the Reformation Luther's and Calvin's writings had circulated freely throughout Europe. Now Protestant writings were put on the Index, and the spread of Protestant ideas was seriously curtailed.

The Inquisition or "Holy Office" was the court of the Roman Church for the detection and punishment of those whose opinions differed from the doctrine of the Church. The head of the Holy Office was the grand inquisitor who was ac-

countable directly to the pope. Under him were many inquisitors, notaries, and legal consultors, as well as servants and jailers. The Inquisition quickly put out the feeble sparks of Protestantism in Italy and Spain. Those who had joined the Reformation were jailed, killed, or driven to flight.

Loyola, a Spanish soldier, was wounded in battle in 1521. While recovering his health, he was given *The Lives of the Saints* to read. The result was that he resolved to give up his life of soldiering and become an active follower of Christ. After making a pilgrimage to Palestine, he went to the University of Paris in 1528 to study for the priesthood.

Here he met Francis Xavier. In 1534 these two established the Society of Jesus. Their purpose was to win people back to the Catholic Church. They were largely responsible for the recovery of most of

The Formation
of the Order
of Jesuits

Poland and Austria and parts of Southern Germany for Catholicism and for keeping Bavaria, Belgium, and Ireland in the Catholic fold. The Jesuits performed extensive missionary work in North and South America.

The name *Counter Reformation* is often given to these various factors which checked the progress of the Reformation and won back much of the territory and prestige which the Catholic Church had lost. In a narrower sense the name *Counter Reformation* refers only to the reform and revival of the Roman Church.

The Roman Church now set about regaining what it had lost. The protecting shield of the Peace of Augsburg covered only the Lutheran Protestants in Germany. It did not cover the Calvinistic Protestants in France and the Netherlands. These now had to bear the brunt of Catholic attack. And Calvin, their great and inspiring leader, was dead.

In one of the inner courtyards of a Jesuit seminary, students kneel and pray the "Angelus." In the center of the courtyard is a statue of Ignatius Loyola.

Philip Gendreau

Charles IX aids in slaying the Huguenots. The frenzied king fires on the fleeing victims of the St. Bartholomew's Day massacre.

4. The Huguenots Fight for Their Lives, 1562–1629 • France, like Germany, was divided between Catholics and Protestants. The Huguenots formed a strong party. They were a prosperous, intelligent class and many of them belonged to the nobility, but they were in a minority.

Both Catholics and Protestants tried to control the government. Young Charles IX and his regent mother, Catherine de Medici, favored first one side and then the other. Civil war broke out between the two religious parties in 1562. The Huguenots defended themselves with varying success.

In 1570 a brief peace was made. The Huguenots were given certain towns in which they were free to defend themselves. For a time Admiral de Coligny, the leader of the Huguenots, acted as a sort of prime minister to Charles and his mother. Henry of Bourbon, a Protestant, was to marry Margaret, the sister of Charles. Thus it was possible that this Henry might become ruler of France.

The Catholic extremists alarmed Catherine with reports that the Huguenots were plotting to take the throne. Catherine convinced the innocent king of this, and a plot was formed for a treacherous and wholesale massacre.

All of the leading Huguenots were invited to Paris for the marriage of Henry and Margaret. In the early morning of August 24, 1572, Saint Bartholomew's Day, bells were rung in the city of Paris as a signal for the massacre to begin. For three days and nights the massacre went on. No fewer than two thousand Protestants were murdered in Paris, and, as the massacre extended to other cities, over ten thousand throughout the country. One of the first victims was the noble leader of the Huguenots, Gaspard de Coligny. Henry of Bourbon, however, escaped. It was one of the foulest crimes recorded in history.

Rather than ending the civil war, the massacre of St. Bartholomew gave it new impetus. The conflict continued into the reign of Henry III who succeeded his brother Charles. It was a three-cornered conflict between three Henry's: Henry of Guise, the Catholic leader; King Henry III, who tried to follow a moderate course; and Henry of Bourbon and Navarre, the Protestant leader.

Henry of Guise was murdered on orders of Henry III, who in turn was assassinated in revenge. Thus in 1589

Catherine de Medici
views the victims
of the St. Bartholomew's
Day massacre.

Ewing Galloway

Henry of Bourbon had a clear title to the throne. Because most of the people were Catholic and would not tolerate a Protestant king, Henry declared himself a Catholic in 1593 and in 1594 entered Paris in triumph as King Henry IV.

Though no longer a Protestant, Henry did not forget his former comrades. In 1598 he issued the *Edict of Nantes,* which granted the Huguenots freedom of private worship, civil rights, and the right to public worship in two hundred towns and three thousand castles. Henry IV was assassinated in 1610 and the kingdom was again torn by warring factions. Many of the finest citizens of France fled to other countries and to the New World.

With the capture in 1629 of La Rochelle, the last Protestant stronghold, the political power of the Huguenots in France was broken. They continued to exist, however, as a religious Protestant body.

5. The Protestants in the Netherlands, 1568–1609 • Protestants were burned at the stake as heretics in Italy, Spain, France, England, and Scotland. But in no country did so many persons suffer martyrdom for their faith as in the Netherlands.

Charles V, Emperor of Germany, was also king of Spain and lord of the Netherlands. In his reign and the first years of the reign of his son Philip II, King of Spain, more than 18,000 persons in the Netherlands fell victim to the Spanish Inquisition. In an attempt to force them to a confession of heresy both men and women were horribly tortured. Then the

Members of a tribunal attempt through torture to make a prisoner confess heresy.

Ewing Galloway

men were burned, the women were drowned or buried alive.

The tyranny and cruelty of King Philip II of Spain became unbearable. Spain was at that time the most powerful country in Europe. Holland was a very small country. But at last in 1568 the people of the Netherlands under the leadership of one of the greatest heroes of the Reformation, William the Silent, Prince of Orange, rose in revolt against Spain. The Calvinists of Holland became the champions of Protestantism for all the world. Through long dark days the Dutch went on fighting in the face of terrific odds. In 1584 William the Silent fell victim to an assassin's bullet.

Elizabeth, Queen of England, was friendly to the Protestant cause. Without declaring war against Spain, she had been

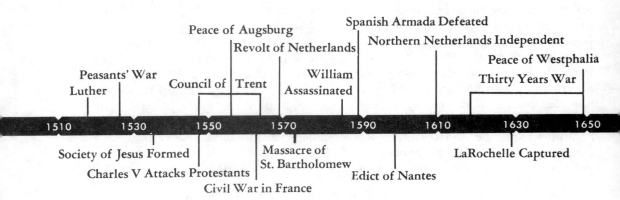

Courtesy Netherlands
Information Center

William the Silent
Prince of Orange and Count of Nassau

terrible blow. The Dutch under Prince Maurice, son of William the Silent, continued the war until 1609 when Spain, in a Twelve Years' Truce, practically acknowledged the independence of the Northern Netherlands, the Dutch Republic.

6. The Thirty Years' War in Germany • Since 1555 Germany, under the terms of the Peace of Augsburg, had been enjoying comparative peace. Then, in 1618, the Peace of Augsburg was broken. More than once the struggle looked hopeless for the Protestants. At the most

"The Lily Among the Thorns" was the symbol used by the Reformed Church in the sixteenth century. The quotation around the margin is from the *Song of Solomon.*

Courtesy Church Herald

lending aid to the Dutch. The Catholics laid many plots to assassinate her, but all were in vain.

Now King Philip of Spain formed a grandiose plan. He built an enormous fleet, which the Spaniards called the "Invincible Armada." With this fleet Philip would invade England. And with that country conquered, so he thought, it would be easy to put down the rebellion in the Netherlands. But the English with the help of the Dutch defeated the Spanish Armada. Most of what was left of it was wrecked by storms on the coasts of Scotland and Ireland. Only a miserable remnant of the once proud Armada returned to the ports of Spain.

The power of Spain had suffered a

SCOTLAND

SWEDEN

IRELAND

ENGLAND

Lutherans
Anglicans
Roman
Catholics
Calvinists

GERMANY

POLAND

FRANCE

HUNGARY

PORTUGAL

SPAIN

ITALY

THE
RELIGIOUS SITUATION
IN 1648

critical moment Gustavus Adolphus, King of Sweden, another great hero of the Reformation, stepped in to save the day for Protestantism. After thirty years of the most savage fighting the Peace of Westphalia was concluded in 1648. The terms of this treaty were much like those of the Peace of Augsburg, except that religious toleration in Germany was now extended to include the Calvinists as well as the Lutherans. As under the former treaty,

each ruler was to determine the religion of his own realm. It had been a devastating war. In Germany alone the population was reduced from fifteen million to less than five million.

7. The Boundaries Become Fixed • As we look back over the period we have studied, we see that the churches of the Reformation passed through a period of bloody martyrdom between the years

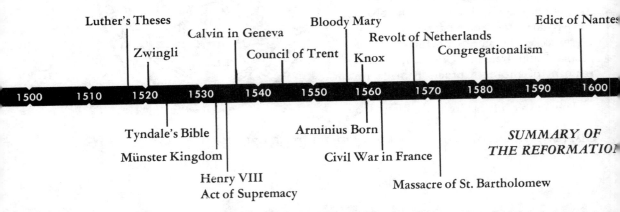

Luther's Theses

Bloody Mary

Edict of Nantes

Calvin in Geneva

Revolt of Netherlands

Zwingli

Council of Trent

Knox

Congregationalism

1500 1510 1520 1530 1540 1550 1560 1570 1580 1590 1600

Tyndale's Bible

Arminius Born

SUMMARY OF

Münster Kingdom

Civil War in France

THE REFORMATION

Henry VIII
Act of Supremacy

Massacre of St. Bartholomew

Courtesy Netherlands Information Bureau

The University of Leyden was established by William the Silent to memorialize the heroism of its citizens. Leyden was besieged by Spanish troops from October 31, 1573, to March 21, 1574. When the siege was lifted, the city did not expect a resumption, and it was unprepared for the terrible siege from May 26 to October 3, 1574. Starvation and the plague took a high toll, but the city refused to surrender. Its fall would have doomed all of Holland. William ordered dikes broken in July, but months of fighting were needed to capture key dikes. Even then a strong west gale had to bring the ocean in before the "Sea Beggars" could relieve the city.

1520 and 1562. And following that, from 1562 to 1648, the Protestants had to wage war for their very existence. Martyrdom was suffered mainly by the Calvinistic Protestants, and it was they who from 1562 to 1618 bore the brunt of the war against the Catholics. Then from 1618 to 1648 the Lutherans were also forced into war. During these years German, Danish, and Swedish Lutherans and the Dutch Calvinists defended the Protestant cause.

When the wars between Catholics and Protestants came to an end with the Peace of Westphalia in 1648, the geographical extent of the Roman and Protestant churches had become fairly well fixed. There have been no major changes since, and the boundaries are today pretty much what they became at that time. (See map.)

At this time little was heard of the Church in the East. Under the Turks the members of the Greek Church in Asia Minor and the Balkan Peninsula were heavily oppressed. In spite of persecu-

The Archangelsky Cathedral in the
Moscow Kremlin

Patriarch Alexis of Moscow and All Russia greets
and blesses the believers on Easter Sunday, 1959.

tion, however, which was met with heroic resistance, the Church continued to exist in the Balkan countries through the centuries and down to the present time. But although the Greek Orthodox Church was heavily oppressed in the countries of its origin, in Russia it grew until it embraced nearly the entire population.

1. *What were the provisions of the Peace of Augsburg?*
2. *List and explain the causes for the halt in the progress of the Reformation.*
3. *Does the division of Protestant churches still do them harm?*
4. *What Catholic forces worked toward regaining their losses?*
5. *Why did Spain as a nation have something to say about religious affairs in the Netherlands?*
6. *The Thirty Years' War (1618–1648) was one of the most destructive wars ever fought in Europe. Was this really a religious war, or were there political complications?*
7. *Identify: Peace of Westphalia, 1572, Edict of Nantes.*
8. *Investigate the story of the St. Bartholomew's Day massacre.*
9. *Do you think that Henry of Bourbon did right in renouncing his Protestant faith in order to become King of France, where he was instrumental in helping the Protestants?*
10. *Find out what you can on the Peasants' War to decide what attitude you would have taken if you had been Luther. To what extent is Christianity today a middle and upper class religion?*
11. *Make a report on "The Lost Colony" of Huguenots which Coligny as Admiral of the French fleet brought to Florida.*

part four

The Church
After the Reformation

Part Four

THE CHURCH AFTER THE REFORMATION

The Reformation was a tremendous upheaval. It was an upheaval not only in the Church, but also in the State, in economics, in education, and in culture. The age of the Reformation was the sixteenth century, but all through the seventeenth century the life of Church and State continued to ferment, especially in England.

The Word of God, whether spoken or written, has always been a basic factor in the life and growth of the Church. From the preaching of Peter at Pentecost through the days of Chrysostom and Ambrose to the preaching of Luther and Calvin, the Word has been of prime importance in maintaining and building the Church.

All Christians claim that they derive their teachings from the Bible, and yet there are many great differences in understanding and explaining the Bible. The final question is therefore: What does one think is the *meaning* of the Bible? Many of the developments in the Roman Church were due to faulty explanations of the meaning of the Bible that came to be accepted by that church. The Reformers acted because they came to a different understanding of the meaning of the Bible.

Since the Reformation the various branches of the Church have moved along one of these four lines: some hold to the confession as formulated by the Council of Trent, some hold to the confessions of the great historic Protestant churches, some have departed more or less from these explanations, and some have entirely given up the Bible as the infallible Word of God.

In this section of our book we shall see the rise of the Congregational, Baptist, Methodist, and Moravian Churches. We shall note many departures from historic Protestantism and the emergence of a false theology called Modernism. Conditions and movements in the established churches of western European countries will conclude this unit.

CHAPTER *31*

The Church in England
Continues to Ferment, 1558-1689

1. The Reformation in England Is Prolonged • We have seen that the history of the Church in England presents certain peculiarities. One of these is that the Reformation in England was more political than religious, and stressed organization more than doctrine.

The continued unrest and change in the Church of England, after the life of the other churches of the Reformation had become more or less settled, is another peculiarity. This peculiarity is due to the fact that the mighty influence of Calvin came to be felt strongly in the

Brown Brothers

Queen Elizabeth

Church of England a good deal later than in the churches in France, the Netherlands, and Scotland.

2. The Influence of Calvin Is Felt • The Elizabethan Settlement of 1563 did not settle the affairs of the Church in England. During the persecutions of Bloody Mary many Protestants who had fled to Geneva came under the spell of Calvin. When in 1558 Elizabeth succeeded Mary to the throne of England, they returned, fired with enthusiasm for the ideas and ideals of the great French Reformer. So almost from the beginning of Elizabeth's reign, voices were heard advocating a much more thoroughgoing reformation. The Settlement of 1563 did not satisfy

them at all. Because they wished to see the Church purified much more thoroughly, these members of the Church of England were called *Puritans.*

3. The Puritans Desire to Reform the Church of England • The Puritans wished to see installed in every parish an earnest and spiritually minded pastor able to preach. They demanded the abolition of the clerical dress then in vogue, of kneeling at the Lord's Supper, of the ring ceremony at weddings, and of the use of the sign of the cross at baptism.

In the clerical dress then in use they saw the claim of the clergy to powers which reminded them of the power of Catholic priests. In kneeling at the Lord's Supper they saw adoration of the physical presence of Christ as taught in the Catholic doctrine of transubstantiation. The ring ceremony at weddings signified to them the claim of Catholics that marriage is a sacrament. The sign of the cross at baptism was to them a Catholic superstition. They wished to see the Church purified of this old leaven of Catholicism.

Before long they went even further in their demands for the purification of the Church. They wished to see in each parish elders chosen to exercise discipline. They wished to have the ministers chosen by the people and the office of bishop abolished. All ministers, they believed, should be on an equal footing. This amounted to a demand for the presbyterian form of church government in place of the episcopalian.

The leader of the Puritan movement was Thomas Cartwright. He was a theological professor in the University of Cambridge. The chief opponent of Puritanism in its early stages was John Whitgift, and through his influence Cartwright was deprived of his professorship. Thereafter Cartwright led a wandering and persecuted life, but he continued to labor tirelessly for the cause of Presbyterian Puritanism.

Although the Puritans objected strongly to the episcopalian form of church government and to many of the rites and ceremonies of the Church of England, they were strongly opposed to separation from that Church. They wished to stay in that Church and to reform it from within, molding it after the pattern of Calvin's church in Geneva.

4. The Separatists Leave the Church of England

The Separatists saw that the process of reforming the Episcopal Church of England from within would at best be long and tedious, if not entirely hopeless. They therefore separated themselves from the Church of England and became known as *Separatists* or *Dissenters*. In the matter of church government they believed not only that each local church or congregation is a complete church in itself, but also that no church should have anything to say about any other church. Because they believed that all local churches should be independent of each other, they were called *Congregationalists* or *Independents*.

Both those who remained in the Church of England and those who separated from it were Calvinists in doctrine.

Those American colonists who established the Plymouth Colony in 1620 were Separatists and were called Pilgrims. Those who came nine years later and established the Massachusetts Bay Colony were Puritans.

5. The Puritans Gain the Upper Hand

For almost forty years after the death of Queen Elizabeth the Puritans were oppressed and persecuted. But in the "Long Parliament" which met in 1640 the Presbyterian Puritans finally found themselves in the majority. They immediately set themselves the task of "cleaning house." The two chief oppressors of the Puritans—the Earl of Strafford and Archbishop Laud—were brought to trial, condemned, and executed by beheading.

King Charles did not like the turn of events. He decided to seize on a charge of high treason the five members of Parliament who were the leaders of the opposition. The House of Commons refused to give them up.

The king resolved to use military force to compel Parliament to submit. He left London and raised the royal flag at Nottingham. With this act he plunged England into civil war.

On the side of the king were the majority of the nobles and the country gentlemen. Because of their daring horsemanship the king's men were called *Cavaliers*. On the side of Parliament were the shopkeepers, small farmers, and a few men of high rank. Because the king's Cavaliers wore long flowing locks, those opposing them wore their hair closely cropped so that it showed the shape of the head. For that reason they were, in ridicule, called *Roundheads*.

The course of the war at first favored the king. One of the gentlemen farmers in the army of Parliament was Oliver Cromwell. With the eye of genius he saw at a glance what was the trouble. Said he to Hampden, who was a Puritan and a

Brown Brothers

Cromwell at Marston Moor

member of Parliament, "A set of poor tapsters and town apprentices cannot fight men of honor successfully."

Cromwell is one of the great characters of history. As colonel of a troop of cavalry he showed great skill and courage. His regiment became famous as Cromwell's Ironsides. It was never defeated. It was composed entirely of "men of religion." They did not swear or drink. They advanced to the charge singing psalms.

An army of twenty-one thousand men, patterned after the Ironsides, was organized. It was called the New Model. It was a body of religious enthusiasts such as the world had not seen since the days of the Crusades. Most of the soldiers of this army were fervent, God-fearing, psalm-singing Puritans. When not fighting they studied the Bible, prayed, and sang hymns.

The Cavaliers were scattered as chaff

before the wind in the Battle of Naseby. The king surrendered; he was tried and found guilty as a tyrant, traitor, murderer, and public enemy, and was condemned to death. On January 30, 1649, Charles I ascended the scaffold in front of the royal palace of Whitehall in London, where a great multitude had assembled to witness the execution.

6. The Westminster Assembly • While the war was running its course, Parliament set itself the task of making changes in the Church. In 1643 it abolished the episcopal form of church government. It called an assembly of one hundred twenty-one clergymen and thirty laymen to provide a new creed and form of church government. This Westminster Assembly (so called because it met in Westminster) contained a few Episcopalians and Congregationalists, but the overwhelming majority were Presbyterian Puritans. Since the Scotch were giving aid in the war, a number of Scottish commissioners were given a seat in the Westminster Assembly. They had no vote, but they exercised a strong influence.

The Westminster Assembly turned out to be one of the history-making assemblies of the Church. It prepared a *Directory of Worship* to replace the Episcopal Prayer Book. This order of worship is still used in orthodox Presbyterian and Congregational churches today. The Assembly drew up the confession which has become famous as the *Westminster Confession*. It was the last of the great creeds of Protestantism to come out of the Reformation. The Assembly also prepared a *Larger Catechism* for pulpit exposition, and a *Shorter Catechism* for the teaching of children.

PART FOUR: THE CHURCH AFTER THE REFORMATION

King Charles I walks from St. James Palace to his execution at Whitehall on January 30, 1649.

Bettmann Archive

The Westminster Assembly did its work thoroughly and well. The Westminster Confession and the two Westminster Catechisms are excellent presentations of Calvinistic or Reformed doctrine.

Ewing Galloway

Oliver Cromwell

By 1648 Parliament had accepted these various documents—although certain modifications were made in the Westminster Confession. The Confession was also adopted by the General Assembly of Scotland. The work of reforming the Church in England in the Calvinistic sense was completed in the same year that the Thirty Years' War on the Continent came to an end with the Peace of Westphalia.

7. Puritan Domination Ends • After its victory at Naseby and the death of Charles I, the army was supreme. It was composed mostly of Independents. Cromwell himself was sympathetic toward Congregationalism. Parliament had decreed that the form of government of the Church of England should be presbyterian. But due to the pressure of the army the full establishment of Presbyterianism in England was not possible.

From 1649–1653 England was a commonwealth or republic. Then Cromwell was made Lord Protector, and England had practically a military dictatorship.

Charles II is
brought back
to England.

Under Cromwell's rule there was a large measure of religious liberty for all religious bodies, especially for all Nonconformists and Dissenters. Cromwell even befriended the Quakers, who were, generally speaking, hated of all men. Since the beginning of the Civil War, however, some two thousand members of the Episcopal clergy had been deprived of their means of livelihood and had suffered great hardship.

8. The Restoration • On September 3, 1658, Cromwell died. His son Richard could not fill his father's shoes. The great mass of the English people were dissatisfied under the yoke of rigid Puritanism, and the son of Charles I was brought back to England and crowned king as Charles II. This return of the House of Stuart to the throne of England is known as the *Restoration* of 1660.

The first act of the Parliament chosen after the Restoration was to proclaim a pardon to all who had fought against King Charles I in the Civil War. The only persons excepted were the members of the High Court of Justice which had sent Charles I to the block.

In May, 1662, Parliament, now strongly Anglican, passed a new Act of Uniformity. Some six hundred changes were made in the *Directory of Worship* or *Prayer Book,* all in the direction away from Puritanism. The use of any form of church service other than that prescribed in this newly revised *Prayer Book* was forbidden. Those who refused to obey were heavily punished. Two thousand Presbyterian clergymen who had refused to conform were driven from their parishes and reduced to poverty.

The Scottish Parliament vied with that of England in persecution of the Dissenters. The Covenanters, as the Scottish Protestants were called, were hunted with bugles and bloodhounds like so many deer. Those who gathered secretly in glens and caves to worship God were hanged and drowned without mercy.

Among the multitude who suffered in England for the sake of their faith was a poor tinker named John Bunyan. He had served against the king in the civil wars. Later he was converted to Puritanism and became a traveling preacher. He was arrested and convicted of having "abstained from coming to church," and was thrown into Bedford jail—a "squalid Denn." While lingering in that jail for twelve years he wrote his famous *Pilgrim's Progress.*

Another Puritan, a man of high rank, excellent education, and rare gifts, was John Milton. In blindness, loneliness, and poverty he wrote *Paradise Lost,* the great Christian epic poem.

As a result of persecution the Puritans now became a party outside the Church of England. They had been a group who wished to stay in the Church of England and reform it. Now they were forced into the position which had been taken by the Separatists. They too had become Dissenters.

During his entire life Charles II swayed

John Bunyan and His Blind Child at the Gate of Bedford Gaol

between unbelief and superstitious Catholicism, but on his deathbed in 1685 he professed the Roman Catholic faith. He was succeeded by his brother James II, who was a professed and earnest Catholic. The new king's great object was to restore England to Catholicism. He plotted with Louis XIV, the king of France who re-

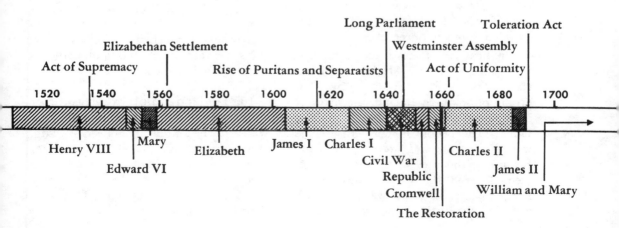

Brown Brothers

The Tower of London had many occupants and many changes of occupants
during these times of turmoil.

voked the Edict of Nantes, to bring this about. Religious and political liberty were at stake.

9. William and Mary • Now in this dark hour William III of the Netherlands came forward as the champion of Protestantism against Louis XIV of France. His wife, Mary, was the daughter of James II. In their distress the English appealed to William. Accompanied by an army he crossed the sea from Holland in 1688 and drove out his father-in-law, James II. He and Mary were crowned king and queen of England.

The next year James made an attempt to regain his throne. He landed in Ireland supported by a French army. The people of southern Ireland, the majority of whom were Catholics, took the side of James. The people in northern Ireland were Protestants and stood by William. Because of this they were called Orangemen. In 1690 the decisive battle of the Boyne took place. James waited on a hill, watching the battle from a safe distance.

When he saw that his army was utterly defeated he fled to France. William, on the other hand, showed great courage and leadership. Although wounded, he led his soldiers in person. An Irish officer cried to one of William's soldiers, "Change kings with us and we'll fight you over again."

As a result of his brave and determined stand William had saved Holland, England, and America for Protestantism and liberty against the Catholicism and despotism of Louis XIV of France and James II of England. After this there were no more wars in which the religious differences between Protestants and Catholics were the main issue.

10. England Enjoys a Measure of Toleration • When William and Mary were crowned king and queen of England, four hundred members of the clergy of the Church of England, among them seven bishops, refused the oath of allegiance to the new sovereigns. They were deprived of their offices.

PART FOUR: THE CHURCH AFTER THE REFORMATION

Courtesy
Netherlands Information Service

William III

Religious toleration was now granted to all Protestant Dissenters. By the Toleration Act of 1689 freedom of worship was granted to those who were willing to: (1) swear the oath of allegiance to William and Mary; (2) reject the jurisdiction of the pope, transubstantiation, the mass, the invocation of the Virgin and saints; and (3) subscribe to the doctrinal portions of the Thirty-nine Articles. Various denominations of Protestant Dissenters could exist freely and openly alongside the established and endowed Episcopal Church of England. The Dissenters—Presbyterians, Congregationalists, Baptists, and Quakers—formed about one-tenth of the population of England at this time.

The Toleration Act did not cover the Roman Catholics or those who denied the Trinity.

1. *In what ways did the Puritans wish to change the Church of England? Were these changes meaningful or merely matters of form? Why was there a strong reaction against Puritan domination?*

2. *In what respect did the ordinary Puritans and the Congregationalists differ?*

3. *Notice in the Revolution of 1648 how religion and politics were mixed in England. Was Cromwell a military, political, or religious leader?*

4. *Be sure to read some of the Westminster Catechism. In what ways does it differ from the Heidelberg Catechism?*

5. *Identify: Westminster Assembly, Long Parliament, Separatists, Thomas Cartwright, John Bunyan, Charles II, Roundheads, Cavaliers, Toleration Act.*

6. *Why was William III, a ruler of Holland, invited to become king of England?*

7. *Why was England among the first of the nations to give a large measure of religious toleration?*

On May 21, 1536, the *Edicts of Reformation* were ratified by the people of Geneva.

German bas-relief: Frederick, the founder of the Prussian state, is shown welcoming the Huguenots exiled when the Edict of Nantes was repealed. Above is engraved part of the *Edict of Potsdam*.

Frederick William (1620–1688)

Holland bas-relief: On July 26, 1581, the States-General at the Hague adopted the *Declaration of Independence of the United Provinces* (Northern Netherlands).

Willi the Sil (1533–1

The background is a section of the former city wall. In front of the entire monument is the water-filled moat. On each side of the monument, two stones bear the names of Luther and Zwingli.

THE INTERNATIONAL MONUMENT

Scottish bas-relief: John Knox is shown preaching the Reformation in St. Giles Church, Edinburgh, Scotland.

Roger Williams (1604–1638)

American bas-Williams had sa the *Mayflower* i on which shi *Mayflower Co* was signed

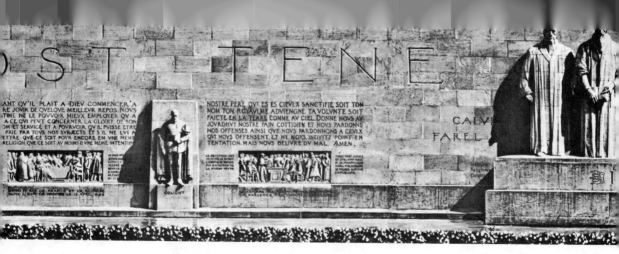

ench bas-relief: enry IV, King of ance and Navarre, gning the *Edict of antes,* April 13, 1598. e inscription is the eamble of the Edict.

Gaspard de Coligny (1517–1572)

Swiss bas-relief: On February 22, 1534, the first child is presented for Reformed baptism. Viret is in the pulpit; Farel is seated behind him.

Contributions for the construction of this memorial came from Reformed congregations throughout the world. After Geneva itself, the largest contribution came from the Reformed churches in Hungary.

EFORMATION: *POST TENEBRAS LUX*

Oliver romwell 99–1658)

English bas-relief: William and Mary are presented with the crown, together with the *Declaration of Rights of the English People.*

Etienne Bocskay (1556–1606)

Hungarian bas-relief: Bocskay brings to the Diet of Kassa the signed *Treaty of Vienna.*

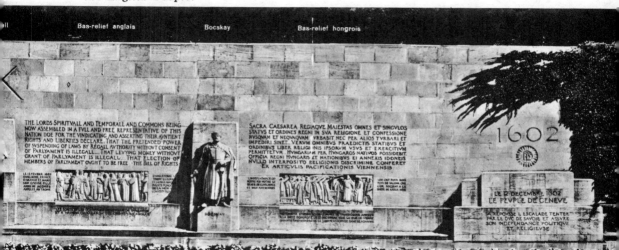

CHAPTER 32

The Congregationalists;
The Baptists

1. Robert Browne • Of all the new denominations that arose since the Reformation, the Congregationalists, or Independents, departed the least from historic Protestantism. In doctrine and worship they were Calvinists. Their departure was in the matter of church government.

In order to trace the history of this important group we shall have to go back to the sixteenth century.

The first one who really spread the Congregational ideas in England was Robert Browne. In 1581, during the reign of Queen Elizabeth, he organized a Congregational church in Norwich, and was cast into prison. When he was set free, he and the majority of his congregation fled to Middelburg in the Netherlands. That little country was a haven of refuge for all the persecuted of Europe. In course of time many other groups of English Separatists found safety there.

While he was in Middelburg, Browne published *A Booke Which Sheweth the Life and Manners of All True Christians.* In this work Browne gave an exposition of Congregational principles. The principles of church government expressed and explained by Browne are held by the Congregationalists to this day.

Briefly stated, the main ideas of Congregationalism are these: Each local church is self-governing. It chooses its own pastor, teacher, elders, and deacons. Churches have no authority over each other, but it is their privilege and duty to help each other. It is highly desirable that from time to time they hold assemblies in which all the churches are represented, and in which matters of concern to all are carefully considered and discussed. The churches, however, are not required to adopt the decisions of the assemblies.

2. Congregationalism Grows • History has proved again and again that imprisonment is a means of encouraging rather than stopping a movement. In 1587 Henry Barrowe, a London lawyer, and John Greenwood, a clergyman, were imprisoned for holding Separatist meetings in London. While they were in prison they wrote certain treatises in which they attacked both Anglicans and Puritans, and set forth the principles of Congregationalism. These treatises were smuggled into Holland, where they were printed. By means of these, the principles of Congregationalism were spread and a number of followers were gained.

One of those converted to Congregationalism by the writings of Barrowe and Greenwood was a Puritan minister, Francis Johnson. In 1592 a Congregational Church was organized in London; Johnson was chosen to be its pastor and Greenwood its teacher. In the spring of the following year Barrowe and Greenwood were hanged for denying the supremacy of Queen Elizabeth in church affairs. Parliament then passed a statute decreeing banishment for all who would not submit to the supremacy of the queen's authority over the Church, refused to attend services in the established Church of England, or attended religious meetings where a form of worship other than that prescribed by the *Prayer Book* was used. Most of the London Congregationalists now fled to Amsterdam, where Johnson continued as their pastor.

3. A New English Bible • In 1603 James I succeeded Elizabeth upon the throne of England. At once the Puritans addressed to the new king a petition in which they set forth some very moderate requests. A conference between bishops and Puritans was held in the presence of the king. No changes in the affairs of the Church desired by the Puritans were granted. But one thing of very great importance was granted—a new translation of the Bible. The result was the *King James Bible,* published in 1611. This Bible is the translation which has until recent times been in universal use among all English-speaking people.

The conference between the Anglican bishops and the Puritans ended in a great

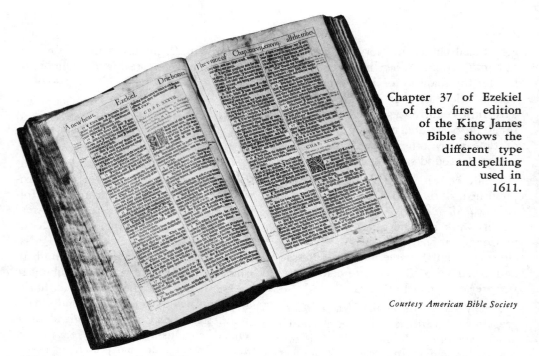

victory for the Anglicans. The Puritans and Separatists were ordered to conform.

4. Smyth, Brewster, and Robinson •

In 1602, the last year of the reign of Queen Elizabeth, there arose a Separatist movement which had a small and humble beginning, but which was destined to have far-reaching results of great importance.

John Smyth had been a clergyman in the Church of England. He adopted Separatist principles, and gathered a congregation in Gainsborough. Soon members were gained in neighboring rural districts, and a second congregation gathered in the home of William Brewster at Scrooby. Around the year 1604 the learned and lovable John Robinson became the pastor of the Scrooby congregation. Robinson, too, had been a clergyman in the Church of England, but he also had adopted Separatist principles.

The hand of oppression was heavy upon the Gainsborough congregation. Probably in the year 1607 this congregation sought refuge in Amsterdam. In 1609 the Scrooby congregation, under the leadership of Robinson and Brewster, removed to Leyden in the Netherlands. The importance of this Congregational church in Leyden will become apparent when we consider the history of the Church in the New World.

5. The Baptists •

John Smyth, who with his Congregational church of Gainsborough had sought refuge in Amsterdam, became acquainted with the Mennonites. Under their influence he adopted Baptist principles. A portion of his church returned to England, and in 1611 or 1612 established in London the first permanent Baptist church in England.

In the Netherlands the Baptists also had been influenced by Arminianism, which rejected the doctrine of election.

The Baptists who adopted Arminianism received the name of *General Baptists.*

Congregationalism was permanently replanted in England when Henry Jacob, who had belonged to the Congregational church of Robinson in Leyden established a Congregational church in Southwark. A portion of this church seceded in 1633, and its members received the name of *Particular Baptists.* They were in many ways Calvinists, but they believed in adult baptism.

6. Cromwell Favors Congregationalism • Cromwell did not belong to any church, but he leaned heavily toward Congregationalism. When he came into power he strongly favored the Congregationalists. He made John Owen, the ablest theologian among the Congregationalists of his day, dean of Christ Church and vice-chancellor of the University of Oxford. Many other Congregationalists were elevated to high positions.

7. The Westminster Confession Is Adopted • Under Cromwell's patronage Congregationalism greatly increased in importance, but to this time the Congregationalists were not organized as a denomination. An assembly of Congregational elders was now summoned to prepare a confession of faith. Twenty-six days after Cromwell's death the Assembly met in the Savoy Palace in London on September 29, 1658. This synod adopted a *Declaration of Faith and Order Owned and Practised in the Congregational Churches.* Almost all the leading members of this synod had been members of the Westminster Assembly. So they adopted the Calvinistic Westminster Confession almost bodily as their confession.

A Plaque in Memory of Rev. John Robinson on St. Peter's Church at Leyden, the Netherlands

The Savoy Declaration includes a section which deals with the "Institution of Churches and the Order Appointed in Them by Jesus Christ." This section declares in favor of the distinctly Congregational form of church organization.

8. Persecution and the Struggle for Freedom • Under Cromwell Congregationalism rode the crest of the waves. This brief period of triumph was followed by the Restoration and a longer period of renewed persecution under Charles II and James II. The Congregationalists shared in this persecution together with Presbyterians, Baptists, and Quakers. These bodies of Dissenters took a prominent part in overthrowing James II, and bringing Wil-

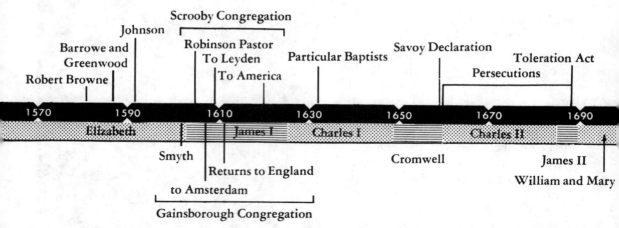

| 1570 | 1590 | 1610 | 1630 | 1650 | 1670 | 1690 |

Robert Browne

Barrowe and
Greenwood

Johnson

Scrooby Congregation

Robinson Pastor
To Leyden

To America

Particular Baptists

Savoy Declaration

Persecutions

Toleration Act

Elizabeth · James I · Charles I · Charles II

Smyth

Returns to England

to Amsterdam

Gainsborough Congregation

Cromwell

James II

William and Mary

liam and Mary to the throne. Together they reaped the benefits of a large measure of religious liberty secured to them by the Toleration Act of 1689.

From this time on the Congregationalists, Presbyterians, Baptists, and Quakers in England continued to labor shoulder to shoulder for complete religious freedom and equality. After a prolonged struggle which extended well into the nineteenth century, their united efforts were at last crowned with success. In 1828 the special laws against Dissenters were repealed, and the universities and all civil and military offices were opened to Protestant Dissenters. Congregationalists and all other Dissenters enjoyed all the rights which it is possible for Dissenters to enjoy in a country where the established and endowed Episcopal Church of England is still the State Church; whose bishops are *ex officio* (by virtue of office) members of the House of Lords; which continues to possess vast endowments and the right to tax all citizens for its support; and which is in control of the universities and to a large extent of popular education. All these things combined give to the members of

the Church of England overwhelming advantages.

English Dissenters are even today still striving for complete religious equality. They feel that the only way this can be achieved is by disestablishing the Episcopal Church as a State Church.

9. Decline and Renewed Growth • During the eighteenth century religious life in England suffered from serious errors which were destructive to church life. Congregational churches dwindled. Some died out altogether. The Baptists also during the eighteenth century underwent the weakening effects of serious errors in doctrine.

But then there took place the great Methodist revival. Together with all other denominations, the Congregational and Baptist churches profited greatly by the new spiritual impulse supplied by this movement. Membership greatly increased. Dying churches gained renewed life, and many new churches were established. A new interest was awakened in home and foreign missions, in Sunday-school work, the circulation of the Scriptures and religious literature, and in various works of charity. In 1832 the Congregational churches of England and Wales formed a union.

The Congregationalists of England and Wales are a numerous, wealthy, and very influential body. They have a large number of learned and able ministers, well-equipped educational institutions, many societies for denominational work, and excellent periodicals.

Presbyterians and Congregationalists sang rhymed versions of the Psalms in their church services. The Baptists were the first to introduce the singing of hymns.

The Congregationalists and Baptists have much in common. Both believe in the independence of local churches. And neither the Congregationalists nor the Baptists think much of creeds. The Baptists go even further than the Congregationalists in rejecting the authority and the binding character of creeds.

During the second half of the nineteenth century there were very few preachers in all the world who could compare with Charles Haddon Spurgeon. In only one respect was Spurgeon a Baptist: he rejected infant baptism. Aside from that he was a thorough Calvinist.

1. *What are the basic teachings of Congregationalists?*

2. *Investigate the origin of the King James Bible. Be sure to read the introduction in which you will find the translators' address to the king.*

3. *What was Cromwell's attitude toward Congregationalism? Why was this relationship to the Congregational Church changed at the Restoration?*

4. *When was toleration for all sects decreed? What does the author mean by saying, "Congregationalists and all other Dissenters enjoyed all the rights which it is possible for Dissenters to enjoy in a country where the established and endowed Episcopal Church of England is still the State Church"?*

5. *Identify: Robert Browne, John Smyth, Charles Spurgeon, Savoy Declaration, 1611.*

6. *What was the difference between the General Baptists and the Particular Baptists?*

7. *What was the importance of the Congregational Church in Leyden, Holland?*

CHAPTER 33

Arminianism;
The Quakers

1. Departures from Historic Protestantism • You will recall that the Congregationalists departed from historic Protestantism in their system of church organization and government, and the Baptists departed in their doctrine of adult baptism.

We come now to a study of other departures from the Christianity of the historic creeds. Quakerism teaches that, in addition to His revelation in His Word as recorded in the Bible, God still grants revelation today to individual believers. Arminianism, while maintaining the doctrine of salvation by faith alone, stresses man's will at the expense of God's sovereignty.

2. Jacobus Arminius • Arminianism received its name from a man named

Arminius, who was born in Oudewater, the Netherlands, in 1560. When Jacobus Arminius was very young the Spaniards came and destroyed his native town, depriving him of parents and relatives. A number of kindhearted Dutch people took him under their care and later had him educated at the University of Leyden, where he showed unusual ability. Because of his talent the burgomasters of Amsterdam supplied him with means for studying abroad. In Geneva he won the high esteem of Beza, the successor of Calvin in the Genevan church and university. He also studied in Italy.

Upon his return to his native country in 1588 he became pastor of the Reformed Church in Amsterdam. He was recognized as a very able and learned minister; his sermons were clear, eloquent, and well-delivered, and they attracted large audiences. Gradually, however, it was noticed that he no longer seemed to be in full agreement with Reformed doctrine. Nevertheless he was installed as professor of theology in the University of Leyden. In his lectures his departure from historic Calvinism became more and more noticeable, although he retained his belief in the Trinity, the deity of Christ, and salvation by faith in Christ's atoning work on the cross.

Pelagius, you will remember, had taught the essential goodness of man. Against him Augustine had defended the doctrine of man's total depravity. Arminius held some ideas which remind us of Pelagius. He denied the total inability and depravity of man.

Arminius did not deny the doctrine of election outright. But he taught that God had elected those who He had foreseen would believe. His teaching was a some-

Three Lions

Jacobus Arminius

what subtle and indirect denial of election. He made God's election depend on the action of man. In that way, while seemingly holding to the doctrine of election, he actually denied and destroyed it. He also taught that Christ died for all men, and that it is possible to fall from grace. He denied that the work of the Spirit is irresistible.

The young ministers whom Arminius had trained brought his teachings into the churches. Before long the whole country resounded with theological controversy. In 1609, in the midst of the uproar which he had caused, Arminius died.

3. The Synod of Dort • To settle the questions in dispute a synod was held in Dort from November 13, 1618, to May 9, 1619. The Synod of Dort was the

Delegates to the historic Synod of Dort
meet in a large recreation hall in Dort,
the Netherlands.

greatest synod of Reformed churches ever held. Present were delegates not only from the Reformed churches in the Netherlands, but also from the Reformed churches in England; in the Palatinate, Hesse, and Bremen in Germany; and in Switzerland. Delegates from France and from other parts of Germany had also been invited but were unable to attend.

The Synod unanimously rejected and very positively condemned the teachings of the Arminians, and stated the true Reformed doctrine in the *Canons of Dort.* The formulation of the *Canons of Dort* is the high-water mark in the creed-making of the Reformed churches.

The *Belgic Confession,* the *Heidelberg Catechism,* and these *Canons of Dort* are to this day the creeds or doctrinal stand-ards of the Reformed churches in the Netherlands and America.

4. Arminianism Lives On • There is still today a small group of Arminian (or Remonstrant, as they were also called) churches in the Netherlands, with a seminary in Amsterdam. However, Arminianism acquired a far greater influence in England. It invaded the Anglican Church and nearly all the dissenting denominations. John Wesley adopted Arminianism, and it became the creed of the Wesleyan Methodists. Today it has become the accepted doctrine in most of the churches in America.

5. George Fox, Founder of the Quakers • In England the seventeenth century was a time of unrest and change. This period produced some remarkable characters, one of whom was George Fox, the originator of Quakerism.

Fox was the son of a weaver. He himself became a shoemaker. Practically the only book he knew anything about was the Bible. In the England of that day there was much religious insincerity and unreality among church people. So it happened that at the age of nineteen Fox was invited by a number of church members to a drinking party. Young Fox was downright distressed at their lack of integrity. They professed to be Christians, but they acted like worldlings. The soul of Fox thirsted for truth and sincerity in religion.

6. Fox's Teachings • Fox was a deeply serious, religious man. He believed in the Bible. But he also believed that the Bible remains a closed book unless the mind of man is illumined by the Holy Spirit. Fox called this illumination by the

This famous painting by Benjamin West shows a Quaker family waiting in silence before making a decision.

Brown Brothers

Spirit the Inner Light. The first name of the people who accepted the teachings of Fox was "Children of Truth." But later they were called "Children of Light." They believed that something within them told them what was right and what was wrong. That something within them drew them away from the false to the true, from the low to the high, from the impure to the pure. They called it "Christ's Light." Not only did it give illumination to mind and heart, it also gave life and power and joy. Therefore they called it the "Seed of God."

Fox had no use whatsoever for any of the existing churches, nor for their creeds or their theology. He did not believe in theological schools, in formal training for the ministry, or in engaging professional ministers.

The origin of the name *Quakers* is not certain. Possibly it comes from the time that Fox told an English magistrate to "tremble at the Word of the Lord." Others say that because in the first days of enthusiasm the followers of Fox trembled with emotion when they were assembled in their meetinghouses, especially when they prayed, their opponents nicknamed them *Quakers*. But they resent that name. They love the text in the Gospel of John: "I have called you friends," and by the name of *Friends* they wish to be known and addressed. Their organization is not called a church, but the *Society of Friends*.

Their meetinghouses are exceedingly plain. There is no pulpit. They do not sing. There are no musical instruments. They sit down and wait in silence for the Spirit to move them. If there is no moving by the Spirit within a certain length of time, they leave without a word having been spoken. But the Spirit may move one of the Friends present, be he man or woman, and He may move several. Then those so moved get up and give their messages. Between messages a considerable time of complete and sometimes painful silence may elapse.

The Friends do not believe in oaths or war. They believe and act on the principle that kindness produces kindness. Friends show their firm belief in divine guidance not only in their meetings but also in their daily lives; they will often wait in silence for guidance in daily problems and decisions. Quaker respect for the dignity and value of all people led William Penn to deal fairly with the Indians, prevented their supporting any war, made them leaders in the agitation against slavery, and made them famous for their relief work in wars and disasters.

7. The Quakers Increase in Numbers • The followers of Fox increased rapidly in numbers, for there were many people in England who were disgusted with the lukewarm and worldly churches. In 1654 there were sixty Quakers. Four years later there were thirty thousand!

They were severely persecuted, but their numbers continued to grow. Possessed of an ardent missionary zeal, they went to Europe, Africa, and America, everywhere proclaiming the ideas of George Fox. When the persecutions ceased, zeal waned, and very strict discipline on their membership caused few converts and lost many former members.

They distinguished themselves by a peculiar mode of dress. You will recall seeing pictures of the Quaker dress which was common in the Quaker colony of Pennsylvania.

Today there are approximately twenty-two thousand Friends, or Quakers, in England, two thousand in Ireland, and one hundred fifteen thousand in America. Herbert Hoover, a former president of the United States, came from a Quaker family.

1. *What was the doctrinal position of Arminius as he taught it? Which churches follow his teaching? Why has this doctrinal question not been solved?*

2. *Read the Canons of Dort and list the five statements in which the Reformed faith is taught. What do the letters T. U. L. I. P. stand for?*

3. *Comment on this statement: New movements that arise in the Church are a criticism of some failing in that organization.*

4. *The followers of George Fox have been known by various titles. Give several of these names and the reasons they were chosen. Which, do you think, is the most appropriate?*

5. *Give specific examples which show that the Quakers put into practice their respect for the dignity and value of all people. Why, until recent times, has the Christian Church been slow in applying the social teaching of the Bible?*

6. *Identify: Pelagius; total depravity.*

7. *Why were the Quakers persecuted in England and America?*

CHAPTER *34*

Pietism;
The Moravians

1. A New Movement in the Lutheran Church • The father of Pietism was Philipp Jacob Spener. He was born in western Germany in 1635, and was therefore a contemporary of Bunyan and Fox in England. He belonged to the Lutheran Church.

In Spener's time dead orthodoxy had come to prevail in the Lutheran Church. All emphasis was on purity of doctrine and defense against any departure from Lutheran doctrine. There was no appeal to the emotions—no call to conversion and Christian service and a devoted Christian life. All that was expected of church members was that they should know their catechism, attend church service, listen to doctrinal sermons, and partake of the sacraments. They were not asked to take part in church work. Nothing was ever said about the inner Christian life and warm religious experience. Some members of the clergy did not lead lives worthy of their sacred office. Many of them were not converted men. Among the members of the church there was much drunkenness and immorality.

Such was the religious atmosphere in which Spener grew up. But in his early years influences of another nature began to mold him. He read a book called *True Christianity,* written by the German mystic Johann Arndt. The impression produced by this book was deepened by the study of devotional works of certain English Puritans, notable among them Richard Baxter. For a time Spener lived in Geneva and other Swiss cities, where he associated with ministers of the Reformed Church. All this time he remained a loyal Lutheran, however.

In 1666 Spener became chief pastor in Frankfort. He soon made improvements in catechetical instruction. In his own house he gathered a small group of people who, like himself, were not satisfied with merely formal religion. In these meetings they read and studied the Bible, prayed, and discussed the sermon Spener had preached the previous Sunday. The purpose of these meetings was to foster a deeper and warmer spiritual life. To these meetings was given the name *collegia pietatis,* or gatherings for the purpose of fostering piety. Because of that name the movement in the Lutheran Church started by Spener became known as *Pietism.*

Historical Pictures
Service—Chicago

Philipp Jacob Spener

2. Spener Believes Christianity Is a Life • As a means of promoting a warmer and more spiritual Christianity, Spener proposed the establishment of *ecclesiolae in ecclesia,* little churches within the church. These were to be circles of people in the local churches formed for the study of the Bible and for watching over each other and helping each other. Christianity, he taught, is more a life than an intellectual knowledge. Doctrinal controversy is unprofitable. The training of ministers should be improved. He wanted ministers who personally had Christian experience, and who lived in a way befitting their high calling. Preaching should not be doctrinal or controversial, but should be designed to build up the Christian life of the hearers. Only that Christianity is genuine which reveals itself in a

PART FOUR: THE CHURCH AFTER THE REFORMATION

life of devotion and service. It has its beginning in a conscious new birth and conversion.

Like the English Puritans, Spener also was against theater-going, dancing, and card playing, while the Lutherans generally looked upon these practices as belonging to the "indifferent things." He also favored moderation in eating and drinking and in dress.

Spener's activities called attention to the unwholesome conditions prevailing in the Lutheran Church of that day. He met bitter opposition. After difficult pastorates at Frankfort and Dresden, he worked with joy in Berlin until his death in 1705.

3. August Francke • At this time one of the younger instructors in the University of Leipzig was August Hermann Francke. In 1687, when he was twenty-four, he experienced what he regarded as a new birth. He went to Dresden, spent two months with Spener, and joined the Pietist movement. In 1689 Francke went to Leipzig and began to lecture to the students and townspeople. He soon had a large following. But trouble started. The students began to neglect their regular studies and started criticizing the other professors and the local ministers. Opposition made Leipzig an uncomfortable place for Francke. He moved to Erfurt, where he also ran into trouble. Spener

then secured for him an appointment to the newly founded university at Halle. Francke now made the University of Halle a center of Pietism. There he labored until his death in 1727.

Francke was a man of tremendous energy who had also a talent for organization. In 1695 he founded a school for poor children, to be conducted in the spirit of Pietism. He also established a home for orphans.

Francke had no money, but he believed in answers to prayer. It was not long before donations began to pour in from every part of Germany. Although Francke depended on prayer, he did not neglect means. He used every means of publicity, and knew how to interest others in his enterprises. His school soon became known, and from a small beginning it grew into a large educational institution.

In 1710 Francke induced a friend to establish a Bible Institute for the publication of Bibles in inexpensive form. This work, too, is still being carried on.

4. Francke Encourages the Work of Missions • From the beginning the Protestant churches did not entirely neglect the work of missions. Yet, for the first two hundred years after the Reformation, their strength was consumed largely in the struggle with Catholicism and the Wars of Religion. With the dawn of

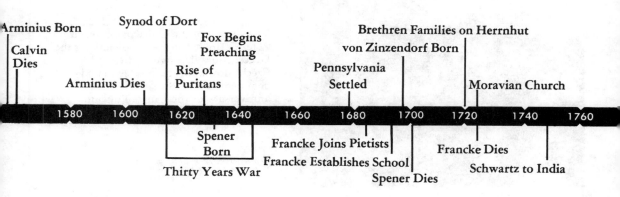

the eighteenth century a new era opened in the history of Protestant missions.

Frederick IV, king of Denmark, wished to establish mission posts in his colony in India. Pietism, with its interest in the salvation of souls, naturally was favorable to the work of missions. Francke, as professor in the University of Halle, had aroused missionary zeal in the hearts of many of his students. So when the Danish king looked around for missionaries to send out to his colony in India he found them among Francke's students in Halle.

During the eighteenth century no fewer than sixty missionaries went forth from the University of Halle to the foreign field. The most famous of these was Christian Friedrich Schwartz. He preached the Gospel in India from 1750 to the end of his life in 1798.

5. Pietism Has Serious Defects •
When Francke died in 1727 Pietism had reached its height. After that no leaders equal to Spener and Francke appeared. The Pietists did not separate from the

Lutheran Church; consequently we do not know how large their number was. Without question, however, the movement did much to arouse the Lutheran Church in Germany from its spiritual coldness.

Although Pietism in many ways was a blessing to the Church in Germany, it had certain serious defects. Before the appearance of Pietism, Lutheranism suffered from a one-sided *intellectualism* (emphasis on knowledge). Pietism was a reaction against this cold and inactive religion. But Pietism too was one-sided. It was ascetic, and emphasized severe self-denial. Francke allowed the children in his institutions very little opportunity for play. Pietism was critical and uncharitable; it condemned as irreligious everyone who was not a Pietist. It denied the name of Christian to all those who could not tell a story of conscious conversion through an intense struggle. Pietism had but little regard for doctrine. The Lutheran Church of the seventeenth century laid one-sided emphasis on doctrine; Pietism laid one-sided emphasis on life. By underestimating the value of sound doctrine, it helped to ease the way for Liberalism and Modernism.

6. Unitas Fratrum •
Persecution in Bohemia (now western Czechoslovakia) following the death of Huss in 1415 had

The church of the Unity of Brethren in Zelezny Brod, Northern Bohemia, is the largest Moravian church in Czechoslovakia. The jubilee Synod commemorating the 500th anniversary of the Unitas Fratrum was held here in 1957.

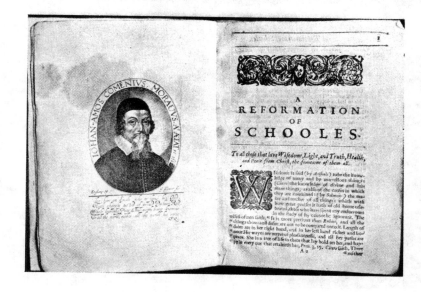

Comenius' book
on school reforms
was translated
into English in 1642.

Courtesy
University Library, Prague

driven the Hussites into hiding, but had not completely destroyed them. They separated from the national church, and deep in the dense forests of their native land they formed an organization in 1457 for which they adopted the name *Unitas Fratrum,* which means "Unity of the Brethren." Individually they called themselves *Brethren* and are generally known as the *Bohemian Brethren.* They are not to be confused with the Swiss Brethren as the Anabaptists in Switzerland were called after 1530.

By Luther's time the Unitas Fratrum had grown to number four hundred churches with 200,000 members. This church in Bohemia engaged in evangelism and education. In 1501 it adopted a hymnal; it was the first church to do so. The leaders of the Unitas Fratrum made contact with Luther and Calvin, and as a result their doctrinal views became more clear and sound.

Through the Counter Reformation and the Thirty Years' War (1618–1648) this church was almost wiped out. Only a remnant survived. The last bishop of

the original Unitas Fratrum, Comenius (1592–1670), who is famous in the history of education, called this remnant the "Hidden Seed." And such it later proved to be.

7. Count von Zinzendorf • Nikolaus Ludwig von Zinzendorf, descendant of an ancient Austrian noble family, was born in Dresden in the year 1700. His father was a high court official in Saxony and a close friend of Spener, who became the boy's godfather. As a child Von Zinzendorf showed strong religious feeling. A picture of Christ on the cross, with the words, "This I did for you. What do you do for me?" made a profound and lasting impression on him. His entire life was controlled by love for Jesus and a burning desire to save souls by winning them for Christ.

When he was ten years old he was sent to Francke's school in Halle. Here he soon displayed gifts of leadership. He organized among the boys a club which he called "The Order of the Grain of Mustard Seed." The purpose of this club was

Count von Zinzendorf

The chapel on Herrnhut where
on August 13, 1727, the Unitas
Fratrum was renewed.

Christian David

the promotion of personal piety and the evangelization of the world. Even before he came to Francke's school, when he was a boy nine years old, he had read a missionary paper about the East Indies. "Then and there," he told later, "the first missionary impulse arose in my soul." When he was fifteen years old, he and some of his schoolmates made a solemn promise that they would on every occasion confess Christ, and seek the conversion of all sorts and conditions of men.

But his family did not wish him to become a missionary. They wanted him to enter the service of the government. In obedience to their wishes he studied law at Wittenberg University from 1716 to 1719. He was a decided Pietist, but while in Wittenberg he learned to appreciate the orthodox Lutherans. He entered the service of the government of Saxony. The next year with part of his patrimony he

bought from his grandmother the large estate of Berthelsdorf, seventy miles east of Dresden.

8. Herrnhut • For many years a simple carpenter, Christian David, had been doing what he could to keep a remnant of the Unitas Fratrum together. In the meanwhile he had become a Pietist. He now begged Count von Zinzendorf to permit the Hidden Seed to take refuge on his Berthelsdorf estate. The count had only the haziest ideas about the Brethren, as the members of the Unitas Fratrum were also called, but he did know that they were being persecuted for religion's sake, and this aroused his sympathy. In 1722 he gave permission to David to bring two families of the Brethren. By 1727 several hundred of the Brethren had come to Berthelsdorf. At this time Zinzendorf read a book by Comenius describing the principles and the practices of the Brethren. The reading of this book gave him the conviction that he was called to devote his life to the reorganization of the ancient Unitas Fratrum, so that its members might become the agents of a great missionary enterprise.

He assigned to the Brethren a corner of his wide estate, where they built up a community which they called *Herrnhut,* or the "Lord's Lodge." Zinzendorf resigned his government post and settled in Herrnhut. He took advantage of the law which permitted a newly established village to establish its own rules of living, enabling it to form a community within the Church. This followed Spener's idea in its deepest import of establishing *ecclesiolae in ecclesia.*

Because they had come from the province of Moravia next to Huss's land of Bohemia, the Brethren, a mere remnant of the once flourishing and numerous Unitas Fratrum, from this time on became known to history as the *Moravians.*

9. The Moravians Organize as a Church • During a communion service in Herrnhut on August 13, 1727, the Spirit's power was so strongly felt that that date was accepted as the date of the rebirth of the ancient Unitas Fratrum under the name of the *Moravian Church.*

Zinzendorf with some of the Moravians developed some unique ideas. He laid extreme emphasis on Christ as the heart of religion. This led to great sentimentality in sermons and in hymns. The sufferings of Christ occupied the mind of Zinzendorf a great deal. His ideas were often both fanciful and sentimental. This was especially true of his ideas concerning Christ's wounded side. Gradually, however, Zinzendorf and the Moravians discarded many of these peculiar ideas.

Zinzendorf was a Pietist Lutheran. He had wanted the Moravians to become members of the Lutheran Church on the basis of Spener's idea of *collegia pietatis* and *ecclesiolae in ecclesia.* In the end, however, the Moravians organized them-

The idea of service is manifested in the "Washing of Feet." Notice the picture on the wall of Christ's side being pierced.

Archives of Herrnhut

After the initial settlement in Bethlehem, Pennsylvania, the Moravians spread to other localities. This is the present Moravian church building in Lititz, Pennsylvania.

Archives of Bethlehem, Pennsylvania

Note the typical dress of the Moravian sisters in this church service today in Herrnhut.

Archives of Herrnhut

selves as a separate church with bishops, elders, and deacons. Actually their form of church government became more Presbyterian than Episcopal.

Zinzendorf favored the founding of exclusive Moravian towns where no one but a member might own real estate and where the Church controlled all industrial pursuits. Bethlehem, Nazareth, and Lititz, Pennsylvania, were founded on this plan. The Moravian Church today is found in Germany, England, and America. Herrnhut in Saxony remains the center of administration. Every ten years a general convention is held there.

10. The Moravians Pioneer in Missions • Zinzendorf looked upon the members of the Moravian Church as soldiers of Christ, who were to go out to all parts of the world to conquer it for the King. To the Moravians belongs everlastingly the honor of being the first Protestant body to take seriously the Great Commission. Eventually they established missions in Africa, Asia, Greenland, Lapland, and among the American Indians. They were also very active in home mission work. Their most outstanding missionary was perhaps David Zeisberger. When in 1808 he reached the age of

Archives of Herrnhut

Moravian missionaries arrive in
Greenland in 1733.

Brown Brothers

David Zeisberger brings the
Gospel to American Indians.

eighty-seven, he had labored among the North American Indians for sixty-three years. This is the longest missionary career on record.

Today the Moravians are carrying on mission work in Greenland, Labrador, Alaska, the West Indies, in South and East Africa, Victoria, Queensland, Tibet, and among the North American Indians.

The Moravian Church is still small. The churches in the United States number less than 70,000 members. But their influence upon other denominations, especially in the way of arousing them to their responsibility for carrying out Christ's last commission, has been entirely out of proportion to the smallness of their number. It was the Moravians, under the leadership and inspiration of the Pietist Zinzendorf, who first lighted the torch of Protestant missionary zeal.

1. *In what ways was Pietism a response to the conditions that prevailed in the Lutheran Church?*

2. *Why was strong missionary activity found among the Pietists?*

3. *What were the weaknesses of Pietism?*

4. *How were Spener's work, the Unitas Fratrum, and the Moravian Church related?*

5. *List the many influences in the life of Von Zinzendorf that kept him from being a traditional Lutheran and led him to become an influential Pietist. What were some far-reaching results of his life?*

6. *Identify: John Huss, August Francke, collegia pietatis, ecclesiolae in ecclesia, Herrnhut, Bohemian Brethren, Swiss Brethren.*

CHAPTER *35*

Socinianism;

Unitarianism; Modernism

1. Distinctive Doctrines of Christianity

2. Socinianism Denies the Trinity

3. Socinianism Becomes Unitarianism

4. Modernism Rejects the Supernatural

1. Distinctive Doctrines of Christianity • We have seen that several Protestant bodies departed from historic Protestantism. But they did not all depart equally far.

All the religions in the world can be divided into two classes: *polytheism* and *monotheism.* Polytheism is the belief that there are many gods. Monotheism is the belief that there is only one God. If you meet a man who believes in many gods, you know at once that he is a heathen.

On the other hand, not all monotheists are Christians. If you should meet a Jew or a Mohammedan and say to him, "Let me tell you something. There is only one God," he would reply, "You are not telling me anything new. I believe that too." So Jews and Mohammedans are monotheists just as truly as we are. But if you should continue, and say to the Jew or the Mohammedan, "Let me tell you something else. In the one being of God there are three divine persons: God the

Father, God the Son, and God the Holy Spirit," he would turn his back upon you, and say, "I do not believe that." And with that he would also confess that he was not a Christian; for no person can deny that Christ is God, and still be a Christian. So you see that the doctrine of the Trinity is the most distinctive of all Christian doctrines. It marks Christians off from the polytheistic heathen. It also distinguishes the Christian from the non-Christian monotheists, such as the Jews and Mohammedans.

In the Creed of Nicaea the Church universal confessed its belief in the deity of Christ. To that creed subscribe not only all the Protestant churches worthy of the name, but also the Greek Eastern churches and the Roman Catholic Church. But the Socinians rejected the Nicene Creed.

Congregationalists and Calvinistic Baptists departed the least. Each departed in only one matter. The Congregationalists departed in one point of church government. The Baptists rejected infant baptism. The departure of the Baptists was a good deal more serious than that of the Congregationalists.

Quakers, Pietists, and Moravians departed by placing a one-sided emphasis upon Christian life at the expense of Christian doctrine. The Arminians departed from one of the historic doctrines of the Church. Augustine and Calvin's doctrine of predestination and election means simply that God is really God, that God and not man decides man's destiny. Arminianism with its doctrine of man's free will teaches that man has a part, the final, deciding part, in his salvation. According to the Arminians the issue of life and death lies, in the end, not in God's but in man's hands.

Martin Luther was buried in the Castle Church in Wittenberg after his death on February 18, 1546.

2. Socinianism Denies the Trinity • Socinianism receives its name from two Italians, Laelius Socinus and his nephew, Faustus Socinus. Although outwardly they conformed to the Catholic Church, they were nevertheless responsible for errors in doctrine which contradicted some of the basic truths held by that church. Laelius gave up the study of law for that of theology. From 1550 to 1551 he lived in Wittenberg, where he enjoyed the friendship of Melanchthon.

The death of Servetus at the stake caused Laelius Socinus to give serious thought to the doctrine of the Trinity. For his own satisfaction he wrote down his ideas on the subject. His ideas differed radically from the teachings of the historic Church, and he did not publish his notes. It is probable that fear of a fate similar to that of Servetus kept him from doing so.

The method which Laelius Socinus used in making propaganda for his erroneous views was peculiar. He did not openly and frankly proclaim them, but tried to open the way for their acceptance by undermining belief in true doctrine by means of clever questions.

While the nephew, Faustus, was studying the Scriptures at Basel, in Switzerland, the unpublished manuscripts of his uncle came into his hands. They greatly influenced his thought. In 1579 Faustus Socinus went to Poland and began to publish his unorthodox views on the Trinity. As a result he became involved in many controversies.

In 1605, a year after the death of Faustus Socinus, there was published in the city of Rakow in Poland the *Racovian Catechism*. It was largely the work of Faustus Socinus and set forth the basic teachings of Socinianism. Laelius and Faustus Socinus denied the deity of Christ. They taught that Christ was only a man, though He was the best man who ever lived. They also attacked the doctrine that Christ's death on the cross was an atonement for man's sins. They likewise denied the doctrine of *total depravity* (that man by nature is totally corrupt). The followers of Faustus Socinus in Poland caused to be inscribed on his tomb: "Lofty Babylon [by this they meant the Catholic Church] lies prostrate. Luther destroyed its roofs, Calvin its wall, but Socinus its foundations."

His writings were widely read and had great influence in the Netherlands, England, and America.

3. Socinianism Becomes Unitarianism • In England during the eighteenth century Socinianism came to be called Unitarianism.

Theophilus Lindsey, a Socinian clergyman in the Episcopal Church of England, circulated a petition that clergymen might be relieved from the obligation to subscribe to the Thirty-nine Articles and pledge their fidelity to the Bible only. You can readily understand the motive back of this petition. Socinian clergymen could not honestly subscribe to the Thirty-nine Articles, for this document teaches the deity of Christ. But they could interpret the Bible to suit their purpose. The petition received some two hundred fifty signatures. It was presented to Parliament in 1772, but Parliament refused to receive it.

Lindsey then did the honest thing. He withdrew from the Episcopal Church and in 1774 organized a Unitarian Church in London.

In 1779 the English Parliament did what it had refused to do in 1772. It amended the Toleration Act by accepting as satisfactory the profession of faith in the Scriptures instead of subscription to the Thirty-nine Articles. This set the door of the Established Anglican Church wide open for every kind of heresy. Later Parliament removed all penal acts against those who denied the Trinity.

English Unitarianism insisted on salvation by character rather than through the atoning blood of Christ, and claimed to reject "all creeds of human composition." But it had, of course, its own creed. That was unavoidable

Unitarianism made heavy inroads among the Presbyterians and the General Baptists. It was a blight upon their religious life, and their churches declined greatly. On the other hand the Congregationalists and the Particular Baptists were influenced only a little. Their numbers increased, and their churches flourished. At the time of the Toleration Act the Presbyterians had been the most numerous of the non-conformist groups. Now the Congregationalists and Particular Baptists outnumbered them.

4. Modernism Rejects the Supernatural • The Protestant bodies mentioned in this chapter had a tendency to place too much emphasis on human reason. Still, they placed the authority of the Bible above that of human reason. But the Modernists place the mind of man above the Bible, and *they place reason above faith.* This attitude is an outgrowth of the spirit of modern science and philosophy.

The Modernists do not believe in the supernatural. They do not believe in miracles. Consequently they do not believe in the virgin birth and the deity of Christ. They do not believe in a special revelation from God and in an infallibly inspired Bible. They consider the Bible to be not a revelation of God, but a record of man. However, according to them it is a record not of the entire human race, but only of the religious ideas and experiences of the ancient Jews.

Modernism is a departure from historic Protestantism. But it is much more. It is a definite break with historic Christianity all along the line. And it has invaded in greater or lesser degree most Protestant churches.

1. *What is the basic teaching of Socinianism and Unitarianism?*
2. *Comment on the following statement: Modernism thinks of religion as man's search for God; Christianity thinks of religion as God's revelation to man.*
3. *In what respects were the views of Michael Servetus and Laelius Socinus alike?*
4. *Who was the founder of Unitarianism? In what area did it spread?*
5. *What is "modern" about Modernism? What do we mean by neo-orthodoxy? Who is Karl Barth?*

The Methodists

1. The Wesleys • Samuel Wesley was a minister in the Church of England in the rough country parish of Epworth. His wife was Susanna Annesley, a woman of unusual strength of character. To this couple there were born nineteen children, eight of whom died in infancy. The fif-teenth child, John, and the eighteenth child, Charles, were destined to become important in the history of the Church.

In 1709 the Epworth parsonage burned to the ground. Both John and Charles were saved from death in the flames with only the greatest difficulty. John was then

PART FOUR: THE CHURCH AFTER THE REFORMATION

Susanna Wesley was a truly remarkable woman. In addition to giving her eleven children a careful Christian training, she found time to give instruction to her neighbors in the Epworth rectory.

a boy of six. His rescue from a fiery death made an impression upon him which time could not erase. He regarded himself as "a firebrand plucked out of the burning."

2. The "Holy Club" • Both boys were good students, and both entered Christ Church College in Oxford, John in 1720 and Charles six years later. John was such an outstanding student that he was chosen a Fellow of Lincoln College. In order to be a candidate for this honor it was required that one be in holy orders. John was therefore ordained a deacon in 1725, and three years later he was ordained a priest in the Episcopal Church of England.

His father, Samuel Wesley, was now getting on in years, and for a time John left Oxford to be his father's assistant in the parish of Epworth.

While John was absent from Oxford, his brother Charles, together with two other students, formed a club for the promotion of their studies. Soon they were spending a good deal of time in reading books that might be helpful to the Christian life. When in 1729 John returned to Oxford, he became the leader of the club, and other students joined. More and more it became the purpose of the club to realize the ideal of a consecrated Christian life.

The members of the club began to visit the prisoners in the Oxford jail. They

John Wesley and his university friends gather for a Sunday evening meeting of the "Holy Club" at Oxford.

also began to practice systematic fasting. The other Oxford students made fun of John Wesley and his fellow club members. They called the club the "Holy Club." Most of the students lived wild and irregular lives. The members of the club were known to live very regularly according to a definite method. Some student started to call them *Methodists*. This nickname stuck.

3. In America the Wesleys Meet the Moravians • In 1735 Samuel Wesley died. John would have been glad to succeed his father in the Epworth parish, but it was at this time that Count Oglethorpe issued a call for missionaries to come to America and preach in his newly established colony of Georgia. The widowed mother of John and Charles urged them both to go. Said she, "Had I twenty sons I should rejoice that they were all so employed, though I should never see them more." The two brothers sailed in October, 1735.

The voyage was stormy. At times the ship seemed on the point of foundering. Aboard ship was a company of twenty-six Moravians. In the midst of the storm they were calm and even cheerful. They not only prayed for protection, but as sea after sea washed the deck they sang hymns of praise with undaunted joy. John Wesley felt that these Moravians had a quiet trust in God far beyond his experience. From their behavior and his conversation with them he learned much.

Soon after his arrival in Georgia he met August Spangenberg, who was associated with Zinzendorf in the work, and the leader of the Moravian settlement in the colony. Spangenberg asked Wesley, "Do you know Jesus Christ?" Wesley answered: "I know He is the Savior of the world." Said Spangenberg: "True, but do you know He has saved you?" For three years Spangenberg's question preyed on John Wesley's mind. He was not sure of the answer.

John and Charles Wesley labored with all their might in Georgia. John was a wonderful linguist; he knew many languages well. He preached in German, French, and Italian, as well as in English. He also founded a small society for the cultivation of a warmer Christian life, undoubtedly patterned after his college club.

Wesley Preaching to the Indians

But he lacked tact and tried to enforce the regulations of the church very strictly. The labors of the brothers were most unsuccessful. Charles fell ill, and the year after their arrival he left the colony and returned home. On February 1, 1738, John too was back in England.

The trip to America was for the Wesleys a failure as far as mission work was concerned. Yet the Georgia episode was of great importance in the life of John Wesley, because of his experiences and the people he had met.

For ten years John Wesley had fought against sin and had tried to fulfill the law of the Gospel. But he had not, he wrote, obtained freedom from sin, nor the witness of the Spirit, because he sought it, not by faith, but "by the works of the law."

4. The Wesleys Are Converted • Within a week after John's return, the brothers became acquainted with a Peter Böhler, also a Moravian, who was in London awaiting passage to Georgia. Böhler taught a faith of complete self-surrender, instantaneous conversion, and joy in believing. Before he sailed he founded in London the Fetter-Lane Society, of which John Wesley became a charter member. But neither John nor his brother had as yet found peace for their souls.

On May 21, 1738, Charles, then suffering from a serious illness, experienced conversion. Three days later that same experience came to John. Unwillingly he had gone to a meeting of an Anglican society in Aldersgate Street. Luther's Preface to his *Commentary on Romans* was being read. Wesley has left a record of his experience at this time: "About a quarter before nine, while I was listening to Luther's description of the change which God works in the heart through faith in Christ, I felt my heart strangely warmed. I felt I did trust in Christ, Christ alone, for salvation: and an assurance was given me, that he had taken away my sins, even mine, and saved me from the law of sin and death."

This experience of John Wesley had a far-reaching effect. It determined his idea of how conversion takes place. From this time on he thought of conversion as an instantaneous experience preceded by a long and hard struggle. He believed that a person should be able to tell the exact circumstances and the time and place of his conversion. Yet even after this experience considerable time passed before Wesley came to know complete freedom from fear and full joy in believing.

The Moravians had been a great aid to Wesley, and he wanted to know more about them. Less than three weeks after his conversion he went to Germany. He met Count von Zinzendorf and spent two weeks in Herrnhut. Wesley owed much to the Moravians, but he was not entirely satisfied with them. He was too active in his religion and not mystical enough to feel entirely at one with them. The Moravians were thoughtful and meditative, and stressed their dependence upon God.

5. Religious Conditions in England • Wesley's long life spanned almost the entire eighteenth century. During this century England engaged in a long and bitter contest with France for supremacy among European powers. During this same century England laid the foundations of her vast empire in India, North America, Australia, and South Africa. The Industrial Revolution also took place

Bettmann Archive

John Wesley and Count von Zinzendorf

men shamefully neglected their work. They hobnobbed with the landowning gentry, and were companions of the squires in their fox hunting, drinking, and card playing.

Especially in the first part of the eighteenth century moral conditions in England were deplorable. Widespread unbelief went hand in hand with coarseness and brutality. Public amusements were of a low character. Drunkenness was common among high and low.

However, it was not all dark in eighteenth-century England. Bishop Berkeley of the Anglican Church, who lived for a short time in the colony of Rhode Island, was filled with missionary zeal. William Law wrote *A Serious Call to a Devout and Holy Life,* a book which had a profound influence on John Wesley. Up to this time the English-speaking people were opposed to singing in their services anything but rhymed passages from Scripture. Their attitude changed with the publication in 1707 of Isaac Watts' *Hymns,* and in 1719 of *The Psalms of David, Imitated in the Language of the New Testament.* The songs of Isaac Watts give expression to a deep and vital piety. He has very appropriately been called "the founder of modern English hymnody."

In many places in England "societies" were organized for prayer, the reading and study of the Bible, and the cultivation of a more earnest religious life. Thomas Bray saw the people's need of Bibles and religious literature, and in 1699 he founded the Society for Promoting Christian Knowledge. This led in 1701 to the foundation of the Society for the Propagation of the Gospel in Foreign Parts, an organization which has devel-

at this time. England had been an agricultural country, but now, with the invention of new machines and the emphasis on manufacturing, large cities sprang up in many places. This new industrial age brought with it great changes in the lives of the English people.

Religious conditions in England at this time were deplorable. Both the Established Anglican Church and the dissenting denominations of the Presbyterians, the Congregationalists, and the Baptists were shot through with Socinianism and Arminianism. Most of the sermons lacked warmth and enthusiasm. They were dry, cold, colorless talks on morality. With a few praiseworthy exceptions the ministers did no more than was absolutely required of them, and that little they did in a purely routine way. The highly paid church officers had poorly paid helpers, called vicars, to do the work. Many of the clergy-

PART FOUR: THE CHURCH AFTER THE REFORMATION

John Wesley is shown preaching to the poverty-stricken Bristol miners who had been forgotten by the Church. This scene is from the film "John Wesley" produced by the Methodist Church.

Religious News Service Photo

oped into a great missionary society. Both these societies were strictly Episcopal Anglican institutions. They have carried on their work with increasing energy to the present day.

It was in this England, growing in wealth and power but religiously stagnant and morally corrupt—an England lighted by only a few stray and feeble gleams—that John Wesley, with the help of his brother Charles and their friend George Whitefield, began his mighty work.

6. John Wesley Is a Remarkable Preacher • Though most of the pulpits in the Established Church were closed to them, John and Charles Wesley began to preach. The societies which we mentioned in the previous section turned out to be a great help to them. It was in these societies that they found their first opportunity to deliver their message.

In 1739 George Whitefield began to preach in the open fields to the miners in the neighborhood of Bristol. Soon he invited the Wesley brothers to join him. Preaching in the open fields instead of in a church was something entirely novel. John Wesley hesitated very much to engage in that kind of preaching. To preach anywhere but in a church seemed to him to be below the dignity of religion. But he learned that these coal miners were poor people who had never been inside a church and who knew nothing about the Gospel. He could not resist the appeal of their need. It also came to his mind that Jesus frequently preached in the great out-of-doors. On April 2, 1739, Wesley preached his first sermon in the open air.

This was the beginning of John Wesley's remarkable preaching career, which extended over fifty years, and which took him on horseback in every kind of weather many times through England, Scotland, and Ireland. Wesley did not possess

John Wesley
Facing a Mob

Methodist Prints

Whitefield's dramatic power. But he was earnest, practical, and fearless. Few preachers have ever equaled him in popular effectiveness. Nevertheless, he stirred up much antagonism, and his preaching often caused mob action to be taken against him.

7. Methodist Societies • John Wesley was not only a great preacher, he was also a great organizer. His first Methodist society he founded in Bristol in 1739. On May 12 of that year he began the erection of the first chapel there. In London the Methodists at first joined the Moravian Fetter-Lane Society (sec. 4). But after a time Wesley and his adherents withdrew, secured an old foundry as meeting place, and there in July, 1740, established the purely Methodist "United Society." Wesley continued on friendly terms with the Moravians, but from this time on Moravians and Methodists went their own ways.

Wesley had no desire or intention of separating from the Established Episcopal Church in England. He did not found a new church or denomination until near the end of his long life. Yet at the same time he could not bear the thought of letting the fruit of his work go to seed. He was determined to conserve and develop the religious life of those who had responded to the call of the Gospel. As we have seen, before Wesley launched out on his great preaching career there already existed in many parts of England religious "societies." Wesley now adopted this device and employed it in his work. He gathered the people who had responded to his preaching into such "societies."

Anyone who was interested could be-

PART FOUR: THE CHURCH AFTER THE REFORMATION

John Wesley
Preaching in a
Double-decked
Cottage

Methodist Prints

come a member of the societies that existed before Wesley. But Wesley made it a rule that only converted persons should belong to his societies. The new converts were expected to go out and convert others. To the converts Wesley issued "society tickets." These tickets had to be renewed quarterly. That provision put into Wesley's hand a simple means for weeding out members whose conversion proved to have been only temporary or not genuine at all.

There was a debt on the chapel in Bristol. This led to an important arrangement which became one of the basic features of Methodist organization. The members of the societies were divided into classes. Each class was made to number about twelve, and had a class leader. It was one of the duties of the class leader to collect a penny weekly from each member. In this way considerable sums of money for the work were gathered in. More important even was the means this system provided for the spiritual oversight of the members of the societies.

Before long Wesley needed help in his work. He would very much have preferred having all the preaching done by ordained men, but none were to be had. In 1742 Thomas Maxfield became the first *lay preacher* (a man who is not trained and ordained as a minister). Soon Wesley employed quite a number of lay preachers. As the work continued to grow, other lay officers were used: stewards to care for property, teachers for schools, and visitors of the sick.

Originally the societies were almost all in London and Bristol and neighboring territory, and Wesley visited each one of them personally. As the work expanded this task became too great. In 1744 Wesley for the first time had the preachers meet him in London. That was the beginning of the Annual Conferences, which have been called the crown of the Methodist system of organization.

Two years later the field was divided into circuits. To each circuit a number of traveling preachers was assigned. After awhile assistants were appointed, each one of them to have general charge of a circuit. Later these assistants were called superintendents.

Because his lay preachers had but scanty intellectual equipment, Wesley thought it best that they labor not more than six or eight weeks in one place. Thus began the system of *itinerant* (traveling) preachers, which has since then become an important feature in the life of a number of denominations.

Charles Wesley also rode the circuit for many years. His wife, who was a woman of wealth, accompanied him on his travels, riding behind him on his horse. She led the song services at the meetings her husband conducted. Charles was the hymn writer of Methodism. He wrote thousands of hymns, many of which have become famous. They are sung even today, not only by Methodists but by all English-speaking Christians. Charles did not have the iron constitution of his brother John. After 1756 he seldom traveled. First he labored in Bristol, but from 1771 until his death in 1788, he preached in London.

8. The Methodist Church Comes Into Existence • Wesley urged his lay preachers to apply themselves to serious study. He did not establish seminaries, but he wrote and published material for these men to study at home. John Wesley's writings were a considerable influence in the intellectual development of the lay preachers.

Wesley tried in vain to have these preachers ordained by the bishops of the Anglican Church. Failing in this he remained steadfast in not permitting his lay preachers to administer the sacraments. But the need for ordained ministers became greater and greater. At last Wesley could withstand the pressure no longer. He himself was a presbyter in the Church of England. Only bishops had the authority to ordain, but Wesley had long held the conviction that presbyters and bishops in the Church of New Testament times were of the same order. So on September 1, 1784, in Bristol, Wesley ordained two men. He himself did not think so at the time, but actually this act of his was a break with the Church of England. The Methodist Church had come into existence.

What was true of Moses was true of John Wesley. His eye was not dim and his natural force was not abated when in his eighty-seventh year he died in London on March 2, 1791.

9. Wesley's Methods • Wesley's methods were not only new, they were revolutionary. In three ways they were a wide departure from the usual church practice.

First of all, Wesley preached in the open air. That certainly was not the usual thing. It is true, Christ had preached not only in the synagogues but also on the mountain slopes, at the seaside, in country highways and city streets. After the Christian Church was established, preaching had been done for the most part in

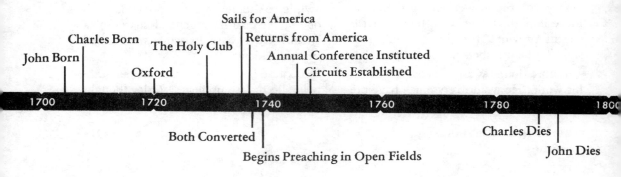

John Born | Charles Born | Oxford | The Holy Club | Sails for America | Returns from America | Annual Conference Instituted | Circuits Established

1700   1720   1740   1760   1780   1800

Both Converted | Begins Preaching in Open Fields | Charles Dies | John Dies

The Wesley Tablet in Westminster Abbey shows John Wesley preaching on his father's tomb at Epworth when he was barred from preaching in the church. The tablet also carries two quotations from Wesley:

THE BEST OF ALL IS, GOD IS WITH US
and
I LOOK UPON ALL THE WORLD AS MY PARISH

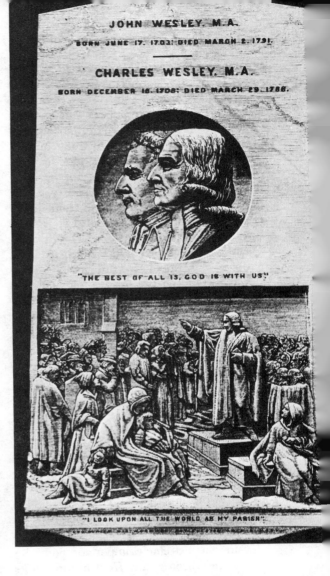

Methodist Prints

churches. Preaching in the open was not a matter of principle with Wesley. When the churches were closed to him, he turned to the unchurched. Preaching in the open was practically the only way to reach them.

Next, Wesley preached anywhere that he saw the need for his preaching. That too was unusual. In England, as in other countries, each minister was expected to preach and perform pastoral work only in his own church or parish. Wesley invaded the parishes of other ministers all over England, Scotland, and Ireland. When criticized for this he answered, "The world is my parish." Again this method of Wesley was the result of his efforts to reach especially the unchurched. There was a great need for this work. The ministers of the established churches had woefully neglected it. A very large number of them had sadly neglected the work among the members of their own parishes. It was Wesley's passion for saving souls that drove him to invade the parishes of other ministers. He often met with harsh criticism.

Third, Wesley engaged unordained men to preach. This was contrary to common practice. Only ordained men were allowed to preach in the established churches. Once more it was the crying need of the starving souls of the unchurched and the lack of ordained men that drove Wesley to adopt this unchurchly method. And he adopted it only very reluctantly.

CHAPTER 36: THE METHODISTS

When Thomas Maxfield, a layman, began to preach in London, Wesley hastened back from Bristol to put a stop to this unheard-of procedure. His mother talked to him. "John, you cannot suspect me of favoring readily anything of this kind. But take care what you do with respect to that young man, for he is as truly called of God to preach as you are. Examine what have been the fruits of his preaching, and hear him also yourself." Wesley followed the advice of his mother, and exclaimed, "It is the Lord; let Him do what seemeth to Him good!" Thus was introduced the practice of using lay preachers, which is followed in many churches today. Long before the time of Wesley, Article 8 of the *Church Order of the Reformed Churches* had opened a way for laymen of exceptional gifts to be ordained as ministers. In the Reformed churches this method has been used rarely, but Wesley made it common practice.

Methodist Prints

Statue of John Wesley Bearing His Well-known Words, "The World Is My Parish"

10. Wesley's Doctrine • Generally speaking, Wesley's theology was that of orthodox Protestantism. He believed firmly in the deity of Christ, in miracles, and in the supernatural character of religion. In opposition to the Baptists he believed in and practiced infant baptism.

In one extremely important point he departed theologically from historic Protestantism. In the Anglican Church of his day Arminianism was widely accepted. Wesley was an Arminian. He declared it openly and opposed Calvinism. Whitefield, who was a convinced Calvinist, died in 1770. In the annual conference of that year Wesley took a strong Arminian position.

As it was his passion for saving souls that had made him break with centuries-old church practices, and had led him to introduce entirely new methods, so it was that same passion that made him so bitter against Calvinism. He believed with all his heart in the power of sin and in the power of Jesus' blood. Fearlessly he preached against the many gross sins of his day, especially against drunkenness and gambling, and he sought to bring sinners to conversion. But he felt that Calvin's doctrine of predestination and election would stifle the call to repentance and conversion. For that reason he rejected Calvinism and embraced Arminianism with its doctrine of the freedom of the will. He believed that people accepted Christ through their own will or choice.

11. Wesley's Influence • Today there are Methodists in England, Scotland, Ireland, and America. They are divided among many Methodist denominations. The total membership of these denominations, huge though it may be, gives only a scant idea of the effects of Wesley's work. Those effects are stupendous.

The England Wesley left behind him was so different from the England he found that it was almost unrecognizable. He had transformed it. He had built up a large, entirely new denomination. He had gained many members from the Anglican, Congregationalist, and Baptist churches. But chiefly he had built up his church out of people who before had not belonged to any church.

But that is by no means the whole story. He breathed new life into many of the existing churches. A number of these churches Wesley imbued with the spirit of evangelism, so that they themselves not only enjoyed a new growth and prosperity, but helped Wesley's Methodist Church considerably in improving the national life of England.

Much of the ignorance, coarseness, brutality, and drunkenness disappeared from English life. Some outstanding people were influenced by Wesley's work. Among them were John Newton, a hymn writer; William Cowper, the greatest English poet of the latter half of the eighteenth century; William Wilberforce, who helped bring the fight against slavery to a victorious close; John Howard, who did so much for the reform of the unspeakably bad prison conditions; and Robert Raikes, the father of Sunday schools.

The influence of Wesley and the Methodists, particularly in the English-speaking world, is indeed immeasurable.

1. *What were the weaknesses and the strengths of the churches in England in John Wesley's day?*
2. *Did the Wesleys make changes by conscious, theological thought or by the requirements of circumstances?*
3. *How did the Wesleys organize their followers?*
4. *List as many hymns as you can find that were written by Charles Wesley.*
5. *Why was Wesley deeply concerned about the practice of laymen preaching? Should qualified laymen be ordained without formal education?*
6. *Why was Wesley opposed to Calvin's teaching of predestination?*
7. *List, with a brief statement of explanation for each, the effects of Wesley's work.*
8. *Identify: the "Holy Club," Fetter-Lane Society, Moravians, Epworth.*
9. *How did George Whitefield influence Wesley?*
10. *How was John Wesley influenced by the Moravians?*

CHAPTER 37

The Eastern
And the Roman Church

1. The Eastern Greek Orthodox Church

2. The Roman Catholic Church

1. The Eastern Greek Orthodox Church • The Church had its origin in the East, and the eastern Greek Orthodox branch is its oldest part. It has had a continuous and unbroken existence down to the present time. Yet to other Christians the Greek Orthodox Church is almost nonexistent. It is, however, a very important part of the Church universal, for it represents Christianity to some two hundred million people. These Greek Orthodox Christians are to be found mostly in Turkey, Syria, Greece, the Balkan countries, and Russia.

The eastern Greek Orthodox Church knows nothing of such a tremendous upheaval as the western Latin Church ex-

perienced in the Reformation. Its theology is that of the ecumenical councils of Nicaea, Constantinople, Chalcedon, and Ephesus.

For centuries the Greek Orthodox Church has held the eastern frontiers against Arab and Turkish Islam. It has been a mighty dam which has prevented the waters of Islam from flooding western Europe. Millions of Greek Orthodox Christians have lived for centuries under Muslim rule. Thousands upon thousands of these Christians have sealed their Christian faith with their blood. No other branch of the Church universal has given so many martyrs. For centuries the

Archbishop Damaskinos of Athens (standing at the head of the table) speaks at a meeting of the hierarchy of the Greek Orthodox Church.

Religious News Service Photo

Greek Orthodox Christians have lived in direct personal contact with people of a non-Christian religion. As a result their belief in the Trinity has come to be more to them than a mere creed. It has entered into their very bone and marrow and become a part of them. They are willing to suffer and die for it.

Christianity in its Greek Orthodox form was introduced into Russia by missionaries from Constantinople. It was the state religion of Russia until the Revolution in 1917, when religion was declared to be an opium and a hindrance to progress. The churches were closed, and the government promoted the teaching of atheism (denial of God) throughout the land. Although religion is officially "tolerated," opportunities for worship are very limited. By encouraging children to take part in antireligious activities and by emphasizing the antireligious aspects of science, Soviet leaders hope that religion will eventually die out.

At its 1961 meeting in New Delhi, India, the World Council of Churches was joined by the Eastern Orthodox Church. The Eastern Church has become active in this predominantly Protestant organization.

2. The Roman Catholic Church • Since the Council of Trent the Roman Church steadily pursued its course for almost four hundred years. Until very recently there had been little change in its traditional practices. There have been scattered conversions of Protestants to Catholicism and of Catholics to Protestantism. In Italy, Spain, and France thousands have left the Catholic Church, but they have not become Protestants. They have broken with the Church and religion in every form. They are the bitter enemies of all religion. A great many of them are Communists. Modernism has also made inroads into the Roman Church.

Worshipers at the Orthodox Church at Vrlika, Jugoslavia, leave the service.

Philip Gendreau

In the seventeenth century Cornelius Jansen, bishop of Ypres in the Southern Netherlands (now Belgium), was the leader of a dissenting movement. His views attracted followers among the more serious Catholics in France. The nunnery of Port Royal near Paris became the center of this movement. The Jansenists were strongly opposed by the Jesuits. Under the influence of the Jesuits, Louis XIV persecuted the Jansenists. In 1710 the buildings of Port Royal were torn down. In the eighteenth century the Jansenist movement resulted in the establishment in the Netherlands of a small Jansenist Catholic Church. It exists today. But the Jansenist movement caused only a passing wave on the waters of Catholicism.

In 1773 Pope Clement XIV abolished the Order of Jesuits. The order was restored by Pope Pius VII in 1814. From that time down to the present the Jesuits have been the power behind the papal throne.

Under the influence of the Jesuits, the Vatican Council of 1870 declared the infallibility of the pope. That is, it declared that the pope in all his official statements and decisions regarding the Church is free from error. Thereby the claims so insistently made in the fifteenth century, that general councils are supreme over the popes, were denied once and for all. Although the authority is seldom used, it was invoked in November, 1950, when Pope Pius XII, speaking ex cathedra, proclaimed the Assumption of Mary to be a Roman Catholic doctrine. This is to say that she, body and soul, was taken up to heaven.

Although the Roman Catholic Church did not accept the Reformation, it nevertheless felt its influence. The Catholic Church after the Reformation, though it

Pope Paul VI with
Amleto Cardinal Gicognani,
Papal Secretary of State,
Formerly Apostolic Delegate
to the United States,
September 16, 1963

retained its essential Roman Catholic character, became in many ways a much better church than it had been before. And the life of both clergy and members of the Roman Church today is on a higher level in strongly Protestant countries than in countries that are entirely or mainly Catholic. This is evident from the Roman Catholic Church's activities today. In spite of some statements of the Church to the contrary, it did in times past fail to encourage Bible reading. Several official pronouncements strictly forbid the use of the Scriptures to the layman. Now it is adopting a more lenient policy, and even at times urging Scripture reading, with the familiar restriction to the use of the Church's own version. The widespread distribution of the Bible by Protestant Bible societies has undoubtedly had its influence. The Knights of Columbus advertisements also emphasize proof of their points of view by referring to Scripture.

Pope John XXIII proved to be an in-fluential man, not only in world politics, but in liberalizing some of the Church's relations to Protestantism and the Greek Orthodox Church. His ecumenical efforts have met with some resistance, particularly from the Curia cardinals, but they have been approved most enthusiastically by the American cardinals. In 1962 he convened the first Council since 1870, but he died before his liberalizing efforts bore fruit in Council decisions.

The election of Paul VI, former cardinal-archbishop of Milan, indicates that this policy has the endorsement of broad segments of the church, as do other modernizations. Mass is being said in the vernacular, free discussions with Communists are in progress, official new attitudes toward the theory of evolution are being considered. All of these show that this church is not as set in its ways as it has been in the past.

In 1962 the Catholic segment of the United States was about thirty-six percent of the total population. The large cities in this country have become great centers of Catholicism, and Catholic influences in politics have drawn into the foreground many problems on the relation of Church and State. The election of the first Roman Catholic President stirred deeply the Protestant groups who feared domination by a foreign (papal) power through the Chief Executive. The relation of the State to church schools or parochial schools also forced the government to express itself through the Supreme Court or the Chief Executive on such issues as State aid for non-public schools, time allotment for religious education, etc. Though these problems cannot be settled easily and quickly at present, it is evident nevertheless that a more tolerant attitude toward fellow religions has developed, and frank discussions are becoming more common in both political and ecclesiastic spheres.

What Protestants have found difficult to understand is the present Roman Catholic emphasis on ecumenicity at the same time that it announces new extra-Biblical doctrines such as the Assumption of Mary, which tend to widen the very breach it is seeking to bridge.

1. *What areas are included in the sphere of the Greek Orthodox Church? Why has this church been less influential in the religious world than the Western Church?*

2. *In what sense does the Roman Catholic Church speak of the pope as being infallible?*

3. *To what degree is the American Roman Catholic Church independent of the papacy?*

4. *The Roman Church claims that there can be only one Body of Christ, the Church. Can you justify the many divisions of denominations? Investigate the differences in faith and practice among Roman Catholic churches in various parts of the world.*

5. *What new developments are significant in the Roman Church today?*

6. *Identify Jansenists, Knights of Columbus, ecumenical, Curia, New Delhi.*

CHAPTER *38*

Religious Life
In Germany and England

1. Doctrinal Differences in the Lutheran Church • Philipp Melanchthon had from the very beginning of the Reformation movement been Luther's closest friend and helper. But he also became acquainted with Zwingli; and with Calvin he formed a warm friendship. In course of time he came to disagree with Luther on certain points of doctrine. As long as Luther lived he kept these ideas to himself. After Luther's death, however, he allowed his views to become known, with the result that the first considerable controversy among Lutherans arose.

Many years after Melanchthon's death the *Formula of Concord* (1577) was drawn up. This was a statement of agreement on most of the essential doctrines of Lutheranism.

Later there arose another controversy. George Calixtus (1586–1656), a leading Lutheran theologian, had come in close touch with thinkers of the Reformed, Anglican, and Catholic Churches. He disapproved of the spirit of bitterness that characterized the doctrinal discussions in his denomination. He came to regard the differences between the Lutherans, the Reformed, and the Catholics of very small importance. He felt that a Christian life was more important than pure doctrine. He thought the Church should be satisfied with the Apostles' Creed and the Bible. This idea of the great theologian Calixtus showed a surprising lack of insight. But Calixtus gained numerous followers. People were weary of doctrinal controversies and the spirit of bitterness in which they were carried on.

At a conference in 1645 Calixtus heard his ideas strongly opposed. The controversy that began here continued for many years. We have the strange spectacle of a controversy on the thesis that there should be less controversy. The dispute went on for many years after the death of Calixtus. At last it wore itself out.

In the meanwhile Germany was suffering from the results of the Thirty Years' War. Time and again armies had swept over Germany in every direction. Cities and farms alike had been ruined. Many had been massacred. City and country folk were plunged into poverty. In these unhappy circumstances people became indifferent to doctrine. Pietism, with its emphasis on Christian life at the expense of doctrine, found fertile soil.

The way was now open for Modernism. Nourished by modern philosophy it spread through the Lutheran Church and the universities in Germany. Luther would not have recognized the Church which he founded in deep struggles of soul.

But orthodoxy in the nineteenth century still had very able defenders in men like Ernst Wilhelm Hengstenberg and Theodor Zahn. These were men of tremendous learning, but they had a firm and simple belief in the Bible as the infallible Word of God.

2. Deism • The prevailing influence in English religious life during the eighteenth century was Deism. The hopes of the Presbyterians in the seventeenth century to make their faith the state religion turned out to be only a passing dream. In the course of the eighteenth century the Trinity-denying Socinians gained the upper hand in the Presbyterian churches. Those who embraced Socinian views left the Presbyterian Church and organized Unitarian churches. Presbyterianism ceased to be an important factor in England.

Deism had its origin in England, but it exerted a profound influence in France, the Netherlands, and Germany. The Deists do believe in the existence of God, and they believe that He made the world. But they think that God's relation to the world is like that of a watchmaker to a watch. A watchmaker makes a watch and winds it, and then the watch runs by itself. So God made the world, a most marvelous piece of mechanism, and now has nothing more to do with it. It runs by itself according to certain laws, the laws of nature.

Thus Deism denies miracles, the atoning work of Christ, and the regenerating work of the Spirit. Deism discredits the Bible and robs religion of its supernatural character.

The morality, or sense of right and wrong, taught by Deism is of a low order. Over in the English colonies in America Benjamin Franklin and Thomas Jefferson, who were in many ways great men, were Deists. This influence is revealed in Franklin's maxim: "Honesty is the best policy," which implies that we should be honest because it pays, rather than because it is right and because God commands it.

3. A Low, a High, and a Broad Church Movement

It was in this England under the sway of Arminianism, Socinianism, and Deism that the Methodist movement arose. The Methodist movement was a mighty spiritual and religious revival. This revival shook the life both of the Anglican State Church and of many of the Dissenting churches. It brought about a tremendous change in the religious and moral life of England. Under the fervor of this revival the ice of Deism melted. The frozen waters of English religious life again began to flow freely.

The Methodist movement had two great leaders: John Wesley and George Whitefield. We have learned something of the life and work of John Wesley. The work of Whitefield is also well worth our attention.

Wesley and Whitefield in many ways resembled each other, but in some important points they differed. Both were Oxford men, and both were ministers in the Established Anglican Church. Both men were fired with a zeal for saving souls. Neither Wesley nor Whitefield confined himself to just one parish. Both men sought especially the unchurched, and they preached to them everywhere throughout England in the open air. They both were great preachers, but Whitefield was the more magnetic of the two.

Wesley was an Arminian. Whitefield was a Calvinist. Wesley had a genius for organizing, Whitefield lacked all talent for organizing. The outcome was that Wesley left behind him a great church, the Methodist Church. Whitefield powerfully influenced thousands of people, but they never formed a church. They re-

Religious News Service Photo

George Whitefield

mained in the Anglican Church, and there they formed the *Low Church* or *Evangelical party*.

In their views these Evangelicals or Low Church people were moderate Calvinists. They were opposed to elaborate ritual in church services. They were filled with religious zeal, and they lived lives of strict piety. If Whitefield had possessed the organizing genius of Wesley, Calvinism might have been today a far greater power in England than it is.

The trend of events in the Anglican Church soon became a cause for deep concern. The great Methodist revival led by the Wesleys had resulted in the withdrawal of thousands from the Anglican Church. The Low Church party under the leadership of Whitefield was moving away from the traditional Anglican practices. Dissenters, Catholics, and

Methodist Prints

**John Wesley Preaching from
a Market Cross**

the Low Church party were all working for repeal of the laws which gave the Anglican Church many advantages over the other churches. It began to look as though the Anglican Church might soon cease to be the State Church of England. As a result, many leaders in the Anglican Church became frantic with alarm. A number of them met to consider what could be done to stop this trend. They and their supporters became known as the *High Church party.*

In the first half of the nineteenth century the High Church party represented a movement back in the direction of the Roman Catholic Church. The foremost leaders were John Keble, John Henry Newman, and Edward Pusey. Because these men were affiliated with Oxford University, the movement came to be known as the Oxford movement.

The High Church party emphasized those features in the Church of England which were a continuation of Roman Catholic tradition and practice. They held that their priests had the power to forgive sin. They were distressed that the Church should be under the authority of the State.

The movement was formally started by Keble when he preached a sermon in Oxford on "The National Apostasy." In the same month the publication of a series of tracts was begun. In all, ninety tracts appeared, most of them written by John Henry Newman. These tracts gave to the movement another name—the Tractarian movement.

To Newman the Church of England was the golden mean between Protestantism and Catholicism. But as the series of tracts progressed, the writings became more and more Roman Catholic in the principles they set forth, until finally the bishop of Oxford ordered their publication be stopped.

On October 9, 1845, Newman joined the Catholic Church. Thousands followed him. But the majority of the High Church party remained in the Church of England, and there they continued to exercise their influence. The ritual in the church service became more and more elaborate, after the Roman fashion. The High Church movement is still a growing force in the Anglican Church.

A *Broad Church party* also arose in the Church of England. It developed under the influence of German thought. The man who introduced the new ideas from Germany into England was the poet Coleridge.

The Broad Church party strongly believed in having a State Church. Members of this party considered the Church to be a department of the State, like the army and the navy. Believing as they do in a State Church they would like to see every citizen a member of it. In order that this may be possible they wish to see every form of belief tolerated in the State Church. There should be no creeds with binding force. Everyone should be free to believe whatever he pleases. That is why this group is called the Broad Church party.

The members of this movement have become more and more liberal in their doctrinal views. They do not realize that truth and error, light and darkness, faith and unbelief cannot exist side by side in the same organization.

4. Three Nonconformist Movements Arise • Step by step during the nineteenth century the Nonconformist or Dissenting bodies in England achieved more nearly a status of equality with the Episcopal or Anglican Church. The number of Nonconformists has grown steadily until at the present time they make up at least half of the population of England. They are found mostly among the middle class. These churches possess many great preachers and a number of scholars; however, in scholarship and in work among the unchurched they do not equal the Anglican State Church.

Among the Nonconformists in England during the past century three new movements of varying importance arose. The first of these movements began when Edward Irving, a Presbyterian minister, began to preach that the *gifts of the apostolic age* (speaking in tongues, prophesying, and healing the sick) would be restored if people only had enough faith.

He soon came to believe that some of the members of his church had received these "gifts." He was deposed as a Presbyterian minister but continued his preaching. After some time, twelve members of his church were designated as "apostles." The "apostles" were believed to be organs of the Holy Spirit.

The people who held the views of Edward Irving took the name of the *Catholic Apostolic Church* and adopted an elaborate ritual. This Church expected the speedy return of the Lord. The last apostle died in 1901 but the Apostolic Church carries on to this day.

A second movement arose as a reaction against the lack of spirituality and warmth in the Anglican Church. Groups of *Brethren* sprang up in Ireland and western England. They claimed faith and Christian love to be their only bonds of union.

The great increase in the number of Brethren was due to the labors of John Nelson Darby, who had been a minister in the neighborhood of Plymouth, England. Because of him the Brethren received the name of *Darbyites* or *Plymouth Brethren*. Darby worked hard to spread his ideas. He organized churches of the Brethren in Switzerland, France, Germany, Canada, and the United States.

Because the Bible teaches that all believers are priests, the Brethren do not believe in ordained ministers. They are against creeds. They hold that the Holy Spirit guides all true believers and unites them in faith and worship after the apostolic model. They claim to reject all denominationalism. But early in their history they were compelled to adopt certain acts of discipline. Today they are divided into six groups.

Evangeline Booth (1865–1950), daughter of the founder of the Salvation Army, distributes baskets of food on Christmas Day to the poor of New York City. After being Commander-in-chief of the Army in the United States from 1904 to 1934, she was General of the world Army from 1934 to 1939.

Brown Brothers

One of the outstanding members of the early Brethren group in England was George Müller of Bristol. Inspired by the example of August Francke, he established an orphanage which became famous as a work of faith.

A third movement, the *Salvation Army,* was founded by William Booth, a former Methodist minister. He first carried on a successful revival in Cardiff, Wales. Later he began a similar work in London. Out of this there developed (in 1878) an organization in military form which soon received the name of the Salvation Army. It is found today in eighty-one countries throughout the world.

The Salvation Army engages in street preaching and in works of mercy. It is not a church. In almost every city it maintains a service center, where the lonely and homeless can find help and where evangelistic services are regularly held.

1. *What was the position of Calixtus? Why should this problem arise?*
2. *Are the basic views of the Pelagians, Socinians, and Deists different?*
3. *What were the differences that led to the formation of the High Church party, the Low Church party, and the Broad Church party?*
4. *Indicate the particular religious emphasis of each of the three new Nonconformist groups: the Catholic Apostolic Church, the Plymouth Brethren, and the Salvation Army.*
5. *Identify: Formula of Concord, William Booth, John Newman, Nonconformist.*

CHAPTER 39

The Reformed Churches
Survive Persecution

1. The Huguenots Prosper • The Edict of Nantes in 1598 secured to the Huguenots—the French Calvinists—a considerable measure of freedom. From that time until the revocation of that Edict in 1685 there were about a million Huguenots in France, with eight hundred churches and about that number of ministers. These Huguenots were found among all classes of society: nobles, gentry, craftsmen, professional men, and farmers. But the bulk of them belonged to the middle class. They were the leaders in business, banking, manufacturing, and the professions. In many communities in which the Huguenots were only a small minority they yet were the most influential element. "Rich as a Huguenot" became a common saying.

The meetinghouses of the Huguenots were for the most part plain wooden structures. Some of them were very large. They had a seating capacity of seven to eight thousand, and they were always filled with eager hearers. Often four long sermons were preached on a Sunday. The Huguenots were very liberal in their fi-

nancial support of the work at home and of the persecuted abroad. Strict church discipline was maintained. Sabbath desecration and frivolous conduct of every sort were severely discouraged.

The Huguenots at this time had four great institutions of learning—at Sedan, Montauban, Nimes, and Saumur. These schools had large enrollments of students, and their faculties counted among their members some of the foremost scholars of the time.

2. Louis XIV Persecutes the Huguenots • By 1648 Spain had lost its place as the most powerful country in Europe. The Dutch Republic was enjoying its golden age, and the Dutch and English were keen rivals for supremacy in commerce and sea power. Germany was exhausted by its Thirty Years' War. The foremost power in Europe at this time was France.

France, a Catholic country, had in Louis XIV an unusually ambitious king. It was Louis's lifelong aim to extend the boundaries of France. He wanted especially to add to his realm Spain, the Netherlands, and the lower Rhine valley belonging to Germany. He also wished to humble England.

As a despotic ruler Louis XIV hated Protestantism, particularly Calvinism. He realized that Calvinism is the strongest bulwark of religious and political liberty.

The proclamation is read revoking the Edict of Nantes which had protected the French Protestants since 1598.

In 1685 Louis XIV revoked the Edict of Nantes. Persecution was renewed. Thousands of members of the French Reformed Church suffered martyrdom. Hundreds renounced their faith. Between five and eight hundred thousand Huguenots fled to Germany, the Netherlands, England, and America. The loss of their skills and industry was a serious blow to France.

The French Reformed Church lost nearly all its members. The feeble remnant of only a few thousand reorganized themselves. What now follows is one of the most heroic episodes in the whole history of the Church.

This remnant retreated to the fastnesses of the wild mountain country of the Cevennes known as the *Desert*. A government order decreed the massacre of the Huguenots. Women were not excepted. Nearly all of the few ministers who remained were killed. Of those who had fled into other countries some recrossed the border to visit the scattered flocks, and were received with inexpressible joy. Even without ministers the Huguenots continued to hold their meetings at the peril of their lives. One of the bravest ministers was Brousson. He crossed and recrossed the border many times, and had many marvelous and narrow escapes. But at last he was captured and executed in the presence of a crowd of ten thousand persons. They wept in sympathy with his courageous witness-bearing. Many Catholics were converted by his example of heroic faith.

At last the fearful persecution drove the Huguenots to desperation and fanaticism. From 1702 to 1710 they carried on a terrible guerilla warfare against their persecutors. They themselves suffered severe losses.

3. Antoine Court and Paul Rabaut

After the death of King Louis XIV in 1715 there was a letup in persecution, but in 1724 it broke out again with new vigor. Men attending Protestant services were made galley slaves, women were imprisoned for life. Parents who did not send their children to a Roman Catholic school were heavily fined. Entire communities were fined for permitting Protestant services to be held.

In spite of persecution the churches in the Desert began to grow again. But their church life had become entirely disorganized. The man who did much to bring about better conditions was Antoine Court. He is known as "the Restorer of the Reformed Church in France." He was born in 1695. When he was five years old his father died. His mother, a woman of heroic character, trained him carefully in the faith of his fathers. When he was still a young child she took him to the secret Huguenot meetings. From infancy the fear of God dwelled in his heart, and when he arrived at young manhood he resolved to devote himself to the preaching of the Gospel.

Court visited many of the scattered groups of Huguenots, and observed their disorganized and confused condition. In August, 1715, when he was only twenty years old, he called together a synod. He had no college education, but through much reading he had educated himself. He had acquired a firm and thorough grasp of the system of Reformed doctrine. In spite of his extreme youth, his great natural ability and powers of persuasion soon made him a recognized leader among the Huguenots. His address before the Synod put new courage and enthusiasm into them.

Persecution had deprived the poor and oppressed Reformed Church of France of all its ordained ministers. The French Reformed Church, true to its Calvinistic tradition, would have nothing of lay preachers. As a temporary measure, preaching by candidates, students who had successfully completed their theological course, was resorted to. But the Reformed rule that preaching should be done by ordained men only was maintained. It was agreed among the members of the French Reformed Church of the Desert that there were among them two who were qualified for the ministry: Court and Corteiz. Corteiz was the older of the two. He was sent to Switzerland to obtain ordination. Upon his return he ordained Court.

The need of a school for the training of ministers led Court in 1730 to found a seminary in Lausanne in Switzerland. There it was beyond the reach of the persecuting government of France. The place where the seminary met was exceedingly humble. A room on a second floor served as a lecture room. Many gifted and devoted young men were trained for the ministry of the Gospel in that small and simple room. That Lausanne seminary became known as "a school of death." Most of the men trained there for the ministry of the French Reformed Church sooner or later lost their lives as victims of persecution.

Paul Rabaut was twenty-three years younger than Court. When he was twenty years old he consecrated himself to the cause of the Reformed Church in France. Court once defined the spirit of the "Desert" as "a spirit of mortification, a spirit of reflection, of great wisdom, and especially of martyrdom, which, as it teaches us to die daily to ourselves, to conquer and overcome our passions with their lusts, prepares and disposes us to lose our life courageously amid tortures and on the gallows, if Providence calls us thereto." Paul Rabaut was the embodiment of that spirit.

Rabaut studied for a time in the seminary established by Court in Lausanne. He was full of zeal and a gifted speaker, endowed with a high degree of personal magnetism. For fifty-six years he labored in behalf of the French Reformed Church. He suffered untold hardships. His life was constantly in danger, but with the wisdom of a serpent he always managed to elude arrest. He abundantly earned the title of "Apostle of the Desert."

4. The Church Survives the French Revolution • Philosophers and leaders in France were promoting a spirit of tolerance, and Anne Robert Turgot, one of the influential thinkers of the day, induced the young king Louis XVI, who came to the throne in 1774, to decide against persecuting Protestants. Consequently after ninety years of persecution the Huguenots were recognized by the government.

Lafayette returned from America, where he had given help to Washington in the War for Independence. Filled with the spirit of civil and religious liberty, he used his influence to have all the laws against the Protestants removed. This was accomplished with the Edict of Toleration in 1787.

Two years later the French Revolution brought a new government into power. The newly formed National Assembly granted the Reformed liberty of worship and restoration of property. But in 1793 the atheists secured control of the government. They hated all religion and persecuted Catholics and Protestants alike. So

PART FOUR: THE CHURCH AFTER THE REFORMATION

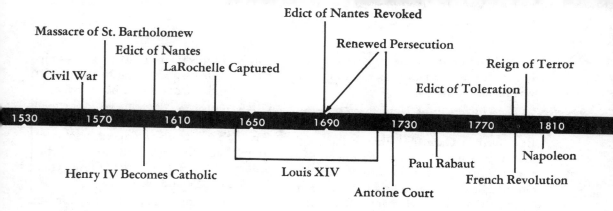

Massacre of St. Bartholomew

Edict of Nantes

LaRochelle Captured

Edict of Nantes Revoked

Renewed Persecution

Reign of Terror

Edict of Toleration

Civil War

1530 1570 1610 1650 1690 1730 1770 1810

Henry IV Becomes Catholic

Louis XIV

Antoine Court

Paul Rabaut

French Revolution

Napoleon

complete was the horror of the period from 1793 to 1794 that it is called the Reign of Terror. Many Huguenots who had escaped the Catholic persecution fell victim to the atheists. The old and venerable Paul Rabaut was cast into prison. It is not possible to say how many Protestants as well as Catholics renounced their faith at this time, but the number was large.

When the storm of the French Revolution had blown itself out the Reformed reorganized their churches, which had been scattered and wasted. Napoleon, who at this time became master of France, granted the Reformed and Lutherans equality before the law with the Catholics. The government provided all churches

A Reformed Church in Paris

alike with financial support. In return it demanded a large measure of control over the churches and their educational institutions.

Of the 700,000 Protestants in France today, about 629,000 are Reformed. The rest are Lutheran.

Modernism has also invaded the ranks of the Reformed Church in France. Only a few churches are thoroughly Reformed in the historical sense.

5. The Reformed Church in Germany • The Treaty of the Peace of Westphalia in 1648 gave to the Reformed in Germany the same rights and privileges enjoyed by the Lutherans. The Reformed were a large and important element in the population of the Rhine provinces and in the province of Brandenburg, now known as Prussia. After the revocation of the Edict of Nantes in 1685, thousands of Huguenots or French Reformed found refuge in Brandenburg. (See p. 258.)

The province of the Palatinate on the upper Rhine probably contained the largest number of Reformed people in Germany. In this province is located the city of Heidelberg with its renowned university. Here in the sixteenth century two professors, Ursinus and Olevianus, wrote the Heidelberg Catechism—one of the clearest and most complete expressions of Reformed interpretation of the Bible. It was published in 1563.

The University of Heidelberg was the stronghold and educational center for the Reformed in Germany. By the Peace of Westphalia it was guaranteed to the Reformed as their university. But the Jesuits wormed their way in and cunningly began to undermine the position of the Reformed professors. In 1719 a new edition of the Heidelberg Catechism was published. This Catechism contains the expression that "the Popish mass is an accursed idolatry." The Jesuits used all their influence to have this new edition suppressed. In this they were unsuccessful, but the Reformed were robbed of the largest of the two Heidelberg churches that were left to them.

In process of time Modernism crept in and increased its influence among the Reformed in Germany. The University of Heidelberg, once a nursing mother of Calvinism, by the beginning of the nineteenth century had become one of the chief centers of Rationalism in that country.

In 1817 the King of Prussia by royal decree forced the union of the Lutheran and Reformed churches. The weakened Reformed Church offered but feeble resistance. Since this union the Reformed Church has practically ceased to exist in Germany, except in two small districts bordering on the Netherlands.

6. The Presbyterian Church in Scotland • During the reign of William and Mary the Presbyterian Church became the State Church of Scotland. Under their successor, Queen Anne, Parliament passed a law which was to cause endless difficulty. It was the act restoring the principle of lay-patronage, which gave to the king and lords the right to appoint ministers of their own choosing to the pulpits of Scotland whenever they became vacant. Often ministers were appointed whom the congregations did not want. In this way the act caused an immense amount of trouble, and to a large extent shaped the history thereafter of the Presbyterian Church in Scotland.

The first rupture in the Scottish Church took place when Ebenezer Erskine and several other ministers were deposed because they boldly denounced lay-patronage (1740). Another secession took place as the result of the refusal of Thomas Gillespie to take part in the installation of a minister appointed according to the principle of lay-patronage.

The various secessions received strong support especially among those who took their religion seriously. In 1847 the groups that had withdrawn joined to form the *United Presbyterian Church*.

The State Church through these withdrawals was tapped of much of its spiritual strength. Besides, Liberalism crept into Scotland also, and resulted in what was called Moderatism. The system of lay-patronage favored the appointment of ministers who were Moderates, or Liberals, even though the congregations wanted men who were true to the historical faith. Rather than submit to this system, some 474 ministers under the leadership of Thomas Chalmers withdrew from the Presbyterian State Church in 1843 and organized the *Free Church of Scotland*.

Chalmers, a true champion of the historical faith in Scotland, was outstanding as a preacher, social reformer, theological teacher, and leader.

The most religious and devoted element had now left the State Church. In all, about one third of the membership had withdrawn. But it was not all to the disadvantage of the State Church. The spirit and enthusiasm of the seceders in time aroused new zeal in the State Church itself. And in 1874 the system of lay-patronage was finally abolished.

In 1900 the Free Church of Scotland and the United Presbyterian Church joined to form the *United Free Church of Scotland.*

7. The Reformed Church in Switzerland • The Reformed Churches in Switzerland, France, Germany, the Netherlands, and Scotland also fell prey to Modernism and unbelief.

In Switzerland a great revival took place in the early part of the nineteenth century, under the ministry of César Malan, Alexandre Vinet, and Frédéric Godet. Once again the great truths of Calvinism were being taught in the pulpits.

But soon Malan was forbidden to preach, and he and his followers left the State Church and organized the Free Church. Gradually, however, Modernism became dominant in this church also. Today the Free Church in Switzerland numbers only about ten thousand members.

8. The Reformed Church in Hungary • Calvinism was enthusiastically received in Hungary already in Calvin's time. In 1567 the Hungarian Reformed Church adopted the *Confession Helvétique.*

When Rudolph of Hapsburg decided to suppress the movement, the Hungarians took up arms for their liberty under the leadership of Etienne Bocskay. His success forced Rudolph to sign the *Peace of Vienna* giving religious freedom. Bocskay's role is memorialized on the Reformation Wall in Geneva. (See p. 258.)

Throughout the centuries the largest group of Reformed churches has been found in Hungary. Although the country today is predominantly Catholic and the situation under communistic domination is obscure, the membership in the Reformed churches is some two million.

This bas-relief on the Reformation Wall shows Bocskay bringing the signed Treaty of Vienna to the Diet of Kassa. At his side stands Pastor Alviczi with a Bible in his hand. Bocskay died, in all probability poisoned, a few days after this achievement.

Kiosque Biblique

VICTORIEVX ETIENNE BOCSKAY PRINCE DE TRANSYLVANIE APPORTE A LA DIÈTE HONGROISE LE 13 DÉCEMBRE 1606 LA PAIX DE VIENNE. GARANTIE FONDAMENTALE DE LA LIBERTÉ RELIGIEVSE DANS LE ROYAVME

Relatively few Calvinistic Hungarians came to America. The small denomination of forty churches called the Free Magyar Reformed Church changed its name in 1958 to the Hungarian Reformed Church.

9. The Reformed Church in the Netherlands •

The Synod of Dort, held in the Netherlands in the years 1618 and 1619, condemned Arminianism and clearly set forth the Reformed doctrine in a statement of faith called the *Canons of Dort*. These Canons together with the Heidelberg Catechism and the Belgic Confession form the doctrinal standards of the Reformed Church in the Netherlands.

But the Synod of Dort was not able to remove Arminianism from the Netherlands, nor was it able to prevent the rise of new departures from historic Protestantism. When the nineteenth century opened, the life of the Reformed Church was at a very low ebb. Reformed doctrine was ridiculed as out-of-date.

However, before the nineteenth century was many years old, signs of new life began to appear, and by the time it drew to a close the situation had changed completely. There were many influences affecting the Church at this time.

First of all there was the influence of César Malan and Alexandre Vinet, which made itself felt also in the Netherlands and resulted in an important revival of religion among the higher classes in that country.

Then there were a few ministers in the Reformed State Church and thousands of its members, especially among the lower and middle classes, who had remained true to the faith of the fathers. These tried to make the Church again live up to its Creed and Church Order; but they met with strong opposition from authorities in the State and Church. In 1834 a large secession from the State Church took place. In spite of persecution by the authorities and by mobs, the seceders organized themselves as the *Christian Reformed Church* and in 1854 founded a theological school in Kampen for the training of their ministers. Two of the outstanding leaders of the Secession were H. P. Scholte and A. C. Van Raalte who in 1847–1848 led their congregations to Iowa and Michigan. Thus the Secession movement of 1834 in the Netherlands and its theological school of Kampen became of importance for the history of the Church not only in that country but also in the United States.

But God's great instrument for bringing about a very remarkable revival of historic Calvinism in the Netherlands was Abraham Kuyper.

10. Abraham Kuyper Is Converted •

Abraham Kuyper was born on October 29, 1837, in the little town of Maassluis. As a student he attended the University of Leyden. Here a book which he wrote in Latin won the first prize in a nationwide contest. Meanwhile in the university he imbibed the principles of Modernism.

Upon graduation Kuyper became minister in the country church of Beesd. In this church there were many members who clung steadfastly to the old Reformed truth. In talking over the Sunday sermons with him they were not afraid to contradict their learned, university-trained pastor. Especially his frequent conversations with one old lady of the church made a deep impression upon the young minister. He now turned to the works of Calvin and made a serious study of them in the original Latin. This study changed the young Kuyper from a Modernist to a convinced Calvinist. From that time on to the end of his life he was the great champion of a revived Calvinism.

11. Kuyper Gives Strong Leadership • Fired with a deep religious zeal and enthusiasm, and consumed with a desire to restore the Reformed Church of the fathers that it might again bless the nation of Holland, Kuyper began an activity which was to stretch over half a century and amaze both friend and foe. As St. Augustine's *City of God* had inspired Charlemagne, Pope Gregory VII, and Calvin, so it inspired Kuyper. He entered upon his tremendous labors not only to restore the Church, but to apply the principles of Christianity to every domain of life: the political, the social, the industrial, and the cultural, as well as the ecclesiastical.

From the little country church of Beesd he went to the big city church of Utrecht, and from there to the still larger church of Amsterdam. He organized a Christian political party and entered the Dutch Parliament. In 1880 he founded in Amsterdam the Free University, based upon Reformed principles. It was given this name because it was free from the control of Church and State. Kuyper became the leading professor.

In 1886 he led a second large secession from the State Church of the Netherlands. And in 1892 he was foremost in helping to bring about in the Synod of Amsterdam the union of the *Christian Reformed Church* with this new seceding group, under the name of the *Reformed Churches in the Netherlands*. This new

Abraham Kuyper

denomination consisted of seven hundred churches and three hundred thousand members.

From 1901 to 1905 he was prime minister of the Netherlands. Kuyper preached, lectured, taught, took part in the debates of the Dutch Parliament, and wrote. He was great as a speaker, but he was even greater as a writer. He issued pamphlet after pamphlet. He also wrote many books, besides editorials for weekly and daily papers.

There were thousands who heard his voice. In 1898 he made a speaking tour through the United States. There were hundreds of thousands—in the Netherlands, in Germany, France, Switzerland, England, Scotland, the United States, Canada, South Africa, and the East Indies— who read his writings. Many of Kuyper's works have been translated into English. Several Americans have learned Dutch in

Netherlands Information Service

Like so many old churches in the Netherlands, this structure in Middelburg, now belonging to the Reformed Church, was in its beginning a Roman Catholic cathedral. It was occupied by the followers of the Reformation as early as 1574. The stately tower, almost 300 feet high, is familiarly known as the "Lange Jan," or "Tall John."

order to be able to read Kuyper's books in the original.

Kuyper possessed in a very high degree the marvelous gift of expressing deep thoughts in a clear, simple, and interesting way. He was a great scholar of enormous learning, a keen and profound thinker, and a superlative stylist.

12. Kuyper's Method of Reform •

Since the Reformation there had been many departures from historic Protestant doctrine. A number of these departures had three things in common. In the first

place, the Baptist, Quaker, Pietist, Moravian, and Methodist movements all originated in a reaction against the deadness and inactivity of the historic Protestant churches. In the second place, they adhered to the fundamental doctrines of Christianity. In the third place, they tried to cure the admittedly bad conditions in the historic Protestant churches by unchurchly methods.

Kuyper's work was also a reaction against the conditions of the times, but to make that reaction effective he employed an entirely different method. In the first place, he returned to historic Protestantism. He battled against ancient and more recent heresies. And while none of the groups that had departed from historic Protestantism did much or anything to stem the rising tide of Modernism, Kuyper opposed it with all his might.

In the second place, he fought persistently against the bad conditions in the Church by laboring to reform the Church itself; and—this is the important thing—in doing so he employed churchly methods. He did not disparage or bypass the Church; rather he operated within the machinery of the Church and when this became intolerable to the Church, he was put out.

In the third place, he devoted himself untiringly to arousing the Church from its deadness; he spurred the members on to an activity far surpassing Methodist zeal. He inspired them not only to carry on home and foreign mission work, but to carry the banner of the cross also into the fields of education, politics, social reform, and labor. He did not, as did the other groups, slight doctrine; he knew that the life and growth of the Church depends upon a steady, systematic teaching of

PART FOUR: THE CHURCH AFTER THE REFORMATION

Scriptural truth in all its breadth and depth and richness.

In striving to carry the banner of the cross into all spheres of life, Abraham Kuyper avoided the mistake of trying to accomplish this by having the Church dictate to the State. Instead he came forward with an entirely new solution. He accepted the Baptist demand of separation of Church and State but he would not, as they did, separate religion from politics. He organized a Christian political party. This party was to work out a Christian political program without interference or dictation by the Church.

Kuyper had many co-laborers. Some of them, as for example F. L. Rutgers and Herman Bavinck, were men of extraordinary ability. But Kuyper stands alone as the pioneering genius. Nowhere else in the world did such a wonderful revival of historic Protestantism take place as in the country of Holland.

In the revival of a sound and active Christianity, his influence is felt today far beyond the narrow boundaries of his small native land—in South Africa, in the East Indies, in certain parts of South America, in Canada, and in the United States of America.

1. *In what ways did the Huguenots respond to the persecution in France?*
2. *What were the attitudes of various French governments to the Huguenots? To the Catholics?*
3. *Who were the authors of the Heidelberg Catechism? When was it first published? When was it revised?*
4. *What is meant by lay-patronage? How does this compare with lay-investiture, the great problem of Hildebrand's age? Why did the Church in Scotland object to this practice?*
5. *What confession did the Hungarian Reformed Church adopt? List the Reformed confessional statements and the major groups which subscribed to each.*
6. *What signs of new life appeared in the Reformed Church of the Netherlands during the nineteenth century?*
7. *List and briefly explain Abraham Kuyper's contributions toward the Reformed faith.*
8. *Identify: Bocskay, Antoine Court, Paul Rabaut, the Desert, Lafayette, Edict of Nantes.*
9. *Why did the Reformed Church of Germany virtually disappear from the scene?*

CHAPTER 40

The Church Grows Once More,
1500 to the Present

1. The Growth of the Church •
The first period of great growth of the
Church was from the year 1 to 400, from
Pentecost to Augustine. In that period the
Church, the army of Christ, conquered the
civilized heathen Roman Empire around
the Mediterranean Sea.

The second period of great growth was,
roughly speaking, from the year 500 to
1000. In that period the Church conquered the new uncivilized heathen nations of northern Europe. But in this second
period of growth the Church lost to the
Arab Muslims much territory previously
conquered, and to this day has reconquered
only part of it. In this period the Muslims
also conquered much territory in India.
That territory they still hold.

After the year 1000 the Church lost much
additional territory in the East to the
Turkish Muslims. Spain in the southwestern
corner of Europe was regained from the

Moorish Muslims. That reconquest had important and far-reaching consequences. But it was the only gain made by the Church in this period.

From 1000 to 1500, roughly speaking, the Church made no new conquests. It could not, for it was fenced in. To the north there was nothing further to conquer. To the west lay the Atlantic Ocean, and to the south and east the wall of Islam formed an impassable barrier.

2. Exploration Opens the World to the Church • The voyages of discovery radically altered the entire situation. They changed the oceans from barriers into highways. And that change made it possible for the Church to get around the Muslim barrier.

Moreover, the further advance of the Turkish Muslims into western Europe was decisively checked in 1683 before the walls of Vienna, by the Polish hero John Sobieski. After that, Hungary and the Balkan countries were regained from the Muslims for Christendom.

Still, although the expeditions of the explorers enabled the Church to circumvent the Muslim barrier, all attempts to take that line itself have so far met with only indifferent success. The Muslims, on the other hand, have in the meanwhile gained considerable heathen territory in Africa. To the present day the great mass of Jews also remain enemies of the cross, and in many cases they are very active and dangerous opponents of the Church. However, the great fact remains that the voyages of discovery opened up all the world to the Church for the first time in history, and gave the Church access to all the remaining and as yet unconquered heathen nations. The way was now open for the third period of great growth of the Church.

3. The Catholics Do Mission Work • From 1500 to 1600 the voyages of discovery were conducted mostly by the Portuguese and the Spaniards. These were Roman Catholics. The Reformation started in 1517. Up to the Peace of Westphalia in 1648 the Protestants were completely occupied with their struggle with the Catholics. So for the first 150 years of the new missionary era the Roman Catholic Church had the newly opened mission fields all to itself.

Ignatius Loyola, the founder of the Order of Jesuits, was the man who aroused the Catholic Church to a sense of its missionary duty and opportunity. The Catholics were stirred with zeal for winning the heathen in the newly discovered lands for the Church. In this way the

Ignatius Loyola
After a painting by Rubens

Eastfoto-China Photo Service

Bishop John Chang is shown officiating at the midnight high mass in Peitang Cathedral on Christmas Eve, 1955.

Catholic Church would make up for the losses it had suffered as a result of the Reformation.

Inspired by Loyola, Francis Xavier became the first great Catholic missionary of the new era. In 1542 Xavier reached Goa in India, where he labored until 1549, when he went to Japan. There his work gained many converts. In 1552, as he was about to begin work in China, Xavier died. His work was taken up by other missionaries.

Spanish missionaries won the Philippines, South and Central America, and Mexico for the Catholic Church. French Jesuits established the Catholic Church in the province of Quebec in Canada, around the Great Lakes, and down the Mississippi River into Louisiana. Spanish missionaries also built up Catholic churches in Florida and along the coast in California.

Today Catholic mission work is being carried on in Ceylon, India, Japan, Korea, Mongolia, Africa, Australia, the islands of the Pacific, and among the North American Indians. Catholic missions are conducted almost entirely by the monks of the different orders.

4. **The Protestants Spread the Gospel** • The first great impulse to the work of missions by Protestants in the new era was given by August Francke and the Pietists. Their greatest missionary was Christian Schwartz, who from 1750 until his death in 1798 labored in India. From 1732 to the present day Moravian missionaries have carried on missionary work with utmost devotion in every part of the world.

World-wide Protestant missions received their impetus from the work and writings of William Carey (1761–1834), called the *Father of Modern Missions.* In 1792 Carey organized the first Baptist missionary society and in 1793 he and his family sailed for India. Neither the loss of all his goods nor the opposition of the British East India Company daunted him in the establishment of a mission. His greatest work was the translation of the Bible, in whole or in part, either alone or with others, into some twenty-six Indian languages.

Today all Protestant Churches participate in the work of missions. In our day the great missionary command of Christ

"Discovery of the Mississippi by Marquette, A.D. 1673" is the title of this painting by J. N. Marchand.

to preach the Gospel to the ends of the earth is at last being obeyed. The Christian Church is being planted in Africa, India, Korea, Japan, South America, and the islands of the Pacific.

5. Missionary Results • The work of missions, strictly speaking, consists in nothing else but in the preaching of the Gospel. But in speaking of missionary results we think of the effect of the preaching of the Gospel. We ask the question: To what extent are non-believers being truly Christianized as a result of the preaching of the Gospel?

The results are often meager as to the number who accept the Gospel and live transformed lives. The results are often so discouraging that many ask the question: Is it worth while?

To judge fairly the results that have been achieved we must understand what difficulties and obstacles stand in the way.

First of all, many missionaries have lacked the necessary qualifications. There was a time when it was thought that men who lacked the ability to become good ministers could nevertheless work success-

fully on the mission field. Today it is realized that a missionary must have fully as much knowledge and ability as a minister, besides specialized knowledge and talents not required of the minister who works in his homeland. The missionary must learn to understand the people to whom he brings the Gospel; especially must he know their language, their history, their customs, and above all their religion.

Other obstacles to successful mission work are these: The vast majority of people to whom the missionaries preach are suspicious of another culture. Some cannot read or write. Some are superstitious. Then, too, like people the world over, they may have a dislike for foreigners; and mis-

William Carey translates the Bible into one of the Indian languages.

sionaries are usually foreigners in the lands where they work.

We must also remember that others, like us, want to cling to the religion of their fathers. We love to sing, "Faith of our fathers, we will be true to thee till death." We are not willing to give up the faith that our fathers have taught us. So, too, non-Christians are not readily willing to give up the religious beliefs that their fathers have taught them. Only the work of the Holy Spirit in their hearts can cause them to give up their traditional beliefs and accept the Gospel of salvation through faith in Christ Jesus.

Another difficulty is that non-Christians often gain wrong ideas regarding Christianity by observing so-called Christians from Christian lands, who are really not Christian, and by coming to our universities and learning the religion of the Modernists who falsely claim to be preaching the Gospel of Christ.

Also there are many missionaries out on the foreign fields who are Modernists and who under the name of Christian missions are spreading their false gospel.

When all these things are kept in mind, it can be said that missionary results are simply marvelous. The results obtained in the face of the many and great obstacles can be explained only by the fact that Christ, who founded the Church and whose it is, has been constantly active from heaven from age to age, maintaining and extending His Church. He is doing this in our day in spite of all obstacles and all the weaknesses and sins of His Church. He will continue to do so to the end of time.

The missionaries in foreign lands are in the thick of the battle, and that battle between Christ and the devil is hard. The heralds of the Gospel sense and experience the power of both these captains.

The list of great missionaries is a long one. You should know of Carey, Brainerd, Livingstone, Taylor, Zwemer, Huizenga, and many others.

1. *Why was the discovery of new lands during the sixteenth century of great importance to the missionary effort of the Christian Church? Who did this missionary work for the Roman Catholic Church?*

2. *Why did not Protestants take on the work of preaching in the newly discovered areas?*

3. *Why do missionaries require broad training for their tasks?*

4. *Investigate the work done by one or two of the missionaries listed among the great men in this field.*

5. *Identify: Loyola, Xavier, Carey, Francke.*

6. *List four difficulties or obstacles to mission work.*

Part Five

THE CHURCH IN THE NEW WORLD

In this final section we shall see the Church establishing itself with the first white settlers in the wilderness on the Atlantic Coast, and pushing steadily westward as the frontier advances. Periods of spiritual decline were followed by periods of awakening and revival.

In colonial days there was no distinction between Canada and the United States; only between English colonies and French colonies. After the political separation into two nations, the Protestant denominations continued to establish churches without regard for a physical border. The ease with which men and ideas have moved across this border has made the establishment of national branches for each denomination unnecessary. The war in which the United States gained independence created a sharp issue for the churches whose origins were English and whose ties with the mother country were still strong.

In the nineteenth century the Church became acutely conscious of social problems —to the extent that it was in danger of losing sight of its central purpose. Increasing wealth and a new sense of leisure stimulated the building of beautiful churches and the founding of church colleges. Worship became more and more formal and theology more openly liberal. A reaction set in. Some broke away from the established denominations and organized new churches, where the form of worship was simple and the message was the Biblical doctrine of salvation by faith. Others left the established churches to form religious movements that were far from the teachings of the Bible.

Canada was in the vanguard of the church-union movement. This new impulse toward co-operation among churches has led to a number of international conferences, ecumenical alliances, and actual church unions.

Our book comes to a close, but the Church of Jesus Christ does not. The new chapters that will be written in future years will indicate the road that a victorious Church will tread until the Church militant becomes the Church triumphant.

CHAPTER *41*

The Church Enters the New World

1. Early Explorers Promote Catholicism • Explorers and colonists came to the New World for many reasons: gold, the glory of their nations or the envy of other nations, adventure, political or religious freedom, and a sense of mission. This last was not usually last in the thoughts of the kings who sent these bold people, nor was it last in the minds of those who came. In that day there was a

On the left is the facade of the beautiful La Merced Church in Lima, Peru, which dates back to Spanish colonial days. On the right Indians in Guatamala are burning offertory candles inside a church.

strong sense of duty to seek out and Christianize the natives.

Before any other European nations had colonies in America, the Spaniards had flourishing settlements in Mexico, the West Indies, and Central and South America. A printing press arrived in Mexico City in 1539 and by 1551 two universities were established.

Portugal and Spain had drawn up the *Demarcation Line* in 1494 giving most of the Western hemisphere to Spain. Brazil, however, fell on the Portuguese side of the line. Since both of these countries were strongly Catholic, the Central and South American countries today are predominantly Catholic. The form of the

religious practices, however, absorbed many of the pagan rituals which the natives had long cherished.

In 1565 the Spaniards established St. Augustine, Florida, with the purpose of driving out the French Protestants who had settled in Florida to find religious freedom. This was in the days when De Coligny was admiral of the French fleet. The Spanish commander, in reporting the massacre, stated that he had hanged 142, attaching to each one an inscription: "Not as Frenchmen but as heretics."

2. The Episcopal Church in America • The Episcopal Church was the first Protestant church to be introduced into

PART FIVE: THE CHURCH IN THE NEW WORLD

America. This was the church which the English settlers brought with them to Jamestown in 1607.

The Episcopal Church was from the beginning the Established or State Church of Virginia, and remained so throughout the colonial period. It also became the Established Church of Maryland and of all the English colonies south of Virginia, as well as of New York.

Throughout the first century of colonial history the Episcopal Church made little progress. But a great change for the better came with the opening of the second century of English colonial history in America. In 1701 there was founded in England the *Society for the Propagation of the Gospel in Foreign Parts.* This society became the great missionary organization of the Church of England.

This ivy-covered church tower dates back to the years when Jamestown was first settled by the English. Behind the tower is the restored version of the main section of the church.

3. The Congregationalist Church in New England • King James I of England meant business when he threatened that he would make the Puritans conform, or that else he would "harry them out of the land." He made things so unpleasant for the Nonconformists that the congregation of Scrooby in England was forced to seek refuge in Leyden in the Netherlands in 1609.

These Englishmen did not feel at home in the Netherlands. They found it very hard to make a living in a strange country. What was far worse, they saw their children being "drawne awaye by evill examples into extravagante & dangerous courses, getting ye raines off their neks, & departing from their parents . . . so that they saw their posterietie would be in danger to degenerate & be corrupted." So they decided to seek a new home in America. They sailed from Plymouth in England in the *Mayflower* and landed on the bleak, rocky coast of Cape Cod on November 11, 1620. They named the spot where they landed *Plymouth,* after the English city from which they had sailed. You will remember from your study of American history that these English settlers at Plymouth were called the Pilgrims.

The settlers at Plymouth were for the most part poor and humble folk. They were looked upon as radicals because they had separated from the Church of England and held the Congregational theory of church government. In other words, they were Separatists. Most of the Puritans wanted to stay in the Church of England and regarded the Separatists as self-righteous troublemakers. In fact, the Separatists were despised by all their fellow countrymen. The colony at Plymouth always remained small.

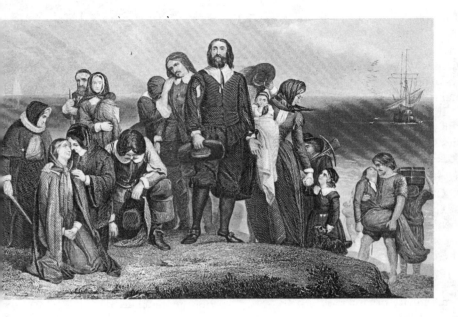

On December 21, 1620, the Pilgrims came ashore on a rocky ledge which was to become known as Plymouth Rock. They bowed their heads in gratitude to God for their safe arrival in the New World.

The great migration of English Puritans to America began in 1628 with the founding of the Massachusetts Bay Colony at Salem. This colony flourished from its beginning. By 1640 around twenty thousand colonists had found a home in the Salem area. A very large proportion of these colonists were men of wealth, social position, and ability.

These Puritans had no desire to separate from the Church of England as did the Pilgrims of Plymouth. One of the first of the Puritan ministers to come to Massachusetts Bay was Francis Higginson. When from the deck of the ship he saw the shore of England fade away, he said, "We will not say as the Separatists were wont to say at their leaving England, 'Farewell, Babylon! Farewell, Rome!' But we will say, 'Farewell, dear England; farewell, the Church of God in England and all the Christian friends there!' We do not go to New England as Separatists

from the Church of England, though we cannot but separate from the corruption in it." Winthrop and the other Puritan leaders considered it "an honor to call the Church of England from whom we rise, our dear Mother."

You would expect this Massachusetts Bay Colony with its wealth and numbers to take the lead in directing the church life and government in New England. But it was rather the little band of poor and despised radicals at Plymouth who laid the foundations of New England, and supplied the model of church government for the Bay Colony and all the New England Puritans. Following their example, the far more numerous and influential Puritans at Salem also broke with their "dear Mother," and adopted the congregational form of church government. In the course of ten years thirty-three churches sprang up in Massachusetts. They all adopted the congregational form of

On Sunday, January 21, 1621, the Pilgrims held their first public worship in a rough, square blockhouse at New Plymouth. Since they had no pastor, they were led in worship by William Brewster, the oldest of the company and an elder of the church.

Schoenfeld Collection from Three Lions

government, though one or two ministers were inclined to the presbyterian form.

In 1636 the foundation was laid for a Christian college at Cambridge in Massachusetts. It was named Harvard College (now Harvard University) in honor of the Rev. John Harvard, who gave a large sum of money to this institution.

In 1701 another college was established in Connecticut. First located at Saybrook, it was removed to New Haven in 1716. Two years later it received the name of Yale in honor of Elihu Yale, who gave generously toward its support. With fond reference to Elihu Yale, Yale University is now often spoken of as Old Eli.

4. The Dutch Reformed Come • The hardy and ambitious Dutchmen were not to be outdone by their English neighbors across the North Sea. In 1623 they established two trading posts in America: the one at the present site of Al-

bany on the upper Hudson River in New York, the other near the present site of Camden on the Delaware River in New Jersey. In 1626 Peter Minuit became the first governor of New Netherlands.

It was only four years after the famous Synod of Dort that the Dutch started their colony in America. The Reformed State Church of the Netherlands was then in full strength and vigor. So it was the Dutch Reformed Church which the Dutch established in the new world. This Church was under the supervision of the Classis of Amsterdam.

The first church was established in 1628 under the leadership of the Reverend Jonas Michaelius. The second minister was Everardus Bogardus, who came in 1633. During his active pastorate two meetinghouses were erected in New Amsterdam. The first was a plain, wooden, barnlike building. The second was built of stone; it was seventy-two feet long and fifty feet wide and cost 2500 guilders (about $1700)—an enormous sum for that time.

The most outstanding of the colonial ministers in New Netherlands was John Van Mekelenburg, usually called Megapolensis. He served the Church faithfully, and also took an interest in the Indians. He learned the language of the Mohawks and preached to them. It is claimed that he was the first Protestant missionary to the Indians.

In 1664, when Peter Stuyvesant was an elder in the Dutch Reformed Church of New Amsterdam and governor of the New Netherlands, this colony was captured by the English and renamed New York. The Dutch Reformed Church was allowed to carry on its work unhindered. Thirty years later there was a great variety of religious faiths in the colony. There were almost as many English Separatists as Dutch Reformed. Besides, there was a sprinkling of French Huguenots, Lutherans, Anglicans, and Jews.

From that time on the Dutch Reformed Church in America made but little progress until it was awakened to new life by Theodore Frelinghuysen. We shall hear more about him presently.

5. Roger Williams Founds a Baptist Church •

In the early months of the year 1631 there landed at the port of Boston with his comely wife a young English minister by the name of Roger Williams. The Congregational Church was the Established State Church of the Massachusetts colony. But Williams believed in the separation of Church and State. Almost immediately this got him into trouble with the church authorities in Boston.

Courtesy First Baptist Church

Roger Williams
A study from the bust in the Hall of Fame by McNeil

He then became minister of the Pilgrim Church at Plymouth. Here he made friends of the Narragansett Indians and learned their language. This was to be of great use to him later on.

In 1634 he was called to the Congregational Church in Salem. He served there for two years, and won a number of the members to his view about the separation of Church and State.

In the fall of the year 1635 the General Court sentenced him to leave the Massachusetts colony within six weeks. But Williams at this time was in poor health, and the court allowed him to wait until the following spring. Williams at once withdrew from the ministry of the church in Salem; but his friends and followers then gathered at his house. There he preached to them on the very points for which he had been censured. This aroused the court to action, and Williams was ordered to leave the colony at once.

Williams took a mortgage on his house to raise money, left his wife and two children in Salem, and plunged into the wilderness. It was the dead of winter. For fourteen weeks he wandered about in the deep snows of the forest. Then the Indians, whom he had befriended back in Plymouth, took him in. Late the following summer he purchased from them a plot of ground at the mouth of the Mohassuck River. Soon followers of Williams came from Massachusetts, and together they founded the town of Providence. This was the beginning of the state of Rhode Island.

In 1638 a church was organized at Providence. A Mr. Holliman, who had been a member of the church in Salem, rebaptized Williams. Thereupon Williams rebaptized Holliman and ten others. The first Baptist church in America had come into being.

When in 1647 the government of Rhode Island was set up, it was founded upon the principles advocated by Roger Williams: separation of Church and State, church membership not a requirement for voting, and complete liberty of religion. These principles have become fundamental American principles of government.

Baptist views were adopted by quite a number of members of the Congregational churches in the older Puritan colonies. Among them was Henry Dunster, the first president of Harvard.

The first Baptist church in Massachusetts was organized in 1663 at Rehoboth by a Welsh Baptist minister, John Myles.

The Enrolement of the wrighting Called the Towne Evidence after it was defaced; (as ffolloweth)

Att Nanhiggansick; the 24th of the first Month Comonly called March the 2nd yeare of our plantation, or planting at Moshosick, or providence,
Memorandum, that wee Caunounicus, & Miantenomu ye 2 cheife Sachims of Nanhiggansick having 2 yeares since Sold unto Roger Williams ye landes & Meaddowes upon the 2 fresh Rivers called Moshosick & wanasquatuckett doe Now by these presentes Establish, & confirme ye boundes of those landes from ye River & fieldes of pautuckquitt, ye great hill of Neotaconckonett on ye Norwest, & ye Towne of Mashappauge on ye West.
in wittnesse where of wee have here unto Sett our handes

ye mᵏᵉ of ⌣ Caunounicus

in ye presence of

ye mᵏᵉ ◯ of Soatash

ye mᵏᵉ of ↑ Miantenomu

ye mᵏᵉ ⌒ of Asotemewitt

Mᵈ 3 Mont: 9 die this was all againe confirmed by Miantenomu he acknowledged this his act and hand up the streame of pautuckett and Pautuxett without limmetts we might have for our use of Cattle wittnesse here of

BENEDICT
ROGER WILLIAMS: ARNOLD
Enroled Aprill ye 4th: 1662: p me Tho: Olney Junr: Towne Clerke.

Photos by Norman S. Watson,
Courtesy First Baptist Church

ciation of Philadelphia adopted a Confession of Faith which was strongly Calvinistic. Up to this time Arminian Baptists had been the more numerous, especially in New England. From this time on the majority of American Baptists have been Calvinistic in their doctrine. The Philadelphia Association became and has remained the strongest Baptist body.

The growth of the Baptist Church in America was not rapid. About a hundred years after Roger Williams landed in Massachusetts there were less than twenty-five Baptist churches in New England, and less than thirty in the Middle Colonies. The rapid growth of the Baptist Church in the South came in a later period.

Roger Williams was not the founder of the Baptist Church in America. The church he organized in Providence was the first of the Baptist churches in America but not their mother, for not a single Baptist church branched off from it; and the part played by Williams in American Baptist history was comparatively small. Most American Baptist churches owe their origin to small groups of men and women who were Baptists before they came to America. The greater number of these were of English and Welsh stock.

The great significance of Roger Williams lies in the fact that he stood bravely and firmly for complete separation of Church and State. This principle of separation was a great contribution on the part of the Baptists to the solving of a problem that had caused trouble ever since the conversion of the emperor Constantine the Great in 312.

The principle of freedom of religion followed naturally from the principle of

Later it was removed to a place near the Rhode Island border called Swansea. This church has had an uninterrupted existence down to the present day. It was, however, not in New England but in the Middle Colonies that Baptist churches flourished most. The first Baptist Association in America, consisting of five churches, met at Philadelphia in 1707.

The year 1742 is considered a turning point in the history of the American Baptists. In that year the Baptist Asso-

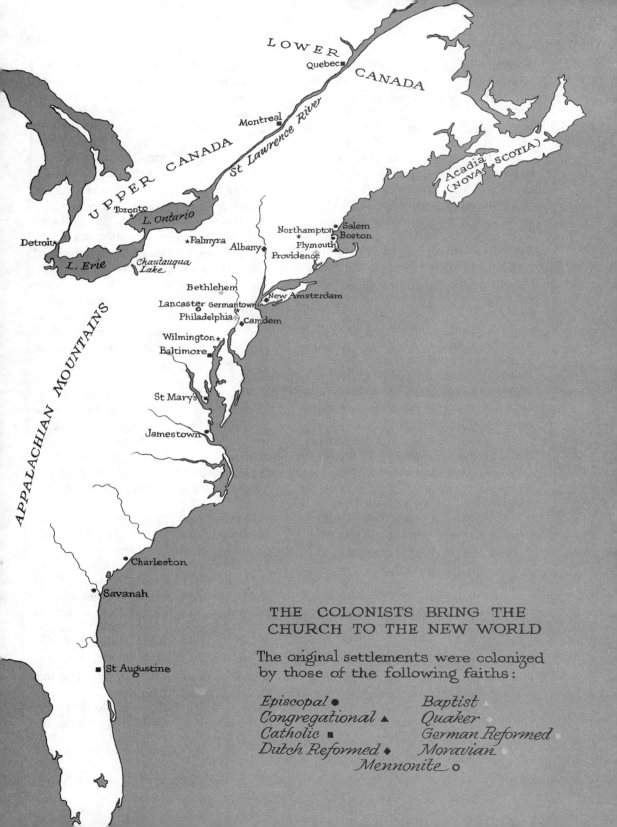

LOWER CANADA

Quebec■

UPPER CANADA

Montreal●

St Lawrence River

Acadia
(NOVA SCOTIA)

Toronto●
★
L. Ontario

Detroit★

●Palmyra

Albany

Northampton●
★
Plymouth
Providence

Salem
●Boston

L. Erie

Chautauqua
Lake

Bethlehem

Lancaster Germantown

Philadelphia●

New Amsterdam

APPALACHIAN MOUNTAINS

●Camden

Wilmington★

Baltimore■

St Mary's

Jamestown●

●Charleston

●Savanah

■ St Augustine

THE COLONISTS BRING THE
CHURCH TO THE NEW WORLD

The original settlements were colonized
by those of the following faiths:

Episcopal ●   Baptist ▲
Congregational ▲   Quaker
Catholic ■   German Reformed ▲
Dutch Reformed ◆   Moravian
        Mennonite ○

separation of Church and State. These principles are among America's most fundamental characteristics. And those who had the foremost part in the fashioning of these principles were the Baptists.

6. The Catholics in the Colonial Era • The Roman Catholic Church came to America with the founding of the colony of Maryland. In 1632 King Charles I of England granted to George Calvert and his heirs the territory around Chesapeake Bay. This George Calvert was made the first Lord Baltimore by the king. He was a recent convert to Catholicism. He named the territory Maryland after the wife of the king.

Soon after having received his grant of territory in America, the first Lord Baltimore died. He was succeeded by his son Cecil Calvert, the second Lord Baltimore, who in 1634 established the first settlement in the new colony, which he named St. Mary after the mother of Jesus.

It is very interesting that the first English colony in America in which religious toleration was established by law was founded by a Catholic. The Catholic Church had nothing to do with this. It was entirely the personal idea of the founder of the colony.

With Lord Baltimore freedom of religion was not a principle, as it was with Roger Williams, but a matter of policy. In order to make his colony profitable, Lord Baltimore needed settlers to whom he could sell the land. A small number of Roman Catholics were among the first settlers, but the great mass of Catholics in England did not care to come to the new country. So Lord Baltimore had to draw his settlers from the ranks of the Protestants. These from the very beginning formed the great majority of the colonists. It was to protect his small minority of Catholics that Lord Baltimore decreed religious toleration for all the religious bodies in his colony—except for people who did not believe in the doctrine of the Trinity. Against the latter he decreed death and confiscation of property.

In 1649 the Maryland Assembly, at the request of Lord Baltimore, passed the Act of Toleration. Although this act was based upon considerations of policy and not of principle, it was nevertheless an important milestone in the history of religious liberty in America.

In 1692 the Baltimore family lost its possessions in America. Maryland was made a royal colony, and the Church of England was set up as the Established or State Church.

Under the rule of the Baltimores the Catholic Church had grown but slowly. At the time they lost Maryland the Catholics formed only one fourth of the population. Yet from these small beginnings there was to develop the great expansion of the Roman Catholic Church in the United States which we see today.

7. The Quakers • The Quakers were among the most interesting of the religious groups which came to America. They were possessed of a strong missionary spirit. Ten years after George Fox started his work in England some of his followers appeared in America. By the end of the century they could be found in every one of the English colonies.

From the beginning many Quaker women did missionary work. The first Quakers to appear in America were two women, Mary Fisher and Ann Austin. They arrived in Boston in 1656; but be-

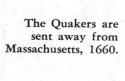
The Quakers are sent away from Massachusetts, 1660.

Brown Brothers

fore they could land, orders were given by the Puritans that they should be kept on board the ship. After that they were put in prison for five weeks. The jail windows were boarded up so that they could neither see out nor be seen. Then they were sent back to Barbados, the place from which they had come.

The ship which took the two women was barely out of sight when another vessel entered the port of Boston bringing eight other Quakers. These were imprisoned for eleven weeks, and then they also were sent out of the colony.

The Massachusetts colony passed several laws forbidding Quakers to enter. In 1661 a law was passed imposing the death penalty upon Quakers who returned after having been banished. In spite of these severe laws the Quakers continued to come. At last the laws against the Quakers were suspended. The story was the same in the other New England colonies.

The Quakers appeared in New York at about the same time that they came to New England. For a short time they were persecuted there. Outside of the so-called Quaker colonies—New Jersey, Delaware, and Pennsylvania—and with the exception of Rhode Island and the Carolinas, the Quakers were persecuted in every one of the English colonies.

The first Monthly Meetings in America were formed in Massachusetts before 1660. The New England Yearly Meeting was established in 1661. It is the oldest Yearly Meeting in America.

George Fox visited America in 1672. He made a number of converts and established several new meetings.

By 1681 more than a thousand colonists had come to New Jersey. Most of them were Quakers. They settled in West Jersey; and Burlington on the Delaware, founded in 1677, became for a time the most important Quaker center.

In 1681 Pennsylvania was granted to

William Penn, and the next year Delaware was added, though later this became a separate colony. No other single Englishman made such a success of his colonial enterprise as did Penn. He not only granted religious freedom, but also advertised his colony in England, Holland, and Germany. As a result a stream of colonists poured into Pennsylvania from all these countries and also from France. While the majority of the early colonists to Pennsylvania were Quakers, Penn estimated in 1685 that only half the population of his colony was English.

The number of *Friends,* as the Quakers are officially called, continued to increase. By 1760 their number was thirty thousand. But as numbers increased, the spiritual life declined. Religion among the Friends was described as lifeless and dry. In the nineteenth century the Friends experienced significant revivals. In 1827–28 the Hicksites, so named after liberal leader Elias Hicks, separated from the orthodox branch. The Friends have established many schools and colleges, and they are very active in missionary work.

8. The German Reformed in Pennsylvania • Between 1727 and 1745 a large number of Germans came to Pennsylvania. For the most part they came without ministers or schoolmasters; consequently several of the earliest German Reformed churches were formed without pastors. The first German Reformed church had been established in 1719 at Germantown, ten miles north of Philadelphia. By 1725 there were three German Reformed churches. These churches asked John Philip Boehm, who had been a schoolmaster at Worms, to act as their pastor. He began to preach and to bap-

A Quaker Exhorter in New England

tize. But there was one difficulty. Boehm had never been ordained as a minister. He and his friends asked the advice of the Dutch Reformed churches in New York, and then of the Classis of Amsterdam. Boehm admitted that he had violated the order of the Reformed Church by preaching and baptizing without ordination. The classis stated that under the circumstances the work of Boehm must be considered lawful, and he was properly ordained as minister in 1729. This was the beginning of a close relationship between the German Reformed and the Dutch Reformed churches in America.

Many Swiss Reformed settled in that area also, between the Delaware and the Schuylkill rivers.

Most of the German immigrants to Pennsylvania were poor. On their way to

America they passed through the Dutch ports, where they aroused the sympathy of the Reformed Church in the Netherlands. An appeal was made to this group to take over the care of the German Reformed churches in America, and they consented. Michael Schlatter, a native of Switzerland, heard of this. He went to Holland and presented himself as a candidate for ministerial work among the German Reformed in America. The Classis of Amsterdam accepted him, and he set sail in 1746.

Schlatter's chief mission was to organize the German Reformed churches in America into a synod. He was full of energy and zeal. He visited all the larger German Reformed churches, and the newly organized synod held its first meeting in Philadelphia in September, 1747. At the request of this synod he went to Holland, and in a short time raised $48,-000 to help the poor German Reformed churches in America. This aid was given on condition that these churches remain under the Classis of Amsterdam. When he returned to America he brought with him besides the money six young ministers and seven hundred Bibles for free distribution. This greatly strengthened the German Reformed Church in colonial America.

In most respects the German Reformed and the German Lutherans in America were much alike in worship and doctrine. They worked harmoniously together. In many places the German Reformed and the German Lutherans held services in the same church building.

9. The Lutherans • Lutheranism in America had its beginnings among the Dutch on the banks of the Hudson and

The Gloria Dei Church is the oldest church in Philadelphia. This Swedish Lutheran Church was dedicated in 1700 and is still in daily use.

among the Swedes on the banks of the Delaware. Two churches are still standing as monuments to the early history of Swedish Lutheranism in America: Old Gloria Dei Church on the bank of the Delaware in South Philadelphia, and Old Swedes Church in Wilmington. Around both churches are graveyards in which rest the remains of these Swedish Lutherans. In the southern end of the graveyard around Old Swedes Church in Wilmington lies buried the body of Torkillus, the first Lutheran minister in America.

But however interesting the history of these Dutch and Swedish Lutheran churches may be, they were historically unimportant in comparison with the German Lutheran churches. As already noted, many Germans came to America between the years 1727 and 1745. Of all the religious groups among these German immigrants, the Lutherans were the most numerous.

All these Germans were desperately poor, and the Lutherans, like the Reformed, came without pastors or schoolmasters. As a result they were slow in organizing churches. But after a time a number of German Lutheran ministers came to the colonies.

One of the Lutherans, John Christian Schulz, returned to Europe to collect funds to obtain ministers and teachers. The appeal struck a responsive chord in Francke in Halle. Francke began looking for a young man suitable for the work among the German Lutherans in America. Finally his choice fell upon Henry Melchior Mühlenberg. Mühlenberg was well-educated and had had experience as a teacher in Francke's orphanage at Halle. Although a Pietist and severely critical of conditions in the Lutheran Church in Germany, he was thoroughly loyal. He loved the Lutheran Church and was deeply concerned about its growth in the new world.

The outlook for Lutheranism in America was not altogether encouraging. The Germans were more numerous than any other non-English inhabitants in the colonies; but they were widely scattered and were divided into many sects—although the Lutherans were the most numerous. Furthermore, at this time Count von Zinzendorf was in America and was working hard to unite all the German religious groups into one body. If his plan should succeed, it would dim the hope of building up in America the Lutheran Church as an independent organization.

Mühlenberg responded to the pleas of Francke, and in 1742 set sail for America. His coming opened a new period in the history of American Lutheranism. He had come out as the pastor of three Lutheran churches in the Philadelphia area. However, he had come unannounced, and when he arrived in Philadelphia in November he found the churches in a disorganized state. The majority of the Philadelphia churches favored Zinzendorf's plan of union. Many congregations had unworthy men as pastors. But Mühlenberg was an energetic and resourceful man. Within one month he was in complete control of the field, and before the end of the year he was installed as pastor of the three German Lutheran churches— in Philadelphia, New Hanover, and the Old Trappe Church in New Providence.

Besides caring for his three congregations he labored far and wide to build up the churches that had no pastors. He regularly sent reports of his work to the authorities in Halle. This kept the American field before the Lutheran churches in Germany, and as a result money and men were sent for the support of the work in the colony. In 1745 three ministers came out from Halle with funds to build new churches. In each one of these churches a Christian day school was opened for children of the parish.

By the year 1748 there were several strong churches and able ministers. New congregations had been organized, and many young men offered themselves as candidates for the ministry. In this same year six ministers and twenty-four members representing ten churches met in Philadelphia and organized the first Lutheran Synod of America. There were around seventy Lutheran churches in

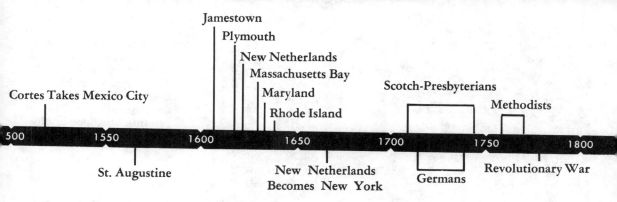

Jamestown

Plymouth

New Netherlands

Massachusetts Bay

Maryland

Rhode Island

Cortes Takes Mexico City

Scotch-Presbyterians

Methodists

| 500 | 1550 | 1600 | 1650 | 1700 | 1750 | 1800 |

St. Augustine

New Netherlands
Becomes New York

Germans

Revolutionary War

America at this time. And when the War for Independence broke out the number of German Lutherans in Pennsylvania alone had reached about seventy-five thousand.

10. Other German Groups • Let us go back, now, to the previous century, and see what other German groups came to America in those early years.

William Penn advertised his colony far and wide. He even made a trip to Europe to tell about it. As a result, in 1683 thirteen German Mennonite families came to America. They made a settlement ten miles north of Philadelphia and named their colony Germantown. Theirs was the first German settlement in America. A number of Swiss Mennonites settled in what is now Lancaster County.

Another religious group to come to Pennsylvania were the German Baptists, who arrived in 1719. The other people in the colony gave them the name *Dunkers,* which comes from the German word *tunken,* meaning "to dip." They first settled at Germantown, but soon left to make other new settlements in that area. From the beginning they held religious services in their homes. A church was not organized until 1723. Within a few years these German Baptist Brethren, or Dunkers, scattered in all directions.

In many respects the Dunkers agreed in doctrine with the Quakers and the Mennonites. They were influenced by the Quakers in that they adopted a very plain style of dress. They practiced trine immersion, that is, threefold immersion in the name of the Father, Son, and Holy Spirit. Adults only were baptized. In their form of church government they were congregational.

The most important Dunker in colonial times was Christopher Sower. He was the first German printer in America. He was also the first to edit and print a German newspaper. After his death his son carried on the work. The Sower Bible was of great importance in the religious life of the early German settlers. Published in 1743, it was the first Bible printed in America in a European language.

The Moravians came to Pennsylvania in 1740 and settled on a tract of five thousand acres at the forks of the Delaware River. Their great object was to do missionary work among the destitute and scattered German settlers in Pennsylvania and among the Indians. In 1741 Count von Zinzendorf himself arrived in Philadelphia. Just before Christmas he came to the Moravian settlement at the forks of the Delaware, and on Christmas Eve he named the place Bethlehem, meaning House of Bread, "in token of his fervent

The home of Christopher Sower, near Philadelphia, served many purposes. The German Baptist Brethren held their meetings upstairs. The printing was done in the building at the rear.

desire and ardent hope that here the true bread of life might be broken for all who hungered." Bethlehem, where today the great Bethlehem Steel works is located, is still the chief Moravian center in America.

11. Presbyterianism Takes Root •
As we saw in Part IV of our book, Presbyterianism in England acquired great strength during the seventeenth century. The moment came when this Church was about to be the Established or State Church. Although in England it did not actually reach this position, in Scotland the Presbyterian Church did become the State Church.

In America several of the foremost Puritan leaders, such as John Eliot, the apostle to the Indians, Increase and Cotton Mather, and others, were favorable toward Presbyterianism. In several of the New England churches presbyterian ideas of church organization were put into operation, and in Connecticut the presbyterian system was fully adopted. There the names Congregational and Presbyterian came to be used interchangeably.

The Dutch Reformed Church in the colonies of New York and New Jersey was presbyterian in its form of church government. When New England Con-

gregationalist Puritans moved into New York and New Jersey their change to Presbyterianism came about easily. And so these New England Congregationalists established in Long Island several churches with the presbyterian form of government.

These were the small beginnings of this denomination in America. Then a mass immigration of Scotch Irish took place and greatly increased the growth of the Presbyterian Church in the new world.

The Scotch Irish were really not Irish at all but Scotchmen who had gone to live in Ireland. They were staunch Presbyterians. Although some came earlier, the mass migration to America began in the early part of the eighteenth century and continued until well past the middle of that century. The earliest parties came to New England, but later groups settled in New York and especially Pennsylvania. From the latter state they gradually made their way into western Maryland, Virginia, the Carolinas, and Georgia.

The man who laid the foundation for organized Presbyterianism in America was Francis Makemie, who came to eastern Maryland in 1683 and established preaching stations in the Scotch Irish communities there. For several years he went up and down Maryland, Virginia, and the

PART FIVE: THE CHURCH IN THE NEW WORLD

Carolinas, preaching in the scattered settlements. Through the work of Makemie and his helpers a number of churches were organized as early as 1706, and by 1716 there were seventeen Presbyterian ministers serving in the colonies. In this year the first synod was held.

Throughout the years when the number of ministers was small and requests for preaching services were many, the Church held steadfast to its rule that only trained, ordained men should serve as ministers. In 1710 a certain David Evans was preaching among the Welsh settlers in Virginia. He was a gifted young man, whose preaching gave spiritual food and guidance to his hearers. Yet, the presbytery decided that he "had done very ill," because he was not ordained. In spite of the great need Evans was told to lay aside all other business for a whole year, and apply himself diligently to learning and study. Once a year the presbytery examined his progress, and five full years passed before Evans was finally ordained.

An important event for Presbyterianism in America was the passing of the Adopting Act by the Synod of 1729. This Act required all Presbyterian ministers to subscribe to the Westminster Confession.

As the Scotch Irish immigration increased, especially after 1720, the church grew more and more rapidly, and by the time the War for Independence began these sturdy Presbyterians were to be found in every one of the English colonies. Everywhere they were in sufficient numbers to be of considerable influence.

12. Methodism Arrives Late in the Period • Since the Methodist movement in England did not get under way until 1739, Methodism was naturally late in making its appearance in America. It was not introduced until almost the end of the colonial period.

The man who brought Methodism to America was Philip Embury. He began work in New York in his own private dwelling in the year 1766. At about the same time Robert Strawbridge labored in Maryland. In 1771 John Wesley sent Francis Asbury over from England to further the work.

But the Methodist Church was not established in America until after the War for Independence.

13. The Spanish Colonize California • Although the Spanish leaders in Mexico sent an expedition of two ships to explore the coast of California in 1542, it

The Preaching
of the First
Methodist Sermon
in Baltimore

was not until 1769 that four groups of settlers were sent out. They met at San Diego Bay. The religious leader was a priest called Father Serra who in the next fifteen years established nine missions. Eventually twenty-one missions stretched from San Diego to San Francisco. The padres, or priests, persuaded the Indians to live at these missions. They taught the Indians about Christianity as well as showing them how to care for crops and raise livestock.

1. *Work out a map showing the religions in the American colonies, Canada, and Florida.*
2. *What was the religious background of the Pilgrims?*
3. *How did the Puritans and Pilgrims differ in their views of the Church of England?*
4. *Why did congregational church government tend to prevail in Massachusetts in spite of the fact that most of the settlers were members of the Episcopal Church?*
5. *What was the purpose for founding Harvard and Yale?*
6. *What principles and practices developed through the work of Roger Williams and the Baptist Church of Providence? Why did the Puritans, who themselves were persecuted, still persecute others who came to their colony?*
7. *What was Calvert's reason for giving religious liberty? What was Roger Williams' reason?*
8. *Where did the Quakers settle in America? Why did they favor religious liberty?*
9. *In which respects were the German Reformed and Lutherans dependent on the homeland churches?*
10. *Which group led the Presbyterian advance in America? What was the Adopting Act?*
11. *Do you think religion is a factor in determining the economic success of a country?*
12. *Identify: Scotch-Irish, Baltimore, the Sower Bible, Father Serra, Yearly Meeting.*
13. *How were the Dunkers, Quakers, and Mennonites alike?*
14. *What group developed a Christian day school?*
15. *In times of stress there are two alternative reactions: maintain basic principles, or adopt expedient practices. Find examples in this chapter showing these reactions in such matters as ordaining ministers and governing churches. Should churches accommodate to changing conditions?*

CHAPTER 42

The Church

Experiences a Great Awakening

1. The Great Awakening • You may recall that in the eighteenth century the winds of Deism and Rationalism blew over England and blighted the religious life of the churches in that country. They likewise chilled much of the religious life of the churches in America into a deep sleep. In the early part of the eighteenth century religious life in America was at a low ebb. The Puritans who had founded the New England colonies were men and women of a deep religious life and strong religious convictions; their grandchildren had lost nearly all religious fervor.

Then a tremendous change came over the religious life of the colonies. It has become known as the *Great Awakening*. A series of religious revivals took place in various colonies. The Great Awakening in America and the Methodist movement in England occurred at the same time. Both of these had for their background the influence of the Moravians and of German Pietism, of which Spener and

Francke were the leaders and the University of Halle became the center. The Methodist movement in England and the Great Awakening in America came together in the person of George Whitefield. Later we shall see how this came about.

2. Frelinghuysen, Tennent, and Edwards • Theodore J. Frelinghuysen, who in the Netherlands had been under German Pietistic influence, arrived in America in 1720 to become the pastor of some Dutch Reformed churches on the frontier in New Jersey, in the valley of the Raritan River. Frelinghuysen was a preacher of outstanding ability. In his sermons he put all the emphasis on the need of conversion, and his fervent preaching soon bore fruit. Many new members were added to his church. Other churches heard about the remarkable changes brought about by his preaching and requested him to preach to them. In this way the revival spread beyond the valley of the Raritan.

William Tennent was the minister of a Presbyterian church in Neshaminy, Pennsylvania. He had four sons: Gilbert, William Jr., John, and Charles. The oldest son, Gilbert, had already been educated by his father for the ministry, when William Tennent built in a corner of his large yard a log cabin to be used as a schoolhouse. In this school, which was nicknamed the "Log College," the Reverend W. Tennent trained his three younger sons and in course of time fifteen other young men for the ministry. He trained his students very thoroughly in Latin, Greek, and Hebrew, in logic and in theology. Above all he stirred in them a fervent evangelical spirit. All four of his

William Tennent and Some of His Students at the "Log College"

sons became ministers in the Presbyterian Church and carried on in the spirit of their father.

In the year in which his father opened his "Log College," Gilbert Tennent became the minister of a Presbyterian church in the neighborhood of the Reverend Theodore Frelinghuysen. The latter helped the younger Presbyterian minister in every way. He permitted him to hold services in the churches of the Dutch Reformed. Tennent, of course, used the English language, and to this some of the members of the Dutch Reformed Church objected strongly. But through the warm evangelical preaching of Gilbert Tennent and the graduates of Log College, a revival got under way which in course of time ran like a forest fire among the Presbyterians from Long Island to Virginia.

The name of Jonathan Edwards is inseparably linked with the Great Awakening in New England. In many ways Jonathan Edwards was the outstanding intellectual figure in colonial America, and one of the greatest minds America has ever produced. He was born in 1703 in East Windsor, Connecticut, where his father was minister of the Congregational Church. He was graduated from Yale at the early age of seventeen years, and in 1727, after several years of further study and of preaching and teaching, he became minister of the Congregational Church in Northampton in central Massachusetts.

The church was in a state of spiritual deadness. In December 1734 Edwards preached a series of sermons on Justification. These sermons were directed against the tendency toward Arminianism, which was then developing in New England. With great vividness the tall, slender, grave young minister pictured the wrath of God, from which he urged sinners to flee. Soon a great change came over the church and the town of Northampton. In the spring and summer which followed the town seemed to be full of the presence of God. There was scarcely a single person, young or old, who was not concerned about the eternal things. During the first year of the revival more than three hundred persons professed conversion.

In the next few years revivals, independent of each other, took place in various parts of New England. By 1740 the revival movement had become general throughout New England. Mass conversions were common. Out of a population of 300,000 between 25,000 and 50,000 new members were added to the churches. The moral tone of New England was lifted to a higher plane.

The revival was attended with strong emotional and physical manifestations. Strong men fell as though shot, and women became hysterical. Edwards preached at Enfield, Connecticut, in July, 1741. His subject was: "Sinners in the Hands of an Angry God." He had to stop and request silence that he might be heard, for there was such loud weeping.

3. George Whitefield • George Whitefield had a large share in the Great Awakening. He was born in Gloucester, England, on December 16, 1714. His father was a tavern keeper. The boy grew up in poverty amidst scenes of low morality. But there was in Gloucester an endowed school. The young George became a pupil there and prepared himself for college. In 1733 he entered Oxford University, where he became a member of the Holy Club. After a serious illness he was converted, and in 1736 he was ordained a minister in the Episcopal Church of England.

You will remember that Whitefield

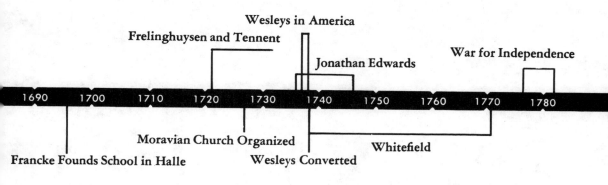

labored with the Wesleys to spread the Gospel in England. But he did his greatest work in America. From 1738 to 1770 he made seven preaching tours to America.

In those years he went up and down the American colonies from New England to Georgia, preaching. Wherever he preached huge crowds came to hear him. Sometimes he spoke to as many as twenty thousand people. Gifted with marvelous eloquence, he was the greatest preacher of the eighteenth century and one of the greatest of all time. Through his preaching thousands were converted, and the spiritual life of many other thousands was quickened.

Whitefield died September 30, 1770, in Newburyport, Massachusetts, where he lies buried under the pulpit of the Old South Presbyterian Church.

4. The Aftermath • In time the interest in spiritual things began to grow less, and the revival called the Great Awakening burned itself out. As early as the years 1744 to 1748 Jonathan Edwards' church in Northampton, according to his own statement, was utterly dead. In those years not a single conversion took place.

As the revival faded away certain disagreements arose. The Congregational ministers in New England and the Reformed ministers in New York were divided as to its value. Some favored it, others were against it. The Presbyterian Church was split over the question, though later it reunited. The Great Awakening also brought about the development of the New England theology, which in the end led to a great weakening of historic Calvinism among the Congregationalists, the Reformed, and the Presbyterians. At the same time a liberal tendency began to show itself, especially in the churches of Boston and vicinity, which in the early nineteenth century resulted in the formation of Unitarian churches.

The Great Awakening powerfully fostered the spirit of revivalism, which has been one of the outstanding features of the life of the Church in America.

1. *Who led the movement that was to develop into the Great Awakening? What did each man contribute?*
2. *You may be able to find a copy of Jonathan Edwards' sermon, "Sinners in the Hands of an Angry God." If so, read it to get the flavor of Edwards' sermonizing.*
3. *Why did the Reformation and the subsequent revivals "burn themselves out" after their initial striking influence?*
4. *What association did George Whitefield have with John Wesley?*

CHAPTER 43 *43*

The Church

As the Young Nation Is Formed

1. Unifying Factors • In addition to the political and economic factors which united the colonists in their purpose to resist and revolt against England, there were two religious factors of significance.

Through the Great Awakening, the colonists experienced for the first time a common religious feeling. They took a common interest in Whitefield, Edwards, Tennent, and others before the names of Washington and Franklin became for them symbols of a common political cause.

Another unifying factor was the common resistance to the long-drawn-out agitation for the appointment of a Church of England bishop for the colonies. A good many Episcopalians themselves were in opposition, feeling that such an appointment would subvert their civil and religious liberties. Starting in 1766 the Congregationalists of New England and the Presbyterians of the

King's Chapel, Boston, was the first Protestant Episcopal church in New England. A Bible sent by James II is still in use. This church was the favorite place of worship among officers of the British army. In 1785 King's Chapel became the first Unitarian church in America.

Middle Colonies united in annual conventions to prevent the establishment of an episcopacy in America.

2. The War for Independence •

When the war broke out, the majority of both the clergy and the members of the Episcopal Church in New England remained loyal to England. In the Southern Colonies they took their stand on the American side. In the Middle Colonies they were about equally divided. Two-thirds of the signers of the Declaration of Independence were Episcopalians. The clergy were in a difficult position, having taken their ordination vow to support the king of England as the head of their church.

The Methodists, who had but recently made their appearance in America, found themselves in a difficult position since John Wesley took the English side. The result was that the American patriots looked askance at all Methodists in America. Yet their number grew from 4,000 in 1775 to 13,000 in 1780.

The Quakers and the Moravians were conscientious objectors to war, but they went as far in its support as their principles allowed.

With few exceptions, the clergy of all other churches gave their hearty support to the war. The Reverend John Witherspoon, an outstanding leader of the Presbyterians, was selected as a delegate to the Continental Congress and was the only minister among the signers of the Declaration of Independence. Many made resistance and independence a holy cause. Many joined the army as officers or chaplains.

3. Disestablishment •

An established church is a State church. It is the legally recognized church of the State. All the citizens of the State are supposed to belong to the State church. In the early days people in Massachusetts who did not wish to belong to the Congregational Church were driven out of the colony. This happened to Baptists and Quakers. In the colonies in which the Episcopal Church was established, that church, through the State, hindered the work of the other churches. The ministers of the Established Church were the only ones given authority to perform certain religious acts. All citizens in the

A Meeting
of Friends
in the Ross Street
Meeting House,
New York

colonies where there was an established church had to pay taxes for its support, whether they belonged to it or not.

At the end of the colonial period and at the beginning of the national period there were two established or official churches in America. The Congregational Church was the Established Church in Massachusetts, New Hampshire, and Connecticut. The Episcopal Church was the established church in New York, Maryland, Virginia, North Carolina, South Carolina, and Georgia. So there was an established church in nine of the thirteen colonies.

Other churches in the colonies were, of course, opposed to the Established Church. The Lutherans, the Reformed, and the Presbyterians each felt that their church should be the State church. The only church that was not in favor of having an established church of any kind was the Baptist Church. The Baptists, as we have seen, believed in the separation of Church and State. The Quakers, or Friends, were like them in this respect.

The reason that Rhode Island, New Jersey, Delaware, and Pennsylvania were without an established church was that in these colonies the Baptists and Quakers were in the majority.

The Baptist Church, supported by the other dissenting churches, led the fight for disestablishment. Naturally, the members of the existing established churches did not like to give up their advantages and special privileges.

Nevertheless, early in the War for Independence disestablishment came easily in New York, Maryland, and the southernmost colonies. But in Virginia there was a long and hard fight. The disestablishment in Virginia was accomplished in 1786. It soon spread throughout the nation. It was made a part of the first amendment to our National Constitution, and thus became a part of the fundamental law of the land.

4. Severing European Ties • In some of the churches there was no official connection between them and Euro-

The Man on Horseback,
a Painting of Bishop
Francis Asbury by
Henry Hayman Cochrane

Chosen by John Wesley as a
missionary to America in
1771, Asbury saw American
Methodism grow from 15,000
to over 200,000 during
his lifetime. He traveled an
average of 4,000 miles a year
on horseback, preached at
least once a day, and preached
a total of 20,000 sermons in
his lifetime.

Methodist Information

pean churches. Some of these churches —the Baptists, the Presbyterians, and the Quakers—organized on a national scale. The Congregationalists, who were the most numerous in the colonial period, refused to organize into even state-wide associations. This failure proved to be a great handicap in their growth.

The Episcopal, Catholic, Methodist, and Reformed churches were subject to European control. The Methodists up to this point had belonged to the Church of England. None of the men who preached were ordained and hence could not administer the sacraments. As a presbyter in the Church of England, Wesley felt he had the right to ordain, and so, assisted by two clergymen of that church, he ordained Thomas Coke as superintendent of the Methodist Societies in America.

In a conference in 1784, Coke and As-

bury were elected superintendents, a number of men were ordained, and a creed and liturgy—thoroughly Arminian—were adopted. These formularies were primarily the work of John Wesley.

The Episcopal Church entered the national period in a weakened condition and still officially connected with the Church of England. Various writings and conferences advocated a separate organization. At an informal meeting of ten Episcopal clergymen in 1783, Samuel Seabury, Jr., was chosen to go to England to obtain consecration as bishop. Refused in England, he obtained it in Scotland. In 1785 a general convention met and prepared the constitution of the *Protestant Episcopal Church in the United States.*

The Reformed churches severed their ties with the Classis of Amsterdam soon after the War of Independence. The

German Reformed Church adopted the name of *The Reformed Church in the United States* and the Dutch Reformed Church took the name *The Reformed Church in America*.

The Roman Catholic Church had been under the control of the vicar apostolic in London. In 1784 the pope appointed John Carroll superior over the Catholic Church in America, and in 1789 he was appointed bishop. Baltimore became the first Roman see.

1. Why was the Great Awakening conducive to the spirit of independence in the colonies?
2. Why would the colonists be opposed to the appointment of an Episcopal bishop for the colonies?
3. How did the church leaders line up their groups in the Revolutionary War?
4. What were the large religious tendencies of this period in American history?
5. State clearly what is meant by the "established church." What were the two established churches in America? What is disestablishment?
6. Do present-day decisions of the Supreme Court follow from disestablishment? Does disestablishment of religion mean that the state is not concerned about religion? Does the federal government pay army chaplains?
7. Trace the development of independence of the Methodists and Episcopalians from the mother country.
8. Why did not the Roman Catholic Church declare its independence?
9. Identify: Loyalists, John Witherspoon, John Carroll, Francis Asbury, Thomas Coke.
10. How did John Wesley want his followers to react to the Revolutionary War?
11. Why didn't Rhode Island have an established church?
12. What handicapped the growth of the Congregationalists?

CHAPTER *44*

The Church
In the Early Nineteenth Century

1. Influences on the Church • Three external events of major consequence influenced the Church in the nineteenth century: the westward movement, new immigration, and the Civil War. Only the first of these will be studied in this chapter.

Internal trends also influenced the Church. The Second Awakening brought many into the Church, but it also promoted the already prevalent trend toward fragmentation. New sects and new branches of established denominations proliferated. And the perennial trend

Philip Gendreau

The Statue "Pioneer Mother" by Proctor in City Park, Kansas City, Missouri

toward apostasy was constantly in evidence. Historic doctrines were watered down, heresy and Modernism crept in, and again the Church seemed dead.

The early years of the nineteenth century saw one of the great sagas of history: the mass movement of people from the old settlements, across the mountains, and into the seething, vigorous West. By 1820 ten new states west of the Alleghenies were added to the Union.

2. The Presbyterians • The Scotch-Irish were the last Europeans to come to America in the colonial era. Naturally, they settled along the western frontier where they founded many Presbyterian churches. They were therefore in the vanguard of the westward movement. By 1802 three presbyteries in Kentucky organized into a Synod.

The *Plan of Union* became of great significance at this time. The Presbyterians and the Congregationalists, if they are both true to their Calvinistic confession, differ only in their forms of church government. When the westward migration swelled to great numbers, both churches came to realize how large was the task facing them in the new West. To perform that task more successfully they adopted in 1801 the Plan of Union. Under this plan the two churches agreed that it would be permissible for Congregational and Presbyterian settlers in the western country to found churches together, and that a church so organized would be free to call a minister of either denomination. If the majority of members were Presbyterians, the church was to be conducted according to Presbyterian rules—even if the minister was a Congre-

Dr. Marcus Whitman,
a physician and
Presbyterian elder,
traveled to Oregon in 1836
as a missionary
to the Indians
of the Northwest.

gationalist; if most of the members were Congregationalists, that form of church organization would be followed.

The Plan of Union worked to the advantage of the Presbyterians. They were more numerous, and they had a strong and active denominational spirit. It has been estimated that in New York, Ohio, Illinois, and Michigan two thousand churches which were originally Congregational became Presbyterian. Throughout the West these churches established schools and colleges.

3. The Baptists • The Baptist and Methodist churches grew in membership far more rapidly than the Presbyterian and Congregational churches. Ministers in the former could be poorly-educated and serve on a part-time basis. Ministers in the latter had to be well-educated, and were required to give full time to the ministry. It cost less to organize a Baptist

or Methodist Church. In addition, these ministers who worked with their hands along with the frontiersmen appealed to them more than the scholarly Presbyterians. Their crude, highly emotional sermons were well-fitted for the rough conditions of life on the frontier.

Often the Baptists came as groups and brought their ministers with them. After meeting in a settler's cabin for a time, a church would be built of logs. The father of Abraham Lincoln helped to build such a church in 1819 on Pigeon Creek in Indiana. It was the custom to hold monthly business meetings. These meetings were generally devoted to matters of discipline for drinking, fighting, stealing, immorality, gambling, and even intimate family relations. South of the Ohio River, where many church members held slaves, the church watched protectingly over the slaves. Slaves could be church members, and they were sometimes per-

PART FIVE: THE CHURCH IN THE NEW WORLD

mitted a voice in church matters. It is clear that the Baptist Church was a powerful factor in maintaining order and decency in the raw western communities.

4. The Methodists • Of all the churches, the Methodist was the most successful in extending itself among the frontiersmen in the new western country. Their greater measure of success in winning men and gathering them into churches was due to two things: their doctrine and their organization.

The Presbyterians and Baptists were both Calvinists, though the Baptists preached a milder form of Calvinism than did the Presbyterians. As Calvinists, both preached the doctrine of predestination, of God's absolute sovereignty and electing grace. They preached that man's destiny lies wholly in the hands of God.

The Methodists were Arminians. They preached the doctrine of man's free will —that man holds his destiny in his own hands. This doctrine had great appeal. The frontiersman felt that he was carving his own destiny out of the western wilderness.

And so the Methodists were able to gain more members and establish a larger number of churches. But a church is not an end in itself. It is only a means to an end. A small church that preaches sound doctrine is more to be desired than a large church whose doctrine has departed more or less from the truth of Scripture.

The form of organization of the Methodists was also better suited to frontier conditions. Under the Presbyterian and Baptist systems the preachers, generally speaking, were confined to their own local churches. It was not so with the Methodist preachers. "All the world is

Methodist Prints

Although the official title of this famous statue of Francis Asbury is "Pioneer Methodist Bishop in America," it is popularly known as "The Circuit Rider." The statue by Lukeman is located at Sixteenth and Mount Pleasant Streets, Washington, D.C.

my parish" was Wesley's motto. Actually, all England was his circuit, and in his pursuit of souls he rode that vast circuit throughout his long life. Thus circuit riding became an established Methodist practice. With Methodism, circuit riding was introduced into America. Nothing could have been better adapted to frontier conditions. And the system of circuit riding was aided and fortified by the system of local lay preachers.

The Methodist circuit riders traveled

on horseback from settlement to settlement. Some of these circuits were so large that it took from four to five weeks to make the rounds. The circuit riders preached every day except perhaps on Monday. At various places they established "classes" with "class leaders" as in England. True to Wesley's slogan, "The world is my parish," the circuit riders did not wait for a number of Methodists to move into a settlement to organize a church. The overwhelming number of frontiersmen did not belong to any church. And so the circuit riders rode across the mountains looking everywhere for frontiersmen to whom they could bring the Gospel and the Methodist doctrines.

As bishop, Francis Asbury was at the head of the Methodist Church throughout the United States. Again and again he crossed the Allegheny Mountains to hold conferences with the preachers and assign them their circuits. He himself also preached.

As a result of the work of the circuit riders and the preaching in the regular churches the Methodists experienced remarkable growth. At the beginning of the nineteenth century there were in the West less than 3,000 Methodists; by 1830 the membership in that area had grown to over 175,000. Of these, 2,000 were Indians and more than 15,000 were Negroes.

5. A Second Awakening Begins in the East • As we have seen in an earlier chapter, the Great Awakening in America was followed by a sharp decline in spiritual life. This was in part the result of the English Deism and French Skepticism, both of which had a deep and widespread influence on the people. Many of the leading men in America were Deists. Perhaps the most influential of these was Thomas Paine, who in a pamphlet entitled *The Age of Reason* boldly swept the Christian faith aside.

The last years of the eighteenth century and the first years of the nineteenth marked the lowest level of vitality in the history of the Christian Church in America. In the new western country the great mass of frontiersmen were sunk in religious ignorance. Quarreling, fighting, hard drinking, and the most shocking profanity were the order of the day.

It was at this time that a revival of religion started in the East, very quietly and gradually. People began to take a renewed interest in Christian life and faith. The membership of the churches increased, and new churches were organized. One of the influences that brought this about in New England was the coming of Methodism with its unique method of evangelization. In 1789 Bishop Asbury appointed the first circuit rider there, and soon all the New England States were covered with a network of circuits.

In 1795 Timothy Dwight became president of Yale. He was a grandson of the great preacher Jonathan Edwards. In a series of lectures and sermons in the college chapel Dwight showed the dangers and evils of Deism, infidelity, and materialism. A revival started in 1802, and one third of the students were converted. Dartmouth, Amherst, Williams, and the College of New Jersey experienced similar revivals.

The religious awakening in the East moved ahead without evangelists or great emotional excitement.

It was not unusual for camp meetings to last night and day for many days. Several ministers from various denominations would address the listening thousands from different stands.

Bettmann Archive

6. Revivals and Camp Meetings •

In the new West the revivals took an altogether different course. One of the early leaders there was a Presbyterian minister by the name of James McGready. Although extremely uncouth, he had within him the power to move his hearers. In 1796 he became pastor of three Presbyterian churches in notorious Logan County in Kentucky. Here, under his preaching, the great western revival began. It became known as the Logan County or Cumberland Revival.

McGready was joined by several Presbyterian and Methodist preachers, and in 1800 the Cumberland Revival reached its climax. In that year a meeting held on Red River was accompanied by excitement. Numbers were converted. The news spread. The crowds grew larger and larger. The people brought provisions with them, and spent several days on the grounds. This was the beginning of the camp meetings which were to become a common practice in American evangelism. One meeting lasted four days and nights, and a hundred people were said to be converted.

Camp meetings were held in every section of the West. Especially at night they were a great sight. Campfires blazed; there were long rows of tents; in the trees hung hundreds of lamps and lanterns. The preachers engaged in impassioned exhortations and earnest prayers. Swelling notes of music floated on the night air as the thousands joined in the singing of hymns. Persons under con-

The Old Cane Ridge Meeting House in Kentucky, where a group of Presbyterian ministers held a sacramental meeting in 1800, became the birthplace of the American camp meetings.

viction of sin sobbed, shrieked, and shouted.

The revivals at the beginning of the awakening in the West were largely a result of the work of Presbyterians, but in the end the Presbyterians suffered because of divisions. The Methodists and Baptists joined in the revival and added great numbers of converts to their membership rolls.

7. New Denominations

• One of the developments which should be noted in the course of American Church history is the tendency of the Church to divide and subdivide. In the first half of the nineteenth century this process had already begun.

Three groups left the Presbyterian Church. The *Cumberland Presbyterian Church* was organized by those who advocated the camp meeting, the circuit system, and a greatly weakened Calvinism. The *Christian Church* left because it could not wholeheartedly accept election and predestination. The *Church of the Disciples* started as a protest movement against all the divisions in the church and a desire to return to the simplicity of New Testament times.

Groups also left the Methodist Church. The *Methodist Protestant Church* was formed by those who wanted greater democracy and lay participation. The *Church of the United Brethren in Christ* and the *Evangelical Church* were organized by German preachers.

While many new denominations were formed by those who desired more piety, activity, or purity in the Church, in New England many Congregational churches and ministers rejected the doctrine of the Trinity and formed Unitarian churches. The birth of this denomination with its false teachings stirred the orthodox Congregationalists to action. As a result many new orthodox Congregational churches were organized.

8. Missionary Societies

• The new religious zeal aroused by the revivals led to the formation of many missionary societies, the publication of many missionary magazines, and the establishment of

Under the sponsorship of the American Board of Foreign Missions, five young men were ordained at Salem, Massachusetts, in February, 1812, to be the first American foreign missionaires. They left soon thereafter for India.

Historical Pictures Service—Chicago

many Christian colleges and theological seminaries.

In the revivals many churches co-operated, and the missionary societies formed were often interdenominational. Nearly every denomination formed its own missionary society. For example, the Congregationalists formed the *American Board of Commissioners for Foreign Missions* in 1810 which sent out 694 missionaries in thirty years.

Particularly dramatic was the beginning of foreign missions among the Baptists. Luther Rice and Adoniram Judson were sent out by the Congregationalists to India. En route they became convinced of Baptist principles and were rebaptized in Calcutta. Judson remained to work in Burma, but Rice returned to organize Baptist missionary societies.

The earliest societies were interested almost exclusively in bringing the Gospel to the unchurched at home—the Indians and Negroes. Later this activity was extended to foreign countries.

To stimulate interest in the work of missions, several missionary magazines were launched. Many were discontinued, but some continue until now.

The frontiersmen were for the most part without Bibles and religious literature. To supply this want the *American Bible Society* was founded in 1816 and the *American Tract Society* in 1825. Many denominations also established publishing societies. These societies were an immense influence in America. They put out a tremendous amount of Christian reading matter which found its way into the cabins of the settlers in the remotest backwoods.

9. The Sunday School • Back in the colonial period there were no Sunday schools. The Methodists were the ones who brought to the United States this appealing way of instructing the children and young people. They began the work in 1786, and were so successful that thirty years later Sunday schools were to be found in every section of the country. In 1824 the American Sunday School Union was organized. The purpose of the Union was to promote the establishment of Sunday schools, and to publish manuals for use in the Sunday schools.

10. Seminaries and Colleges • The settling of the West and the Second Awakening created a growing need for ministers and religious leaders. To fill this need many new seminaries for the training of ministers were founded. Almost every denomination founded one or more schools during this time.

The Congregationalists, whose ministers had been receiving their training at Harvard, established Andover Seminary in 1808, after a Unitarian had been appointed theological professor at Harvard. The Dutch Reformed in 1810 founded a seminary in New Brunswick, New Jersey. Up to that time many of their young men had gone to the Netherlands to be educated for the ministry at the University of Utrecht. In 1812 the Presbyterians founded their seminary in Princeton, New Jersey. Between 1808 and 1840 at least twenty-five such schools were founded. They were all located in the East.

Teachers and leaders also were needed in the new, rapidly growing areas. Throughout the West during this time the churches established many colleges. From these small denominational colleges learning and culture radiated in every direction. Their significance for the life of our nation can hardly be over-estimated.

1. *Which religious groups led the westward movement of colonists? Why was the presbyterian form of church government adopted by these groups?*

2. *Why were the Methodists and Baptists more successful in their growth of membership at the frontier?*

3. *Notice again that revival came to the American scene to counteract a low spiritual level. What two large areas experienced the effects of revival? What methods were used in each to bring about the conversions?*

4. *List the new denominational groups started at this time and the particular emphasis of each one on some phase of church activity or doctrine.*

5. *Look up the origin and history of the Sunday school movement.*

6. *Identify: Plan of Union, circuit rider, Timothy Dwight, James McGready, camp meetings.*

7. *Explain the growth of the Presbyterian Church in the Midwest.*

8. *Note that practically all the great colleges of this period were products of some denomination's plans for training preachers. List ten or twelve of the outstanding universities; then check to find their religious backgrounds.*

CHAPTER 45

The Church in a Time of Turmoil

1. The Presbyterian Church • Under the Plan of Union of 1801 a large number of churches were organized in Central New York, Ohio, Michigan, Indiana, Illinois, and Wisconsin. As you will remember, these churches were made up of two entirely different elements: New England Congregationalists and

Scotch-Irish Presbyterians. Most of the Presbyterians held to a strict Calvinism; but the Congregationalists, influenced by New England liberal theology, were moving more and more away from historic Calvinism.

In 1837 the clash between the orthodox group and the liberal group brought about a split in the Presbyterian Church. This separation lasted for thirty-two years. A year before the two groups divided, the Liberals established Union Seminary in New York City. This school has remained a fountainhead of Liberalism in the United States.

2. The Episcopal Church • As a result of their activities in the Revolutionary War, the Episcopalians were under a cloud for nearly a generation after the War for Independence. They also failed to deal adequately with the problems created by the western movement, so that by 1850 they had only 90,000 members and had slipped from fourth to seventh among the major denominations.

A few individual leaders were exceptions to this negative attitude. Of these, the most outstanding was Bishop Philander Chase. His first parish was on the New York frontier; then he organized the first Episcopal church in New Orleans; later his pioneering work in Ohio led to the formation of a diocese and of Kenyon College; this was followed by missionary work in Michigan and Illinois.

During all this time the gap between the High and Low Church parties was growing. You will remember that the Low Church party was evangelical in spirit and favored simplicity in the church service. The High Church party in America was strengthened by the Oxford Movement in England, and the Low Church party became genuinely alarmed. They feared that their church would be led back into the fold of Rome. A split was prevented at the general convention of 1853 by allowing greater freedom of opinion in the church. From that time on, the Low Church party lost influence.

3. Immigration Strengthens the Lutherans • Among the German Lutherans a conflict broke out on two points: one group stood for the Americanization of the Lutheran Church and a more liberal interpretation of the Augsburg Confession; the other group wished to maintain the German language and hold closely to orthodox Lutheranism.

The first group might have prevailed were it not for the great wave of German immigration which began about 1830 and continued until about 1870. More than a million Germans came to America in the ten years just before the Civil War. While many of these German immigrants were Catholic, and others were hostile to religion of any kind, the majority were Lutherans. They greatly strengthened the conservative element in the Lutheran Church. Their leader was C. F. W. Walther. At this time a number of strictly orthodox synods were organized, among them the well-known Missouri Synod.

Walther became pastor of the Lutheran Church in St. Louis, Missouri. In his German periodical *Der Lutheraner* he ardently instructed his readers to hold fast to orthodox Lutheranism. He also recommended the establishment of parochial schools for the education of the children. A fine system of Lutheran schools in the

St. Louis early became the center of the great branch of the Lutheran Church known as the Missouri Synod. This is how the Trinity Church and parsonage looked a century ago.

Concordia Publishing House

Missouri Synod stands today as a monument to Walther and other leaders. The memory of this great Lutheran is preserved in the name of the Walther League —the youth organization among the Missouri Synod Lutherans.

In the time preceding the Civil War there was also a large immigration of Norwegian and Swedish Lutherans. The latter organized the Augustana Synod and Augustana College at Rock Island, Illinois. This group was also strictly orthodox.

4. The Dutch Reformed Church •
You will recall that the Dutch Reformed had settled in the New York area in the early seventeenth century and had been aroused by the vigorous preaching of Theodore Frelinghuysen in the early

eighteenth century. He founded the first theological seminary to be built in this country. This college, located in New Jersey, was called Queen's College, but is now called Rutgers University.

The great emigration from Europe brought many from the Netherlands also. Many entire congregations came with their pastors. One group led by Dominie Albertus Van Raalte established their first settlement some distance from the east shore of Lake Macatawa in the western part of Michigan in the year 1847 and called it Holland. They joined the Reformed Church of America in 1850. Another colony, led by Dominie Hendrik Scholte, made a settlement in central Iowa to which they gave the name Pella. In 1856 they also merged with the Reformed Church. Other groups of

The Log Church, Holland, Michigan, was built by Dutch immigrants who had participated in the Secession of 1834 in the Netherlands. Later they joined the Reformed Church in America.

Courtesy
Netherlands Information Service

immigrants made themselves homes in Paterson, New Jersey; in Grand Rapids, Michigan; and in Chicago.

The Reformed Church has been greatly instrumental in preserving and spreading the Reformed faith in our own land and in sending out the Gospel to heathen countries. To this day it maintains the Confessions of the ancestral church in the Netherlands. But Liberalism, a foe against which no stronghold can afford to feel secure, has made an invasion here also. However, the larger part of the membership of this church remains orthodox, and hundreds of its ministers are proclaiming the true Gospel. It numbers 230,000 members in 900 churches.

5. The Christian Reformed Church •
Dissatisfaction on the part of some of the Michigan settlers with the hastiness of the union with the Reformed Church and with some of the practices of that church caused discontent to grow rapidly during the years 1850 to 1857.

The use of hymns and choirs in the East was criticized. Questions concerning lodge membership and open communion were introduced at the meetings of Classis Holland. It was claimed that catechism preaching, catechism classes, and house visitation were neglected. A new cause for dispute arose in the recommendation by Van Raalte of Richard Baxter's book, *Call to the Unconverted,* which critics found to be a book containing Arminian sentiments. The discontent was in large part a reaction of laymen against the union fostered by their leaders.

The result of this agitation was that at the meeting of Classis Holland of April 8, 1857, four documents of secession

were presented. On October 7 of the same year five churches with only one minister, the Rev. K. Vanden Bosch, organized themselves into the Christian Reformed Church.

Early growth was slow, but a large number of immigrants from the Netherlands from 1880 to 1890 increased the membership of the denomination. In 1881–1882 eight congregations as well as many individuals left the Reformed Church when it failed to take a positive stand against Free Masonry. These joined the Christian Reformed Church as did the entire Classis Hackensack of the *True Reformed Dutch Church* in 1890.

6. The Catholic Church Aided by Immigration •
The enormous wave of immigration from 1830 to 1870 caused not only the Lutheran and Reformed churches, but also the Catholic Church, to grow. One third of the German immigrants were Roman Catholic. During these years thousands of Irish poured into America. Practically all of these were Roman Catholic.

The Irish Catholics were poor. When they arrived their purses were empty, and they had to settle down where they landed. Consequently Boston, New York, Philadelphia, and Baltimore became great Catholic centers. The German Catholics settled in the new western country north of the Ohio or west of the Mississippi. Missouri and Wisconsin became great German centers.

In 1830 the number of Catholics was somewhat over half a million. Thirty years later the number had increased to four and a half million, and nearly every important city in the country had a Catholic bishop. From that time on the

Roman Catholic Church has remained a powerful influence in America. There are over forty million Catholics in the United States today.

7. The Times Are Ripe for the Rise of Sects • The restlessness of the times produced immigrations from Europe and vast movements of people westward. It produced a setting for periodic revivals and for the new phenomenon of camp meetings. But it also made fertile ground for the germination and rapid growth of several movements which were so far removed from the teachings of the Bible that they are usually called sects or cults.

It is very strange to note that the central western section of New York was the area from which originated the Millerite craze, the spiritualistic movement, and the most unusual sect of all, the Mormons.

It is still more strange that the region also produced the greatest revivalist of the time in Charles G. Finney. And one of Finney's converts established one of the successful communistic communities —The Oneida Community—in this same region.

8. The Mormons • Joseph Smith, a resident of the town of Palmyra, New York, began to have visions at an early age. He professed that the angel Moroni appeared to him and told him that all existing churches were in error and that the Bible of the Western world lay buried in a hill nearby. On September 22, 1827, he claimed that he dug up a stone box in which was a book made of thin golden plates.

For three years Smith was engaged in translating these plates which were pub-

Courtesy
Church of Jesus Christ of Latter-day
Saints Information Service

Joseph Smith, first president of the Church of Jesus Christ of Latter-day Saints, died from assassins' guns at the age of thirty-eight.

lished in 1830 as the *Book of Mormon.* The book professes to be the history of America from its original settlement of people from the dispersion from the Tower of Babel. Moroni, the son of Mormon, was the final survivor of the Nephites, God's chosen people. He buried these plates in the fourth century A.D.

Followers of "Joseph the Prophet" formed a church in April, 1830. From 1831 to 1837 Mormon headquarters were in Kirtland, Ohio, where Brigham Young joined the movement and soon became one of the "Twelve Apostles." Lawsuits and community friction caused the Mormons to move first to Missouri and in 1840 to Nauvoo, Illinois.

Courtesy Church of Jesus Christ of Latter-day Saints Information Service

Leaving Nauvoo, twenty thousand Mormons abandoned their homes and fled
into the wilderness to seek a new home in the Rocky Mountains.

Opposition to a vision which Joseph Smith claimed to have received in July, 1843, authorizing polygamy, caused a general uprising against the Mormons. While Smith and his brother were in jail, a mob broke into the prison and brutally shot the two brothers. Two years later, under Brigham Young's leadership, the Mormons left for the Valley of the Great Salt Lake.

This church influences every phase of the life of every member; it supplies relief in illness or poverty, provides education, recreation, and employment. Young Mormons go out two by two without compensation, giving a year or more to work for their church.

The *Book of Mormon* is considered as equal with and "supporting but not supplanting" the Bible. The Bible is accepted "as far as it is translated correctly." Two other books by Smith are also highly regarded in determining fundamental teachings. Two doctrines peculiar to the sect are baptism for the dead and celestial marriage. The practice of polygamy has been abandoned.

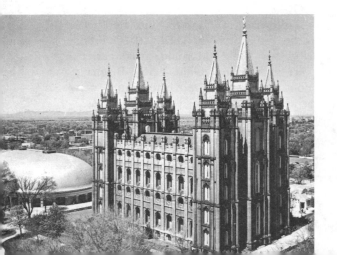

This historic Mormon temple, right, and dome-shaped tabernacle, left, stand "at the crossroads of the West" in Salt Lake City, Utah.

Courtesy
Church of Jesus Christ of Latter-day
Saints Information Service

9. The Adventists • All of the evangelists of this era preached about the second advent (second coming) of Christ. The doctrine that won so many followers for the New England farmer and Baptist lay minister William Miller was that he set an exact time. From certain passages in Daniel and Revelation he fixed the year at 1843 and the day around March 21.

Miller began preaching in 1831 and was invited to preach in many of the villages near his home. Soon he was preaching in the larger cities and requests came from all parts of the country for speakers and literature.

March 21, 1843, came and went. Miller said Christ might come any time during the year. March 21, 1844, came and went. The figures were revised. October 24, 1844, came and went. Each date had been accompanied by extensive preparations.

In 1845 a loose organization of all Adventists was formed and in 1846 the Seventh-day Adventists separated from the main body on the question of the Jewish Sabbath as well as the interpretation of the sanctuary in Daniel 8.

Mrs. Ellen White was the early leader. Growth was slow at first. In doctrine the Seventh-day Adventists are very conservative. They are exemplary in generous giving, abstain from alcohol and to-

Courtesy
Bureau of Public Relations
General Conference of Seventh-day Adventists
William Miller

bacco, and conduct a comprehensive medical and evangelistic program in over nine hundred languages and dialects. The Seventh-day Adventists reported a membership in 1963 of 1,300,000 adult baptized members in 13,369 churches.

10. Spiritualism • Man has always had a desire to speak with the spirit

Adventists maintain strong medical programs at home and abroad. Missionary activity is preceded by a comprehensive health service. This is the Sanitarium and Hospital, Orlando, Florida.

Courtesy
Bureau of Public Relations
General Conference of Seventh-day Adventists

world, but in this era of turmoil the movement expanded explosively.

Andrew Jackson Davis is considered to be the philosophical founder of Spiritualism. He organized the Children's Progressive Lyceum (the Spiritualist Sunday school) some years before the Fox sisters heard rapping noises in their home at Hydesville, New York. Margaret and Kate soon felt that these were signals from the spirit world. Their seances became famous, and interest spread. In 1855 it was claimed that there were two million believers. Permanent national organization came in 1893. Various Spiritualist groups report a total of less than 200,000 members today.

11. Christian Science • Several decades after the rise of Mormonism, Adventism, and Spiritualism, the movement called *Christian Science* arose. In 1866 Mary Baker Eddy recovered almost instantly from a severe injury. She had been a student of mental and spiritual relationships and developed her ideas as a "scientific system of divine healing."

She believed the "Principle of all harmonious Mind-action to be God." Obviously the movement is not biblical, nor is it scientific.

Mrs. Eddy wrote *Science and Health with Key to the Scriptures* which became the textbook of Christian Science. Under her direction a church was established at Boston in 1879. In 1892 it was reorganized under the name *The First Church of Christ, Scientist.* All other Christian Science churches are branches of the *Mother Church.*

Leaders in the local churches are the readers, practitioners, and teachers. Readers read the lesson-sermons prepared by the Publishing Society; practitioners devote their full time to healing; teachers instruct classes of inquirers.

Free lectures are often given by lecturers supplied by the Mother Church. *The Christian Science Monitor,* which is acknowledged to be one of the finest newspapers for unbiased reporting, is an example of the effective literature produced. This group prohibits the publication of its membership statistics.

The Mother Church, the First Church of Christ, Scientist, in Boston, Massachusetts

At the extreme right is a portion of the Christian Science Publishing House.

12. Jehovah's Witnesses • Another sect, now spread throughout the world, are the Jehovah's Witnesses. They were not known as Jehovah's Witnesses until 1931. Before this they had been called *Millennial Dawnists, International Bible Students,* and *Russellites,* after their first leader.

Charles Taze Russell attracted huge crowds to hear his preaching on the second advent of Christ. The first formal organization of his followers was in Pittsburgh in 1872. Over 13,000,000 copies of his books have been circulated. Headquarters of the group was moved to Brooklyn in 1909, and in 1939 the name was changed to the *Watchtower Bible and Tract Society, Inc.* On the death of Russell in 1916, "Judge" Rutherford became president, to be succeeded by Nathan Knorr, the present president, in 1942.

All members are ministers although they will take no titles. All give generously of their time and money for witnessing and missionary activity. The literature they write, print, and distribute is of astronomical proportions. *The Watchtower,* their official paper, has a circulation of 3,700,000. Over 700,000,-000 books and booklets have been distributed since 1920. There are 4,000 congregations in the United States and 20,000 throughout the world.

Witnesses refuse to salute the flag or bear arms, contending that the tyranny of government is one of the three allies of Satan. The other two are the "false" teachings of the churches and the oppressions of business. Although some of the teachings of Russell have been altered by later leaders, the doctrines of the sect conflict with those of historic Christianity on many points. They deny the Trinity, the deity of Christ, His physical resurrection and a physical second coming. They teach a second probation for all in the millennium and the annihilation of the wicked. Their doctrines on the sufficiency of Christ's atonement, on human government, and on the existence of the soul are not biblical.

13. Anti-slavery Sentiment Arises • In colonial times slaveholding was general in America. Many of the foremost Congregational ministers, including Jonathan Edwards, were slave owners. At the beginning of the Revolutionary War there were 6,000 slaves in Massachusetts alone. But although slavery was taken for granted, there were those who disapproved. As early as 1769 Samuel Hopkins, a minister at Newport, Rhode Island, preached strongly against slavery. However, the Quakers were the only religious body in colonial times to take a definite stand against slavery.

Toward the end of the colonial period the attitude of the people began to change. In the South as well as in the North the feeling became widespread that slavery ought to be gradually abolished. The Presbyterian, Methodist, and Baptist churches passed strong resolutions against slavery.

14. The Churches Divide on the Slavery Question • Whitney's invention of the cotton gin in 1792 and the invention of machinery for spinning and weaving cotton brought about a complete change of sentiment toward slavery in the South. Cotton became the most important American product, and by 1830 southern leaders had become convinced

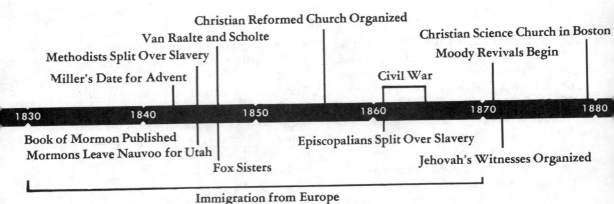

Christian Reformed Church Organized

Van Raalte and Scholte

Christian Science Church in Boston

Methodists Split Over Slavery

Moody Revivals Begin

Miller's Date for Advent

Civil War

| 1830 | 1840 | 1850 | 1860 | 1870 | 1880 |

Book of Mormon Published
Mormons Leave Nauvoo for Utah

Episcopalians Split Over Slavery

Fox Sisters

Jehovah's Witnesses Organized

Immigration from Europe

that the welfare of the nation depended upon cotton. Furthermore, it was felt that cotton could not be raised profitably without Negro slave labor.

In the North the attitude of an ever increasing number of people against slavery became exceedingly intense and fierce. This was due in large measure to the eloquent preaching by Wendell Phillips, the poems of Whittier, and most of all the fiery propaganda of Garrison in his paper *The Liberator*.

Bitter antagonism between the North and the South developed. This feeling of bitterness went so far as to divide a number of the churches.

In May, 1845, the Baptist Missionary

Society decided to discontinue its co-operation with the Baptists in the North. In the same year the southern Methodist churches voted to separate from the northern churches, and adopted the name *Methodist Episcopal Church, South*. A similar break occurred among the Presbyterians.

In 1861 the Episcopalians of the South separated from those in the North; but at the end of the war in 1865 the unity of this church was restored. This early reunion was made possible by the fact that the Protestant Episcopal Church never had taken sides on the slavery question. There was no bitterness to overcome.

In the South as well as in the North

NO SEATS ON THE FLOOR OF HALL

"The first appearance in New York of the revivalists Moody and Sankey, last night was before an audience larger than the metropolis ever witnessed before," reports the *New York Daily Tribune* on February 8, 1876. The vast Hippodrome seated 11,000. Many thousands were turned away.

*Courtesy
Moody Bible Institute*

Billy Graham preaches to vast crowds in many evangelistic campaigns throughout the world.

Courtesy
Billy Graham
Evangelistic Association

the churches felt their obligation to the Negroes who had been set free from the bonds of slavery. They opened schools for the freedmen and their children and provided for their religious instruction and training. As time went on and this education took effect, the Negroes began to organize their own churches.

Of all the agencies devoted to the welfare of the colored people, these Negro churches have perhaps had the most important part not only in the religious and moral but also in the social and intellectual progress of the Nergo race in America.

15. Dwight L. Moody • Among those who carried on Christian work among the soldiers during the Civil War was Dwight Lyman Moody—a young man who had already made considerable progress in evangelistic work in Chicago.

Moody was born in East Northfield, Massachusetts. His education was mea-

ger, for his father died when he was only four years old and his mother had all she could do to provide the necessary things for her children.

When Dwight Moody was eighteen he confessed Christ as his Savior, and a year later he went west to Chicago, where he engaged in business. At Plymouth Church he rented extra pews and invited many young men to come to the service with him. He also opened a Sunday school in one of the poorer sections of the city, gathering the children in from the streets to tell them the truths found in the Scriptures.

Soon he gave up his business to devote all his time to Christian work. From 1865 to 1869 he was president of the Chicago Y.M.C.A. He collected money for the first Y.M.C.A. building in America.

From 1871 on Moody conducted revival meetings in various places throughout the land. He also toured England and Scotland several times. Ira D. Sankey, a singer, assisted him in conducting the meetings. Sankey led the singing and introduced new hymns to the people.

In his preaching Moody stressed the Gospel of salvation through Jesus Christ. The simplicity of his language and the warmth and sincerity of his spirit attracted great numbers. Moody and Sankey became household names in America.

As a result of their ministry thousands professed Christ as their Savior.

Moody's great ability for organizing was again shown in the Christian boarding schools he established in Massachusetts and in the founding of the Moody Bible Institute. Much of his later life was devoted to building up this institution. He died in Northfield in 1899.

1. *Why did the Presbyterian Church divide?*
2. *What important distinctions obtained between the High Church and the Low Church party of the Episcopal Church? Why did this church divide?*
3. *How did immigration affect the German Lutherans? The Roman Catholics?*
4. *What was the general attitude of the religious groups toward slavery during colonial times?*
5. *How did Whitney's invention of the cotton gin affect the use of slaves? Why did the North begin to oppose slavery?*
6. *Why was the practice of revival meetings a significant development in America? How would Billy Graham's campaigns compare with Moody's work?*
7. *Identify: Joseph Smith, C. F. W. Walther, Theodore Frelinghuysen, Albertus Van Raalte, second advent, Mary Baker Eddy, Rev. K. Vanden Bosch, sect.*
8. *Form a committee which will prepare a chart showing the stand taken by the sects on major orthodox doctrines. A good source is* The Four Major Cults *by Hoekema, Eerdmans, 1963.*
9. *Various sects have characteristics or programs that are worth imitation by all churches. Make a list of these.*
10. *What is the Mormon view of the Bible?*
11. *How did the slavery question affect the different church denominations?*
12. *List the contributions of D. L. Moody.*
13. *Find a few of the poems of Whittier and Lowell that express New England's opinion about slavery. How did the development of such sentiments affect the churches?*
14. *Why did the Low Church lose influence in the Episcopal Church?*
15. *What has the Church done for the social and intellectual progress of the Negro race in America?*

CHAPTER 46

The Church

Faces New Problems

1. Immigrants Disregard the Puritan Sabbath • After the Civil War immigration from Europe was resumed on a scale larger than ever before. From 1865 to 1884 more than seven million immigrants entered the United States. Nearly half of them came from Ireland and Germany. The Irish immigrants were practically all Roman Catholic. The German immigrants were Catholic, Lutheran, or Rationalistic.

Up to this time strict Sunday observance was the rule in America. All stores were closed, few trains ran, and all places of amusement were closed. No picnics or outings were held on Sunday, and there was no "week-ending." The great majority of the American people went to church regularly on Sunday morning and again in the evening. Americans had inherited their strict Sunday observance from the Calvinistic or Puritan founders of New England.

Both Lutheran and Catholic Germans brought with them the so-called "Continental Sabbath." Sunday in Chicago, where many of these newcomers made their homes, was described as "Berlin in the morning, and Paris in the afternoon and evening." This meant that people in Chicago went to church in the morning, and went out for pleasure the rest of the day. The new immigrants spoke derisively of the American way of Sunday observance; they called it the "Puritan Sabbath."

2. Tenement Evangelism • The immigrants to a very large extent were poor. As a result there developed in the large cities vast tenement districts inhabited by "foreigners." A large proportion of these immigrants had no church connections.

Many churches saw their need and began to bring them the Word of God. The Baptist Home Mission Society in 1867 had forty-nine ordained "foreigners" working among Germans, Hollanders, Frenchmen, Welshmen, Norwegians, Swedes, and Danes. In three of their seminaries the Baptists introduced foreign language departments so that ministers could be trained for this kind of mission work. Today many denominations carry on a wide program of evangelization in the cities of the United States.

The constantly advancing white man crowded the red man ever farther back. This resulted in several Indian wars, until finally the government adopted the policy of placing the Indians on reservations of available land. The churches carried on mission work among the natives of our country with increasing energy.

3. Wealth Influences the Church • From 1880 on the wealth of the American people increased greatly. This had its effect on the life of the churches.

Revivalism continued, and throughout the eighties and nineties the churches held their annual series of revival meetings, usually during the winter months. Camp meetings were still held in the rural districts, especially in the South. But here and there changes were noticeable.

The camp meeting grounds on Lake Chautauqua in New York showed signs of the increased prosperity: Cottages replaced tents. The meetings that had always been held out under the trees now took place in a large frame tabernacle. In 1874 lectures and entertainment began to take the place of revival sermons.

Lake Chautauqua became widely known for its summer programs, and similar projects combining education and entertainment became popular on camp meeting grounds in other parts of the country. They were known as chautauquas.

Revivalism received sharp criticism in a small book entitled *Christian Nurture* by Horace Bushell, a Congregational minister. This book was also a strong influence in leading the churches to give more attention to the training of their youth. Revivalism received another setback when, in 1902, a book entitled

Primitive Traits in Religious Revivals by Davenport came off the press.

With the new industrial age churches began to place great emphasis on business efficiency. Successful businessmen were given places on the financial boards of the churches.

The increase in wealth brought with it also a desire for more opportunities in education. Denominational colleges increased in number, and their enrollments and incomes multiplied as never before. College presidents became business administrators, and their great aim became the securing of large gifts of money for their schools.

It was during this period that wealthy men founded, in various parts of the country, the University of Chicago, McCormick Seminary, Cornell and Leland Stanford universities, and four women's colleges—Vassar, Smith, Wellesley, and Bryn Mawr. Many of these centers of learning were established as Christian institutions, by men who realized that they were only stewards of the wealth God had given them.

4. Social Problems • During the period of industrial growth and increasing national wealth many churches came to lay great emphasis on social work in the community.

Since the eighties there had been a great movement of population from the country to the cities. Immigration from Europe continuing on a large scale added its numbers to those already in the cities. Slum areas developed, and many persons were affected by the cramped, unhealthy conditions. To meet the problems arising from these conditions the so-called institutional church was developed.

Courtesy Riverside Church

Both the Tower and the South Wing of the Riverside Church were given by John D. Rockefeller, Jr. His father richly endowed the University of Chicago.

The originator of the institutional church was the Episcopal clergyman William A. Mühlenberg, great-grandson of the organizer of American Lutheranism. From 1846 to 1858 he was rector of the Church of the Holy Communion in New York City. Under his inspiration his church sponsored certain social agencies, such as the Sisterhood of the Holy Communion and St. Luke's Hospital.

Thomas K. Beecher, pastor of the First Congregational Church of Elmira, New York, in 1872 equipped his church building with a gymnasium, lecture rooms, and a library. Russell H. Conwell in 1891 introduced institutional features in his Baptist Temple in Philadelphia. In addition to social clubs he introduced sewing classes, reading rooms, a gymnasium, and a night school where volunteer teachers taught the working people. This night school grew into Temple University.

Courses in Christian sociology and in social service were offered in many of the seminaries. In 1908 the Federal Council of Churches of Christ in America adopted the *Social Creed of the Churches.*

All this activity in the realm of social service had the tendency to make the churches forget their main purpose. In their eagerness to fulfill Christ's command to do good to their fellow men, they began to neglect the pure Gospel of salvation through faith.

Social service is a necessity, and Christians must be active in caring for their fellow men. But the central work of the Church is the preaching of the Gospel and the administration of the sacraments. These should never be neglected or given second place.

5. Religious Education • One of the most striking features of the history of the churches in America since 1880 is the growing preoccupation of these churches with the problem of religious education.

At the beginning of the present century many leaders in various Protestant churches were becoming uneasy over the lack of religious education in the public school. Religion had been an important part of all education in colonial days. But gradually the religious content had been removed. Many leaders saw in this a grave danger to the welfare of the nation. And they began to realize that the

home and the Sunday school were falling far short of making up for this lack.

Some attempts had been made to improve the Sunday school. A system of uniform Sunday school lessons had been adopted in 1872. A rich variety of Sunday-school "lesson helps" were published. Some churches put up special buildings especially planned for Sunday-school work. Teacher training courses were given. As a result new enthusiasm was aroused, and the Sunday school enjoyed a remarkable growth. Many of the larger and wealthier churches appointed directors of religious education. In some states a director now has charge of the religious education for the entire state. Weekday and summer vacation church schools have been organized. In many communities children have been dismissed from school for a period each week to attend Bible classes. Departments of religious education have been introduced in denominational colleges and theological seminaries for the training of teachers. The results of all this effort, however, have been disappointing.

The Catholic, Lutheran, Adventist, and Reformed people have followed a different pathway. They are not satisfied with public school instruction for their children. They feel that one hour of religious training a week given by teachers who are more or less inexperienced cannot offset the non-religious teaching of the public school five days a week by thoroughly trained professional teachers. They feel moreover that the salt of religion should not be given to children in separate doses, but should season all the subjects taught throughout the day. They have therefore established schools of their own, in which the children are

Courtesy Kalamazoo Christian High School

The Kalamazoo, Michigan, Christian High School is one of the member schools of Christian Schools International.

taught five days a week, and in which all the subjects from kindergarten to university are taught in agreement with the religious doctrines of their churches.

Between the Catholic, Lutheran, and Adventist schools on the one hand and the Reformed schools on the other there is a difference in organization. The first are *parochial* or church schools. The second are usually not parochial or church schools, but *society-controlled* schools.

The Reformed groups, following in the footsteps of Dr. Abraham Kuyper of the Netherlands, believe that all of life should be controlled by the Christian religion, but they do not believe that all of life should be controlled by the Church. They believe that the Church's function is to preach the Gospel and administer the sacraments. They hold that it is not the work of the Church to operate schools, but that its members as Christian parents should establish, maintain, and control their own Christian schools. Associations of Reformed parents maintain over 350 Christian grade and high schools, with over 70,000 pupils and 3,500 professionally trained teachers. These schools are members of *Christian Schools International (CSI).*

Religious education is one of our most important national problems. Without religion a nation is headed for ruin. The American nation, no matter how strong and powerful at present, cannot, with the non-religious education of the public schools, escape that fate in the end. As the evil effects of the humanist education of the public school become more and more noticeable, Christians in Baptist and other churches feel the need of establishing Christian schools. In 1978 the Western and Ohio Associations of Christian Schools and the National Christian Schools Education Association merged to form the *Association of Christian Schools International (ACSI).* The Episcopalians have a large number of private schools.

From a purely educational point of view Catholic, Lutheran, Adventist, Reformed, Baptist, Assembly of God, Mennonite, Episcopalian, and other schools compare very favorably with the public schools. In the debate over various forms of federal governmental assistance to public and non-public schools, the maintaining of these educational standards

Courtesy
Netherlands Information Service

This photograph taken from a helicopter shows the reconstruction of the St. Laurens Church, Rotterdam, which was completely burned out during the 1940 bombardment.

has been one of the arguments used by those who favor the acceptance of such assistance by Christian schools.

6. Problems of Peace and War •

The suffering and tragedy that are a part of every war, and the ever present danger of new wars breaking out, have led people throughout history to band together to preserve peace. Some of these groups, though they work to guard the peace, will, in the event of unavoidable war, answer the call to service. Others regard all war as sinful and refrain from entering into battle.

The peace movement in America had its origin in colonial days with the coming of the Quakers, the Moravians, the Mennonites, and the Dunkers. Alongside these pacifist religious groups, there were

by 1826 some fifty peace societies in various states. The members of these peace societies were mainly ministers and pious laymen. During the 1830's and 1840's churches often passed resolutions in favor of international peace.

The peace movement was particularly active after the Spanish American War (1898). In 1909 the first Hague Conference was held, with twenty-six nations represented. Andrew Carnegie gave millions to promote the cause of peace, and built the Peace Palace in The Hague. More peace sermons were preached than ever before. Most Christian people in America dreamed of the new era of peace and justice that was about to dawn. Then suddenly that dream was shattered by the explosion of World War I.

How would the advocates of peace be able to hold to their position in the midst of a country and world at war? That problem was settled quite simply for most of them. The war was represented as a war to end war; and the advocates of peace, the American churches with their ministers and members, felt that to be consistent in promoting peace they would have to support the war with all their might.

Those who dared openly to oppose the war were mistreated. In some cases where ministers continued to preach peace, audiences walked out on them. A good many ministers had to resign under pressure. The house of one minister was painted yellow because he refused to participate in a Liberty Loan drive. Fifty-five ministers of various denominations were arrested. One was sentenced to twenty years in prison. A convention of Christian pacifists in Los Angeles was broken up by a mob, and three of the leading pacifists were arrested, tried, fined, and jailed.

After World War I the peace movement became positive and aggressive rather than negative. Reduction of armaments was the tangible goal. But the rise of Hitler with his ruthless treatment of the Jews and his destrutcion of the liberties of peoples required a reevaluation.

The sudden ending of World War II by the use of two atomic bombs gave new impetus to the peace movement. The prospect of nuclear war and the ethics of using weapons of total devastation have led to "Ban the Bomb" demonstrations and the picketing of installations of nuclear weapons.

7. Modernism in Recent Years • The years of World War I and those immediately following were boom years in the United States. Business thrived and money was plentiful. Men of wealth gave large gifts of money to their churches, and many costly and beautiful houses of worship were built. Two of the outstanding examples are the Riverside Drive Baptist Church and the Episcopal Cathedral of St. John the Divine, both in New York City.

In keeping with the beauty of the new buildings, worship was made more formal. The preachers put on gowns and the choir members wore robes. A more

A. Hansen Studio

The Interior of the Cathedral
of St. John the Divine

dignified type of church music was introduced, together with processionals and recessionals, music responses and chorals.

While the church service was thus made more elaborate, church attendance was declining, for in many cases the preaching of God's Word was disappearing. The heart had been removed from the service. The churches had lost sight of their central purpose, to preach the Gospel. A liberal theology and a social gospel had taken its place.

The Liberalism of the present day, often called Modernism, has led thousands of worshippers toward a vague, unfounded, and unsatisfying faith. Because in its teachings many fine sentiments are included it is apt to be attractive to those who are not well-grounded in Scriptural truth.

Present-day Modernism stands in reverent awe before the eternal mysteries. It has profound respect for Christ as a unique religious genius. It admires the books of the Bible as a marvelous collection of sublime literature. But Modernism denies the virgin birth and the deity of Jesus Christ. It denies the truth that man is altogether sinful, and that Christ died on the cross to atone for man's sin. The present-day Modernist denies practically all the fundamental doctrines of the Bible. At the bottom of this lies the fact that he does not believe that the Bible is divinely inspired—that it speaks to man with divine, absolute, and final authority. To the Modernist it is simply the record of the religious thoughts, emotions, and experiences of the ancient Israelites.

The Modernists believe that there is no one certain authority in matters of faith. They have no use for the great creeds of the Church. They differ much among themselves. They say that every man is entitled to his own opinions.

Today Modernists are not so sure of themselves as they used to be. History itself has of late disproved some of their favorite ideas. They had placed man in the center instead of God. Under the influence of the theory of evolution they believed that the human race could in time develop to a state of ideal goodness and usefulness and happiness. All their hopes were pinned on man. Man had within himself the power to live the good life and to build a better world.

Then came the financial crash of 1929, and later World War II with all its horrors and cruelties. It was plain to see that the human race was as sinful and imperfect as it ever had been and was not making steady progress toward a better world.

8. Missionary Activity • The War with Spain in 1898 opened up the Philippine Islands and Puerto Rico to Protestant missions. The churches that engaged in mission work on these islands did so in a co-operative spirit, making an agreement as to the field in which each church would work.

Since 1886 the Student Volunteer Movement had been lending its enthusiasm and support to the cause of missions. John R. Mott became its great leader. In 1906 the Laymen's Missionary Movement was organized. Foreign mission work was going forward among many peoples of the world. Home mission work in the far western states and in Alaska continued to be pushed by all the great churches.

But while missions were extending the Church to the west and in foreign lands, Modernism was seeping in and spreading. Modernism is one of the great obstacles in the work of evangelization. The gospel of Modernism is another gospel than that of the Bible. Modernism cuts the very heart out of the true Gospel: man's need of salvation through the shed blood of Jesus Christ. It destroys the one true and great purpose of Christian missions—to bring the message of this salvation.

The only purpose left to the Modernist missionary is to bring our western civilization to Africa and the Orient. But the people of India, China, and Japan have wonderful civilizations of their

Masses of people
fill the streets of
Bharatpur, India,
during a religious festival.

Screen Traveler, from Gendreau

own. And our western civilization is beginning to show serious faults.

As a result of Modernism in the churches the supply of money and men for missions began to drop at an alarming rate. The Student Volunteer Bands, which once flourished in all the colleges, disappeared. John R. Mott's ideal of the "Evangelization of the World in This Generation" lost its meaning. By 1930 it became clear that the whole missionary enterprise had reached a crisis.

The program of missionary activity changed rapidly in the years following World War II. Many nations, particularly in Africa, received independence. The spirit of nationalism in these emerging cultures made the position of missionaries difficult. They were looked upon as agents of the West. Christianity was regarded as an enemy of native religions. With the end of the services of the alien missionary in sight,

missions placed great emphasis on the training of native leaders and on the organization of the young Church as a native institution.

Nor has the restriction on the missionary effort been confined to emerging nations. The religions of nearly all non-Christian nations are reasserting themselves. The Christian schools in Sri Lanka have been taken over by the government. The number

Native leaders, trained
in Bible schools and
seminaries, go out to
preach, teach, and
distribute literature.

*Courtesy Christian Reformed
Board of Foreign Missions*

of missionaries is limited in India and many other countries. And, of course, Communist governments in China and other countries have curtailed the missionary programs of many churches. Japan and Central and South America have, however, provided new fields of opportunities.

'1. In what ways was the prosperity of the Church evident in the revival program? In education programs?

2. Why did the churches of the late 1800's introduce social activities into their programs? Was this the right procedure? What is the task of the Church?

3. What efforts at Christian education were developed by the various denominations? If there are Catholic schools near you, find out how they are controlled.

4. What part did the Church play in the movement to prevent war? Has your church a statement on the ethics of modern warfare?

5. What influences led to abandoning Sunday observance? Do you think this disregard of older Puritan custom would have come eventually in spite of the cause indicated in this chapter?

6. What programs are the denominations which do not maintain Christian day schools currently following to educate their children in religion?

7. Identify: Continental Sabbath, chautauquas, processional, parochial.

8. Why has missionary activity changed since World War II?

9. What should the Church's attitude be toward education? Toward war, politics, and racial problems?

10. What are the chief theological tenets of the Modernist group? What is meant when men speak of the neo-orthodox? Who are some of the leaders? Why would the liberal theology lead to a falling off of missionary activity?

11. Check the book advertisements of several issues of an interdenominational magazine such as Christianity Today and place the titles in categories of your choice. How many of them deal with problems discussed in this chapter?

12. Could you conduct a research project to determine whether students attending Christian schools are stronger in life and doctrine than others? Why is this very difficult to determine statistically?

CHAPTER *47*

The Church in Canada

1. Early History • The early history of Canada is inextricably interwoven with the histories of France and England and with the missionary zeal of the Roman Catholic Church. For two centuries after the first discovery of the St. Lawrence by Cartier in 1534 the primary motives in exploration were the profits from the fur trade and the conversion of the Indians, rather than colonization. Acadia, now called Nova Scotia, was the first colony. It was settled in 1605.

The prolonged struggle between France and England for the control of North America ended with the Treaty of Paris in 1763 giving all to England.

The French Canadians took little interest in the American Revolution. Many Loyalists, however, left the American colonies under pressure and settled in New Brunswick and in Upper Canada, now Ontario. Most of these and later colonists were Nonconformists or members of the Church of England, while

Isaac Jogues,
French Jesuit,
Preaching to the
Mohawk Indians

Bettmann Archive

Lower Canada (Quebec) remained predominantly Roman Catholic.

Continued suspicion and friction between these two groups led to the separation of Upper and Lower Canada in 1791. The new provinces, Ontario and Quebec, respectively, had their own elected assemblies. Small rebellions led to their reunion by the British government in 1840. In 1867 the two Canadas, Nova Scotia, and New Brunswick joined to form the Dominion of Canada. The basic problem of two languages, two national heritages, and two religions remains to this day.

2. The Roman Catholic Church • From the establishment of the little settlement of Quebec by Champlain in 1608 until the present, the Roman Catholic religion and the French language have dominated in Lower Canada. Although more northerly than Upper Canada (Ontario), it includes the lower reaches of the St. Lawrence River basin.

Champlain in 1615 called in the Recollet Fathers from France who, being unable to man all the mission posts among the Indians, in 1625 called on the Jesuits for help. When Quebec fell to the English under David Kirke in 1629, all the missionaries returned to France until 1632.

Ville Marie, now Montreal, was founded in 1642 for the "glory of God and the establishment of religion in New France." But this was a decade of martyrdom for many an explorer-priest. Montreal owed its salvation on one occasion to a young man who at the head of

This picture, "Martyrdom of the Jesuit Missionaries," was the frontispiece of a book published in 1664. It is not one specific event but a composite of the martyrdoms of ten Jesuit missionaries.

The Public Archives of Canada

sixteen companions for several days faced over 700 Iroquois, and resisted them to the death.

Many missionaries and explorers went throughout the Great Lakes region. From Canada, Joliet and Father Marquette went on their trip which led to the discovery of the Mississippi in 1673. Cadillac and a missionary founded the town and colony of Detroit in 1700. Mission work was carried on in the area between the Illinois and Ohio rivers.

The conversion of the Indian tribes never materialized due to conflicts with traders, conflicts with other Indians, forced returns of the missionaries to France due to British conquest, and the lack of permanent colonists. There were only 3,215 people in New France in 1666; only 18,000 by 1713. The American colonies numbered 260,000 already in 1706.

Although the Treaty of Paris of 1763, which concluded the British victories, guaranteed to all "the free exercise of their religion," it added "so much as the laws of Great Britain will permit." This opened a century of restrictions on the Catholic schools, communities, and activities, followed by conciliation, and followed again by renewed conflict. The British government tolerated the religious orders of women, but directed the gradual extinction of those of men. The huge estates of the Jesuits were confiscated and the Jesuits banned in 1767. The efforts of the British to win the French to Protestantism by Protestant schools resulted rather in the unifying of the French-Catholic community.

Canada, unlike Great Britain, has no Established Church. Freedom of worship is by implication granted in the British North America Act of 1867, whose preamble states that the provinces have expressed the desire to be federally united under a constitution similar in principle to that of the United Kingdom. The right to worship freely is buried deeply in British law.

Of the eighty Canadian religious bodies listed in the *1981 Yearbook of American and Canadian Churches,* the largest is the Roman Catholic, with almost ten million of some fifteen million members listed for these bodies. Separate primary school systems for Roman Catholics and Protestants (meaning those who are not Roman Catholic, including Jews, Muslims, and Hindus) are both supported from the provincial treasuries.

3. The Presbyterian Church • Canadian Presbyterians trace their descent to many sources. A Huguenot settlement in the seventeenth century failed, but Huguenots came along with other Loyalists during the American Revolution. Protestants came to Nova Scotia in 1749 and again in 1755 after the expulsion of the Acadians. Large numbers of Presbyterians came from Scotland and North Ireland during the first half of the nineteenth century. These, as well as those who came from England and the United States, clung to their many ancestral subdivisions.

The trend toward union began in the middle of the nineteenth century and was climaxed by the union of all Presbyterian bodies into the Canadian Presbyterian Church in 1875. This epoch-making event unified the life of the Church and became the starting point of its missionary energy both in the Canadian Northwest and throughout the world. In 1925, a crucial year in the history of Canadian

church life, about two-thirds of the membership of this church united with the Congregational and Methodist churches to form *The United Church of Canada.* The remaining third, under the determined leadership of the Rev. Ephraim Scott, was called *The Presbyterian Church in Canada*, and ranked as the seventh largest religious body in 1980.

4. Other Churches • The Methodist Church followed a similar pattern. Methodists came to Canada in 1770 from England and the United States. Until the War of 1812, Canadian Methodism was closely connected with that of the United States. There were five principal Methodist bodies until they united in 1883. In 1925 they formed one of the constituent parts of the United Church. The United Church is now the largest Protestant Church in Canada, followed in size by the Anglican Church.

Some Baptists came from the colonies before the American Revolution. Their number was augmented by Loyalist refugees. Traditional independentism has made it difficult to form associations. Besides the religious communions listed, the following deserve mention as forming sizable groups in Canada: Lutheran, Jewish, Greek Orthodox, Ukranian (Greek) Catholic, Mennonite, Pentecostal, and the Salvation Army.

5. The Anglican Church • The Anglican Church in Canada began with the settlement of Nova Scotia in 1749. Many of the Loyalists who came from the American colonies during and after the revolution were members of the Church of England.

In 1787 the first bishop was consecrated in England as bishop of Nova Scotia. His diocese included all of Canada that was settled at that time.

The Church was totally controlled from England until, after much discussion, the Canadian bishops in 1857 determined to have their own synods. A

PART FIVE: THE CHURCH IN THE NEW WORLD

bishop was not consecrated on Canadian soil until 1862. The Anglican Church is the second largest Protestant body in Canada, with a membership in 1980 of almost one million. Its characteristic Englishness is viewed by its present-day leaders as a hindrance in fulfilling the Church's mission to the world.

6. The Reformed Churches

Of the churches subscribing to Reformed creeds at least five have organized into separate denominations. The largest and oldest of these is the Christian Reformed, some of whose congregations were established as early as 1905. Until World War II, however, their number was only thirteen, their real numerical growth coming after 1946 when thousands of Reformed people from the Netherlands began to come to Canada. In 1981 membership in the Christian Reformed Church in Canada stood at 80,359 souls, with 196 congregations served by 192 pastors. It is still in transition, troubled by language difficulties, finding its place in Canadian society, and trying to be a Reformed church in a land where religious distinctiveness is not highly prized. Its people have responded to the challenge of a secularized culture by founding Christian primary and secondary schools.

Another denomination to benefit from postwar immigration is the Reformed Church in America. It numbered twenty-three ministers, nineteen congregations, and 5,541 members in 1980.

Maintaining close relations with parent groups in the Netherlands are the Canadian Reformed Churches, whose first congregation in Canada was organized in 1948; the Free Christian Reformed Churches, represented in Canada since 1951; and the Netherlands Reformed Churches who established their first congregation in 1950. The first of these, the Canadian Reformed Churches, lay special emphasis on the institutional oneness and visibility of the true Church of Jesus Christ; the other two stress the necessity of a verifiable spiritual regeneration and an experiential knowledge of saving grace as a requirement for true and effective membership in the Church of Jesus Christ.

1. *What forces kept the North American Indians from being converted to Christianity?*
2. *What did the British North America Act of 1867 provide?*
3. *List the five different Reformed denominations in Canada today.*
4. *What churches joined to form the United Church of Canada?*
5. *What basic problem confronts Canada?*
6. *Identify: Lower Canada, Father Marquette, secularized culture, diocese.*
7. *What is the historical background of Longfellow's poem Evangeline?*

CHAPTER 48

The Church
Seeks to Preserve the Faith

1. Fundamentalism • In the year 1910 a series of twelve small volumes was published under the title, *The Fundamentals: A Testimony to the Truth.* The appearance of these books marked the beginning of the Fundamentalist movement, an organized attempt to uphold the teachings of the Bible against Modernism.

The doctrines set forth in these books as fundamental were: (1) the Bible's freedom from error in every respect, (2) the virgin birth of Christ, (3) the substitutionary work of Christ on the cross (that He suffered and died in our stead to satisfy the wrath of God against sin), (4) the physical resurrection, and (5) the physical second coming of Christ.

More than 2,500,000 copies of these books were circulated, and in all the large churches a sharp controversy developed between the Fundamentalists and the Modernists. It stirred the Methodist, the Episcopalian, and the Disciples churches, but it raged most violently in the Baptist and Presbyterian churches. The struggle began in 1916 and continues to the present day.

2. Many Fundamentalists Accept Premillennialism

The horrors of the First World War led many people to believe that the end of the world was at hand. Believing this, they occupied themselves with the teaching of the Bible concerning the last things. A vast number of people in the various churches accepted the doctrine that the Jews will return to Palestine, and that Christ will come back to earth to rule in Jerusalem as king for a thousand years. This doctrine is called Premillennialism, because it teaches that the second coming of Christ will take place before (pre) the establishment upon earth of a reign of a thousand years (millennial). The people who hold to this doctrine are called Premillennialists or, more commonly, Premillenarians.

A great number of the Fundamentalists in the large churches accepted the Premillennial views. Thus, although the name Fundamentalist would be a fitting one for all those who believe the fundamental truths of the Bible, it has in past years become popularly linked with the Premillenarians. This doctrine of the thousand-year reign is also held by a number of the small sects and the so-called undenominational churches.

3. Holiness Groups Oppose Worldliness

In all the large churches in America there were many people of lim-
ited means who began to feel ill at ease among the wealthy and prosperous members. Moreover, with the triumphant progress of Modernism in the fashionable churches and their formalistic worship, these people felt that heart religion was disappearing. Around the year 1880 the "holiness" question came to the fore especially in the Methodist churches. In his day Wesley had taught the possibility of Christian perfection. But to the great mass of members in the Methodist churches, Christian perfection was no longer a goal for which to strive with might and main. Instead a large measure of worldliness had crept in.

In many churches Holiness groups came into existence. The members of these groups declared that they were true to the founder of the Methodist Church, Wesley, and that they wanted the Church to return to his doctrine and ideal. But the leading men in the Methodist churches looked with disfavor on the Holiness movement. The majority of prominent ministers in the Methodist Church and in other large churches were inclined to accept Modernist views. This filled the orthodox members with alarm. They felt less and less at home in churches that were cold to the desire for "holiness." Before long they began to withdraw and form separate religious organizations.

Between the years 1880 and 1926 no less than twenty-five Holiness and Pentecostal sects were formed. They were most numerous in the rural districts of the Middle West. In that region the Methodists are especially strong, and it was from the various Methodist bodies that the greatest number of people came who joined the Holiness sects. However, other churches and other sections of the country also yielded members to these sects.

The *Church of the Nazarene* was formed in 1894 when eight smaller Holiness groups combined. Other Holiness groups are the *Assemblies of God,* the *Church of God,* and the *Pentecostal Assemblies of Jesus Christ.* All are protests against the increasing Modernism in the large churches of America.

4. Established Churches Oppose Liberalism • Other churches, both old and new, have taken their stand for the true, historical Christian faith. Large elements in the Reformed and Presbyterian churches resisted the tide of Modernism and preserved their creeds. The Southern Baptists have firmly maintained the orthodox position. Growing at a rate of well over 100,000 per year, its membership passed the thirteen-million mark in 1980. Certain Lutheran bodies, too, remained loyal to their confessions—notably the Missouri Synod. The smaller Wisconsin Evangelical Lutheran Synod is even more conservative than the Missouri Synod. It numbered 402,972 in its 1980 membership, compared to two and a half million in the Missouri Synod.

The southern branch of the Presbyterian Church and the United Presbyterian Church have become divided camps because of the liberal beliefs of many of their ministers and members. We should not forget that there are great numbers of true believers in these denominations —people who have been born and bred in the Reformed faith, and who, under unfavorable conditions, are remaining true to their confession.

The northern branch, called the Presbyterian Church in the U.S.A., has stead-

J. Gresham Machen

ily lost ground to the Liberals. Although the historic Westminister Confession continues as its official creed, it no longer has the same meaning for all members. The Modernists are free to read liberal meanings into the statements of the confession, while the orthodox members hold to the true doctrines which it really contains.

Other churches, smaller and lesser known, withstood the tide of Modernism and are today preaching the historic Gospel. Old School Presbyterians carry on in the faith of their Scottish forefathers. The Netherlands Reformed Church is an offshoot of small groups rising out of the Secession of 1834 in the Netherlands. The Reformed Episcopal Church, though episcopalian in organization and church government, is Calvinistic in doctrine and continues as a witness to this faith. And there are others.

And so we see that although Modernism has swept in like a tide during the

PART FIVE: THE CHURCH IN THE NEW WORLD

past few decades, there have been and still are those in many denominations who by God's grace are standing firm and will not be moved.

5. The Orthodox Presbyterian Church •
A fairly recent church to come out of the struggle between Modernism and the historical Christian faith is the Orthodox Presbyterian Church. When the Congregational Church, under the influence of the New England Theology, lowered the Calvinistic banner, the northern branch of the Presbyterian Church, called the Presbyterian Church in the U.S.A., continued for many decades to hold it high. But at last Modernism made its subtle inroads into Princeton Seminary and into the Presbyterian Church.

Then in 1929, under the heroic leadership of Professor J. Gresham Machen, the Westminster Seminary was established in Philadelphia as a protest against the Modernism at Princeton. After a severe struggle, the defenders of the Calvinistic doctrines of the Westminster Confession suffered a decisive defeat at the hands of the Modernists in the General Assembly of 1935. This victory of the Modernists was made possible by the large number of Presbyterian ministers who, although themselves sound in doctrine, played into the hands of the Modernists when they valued peace above truth. Those who were true to the faith of their fathers then organized, in 1936, the Orthodox Presbyterian Church. This small but valiant church continues today its bold fight against Modernism.

6. The Christian Reformed Church •
With very few exceptions the churches

The Ninth Street Christian Reformed Church, Holland, Michigan, was built in 1853 by the Van Raalte settlers. It is known as "The Pillar Church."

in the United States are immigrant churches. The Christian Reformed Church is no exception. It is one of the very last churches to be planted on the North American continent as the result of immigration from Europe.

In doctrine this denomination is Reformed or Calvinistic. Its creeds are the creeds of the Reformed Church in the Netherlands: the Belgic Confession, the Heidelberg Catechism, and the Canons of Dort. The form of its government is presbyterian. Its churches are grouped into *classes,* which correspond to presbyteries. Each church within a classis sends its minister and one of its elders as delegates to the classical meetings, which are held two, and in some localities three, times a year. Minister and elder delegates from each classis meet in annual *synods*. Like all Presbyterian and Reformed churches, the Christian Reformed Church demands a thoroughly and broadly educated ministry.

Its remarkable recent growth is due to strong internal growth as well as to another wave of immigrants from the Netherlands following World War II. In 1981 there were 213,995 members in 626 congregations compared to 126,000 members in 306 congregations in 1943.

Throughout the years denominational leaders have kept in touch with theological developments in the Netherlands. The writings of Kuyper, Bavinck, and others fostered an intelligent and enthusiastic love for Reformed theology and the Calvinistic view of life.

There are several factors that aid in maintaining the orthodoxy of the denomination. One of the two sermons that ministers are required to preach each Sunday must follow the Heidelberg Catechism. Families are visited every year by the pastors and elders. Catechism instruction for the youth of the church is emphasized. Christian day schools are given strong support. Societies for all age groups promote Bible study. And in a day of growing laxity in most denominations, members are disciplined even to the point of excommunication for failure to show evidence of a true faith or failure to live the Christian life.

1. *How does the list of fundamentals mentioned in the first section of this chapter agree with the summary of early Christian faith in the Apostles' Creed?*

2. *Why should premillenarian views be associated with the Fundamentalists?*

3. *What was the object of the founding of Holiness groups?*

4. *Why is Modernism a constant danger to the historic faith of the Church? Is this true of the Roman Catholic Church as well as of Protestantism?*

5. *What was the basis for the separation of the Orthodox Presbyterian Church from the Presbyterian Church?*

6. *List about seven centers of Christian Reformed Church activity. Can you find evidences of the Dutch background of this church?*

7. *Identify: Machen, worldliness, Missouri Synod, Westminster Confession.*

8. *Make a list of Holiness churches in your community or listed in references such as* Yearbook of American Churches, *NCCC, New York, or* Handbook of Denominations *by Mead, Abingdon Press, Nashville, Tennessee.*

9. *When one's denomination becomes modernistic, is it better to organize a new church or remain and seek to purify the established denomination?*

CHAPTER 49

The Churches
Seek Co-operation and Union

1. Two Forces: Separation and Co-operation • From the very beginning of the Reformation a tendency to divide showed itself in Protestantism. Luther, Zwingli, and Calvin did not see eye to eye in all things. But also from the very beginning efforts were made to overcome this tendency. One such effort, though unsuccessful, was the conference between Luther and Zwingli held at Mārburg. John Calvin, through his let-ters and teaching and by means of conferences, succeeded in bringing a degree of unity into the Protestant movement.

The first effort in modern times to encourage co-operation among Protestant churches was the organization in London, in 1846, of the *Evangelical Alliance*. Some fifty evangelical bodies in England and America joined this alliance, and branches were established in nine European countries. The Alliance promoted many co-operative activities. But toward the end of the century its enthusiasm died out.

As time wore on, divisions in the ranks of the Protestants increased. This was the case especially in America with its separation of Church and State and entire freedom of religion. Today there are some three hundred denominations in the United States alone.

Throughout the Protestant world, by the closing years of the nineteenth century, there was a widespread desire for united testimony and action on various questions. This feeling has led to church federation and church union. By *church federation* we mean the formation of an organization composed of separate denominations for dealing with problems common to all. By *church union* we mean the uniting of two or more denominations into one.

Although American churches have been particularly active in this respect, the older European churches and the younger churches in Asia and Africa have also played a very active role. And although this movement has been found primarily among Protestants, the Eastern Orthodox have also taken part in it, and some interest has even been expressed by the Roman Catholic Church.

This movement toward co-operation has become the most striking feature of the life of the churches in the twentieth century.

2. Federations of Churches Are Formed • The Evangelical Alliance had been more an association of Christian individuals than a federation of churches. While this international alliance was dissolving, a new kind of alliance of churches

was formed in America in 1908. It bore the name of the *Federal Council of Churches of Christ in America*. It was very active in considering and making pronouncements on social, economic, and political questions. Most of the larger Protestant denominations affiliated with this council. Modernistic theology exerted a great influence in this organization.

This Federal Council was replaced in 1950 by the *National Council of the Churches of Christ in the U.S.A.* This new council included the churches of the older Federal Council plus various other national groups of Protestant church members. Eastern Orthodox groups were also affiliated with it. This council has become a very influential body, claiming to represent the great majority of Protestants in the United States.

There have been a number of denominations that refused to join the National Council because of its modernism. And within the denominations that did join, there were large numbers of members who felt that the Federal Council, or its successor, the National Council, were not giving expression to their faith or striving after the proper goals.

Many of these Christians, while rejecting the standpoint of the National Council, felt strongly the need of a unified voice for orthodox Protestantism. Among them two organizations sprang up in the years 1940–1944. These two organizations, the *National Association of Evangelicals* and the *American Council of Christian Churches,* agreed in their loyalty to orthodox Christianity, but differed somewhat in their structure and in their attitude toward the National Council of Churches. The National Associa-

tion of Evangelicals, which held its first convention in 1943, includes not only denominations, but other organizations and individuals as well. The American Council of Christian Churches, organized in 1944, restricts its membership to entire denominations which have no connection with the National Council. The former group is more moderate in its criticism of the National Council than is the latter. Both groups have been active in publication and other work, and have provided valuable services to their members.

3. Church Union Proceeds at a Rapid Pace • On very few subjects do all men think alike. They do not all think alike on the subject of religion. Where there are differences of views on fundamental doctrines or on forms of worship and church government, separation of Christians into different groups is unavoidable. This is the more true because matters of religion are the subjects of convictions, not mere casual opinions.

Christians are not agreed as to whether such division is wholly wrong or partly right. While some have defended the division of the Church into denomina-

tions, others have increasingly felt that the extreme divisions are a sin and a scandal.

Many of the leaders in the large denominations have been working for church union. Some have bent their best energies to that task, and with considerable success. For many years the process of unifying the denominations proceeded very slowly, but the pace has quickened. In 1939 the *Methodist Church in the United States* was formed out of three former denominations. *The United Church of Christ* is the product of several mergers which united four earlier denominations. Major Presbyterian bodies have united, and unions have taken place among Lutherans also. These are but samples of many unions, large and small.

Such unions have also taken place outside of the United States. The outstanding ones are the *United Church of Canada,* formed in 1925 out of former Methodist, Congregational, and Presbyterian churches; and the *Church of South India,* which was formed in 1947 and also included bodies with widely differing backgrounds.

Besides the groups mentioned, many others are discussing possible unions with other denominations, and the list of churches engaged in this process grows every year.

While this development has several pleasing aspects, a word of caution is in order. Church *unity* should underlie and precede church *union*. Where there are important differences in doctrine, worship, or church government, these should be settled, not ignored, in coming into union. Otherwise the unity which is professed is not a true unity, and cannot be of real profit to the Church of Jesus Christ.

4. The World Council of Churches •
The largest effort of Protestants toward unity is found in the World Council of Churches. The story of this council begins with a great international missionary conference held in Edinburgh in 1910. Although this was a missionary conference, and not a council of churches, it taught the churches many things about the possibility of discussing problems with each other and working together.

The impulses proceeding from this conference led to the formation of three important movements. The *International Missionary Council* was formed some years later to continue the discussion of missionary problems and to serve mission organizations with advice. *The World Conference on Life and Work* met in 1925 at Stockholm and in 1937 at Oxford to discuss the activities of the churches in society. *The World Conference on Faith and Order* met in 1927 at Lausanne and in 1937 at Edinburgh to discuss differences between the churches in doctrine and church government.

Each of these conferences discovered important differences among the churches.

But the general feeling was that it was profitable to meet together for two purposes: to discuss these differences and to act together when this was possible. And it was further felt that this was a promising road toward true Christian unity which ought to be further pursued.

Therefore, the 1937 conferences on Life and Work and on Faith and Order called for a new organization, which would include their own activities and carry the work of Christian unity closer to its goal. The result of this call was the formation, in 1948, of the *World Council of Churches,* which has as its purpose to carry on the work of the two world movements for Life and Work and for Faith and Order and to encourage cooperation in matters of world-wide concern.

The World Council of Churches held its first assembly at Amsterdam in 1948, with 351 delegates representing 147 churches in 44 different countries. A second assembly was held in Evanston, Illinois, in 1954, and a third in New Delhi, India, in 1961. Its fourth assembly was held in Upsala, Sweden in 1968 with 235 member churches represented as well as eleven associates, i.e. churches with less than 10,000 membership but otherwise eligible for full membership in the Council. The fifth World Council Assembly was held in Nairobi in 1975.

This council is frankly working toward world-wide unity of the Christian Church, but it is still composed of many separate churches. Some orthodox churches have consistently declined to apply for membership in this council, fearing that it is too liberal in its outlook or that it will lead to a super-church in which the biblical truth will not be recognized. Others, however, have felt that it was the duty of orthodox denominations to be members so that the conservative evangelical voice may also be heard in the World Council meetings. The younger churches, newly formed on the mission fields, have steadily risen to greater prominence in this council. Many differences of opinion are expressed within the council, but there is a determination to stay together so that greater unity may result as time goes by.

5. Other Types of Ecumenical Activity
● "Ecumenical," which means "the whole inhabited world," is the term used to describe these various movements toward Christian unity. Besides the movements previously mentioned there have been other ecumenical activities in the past one hundred years. One of these is the formation of world confessional alliances. Churches throughout the world which are similar in confessions and organization have met periodically for discussion and fellowship. The earliest of these was the *World Alliance of Reformed Churches* (formerly called the Presbyterian Alliance), which has existed since 1875. Other world confessional alliances are the *International Congregational Council*, the *World Methodist Council*, the *Baptist World Alliance*, the *Lutheran World Federation*, and the *International Council of Christian Churches*. The *Reformed Ecumenical Synod*, formed in 1946, is a similar organization.

The Roman Catholic Church, which for a long time had ignored Protestants, has shown increasing interest in conversations with them in recent years. The Second Vatican Council, which was held intermittently from 1962 to 1965, invited Protestant observers to be present.

These many streams of ecumenical activity indicate that the churches are seriously concerned with the problem of united Christian witness. On the other hand, they are conscious also of the depth and persistence of the differences which exist among them. This ecumenical movement is the most challenging development in church life in our time.

1. *What is the distinction between church federation and church union? What are the advantages and disadvantages of each?*
2. *What are the major factors that make union difficult?*
3. *Name some outstanding unions in Canada, India, and the United States. What discussions of union are currently being carried on?*
4. *What have the Roman Catholics done toward ecumenical planning under John XXIII and Paul VI?*
5. *Conduct a panel discussion with different members advocating joining the World Council of Churches, the National Association of Evangelicals, and the American Council of Christian Churches. A fourth panelist could present the case for no federation.*

A Look Backward

And Forward

1. A Look Backward • In Philippians 3:12-14 Paul says, "Not that I have already obtained all this, or have already been made perfect, but I press on to take hold of that for which Christ Jesus took hold of me."

The Church can make these words of Paul its own. Its service has not been perfect, for it is composed of sinners in a sinful world. The Church is not *of* the world, but it is very much *in* the world. It has greatly influenced the world; it has been a salt and a savor. But the world has at all times also profoundly influenced the Church. At times the salt has almost lost its savor, and frequently the light has been dimmed.

From the very beginning the Jews have been the bitter opponents of the Church. The Muslims have conquered much territory over which the banner of the cross once flew. The Church so far has not been able to win over many of these opponents.

The Church has never been overpowered. It did not prevent the fall of the Roman Empire, but it brought within its fold the Germanic tribes which destroyed that empire. At times the Church has sunk into error, superstition, corruption, and indifference. But the divine life which is in the Church has always preserved and revived it. Empires and kingdoms have risen and fallen. Systems

Philip Gendreau

of political and social organization have appeared and vanished. As century after century has rolled by, man's ways of living have undergone countless changes. But the Church, under God, has survived.

2. A Look Forward • Together we have traveled nearly two thousand miles of the long road of the Church's history. The road will continue on. Today we behold the strange spectacle, cause for sorrow and joy, of many in the Church repudiating the Gospel while others in the far corners of the earth are accepting it. From Scripture we know that dark days are in store for the Church and for the world. Black clouds are even now rising in the sky. But we know that the Church will continue upon its career of conquest until the return of our Lord. For the Church is the army of Christ. Jesus Christ is the living Head and the great King of the Church.

You have studied the history of the Christian Church. But you must do more. You must help make that history from now on, be your part ever so small. In the bitter warfare that lies ahead, and as the battle mounts, you must prove yourselves loyal and valiant soldiers of Jesus Christ. Help to make the future history of the Church even more glorious than its past.

A backward look through an arch toward the cathedral at Milan, Italy, is contrasted with a forward look represented by the seventeen spires of the U.S. Air Force Academy inter-faith chapel at Colorado Springs, Colorado. Three services can be held simultaneously. The Protestant nave will seat 900 cadets, the Catholic nave 500 cadets, and the Jewish synagogue 100 cadets.

Courtesy United States Air Force Academy

INDEX

Georgia, *map, 67*
Gerbert, archbishop of Rheims (Sylvester II), 85
German Baptist Brethren, 339
German Catholics, 364
German constitution, 137
German immigration, 336–338, 362
German Lutherans, in America, 338, 339, 362, 363
German Reformed: in America, 336, 337, 351; *map, 333*
Germantown, *map, 333*
German tribes, 49, 86, 87
Germanizing of the Church, 87, 88
Germany, 84; Christianized, 56, 57; Reformation in, 235, 236
Gillespie, Thomas, 312
Giralda Tower, *illus., 231*
Gloria Dei Church, Philadelphia, *illus., 337*
Gnosticism, 17, 18
Godet, Frédéric, 313
Godfrey, duke of Tuscany, 100, 102
Gospel, spreading of, 320–322. *See* Missions.
Gothic architecture, *illus., 88*
Goths, 49, 52; *map, 51, 53*
Graham, Billy, *illus., 371*
Granada, 231
Great Awakening, 343, 345–347, 356
Great Schism, 137, 138, 145, 146, 147, 230; *time line, 137*
Grebel, Conrad, 204, 205
Greek Eastern Church, 98; *map, 89. See* Greek Orthodox.
Greek: language, 5, 20; culture, 5, 148; philosophy, 5. *See* Paganism.
Greek Orthodox Church, 152, 296, 297, 299; doctrine, 296, 396; in Russia, 245–247, 297; in Canada, 386. *See* Eastern Greek (Orthodox) Church.
Greenland, 279
Greenwood, John, 261
Gregorian Chant, 58
Gregory I, the Great, Pope, 56–58, 69
Gregory II, Pope, 78
Gregory V, Pope, 85
Gregory VI, Pope, 85, 97, 100
Gregory VII, Pope, Hildebrand, 79, 95, 100–119, 123, 125; *illus., 105, 112, 113*
Gregory XII, Pope, 145
Gregory of Nazianzus, 32
Gregory of Nyssa, 32
Grey Friars, *illus., 129*
Groote, Gerhard, 150
Gustavus Adolphus, 244
Gutenberg, Johann, *illus., 207*

H

Hadrian, 40
Hague Conference, 378
Hampden, John, 251
Hanover, *map, 175*
Harvard, John, 329
Hastings, battle of, 83
Heathen tribes, Christianizing of, 53
Heathenism, in the Church, 44
Hegira, 63
Heidelberg, 165
Heidelberg Catechism, 214, 311, 312, 314, 391, 392
Helvetique, Confession, 313
Hengstenberg, Ernst Wilhelm, 302
Henry III, Emperor, 97–99
Henry III, king of France, 240
Henry IV, Emperor, 99, 103, 104, 106, 109–114, 123; *time line, 111*
Henry IV, king of France, 241; *illus., 259*
Henry VIII, king of England, 220–227
Henry of Bourbon and Navarre, 240
Henry of Guise, 240, 241
Heraclius, Emperor, 61
Heresy, 17, 39, 146, 170, 205, 235, 241, 281, 282, 353; Gnosticism, 17, 18, 21; Montanism, 17, 18, 21; Pelagianism 39; Socinianism, 281, 282, 288, 302. *See* Albigenses; Modernism.
Heretics, 21, 38, 141, 142, 147, 172, 173, 178, 198, 241; punishment of, 127, 170; persecution of, 46, 142, 143; law concerning, 144, 146. *See* Persecution.
Hermas of Rome, 15
Hermit, 45
Heroic Age, 7
Herrnhut, 277, 287
Hicks, Elias, 336
Hicksites, 336
Hierarchical system, 78
Higginson, Francis, 328
High Church party, 304; in America, 362
Hildebrand, *time line, 111. See* Gregory VII.
Hippo, *map, 16*
Hofmann, Melchior, 208
Holbein, 158, 224
Holiness movement, 389, 390
Holy Club, 285, 286, 345
Holy Ka'ba, *illus., 63*
Holy Land, 119, 126; pilgrimages to, 118; monastic orders, 128

Holy Roman Empire, 85, 140
Holy Sepulcher, 121
Holy wars, 120, 121
Honorius II, Pope, 104
Hoover, Herbert, 270
Hopkins, Samuel, 369
Hospitalers, 128
Host, 183, 228
Howard, John, 295
Hugo, abbot of Cluny, 97
Huguenots, 213, 240, 241, 307–310; in Canada, 385
Huizenga, Lee S., 322
Hungarian Reformed Church, 313, 314
Huns, *illus., 50; map, 51, 53*
Huss, John, 143–146, 152, 173; teachings of, 174
Hussites, 174, 275
Hutter, Jacob, 206
Hymns, 34, 200, 288, 364; in Middle Ages, 128; Lutheran, 185; first used in worship, 265; Watts', 288; Wesley's 292

I

Iconoclasm, 192, 217
Iconoclasts, *illus., 218*
Ignatius of Antioch, 8, 9, 15, 20
Images, 44, 45, 192. *See* Iconoclasm.
Imitation of Christ (à Kempis), 151
Independents, 251, 253 260
Index, 237, 238
India, *map, 67*
Indulgences, 153, 158–160, 166, 231
Industrial Revolution, 287, 288
Infallibility of Scripture, 283
Infallibility of the pope, 298
Inner Light, 269
Innocent III, Pope, 71, 79, 124–130; *illus., 143*
Inquisition, 129, 152, 238; Medieval, 142; Spanish, 142
Institutes of the Christian Religion (Calvin), 191, 193, 196, 199, 201, 212, 213
Institution of Churches, 263
Institutional church, 375
Interdict, 125
International Bible Students, 369
International Congregational Council, 397
International Missionary Council, 396
International Monument of Reformation, *illus., 202, 258, 259, 313*
Investiture, 99, 103, 108, 109; definition, 84